The essays in *Exploring the New Testament i*
to the New Testament with Asian ears, he;
the many Asian contexts, and show others,
can learn from and with our brothers and
to read Scripture faithfully.

Michael F. Bird, PhD
Deputy Principal,
Ridley College, Australia

Evangelicals have been late to the starting gate of contextualizing the gospel for diverse cultures around the world. A lot of this has been due to the cavalier approach to the text of Scripture taken by many of those early to the gate. This volume, edited by Samson L. Uytanlet and Bennet Lawrence, represents the very best combination of unswerving faithfulness to the non-negotiables of Scripture with the need to communicate gospel truths in the most relevant way possible in each of the world's cultures and to address the biggest questions spawned by those cultures. The volume falls into two sections of essays. First come treatments of standard doctrines of Christian theology from a specifically Asian perspective. Then come discussions of topics not always given much attention in the West that nevertheless loom large in the thinking of many Asians. Scripture is the touchstone throughout but every author is conversant and interacts with a broad range of other secular or religious thought that proves pervasive in their society. The first section spans topics like Christology, reconciliation, salvation, holiness, gender roles, and eschatology. The second section deals with poverty, ethnic strife, honoring elders, persecution, powers and principalities, authoritarian vs. servant leadership, and hospitality. Focal cultures span most of the countries in East, Southeast, and South Asia, and the authors are theological and sociological experts from those cultures. This book offers a feast for all readers alike, with new and important insights everywhere one turns. A welcome and treasured gift for the church worldwide.

Craig L. Blomberg, PhD
Distinguished Professor Emeritus of New Testament,
Denver Seminary, Colorado, USA

A good way to interrupt our own localized readings of the Bible is to hear from readers in other contexts. The authors of *Exploring the New Testament in Asia* provide an expansive set of lenses for understanding the New Testament. They help readers consider that the first-century world may frequently have more in common with contemporary Asian settings than Western ones. They illuminate important areas for engaging New Testament texts and themes in light of realities in their own locations

– themes such as salvation, holiness, poverty, ethnic tensions, reconciliation, honoring elders, persecution, and hospitality. Taking seriously the inevitability of hermeneutics, this volume seeks to open up avenues for mutual understanding and thoughtful recontextualization.

Jeannine K. Brown, PhD
David Price Professor of Biblical and Theological Foundations,
Director of Online Programs,
Bethel University, Minnesota, USA

Exploring the New Testament in Asia is biblically sound, contextually relevant, and comprehensive in scope for facilitators and students of theological education. Articles by eminent scholars provide exceptional insights as they speak from their excellent learning, teaching experience, and down-to-earth approach in their contexts of Asian realities with global expressions of the New Testament. I highly recommend this compilation of essays for teaching and as an introduction to scholarly research undertaking.

Ashish Chrispal, PhD
Senior Advisor, Overseas Council

If previous generations emphasized historical context for making sense of the New Testament, today we have also learned the importance of our varied contemporary contexts. That is what makes this book so important – to the Asian church that reads the Bible as Christian Scripture and, indeed, to the global church. Exploring Scripture with Asian eyes and ears, these scholars provide us with fresh insight into both the message of the New Testament and the ongoing challenges of faithful interpretation.

Joel B. Green, PhD
Senior Professor of New Testament Interpretation,
Fuller Theological Seminary, California, USA

This book shows how the New Testament continues to speak in Asian contexts. Using "Asian ears" that hear the Scriptures afresh and "Asian eyes" that see Asia today, the chapters in this book re-explore the New Testament's Christology, salvation, visions of holiness, gender relations, and hope for the future. There are also chapters that introduce areas particularly relevant in Asia, such as poverty, persecution, ethnic strife, filial piety, hierarchy, and the spirit world, where the New Testament needs to speak afresh. Questions are asked and answers offered, showing the need for further reflection and research. This is an excellent resource.

Robert M. Solomon, PhD
Bishop Emeritus, The Methodist Church in Singapore

 **FOUNDATIONS IN ASIAN CHRISTIAN THOUGHT**

Series Editor: Stephen T. Pardue

The Foundations in Asian Christian Thought series offers accessible and innovative introductions to key topics that are biblically rooted, contextually engaged and theologically rich. In each volume, a mixture of seasoned and rising scholars from all over Asia with a shared commitment to genuinely contextual reflection and the primary authority of Scripture introduce readers to major issues, identifying the key contributions of Asian Christians to the global theological conversation. In addition to introducing readers to the dynamic landscape of Asian Christian thought, each book also includes constructive proposals regarding how Christians can wisely advance the development of Asian biblical and theological reflection.

TITLES IN THE SERIES

Asian Christian Theology
2019 | 9781783686438

Asian Christian Ethics
2022 | 9781839730740

Exploring the Old Testament in Asia
2022 | 9781839732799

Exploring the New Testament in Asia
2024 | 9781839737114

FOUNDATIONS IN ASIAN CHRISTIAN THOUGHT

Exploring the New Testament in Asia

Langham

GLOBAL LIBRARY

FOUNDATIONS IN ASIAN CHRISTIAN THOUGHT

Exploring the
New Testament
in Asia

Evangelical Perspectives

Editors
Samson L. Uytanlet and Bennet Lawrence

© 2024 Samson L. Uytanlet and Bennet Lawrence

Published 2024 by Langham Global Library
An imprint of Langham Publishing
www.langhampublishing.org

Langham Publishing and its imprints are a ministry of Langham Partnership

Langham Partnership
PO Box 296, Carlisle, Cumbria, CA3 9WZ, UK
www.langham.org

Published in partnership with Asia Theological Association
ATA
QCC PO Box 1454 – 1154, Manila, Philippines
www.atasia.com

ISBNs:
978-1-83973-711-4 Print
978-1-78641-041-2 ePub
978-1-78641-042-9 PDF

British Library Cataloguing-in-Publication Data
A catalogue record for this book is available from the British Library

ISBN: 978-1-83973-711-4

Cover & Book Design: projectluz.com

CONTENTS

ABBREVIATIONS

AB	Anchor Bible
ABD	*Anchor Bible Dictionary*
ABQ	*American Baptist Quarterly*
AsJT	*Asia Journal of Theology*
ATA Journal	*Asia Theological Association Journal*
AThR	*Anglican Theological Review*
BBR	*Bulletin of Biblical Research*
BDAG	Danker, Frederick W., Walter Bauer, William F. Arndt, and F. Wilbur Gingrich. *Greek-English Lexicon of the New Testament and Other Early Christian Literature.* 3rd ed. Chicago: University of Chicago Press, 2000.
BECNT	Baker Exegetical Commentary on the New Testament
BibInt	*Biblical Interpretation*
BibInt	Biblical Interpretation Series
BNTC	Blacks New Testament Commentaries
BR	*Biblical Research*
BTB	*Biblical Theology Bulletin*
BZNW	Beihefte zur Zeitschrift für die neutestamentliche Wissenschaft
CBQ	*Catholic Biblical Quarterly*
DJG	*Dictionary of Jesus and the Gospels.* Edited by Joel B. Green, Scot McKnight, and I. Howard Marshall. Downers Grove: InterVarsity Press, 1992.
DLNT	*Dictionary of the Later New Testament and Its Development.* Edited by Ralph P. Martin and Peter H. Davids. Downers Grove: InterVarsity Press, 1997.
DNTB	*Dictionary of New Testament Backgrounds.* Edited by Craig A. Evans and Stanley E. Porter. Downers Grove: InterVarsity Press, 2000.
DPL	*Dictionary of Paul and His Letters.* Edited by Gerald F. Hawthorne and Ralph P. Martin. Downers Grove: InterVarsity Press, 1993.

ECL	Early Christianity and Its Literature
EuroJTh	*European Journal of Theology*
EvQ	*Evangelical Quarterly*
HTR	*Harvard Theological Review*
HUCA	*Hebrew Union College Annual*
Int	*Interpretation*
ISBE	International Standard Bible Encyclopedia
JAET	*Journal of Asian Evangelical Theology*
JAM	*Journal of Asian Mission*
JBL	*Journal of Biblical Literature*
JBQ	*Jewish Bible Quarterly*
JCTS	Jewish and Christian Texts Series
JIBS	*Journal of International Buddhist Studies*
JRC	*Journal of Religious Culture*
JSJ	*Journal for the Study of Judaism in the Persian, Hellenistic, and Roman Periods*
JSNTSup	Journal for the Study of the New Testament Supplementary Series
JSNT	*Journal for the Study of the New Testament*
JTI	*Journal of Theological Interpretation*
JTS	*Journal of Theological Studies*
LCL	Loeb Classical Library
LENT	Linguistic Exegesis of the New Testament
LNTS	Library of New Testament Studies
NAC	New American Commentary
NCC	New Covenant Commentary
NIGTC	New International Greek Testament Commentary
NICNT	New International Commentary on the New Testament
NovT	*Novum Testamentum*
NovTSup	Supplements to Novum Testamentum
NOTA	Novum Testamentum et Orbis Antiquus
NTS	*New Testament Studies*
NSBT	New Studies in Biblical Theology

NTL	New Testament Library
P. Mich. inv	University of Michigan Inventory of Papyri
RB	*Revue biblique*
RBS	Resources for Biblical Study
RevExp	*Review and Expositor*
RGRW	Religions in the Graeco-Roman World
SBLMS	Society of Biblical Literature Monograph Series
SHBC	Smyth & Helwys Bible Commentary
StBibLit	Studies in Biblical Literature
SNT	Studien zum Neuen Testamentum
SNTSMS	Society for New Testament Studies Monograph Series
SP	Sacra Pagina
TDNT	*Theological Dictionary of the New Testament*
TJ	*Trinity Journal*
TGSS	Tesi Gregoriana, Serie Spiritualita
TynBul	*Tyndale Bulletin*
WBC	Word Biblical Commentary
WUNT	Wissenschaftliche Untersuchungen zum Neuen Testament
WW	*Word and World*

INTRODUCTION

Samson L. Uytanlet and Stephen T. Pardue

Despite ongoing debates about evangelical identity, there is widespread agreement about at least one key element of their theological posture: evangelicals are characterized by a special affinity for Scripture as a unique source of theological authority and guidance.[1] In their churches, seminaries, and personal lives, evangelicals prize Scripture as an authoritative word from God, and seek to live in accordance with its guidance. We are, as some would put it, "people of the book."

One result of this posture is a tendency to be fiercely protective against any perceived threat to Scripture's authority, which often translates to a high level of suspicion of other theological sources, such as tradition, experience, reason, and culture. Spend enough time at evangelical churches or seminaries, and you will likely hear a pastor or scholar declare that they "only teach the Bible." Such statements are generally well-intentioned. As "people of the book," we want to elevate Scripture to its proper place as the unique revelation of the triune God and the means by which we can most readily enjoy communion with him.[2]

Yet this approach can obscure important realities. Teaching the Scriptures requires interpretation, and while we affirm that our source is infallible, there is no guarantee that our interpretation will be. Moreover, while we confess that Scripture is clear and sufficient, we also recognize that we come to the Scripture with a limited perspective that requires us to listen to other interpreters if we are to gain a fuller picture of what the Scripture is trying to convey.

Because our experience and cultural background can either skew or sharpen our vision, or impair or amplify our hearing, self-awareness is necessary to understand that each one can recognize aspects of the text that remain

---

1. Kurt Anders Richardson, "Evangelical Theology," in *Global Dictionary of Theology: A Resource for the Worldwide Church*, ed. William A. Dyrness et al. (Downers Grove: IVP Academic, 2008), 294–97; Gerald R. McDermott and Kevin J. Vanhoozer, eds., "Scripture and Hermeneutics," in *The Oxford Handbook of Evangelical Theology* (New York: Oxford University Press, 2010), 35–52; Michael F. Bird, *Evangelical Theology: A Biblical and Systematic Introduction* (Grand Rapids: Zondervan, 2013), 62–64; Scott R. Swain, "Scripture," in *Evangelical Dictionary of Theology*, ed. Daniel J. Treier and Walter A. Elwell, 3rd ed. (Grand Rapids: Baker, 2017), 790–92.
2. Timoteo D. Gener, "Divine Revelation and the Practice of Asian Theology," in *Asian Christian Theology: Evangelical Perspectives*, ed. Timoteo D. Gener and Stephen T. Pardue (Carlisle: Langham Global Library, 2019), 13–37.

hidden or distorted for others. This is why listening to other voices and the willingness to dialogue is essential. Thankfully, there is a growing recognition among evangelicals that God's design is for us to read Scripture alongside the whole church in all of its cultural and linguistic diversity.[3]

It is in light of this reality that this volume seeks to make a key contribution to students and scholars of the New Testament: namely, by helping the global church hear and see the good news of Jesus with fresh eyes. The modern field of New Testament studies was birthed and nurtured in nineteenth- and twentieth-century Europe and North America, and scholars from these contexts are still the primary voices setting the terms of debate in the field. Modern Western scholarship of the New Testament has certainly yielded important gains, as the essays in this volume consistently note. At the same time, it has increasingly become impossible to ignore the vast cultural distance between modern Europe and North America and the world of the New Testament, and by contrast, the close affinity between many Majority World contexts and the world of the New Testament. Equally important, it is increasingly the case that the majority of the people on earth who are reading, interpreting, and applying the New Testament live outside of Europe and North America, leading to a profound mismatch between the New Testament resources being produced and the needs of most Christians.

A primary goal of this volume is to listen to Scripture with an "Asian ear," recognizing themes, nuances, and elements of the New Testament that have been overlooked in modern New Testament scholarship. Yet, listening to the Scriptures well is only half of the task; we also hope in these pages to offer Asian Christians an example to follow in terms of applying the good news to the distinctive challenges they face. In these tasks, we seek to build on the growing number of resources which seek to understand and apply the good news for the Asian context.[4]

---

3. Thus, e.g. Tat-Siong Benny Liew, ed., *What is Asian American Biblical Hermeneutics? Reading the New Testament* (Hawaii: University of Hawaii Press, 2008); Elizabeth Mburu, *African Hermeneutics* (Carlisle: HippoBooks, 2019); Jerry Hwang, *Contextualization and the Old Testament: Between Asian and Western Perspectives* (Carlisle: Langham Academic, 2022); Stephen T. Pardue, *Why Evangelical Theology Needs the Global Church* (Grand Rapids: Baker Academic, 2023).

4. See, for example Melba Maggay, ed., *The Gospel in Culture: Contextualization Issues through Asian Eyes* (Manila, Philippines: OMF Literature, 2016), as well as the other books in the Foundations in Asian Christian Thought series: Timoteo D. Gener and Stephen T. Pardue, eds., *Asian Christian Theology: Evangelical Perspectives* (Carlisle: Langham Global Library, 2019); Aldrin M. Peñamora and Bernard K. Wong, eds., *Asian Christian Ethics: Evangelical Perspectives* (Carlisle: Langham Global Library, 2022); Angukali Rotokha and Jerry Hwang, eds., *Exploring the Old Testament in Asia* (Carlisle: Langham Global Library, 2022).

INTRODUCTION

PLAN OF THE BOOK

The book proceeds in two parts. The first part focuses on issues often discussed in standard approaches to New Testament theology, with each essay
considering how a traditional topic can be approached with distinctive insight
from the Asian context. In contrast, the second section highlights a variety of
issues that are particularly relevant in Asian contexts, but which often receive
little or no attention in the wider field of NT studies. All of the book's essays
involve careful investigation of theological themes in the NT and thoughtful
reflection on their resonance with and application to contemporary Asian
contexts. Readers will note that each author pursues these tasks with varied
methodology. This variety is intentional, and is reflective not only of the mul-
tiplicity of valid approaches to doing NT theology with attunement to local
context, but also of the wild diversity of contexts encompassed in the region.

The first part begins with Narry Santos's reflection on the central focus of
the NT: the person and work of Jesus of Nazareth. Santos begins by offering
readers a helpful overview of the vast diversity of approaches to studying and
describing the Jesus of the NT, ultimately noting that this diversity begins in
the NT itself, where the Gospel writers adopt differing but complementary
portrayals of Jesus. Santos helps readers understand christological proposals
currently emerging in the Asian context, and concludes the essay with a fresh
vision for christological reflection as a lively conversation "between biblical
and historical traditions and current global realities."

In the book's next essay, Xiaxia Xue reflects a key implication of Christ's
saving work as articulated in the NT: reconciliation not only with God, but
also with other people from every culture and background. The essay reflects on
the pervasiveness of tension and conflict even within Christian communities,
considering the contemporary Chinese church as a case study for understanding the dynamics of these struggles. After reflecting on key aspects of the NT
vision of reconciliation, she demonstrates that despite the enduring conflicts
among God's people, reconciliation is still possible through the miraculous
work of the Holy Spirit.

In the next essay, Johnson Thomaskutty continues the reflection on
the NT's vision of salvation, focusing our attention on the vast variety of
metaphors NT authors use to describe Jesus's saving work. In particular,
Thomaskutty highlights the NT metaphors for salvation which resonate in
special and often unexpected ways in the Asian context. Foregrounding these
ideas can be helpful both in evangelistic work – creating ready-made bridges

3

for explaining salvation to those outside the faith – and in deepening our own spiritual understanding.

A central aspect of salvation in the NT – as well as in major Asian religious traditions – is holiness, which is the focus of Arren Bennet Lawrence's essay. While Christians from various contexts agree that the Bible teaches about holiness, their expressions and the practical expectations vary widely. In this chapter, Lawrence revisits the various ways the NT writers present the concept of holiness, and how they may relate to the ideas of holiness found in the major Asian religions that dominate the Asian context. He also discusses the many ways holiness can be practiced and expressed in today's Christian communities.

Given that the NT envisions our holiness playing out not just in individuals, but in communities of men and women living and working alongside one another, Joyce Wai-Lan Sun focuses her essay on the NT's teaching on gender dynamics. Sun considers the household codes of the NT, considering what they meant in their time as well as how these codes are understood and interpreted in the contemporary Asian context. In the process, she helps readers think through the difficult question about how Christians in Asia can embody a biblical ethic in Asian contexts that often have highly fixed ideals for men and women.

Finally, Siang-Nuan Leong closes the first part of the book with a reflection on the NT's vision of "last things," considering especially the NT's vision of hope in the face of pervasive suffering. In important ways, the contemporary Asian context mirrors the challenging and unstable circumstances faced by Christians in the first centuries. Leong helps readers see how the NT's vision of the coming kingdom can speak a word of hope to Asian Christians today.

As noted above, the second section of the book focuses more squarely on topics that are important to the NT, but are often overlooked in more Western-centric NT theologies. The first essay in this section focuses on the NT's good news and liberation for those in slavery and poverty. Thawng Ceu Hnin helps readers understand the scale and seriousness of poverty across Asian nations, and the similarities between this economic situation and the environment in which the NT was composed and received. He goes on to explore the NT's message regarding the underlying causes of poverty and the appropriate response of God's people.

Alongside poverty, ethnic strife is a profound reality in Asia, where people from a vast diversity of backgrounds live alongside each other, and centuries of conflict often carry powerful weight. Kazuhiko Yamazaki-Ransom encourages readers to learn from the NT's engagement with the ethnic tensions between the Jews and the Samaritans, and taps into the "spatial turn" in NT studies to help us understand the connection between space, the kingdom of God, and ethnic conflict. He goes on to cast a vision for Christians in Asia to address injustice in part by creating space for ethnic others, and centering our communities around the unifying person of Jesus Christ.

In the next essay, Steven Chang addresses a foundational cultural value shared by almost every Asian context, especially those areas influenced by Confucian ideals: honoring elders, both living and dead. Chang helps readers see the ways in which the issue is more complex than it first appears, both in terms of the NT – where the theme of honoring elders is often overlooked by Western scholarship – and in terms of the contemporary Asian context, which is marked increasingly by negotiation between modernity and traditional values. Chang calls Christians around the globe to recognize the central value of honoring elders in a manner that is faithful to the NT and also winsome in our local contexts.

Chee-Chiew Lee's essay addresses another theme extremely pervasive in the NT, but which remains largely overlooked: namely, the persecution and marginalization that Asian Christians often face as a result of their allegiance to Christ. Lee helps readers understand the complex set of reasons for persecution in the first century, and notes the similarities with the causes of persecution in contemporary Asia. She goes on to help readers consider how to respond well to persecution, considering, for example, when to make reasonable adjustments and when to hold their ground even in the face of opposition.

For many Christians in the Asian context, it is a perplexing curiosity that so many resources about the NT reflect so little on a topic both central to the biblical text and of practical significance: the nature of the spirit world, and especially the confrontation between Christians and demonic forces. Samson Uytanlet helps remedy this gap in the existing literature with an essay that considers the NT's historical context as well as the contemporary realities in Asia. He first helps readers understand prevailing beliefs about the spirit world at the time of the NT's writing, which inform a better reading of the NT and its guidance on the subject. Informed by this analysis, Uytanlet helps readers consider how to respond to the spirit world in their faith and practice.

In keeping with a focus on "powers and principalities," but in a different sense, Alroy Mascrenghe takes up the issue of power politics in the NT and in Asian churches. While contemporary Western cultures often bridle at the idea of hierarchy and therefore promote relatively "flat" power structures in their churches, Asian cultures often mirror more closely the world of the NT, in which a small number of authoritative leaders are entrusted with significant sway. Mascrenghe analyzes the ways the first Christians navigated these dynamics, accepting the need for hierarchy and authority, but also adjusting prevailing values in light of Jesus's radical expectations for servant leadership. He then helps readers consider how Asian churches might do the same, retaining their cultural distinctives while also committing to accountability and servanthood in their authority structures.

Finally, the book closes with a thoughtful reflection on the theme of hospitality. Scholars of the ancient Mediterranean world have long noted the central importance of hospitality as a cultural value, and thus Asian Christians find much that is familiar in the pages of the NT. Andrew Spurgeon helps readers not only understand the way that the NT advanced a distinctive vision of hospitality – a call to go far beyond expected levels of welcome to strangers and outcasts – and then helps readers see opportunities for the Asian church to exercise distinctively Christian hospitality today.

ENTA does not promise a comprehensive discussion of various issues in NT theology, nor even of the NT's special resonance in Asian contexts. This is the task of future books and articles, which will no doubt refine and further advance these discussions. Yet we hope that readers will find here the glimpses of a reinvigorating perspective on the good news that God seeks "to reconcile to himself all things, whether things on earth or things in heaven, by making peace through his blood, shed on the cross" (Col 1:20).

CHAPTER 1

MULTIFACETED PORTRAYALS OF JESUS

The Fourfold Gospel and Contextual Christologies

Narry F. Santos

INTRODUCTION

Jesus Christ is valued significantly in God's communities of faith with utmost and urgent relevance. Christ has been regarded as "the basis for much of the worldview projected and reflected by the NT writers."[1] Thus, it is not surprising that Christology, which is the theological interpretation of Jesus's person and work[2] and the evaluation of who he is and the role he played in the divine plan,[3] was the focus of early Christian proclamation and is at the heart of NT witness.[4]

Despite the diversity of cultures and plurality of religions across the continents, Christ has been received, believed, and experienced by the global church as the basis for and focus of Christian life – both in corporate life and in daily living. As Ben Witherington writes, "At the bottom of the Christological well there lie deep waters of religious experience, which we have by no means plumbed the depths of – even 2,000 years after the ministry, death, and resurrection of Jesus Christ."[5]

In this chapter, we will explore the fourfold Gospel as it presents through the four Gospels the various portrayals of Christ, and we will discuss the

---

1. Ben Witherington III, "Jesus as the Alpha and Omega of New Testament Thought," in *Contours of Christianity in the New Testament*, ed. Richard N. Longenecker (Grand Rapids: Eerdmans, 2005), 26.
2. Longenecker., *Contours of Christianity*, xii.
3. Raymond E. Brown, *An Introduction to New Testament Christology* (New York: Paulist, 1994),
3. Christology is also considered the "doctrine of living to follow Jesus," as quoted by Kevin J. Vanhoozer, "Christology in the West: Conversations in Europe and North America," *Majority World Theology: Christian Doctrine in Global Context*, eds. Gene L. Green, Stephen T. Pardue and K. K. Yeo (Downers Grove, IL: IVP Academic, 2020), 117, from William Ames (*The Marrow of Theology* [Durham, NC: Labyrinth, 1983]), 1.
4. Longenecker., *Contours of Christianity*, xii.
5. Witherington, "Jesus as Alpha and Omega," 45.

different ways contextual Christologies are expressed in the Global North and Global South, especially in Asia. To do this, we will briefly scan the state of Christologies in scholarship over the decades, highlight the common and distinctive portraits of each Gospel writer, discuss Asian perspectives in understanding Jesus, and offer some ideas on doing Christology in the future that seeks to read the Bible more culturally and to read cultures more biblically.

Before moving further, we need to understand the use of key terms in this essay. First, we intentionally use the plural term "Christologies." There is no "one" Christology (or "the" Christology) expressed directly in the NT. Christians over the generations have understood Jesus in diverse ways. Frank Matera argues that there is diversity in our christological understanding today because of the diversity of stories about Jesus. He contends, "There are as many stories of Christ as there are Christologies; indeed, there are so many Christologies, because there are so many stories."[6] In addition to affirming these different Christologies, Richard Longenecker prefers to view such differences as "contours" in the overall Christology of the NT – suggesting that the contours are "undulations in the terrain or somewhat differing emphases of the respective authors within a basic commonality of conviction."[7]

Second, we conduct our inspection of the varying portrayals of Jesus through the lens of the fourfold canonical Gospels. The multiple perspectives from these Gospels are not simply diverse; they are also complementary – the differences enhance and enrich the varying Christologies rather than undermine them. As Francis Watson has argued, the fourfold Gospel is in a sense greater than the sum of its parts, retaining a complementary plurality in unity. In this chapter, we will highlight both the commonalities and distinct features of the Gospels with a view to understanding and appreciating better their plural perspectives.[8]

Third, we describe the diverse Christologies in the fourfold Gospel and in the progress of these Christologies in global Christianity as contextual. The four Gospel writers painted their own portraits of Jesus according to their understanding of who he is and what he set out to fulfill, using their own

---

6. Frank J. Matera, *New Testament Christology* (Louisville: WJKP, 1999), 3.
7. Longenecker, *Contours of Christianity*, xiii.
8. Francis Watson, *The Fourfold Gospel: A Theological Reading of the New Testament Portraits of Jesus* (Grand Rapids: Baker Academic, 2016), vii. Cf. Richard A. Burridge, *Four Gospels, One Jesus? A Symbolic Reading*, 2nd ed. (London: SPCK, 2005).

understanding of the terminological and conceptual world[9] of their time, and considering the circumstances and culture of Jesus's followers in their respective locations. In other words, the four Gospels were contextual in the sense that they were sensitive to the realities and needs of their communities.

Similarly, the development of the different Christologies in the West and later in the Majority World were also contextual, addressing the realities and needs in Europe and North America and later in the other countries of the Global South, respectively. This plurality of contexts in the development of diverse Christologies throughout the global church goes in the same way, only differently.

Fourth, aside from exploring the different Christologies from the fourfold Gospel in the West, we will also review the varying Christologies that started and grew in Asia. As a vast continent, Asia is home to many "great scripture religions of the world":[10] Judaism, Christianity, and Islam in western Asia; Hinduism, Buddhism, Jainism, and Zoroastrianism in southern Asia; and Confucianism, Taoism, and Shinto in eastern Asia.[11] Discovering how Asian theologians and reflective practitioners contextualized Christologies in such pluralistic religious settings is an enriching exploration and study for the global church.

Having clarified our crucial terms of diverse, contextualized Christologies from the fourfold Gospel and in Asia, it is valuable to now recall the state or development of Christologies over the decades from the Western church to the Majority World church.

STATE OF CONTEXTUALIZED CHRISTOLOGIES
IN WESTERN CHRISTIANITY

NT scholarship has come to no universally acceptable positions on the relationship of Jesus's Christology to that of his followers.[12] I. Howard Marshall contends that the "teaching of the NT about the person of Jesus (is) a subject vast in scope, unencompassable in its bibliography and daunting in its

---

9. Sigurd Grindheim, *Christology in the Synoptic Gospels: God or God's Servant* (London: Continuum, 2012), xiii.
10. Priscilla Pope-Levison and John R. Levison, *Jesus in Global Contexts* (Louisville: WJKP, 1992), 55. To see the spread of Christianity and missions in Southeast Asia, see Kiem-Kiok Kwa and Samuel Ka-Chieng Law, eds. in *Missions in Southeast Asia: Diversity and Unity in God's Design* (Carlisle: Langham Global Library, 2022).
11. Samuel Rayan, "Reconceiving Theology in the Asian Context," in *Doing Theology in a Divided World*, eds. Virginia Fabella and Sergio Torres (Maryknoll: Orbis, 1985), 126.
12. Brown, *Introduction to New Testament Christology*, 15.

problems."[13] Surveys of recent research on NT Christology abound[14] and present different perspectives on understanding Jesus from various schools of thought and their advocates over many decades.[15] For our purposes, we will look at the contributions in the development of Christologies in Western Christianity through the quest for the historical Jesus.

We can divide the quest for the historical Jesus into three categories. The original or first quest was influenced by Albert Schweitzer (1910),[16] who heightened the impression that scientific research showed differences between the Jesus of history and the Christ of Scripture, the creeds, orthodox theology, and Christian piety.[17] In this first quest, Jesus was seen as the great ethical teacher who valued the fatherhood of God, the brotherhood of all humanity, the infinite worth of a person's soul, and a higher righteousness through love.[18]

In the 1950s, followers of Rudolf Bultmann initiated what was called the new quest for the historical Jesus. In this new quest, they followed Bultmann's intent to show that there is virtually nothing to be known about the historical Jesus because of the interweaving of history and faith in the Gospels. For

---

13. I. Howard Marshall, *The Origins of New Testament Christology*, updated ed. (Downers Grove: InterVarsity Press, 1990), 7. He also argues, "The early history of the development of the church and its thought is so complex that any attempt at a synthetic view of early Christianity would be both speculative and premature," 28–29.

14. Cf. Hendrikus Boers, "Where Christology Is Real: A Survey of Recent Research on New Testament Christology," *Interpretation* 26, no. 3 (1972): 300–27; Norman Perrin, *A Modern Pilgrimage in New Testament Christology* (Philadelphia: Fortress, 1974), especially chapter 4, "Recent Trends in Research in the Christology of the New Testament," 41–56; David B. Capes, "New Testament Christology," in *The State of New Testament Studies: A Survey of Recent Research*, eds. Scot McKnight and Nijay K. Gupta (Grand Rapids: Baker Academic, 2019), 161–81.

15. Marshall (*Origins of New Testament Christology*, 14–30) gives an overview using seven names who addressed main themes and problems of Christology in the NT: H. P. Liddon; W. Bousset; A. E. J. Rawlinson; V. Taylor; O. Cullman; F. Hahn; and R. H. Fuller. Also, Brown (*Introduction to New Testament Christology*, 6–15) categorized approaches to NT Christology into five: (1) non-scholarly conservatism (i.e., the view that identifies the Christology of NT writings with the Christology of Jesus himself); (2) no-scholarly liberalism (i.e. the view that there is no continuity between Jesus's self-evaluation and the exalted Christology of the NT documents); (3) scholarly liberalism (i.e., the view that traced the creative process in NT Christology with careful methodology; (4) Bultmannian existentialism (i.e., the view that there was a functional equivalence between the NT christological proclamations and Jesus's proclamation of the kingdom of God in terms of existentialism); and (5) scholarly (moderate) conservatism (i.e., the view that there is a discernable continuity between the evaluation of Jesus during his ministry and the evaluation of him in NT writings).

16. Albert Schweitzer wrote the influential book, *The Quest of the Historical Jesus: A Critical Study of its Progress from Reimarus to Wrede*, translated in 1910 by W. Montgomery (London: Adam and Charles Black).

17. Colin Brown, "Historical Quest, Quest of," *DJG*, 326.

18. Craig L. Blomberg, *Jesus and the Gospels* (Nashville: Broadman & Holman, 1997), 179–80.

Bultmann, Jesus was a teacher who had demanding ethical standards, but he believed that Jesus was referring to someone else (other than himself) when he taught about the coming Son of Man.[19]

More recently, the term "third quest" has been coined to describe the renewed interest in Jesus in his historical context.[20] In this third quest, scholars rigorously examined historical criteria of authenticity in the use of gospel data. They also focused on understanding Jesus as a Jew, viewing him against the backdrop of religious and sociopolitical issues and institutions of his time.[21]

These quests brought about this valuable benefit: the "study of Jesus and the Gospels in the light of the social, economic, political and religious conditions of his times has immensely enriched our understanding not only of history but also of theological issues embedded in history."[22] In other words, Jesus began to be understood as a Jew rooted in his time, though he continues to be relevant for all times. Another fruit of the quests is the development of standard criteria of authenticity that are considered helpful to enhance confidence in the reliability of the gospel record.[23]

However, a drawback from the various quests is the unfolding of a Jesus who "all too often reflected the image of those who engaged in it."[24] For example, "Harnack's Jesus was the reflection of a liberal Protestant face at the bottom of a well. Schweitzer's Jesus had the demeanor of Nietzsche's superman. The Jesus of the New Quest sounded like an existentialist philosopher summoning his hearers to make existential decisions."[25]

These examples may point to the contextual nature of these Christologies in Western Christianity. Schweitzer's superman image of Jesus came out of a context when scholarly liberalism was flourishing before the First World War, an era marked by an enthusiasm for the achievements of modern technology in bringing a new and better way of life.[26] The reality of the Great War that ensued took away the superman image of Jesus and moved some scholars

---

19. Blomberg, *Jesus and Gospels*, 181.
20. Brown, "Historical Quest," 326.
21. Blomberg, *Jesus and Gospels*, 182. Cf. Ben Witherington III, *The Jesus Quest: The Third Search for the Jew of Nazareth* (Downers Grove: InterVarsity Press, 1995).
22. Brown, "Historical Quest," 341.
23. Blomberg sees the value of the criteria of dissimilarity, multiple attestation, Palestinian environment or Semitic language, and coherence (*Jesus and Gospels*, 186).
24. Brown, "Historical Quest," 341.
25. Brown, "Historical Quest," 341.
26. Brown, *Introduction to New Testament Christology*, 13.

toward the "more traditional Christian emphasis on the need for salvation by God in Jesus."[27]

THE FOUR GOSPELS AND THEIR CONTEXTUALIZED CHRISTOLOGIES

To discuss the four Gospels and their contextualized Christologies, we need to begin with the understanding of the genre (or type of literature) of the Gospels. There is a growing scholarly consensus that the Gospels were written as "biographies" (*bioi*) or "lives."[28] They were not written for the purpose of creating a book of Christologies, though they reveal the points of view of the writers on the person of Jesus through their narratives and theological themes.[29] As Grindheim affirms regarding the synoptic Gospels, "The evangelists, Matthew, Mark, and Luke, did not write 'Christologies' – they wrote Jesus biographies. Such biographies will, of course, tell us a lot about what the authors believed about what kind of person Jesus was."[30]

Aside from understanding their genre, what helps us put in perspective the fourfold Gospel and contextualized theologies is the paired reality of the differences of the four Gospels and the fourfold Gospel's commonalities. In other words, we need to see the creative tension of their diversity and unity, or as Mark L. Strauss expresses in his book title, we are to engage with *Four Portraits, One Jesus*. Strauss also observes the tendency of conservatives to lean on harmonizing the four portraits instead of appreciating their distinctives: "Evangelical and fundamentalist interest in the historicity of the Gospel events has sometimes resulted in a harmonistic approach, where the theology of the Evangelists is ignored, and the Gospels are gleaned solely for data about the historical Jesus."[31]

Craig Blomberg raises a similar sentiment and compares the dichotomizing tendency of conservative and liberal scholars in the way they view the person of Jesus. He observes that conservative scholars tend to harmonize the life of Christ in the four Gospels, while liberal scholars lean toward stressing

---

27. Brown, *Introduction to New Testament Christology*, 13.
28. Mark L. Strauss, *Four Portraits, One Jesus: An Introduction to Jesus and the Gospels* (Grand Rapids: Zondervan, 2007), 28.
29. Mark L. Strauss, "Christology and Christological Purpose in the Synoptic Gospels: A Study of Unity in Diversity," in *Reconsidering the Relationship between Biblical and Systematic Theology in the New Testament*, eds. Benjamin Reynolds, Brian Lugioyo, and Kevin J. Vanhoozer (Tübingen, Germany: Mohr Siebeck, 2014), 41–62, 45.
30. Grindheim, *Christology in the Synoptic Gospels*, xiii.
31. Strauss, "Christology and Christological Purpose," 42.

the theological distinctives of each Gospel. But he argues that "each of these approaches, when employed to the exclusion of the other, leads to a distorted understanding of the texts . . . It is our desire to keep both history and theology in balance."[32]

To read the Gospels with a view to both history and theology, we need to affirm the value of theological distinctives and find appropriate expressions of harmony in their Christologies. Appreciation of the theological distinctives can be done by reading "vertically" (or following the storyline of the Gospel), respecting the integrity of each narrative, reading it on its own terms, tracing the progress of story and discourse from introduction, to conflict, climax, and resolution.[33] In other words, reading vertically is to follow the narrative from top to bottom. Another valuable practice is to read "horizontally" (or comparing the Gospel accounts),[34] in order to discern each writer's unique theological perspective and what they hold in common.

Distinctives in the Prologues of the Four Gospels

Though there are many instances in the narratives when the four Gospels diverge in their portrayal of Jesus, the prologue is a vivid example of their remarkable distinctives. It is important to note that prologues can be a pivotal key to the Gospel.[35] Though the prologues do not serve as summaries of the Gospel nor do they include all the crucial titles of Jesus, they influence the readers on how the Gospel writers want them to view Jesus at the outset of their narrative.

In the prologue of Matthew's Gospel, we see the focus on the genealogy of Jesus, tracing the genealogy of Jesus (Matt 1:1–17) and "confirming his legitimacy as the promised savior and king who will bring Israel's history to its climax."[36] The key identification to Jesus of this opening passage refers to him as the "Christ, the son of David, the son of Abraham" (1:1 ESV). Abraham and David are prominent figures both in Israel's history and the Gospel's purpose. Abraham was not only the father of Israel but also the recipient of God's promise that all the nations would be blessed through him (Gen

---

32. Blomberg, *Jesus and the Gospels*, 177. Cf. Longenecker, *Contours of Christianity*, xiii.
33. Strauss, *Four Portraits, One Jesus*, 32–33.
34. Strauss, *Four Portraits, One Jesus*, 34.
35. See Morna D. Hooker, *Beginnings: Keys That Open the Gospel* (London, UK: Trinity, 1997) and Morna D. Hooker, "Beginnings and Endings," in *The Written Gospel*, eds. Markus Bockmuehl and Donald A. Hagner (Cambridge: Cambridge University Press, 2005), 184–202.
36. Strauss, *Four Portraits, One Jesus*, 220. Cf. M. E. Boring, "Mark 1:1–15 and the Beginning of the Gospel," *Semeia* 52 (1990): 43–91.

12:2–3). David was not only the best king of Israel but also the prototype of the coming Messiah. Jesus is related and identified with Abraham and David as a key understanding of how Matthew wants his readers to view Jesus from the beginning of his narrative.

In the prologue of Mark's Gospel, we observe the highlighted view of Jesus through the title[37] of the Gospel: "The beginning of the gospel of Jesus Christ, the Son of God"[38] (Mark 1:1 ESV). This beginning reveals that Jesus is a character of unique and lofty authority in the narrative as the Christ and Son of God. Though Mark does not elaborate the full significance of these titles in the prologue, they make us anticipate that the rest of the narrative will put meaning into the authoritative designation of Jesus as God's agent.

In the prologue of Luke's Gospel, we note the value of witnesses and ministers of the word (Luke 1:1–4) tied to oral tradition and sources, "rooted in apostolic memory."[39] This theme of witness becomes important to Luke with the resurrection. In relation to the infancy narrative (1:5–2:40), the emphasis in this early segment of the Lukan narrative is on "Jesus as the promised Davidic king who brings peace and light to those in darkness (1:31–35, 78–79),"[40] who is the "Son of the Most High" (1:32), the Savior, Christ the Lord (Luke 2:11). The title "Lord" can be a significant title in the narrative, realizing that Luke employs it "with considerable ingenuity to show that Jesus shares God's name."[41]

In the prologue of John's Gospel, we notice the disparity of its view of Jesus compared to the presentation of Jesus in the synoptic Gospels.[42] John 1:1–18 has been considered as "the most profound statement of Jesus's identity in the NT, identifying Jesus as the 'Word' (*Logos*), the preexistent Creator of the universe, distinct from the Father yet fully divine."[43] It has also been viewed as a literary masterpiece and statement of high Christology summarizing the

---

37. David Garland, *A Theology of Mark's Gospel: Good News about Jesus the Messiah, the Son of God* (Grand Rapids: Zondervan, 2015), 182.

38. The phrase "Son of God" is to be taken as originally part of Mark 1:1. It reappears in critical portions of the narrative (1:11; 3:11; 5:7; 9:7; 12:6; 13:32; 14:61; 15:39). For external and internal evidence favoring the inclusion of this phrase, see Bruce Metzger, *A Textual Commentary on the Greek New Testament* (Stuttgart: United Bible Societies, 1971), 73.

39. Darrell L. Bock, *A Theology of Luke and Acts: God's Promised Program, Realized for All Nations* (Grand Rapids: Zondervan, 2012), 67.

40. Bock, *Theology of Luke*, 68.

41. Grindheim, *Christology of Synoptic Gospels*, 118.

42. Several perspectives explain this disparity. A minority of scholars hold to John's direct dependence of the synoptics (C. K. Barrett, *The Gospel According to St. John*, 2nd ed. [Philadelphia: Westminster, 1978], 15–26).

43. Strauss, *Four Portraits, One Jesus*, 305.

Gospel's main theme: Jesus – the self-revelation of God – who through his incarnation brought life and light into humanity.[44] Andreas J. Köstenberger gives two reasons for this "lengthy, exceedingly well-crafted introduction" this way: (1) to present Jesus and highlight his significance within the framework of antecedent salvation history; and (2) to clarify the relationship between the new messianic community (followers of Jesus) to Old Testament Israel.[45]

Commonalities in the Prologues of the Four Gospels

We have seen the themes about Jesus and his titles in the prologues of the four Gospels. These themes and titles reveal the particular concerns and contexts of the Gospel writers and their communities. However, despite these distinctives, we can still see four commonalities in these prologues. First, as revealed in the prologues, the fourfold Gospel has its origins long ago in the purpose of God (Mark 1:1–3; Matt 1:1–17, 23; 2:6, 15, 18, 23; Luke 1:68–79; 2:29–32, 38; John 1:1). Second, the prologues describe Jesus as the Messiah (Mark 1:1; Matt 1:18; 2:1–6; Luke 1:69; 2:11, 26; John 1:17). Third, the prologues present Jesus as the Son of God (Mark 1:11; Matt 2:15; Luke 1:35; John 1:18). Fourth, the prologues show that in Jesus the Holy Spirit is at work (Mark 1:8, 10, 12; Matt 1:20; Luke 1:35; John 1:15, 30–34).[46]

Another commonality in the prologues of the fourfold Gospel is their use of the word "beginning." In three prologues, the word "beginning" (*archē*) is found at or near their beginnings. In Mark, the word occurs as the first word in the narrative: "Beginning of the gospel of Jesus Christ, Son of God" (Mark 1:1 ESV). In John, the word appears as the second word (*en archē*), "In the beginning" (John 1:1). In this Fourth Gospel, this beginning echoes the beginning in the first book of the Bible: "In the beginning God created the heavens and the earth" (Gen 1:1). In Luke, a reference to "the beginning" is seen halfway through Luke 1:1–4, when the sequence of events is shared by eyewitnesses who took part in these events "from the beginning" (Luke 1:3 NIV). Though the word "beginning" does not occur in Matthew, we find a near synonym, *genesis* ("becoming"). Thus, Matthew's opening words, *biblios*

---

44. Strauss, *Four Portraits, One Jesus*, 305.
45. Andres J. Köstenberger, *A Theology of John's Gospel and Letters: The Word, the Christ, the Son of God* (Grand Rapids: Zondervan, 2009), 176.
46. Hooker, "Who Can This Be?," 84.

geneseōs, do not refer to the name of the first book of the Bible but to the "book of the genealogy of Jesus Christ (ESV)."[47]

Creative Tension for Distinctives and Commonalities

Though there are commonalities in the context of distinctives, as seen in the above discussion on the prologues of the fourfold Gospel, there is no clear-cut way to fully harmonize the prevailing differences in the Christologies of the Gospels, especially in instances of ambiguity. For example, in the Synoptics, Jesus is presented as the Messiah and the Son of David, but he is also David's Lord (Mark 12:35–37). He is perceived as a prophet (Matt 21:11; Luke 7:16; John 4:19) but also the "sender of the prophets."[48] He is called the Son of Man with depictions of a humble human being, but he is also a heavenly figure who will come in glory that is equal with God's.

These ambiguities reveal creative tension in the Gospel portrayals of Jesus, prompting us to recognize the reality of both sides of the tension and to refrain from harmonizing them when the distinctives of both sides need to be emphasized. Such creative tension opens our minds to the need to appreciate the Christologies in the fourfold Gospel and enables us to behold the indispensable images of Jesus's diversity and unity and the unique ways in which Jesus can be understood from distinct perspectives.

CONTEXTUAL CHRISTOLOGIES IN ASIA

So far, we have surveyed the state or development of contextual Christologies in the West and the reality of contextualized Christologies in the fourfold Gospel (using the differences and commonalities in the prologues of the four gospels). In this current section, we will scan the different Christologies in the context of Asia. We will divide the section into the key contextual factors at play in the diverse settings of Asia and the various expressions and examples of contextual Christologies in this vast continent.

---

47. Watson, *Fourfold Gospel*, 96. Aside from commonalities in the beginnings, Watson also observes some similarities in the passion narrative: "The gospel texts converge at their endings. . . . They present readings of episodes from the combined passion narratives – the triumphal entry, Gethsemane, the crucifixion, the empty tomb – in which the same story is told and retold by all four evangelists" (Watson, *Fourfold Gospel*, ix).
48. Grindheim, *Christology of Synoptic Gospels*, 149.

Key Contextual Factors in Asia

There are four contextual factors that shape the contours of Asian portraits of Jesus. The first factor is the plurality of religions in Asia – Judaism, Hinduism, Islam, Buddhism, Taoism, Shinto, and Confucianism. Though Christianity started in west Asia (Palestine), it "left Asia very early and forced its way back several centuries later as a stranger and 'intruder' which Asia consistently refused to entertain."[49] As a result, Asia today is the least-Christian major area in the world by percentage. However, Christianity made significant gains in the twentieth century, rising from 4.5 percent of the total population in 1970 to 8.2 percent in 2010.[50]

The second factor that needs to be addressed in this region is Asian poverty, which is shared with much of the underdeveloped world – though some countries, like China and India, have developed economically recently. The third factor is Christianity's association with the history of colonialism in Asia. Because Christianity received support from colonial governments and powerful nationals, "the gulf between the institutional church and the poor majority widened."[51] The fourth factor, related to the plurality of religions, is the diversity of cultures within the Asian continent. Out of these four factors, Asian religiosity and poverty have been considered as two inseparable realities that must shape a Christology that is truly Asian.[52] The basic question scholars and theologians constantly wrestle with is this: What images of Jesus can bring hope and health to many Asians living in poverty and in religious pluralism?

Various Asian Expressions of Contextual Christologies

Some expressions of contextual Christologies that addressed either poverty or religious pluralism are the cosmic Christ, the liberator Jesus, and the pain-love

---

49. Aloysius Pieris, *An Asian Theology of Liberation* (Maryknoll: Orbis, 1988), 74.

50. Center for the Study of Global Christianity, *Christianity in its Global Context, 1970–2020: Society, Religion, and Mission* (South Hamilton: Gordon Conwell, 2013), 34.

51. C. Lakshman Wickremesinghe, "Alienated Church and Signs of the Times," in *Living Theology in Asia*, edited by John C. England (Maryknoll: Orbis, 1982), 184. In addition, 84 percent of Hindus, Buddhists, and Muslims have relatively little contact with Christians (Benjamin P. Thomas, "Confronted with the Facts," in *Portraits of Global Christianity: Research and Reflections in Honor of Todd M. Johnson*, edited by Gina A. Zurlo [Littleton: William Carey, 2023], 163).

52. John R. Levison and Priscilla Pope-Levison, "Toward an Ecumenical Christology for Asia," *Missiology* 22, no. 1 (1994): 4.

of God. Two examples that engage both poverty and religiosity are the cosmic Lord of history and Jesus's double baptism.[53]

Cosmic Christ

At the base of cosmic Christology is a shared conceptual framework that unites Christianity and other religions. As Paul Devanandan contends, "many Christian truths, abstracted from their original context, are found as unspoken presuppositions in what we may call conceptual framework of non-Christian religious practice."[54] A well-known example of this shared conceptual framework is Raimundo Panikkar's *The Unknown Christ of Hinduism*.[55] Panikkar argues that an unknown reality (which Christians refer to as "Christ") can be discovered at the very heart of Hinduism. This reality (the unknown Christ of Hinduism) can be viewed as the very principle of life and as the light that illumines every person.[56] According to Panikkar, this principle is found in the mediation between the divine world (Brahman) and the created world through Isvara in Hinduism and the cosmic Christ (described in Col 1:15–20). Unfortunately, Panikkar's approach downplays the significance of the historical Jesus: "(the) major obstacle appears when Christianity further identifies, with the necessary qualifications, Christ with Jesus, the son of Mary."[57] Disconnecting the cosmic Christ with the Jesus of history disregards the way Asian Christianity has benefited from the historical Jesus, who is seen as a human model of social justice.

Liberator Jesus

The cosmic Christ addresses the issue of religiosity in Asia, but Jesus Christ as liberator addresses the issue of poverty in Asia. With Christ as liberator, Jesus proclaims the reign or kingdom of God as a declaration of humanization, a new humanity characterized by total human development.[58] The dominant image of this new humanity is Jesus sitting at a table with the marginalized of society, showing that Jesus recognizes the dehumanizing cultural and

---

53. This christological approach is ecumenical. To see how this approach is applied in Asia, see John R. Levison and Priscilla Pope-Levison, *Jesus in Global Contexts* (Louisville: WJKP, 1992), especially the chapter on Jesus in Asia (55–88).

54. Paul Devanandan, "Called to Witness," *Ecumenical Review* 14 (1962): 161–62.

55. Raimundo Panikkar, *The Unknown Christ of Hinduism: Toward an Ecumenical Christophany* (Maryknoll: Orbis, 1981).

56. Panikkar, *Unknown Christ*, 19–20.

57. Panikkar, *Unknown Christ*, 56–57.

58. Levison and Pope-Levison, "Toward Ecumenical Christology," 6.

institutional values of his day. This image of Jesus in Asia is valuable because of how it confronts poverty in Asia. However, many liberation theologians have neglected growing movements for justice within non-Christian religions; thus creating a tendency to isolate Christianity from the liberative streams of other Asian religions.

Pain-Love of God

Another contextual Asian Christology that addresses poverty or suffering is the pain-love of God, as expressed by Kazoh Kitamori in his book *The Theology of the Pain of God*.[59] This Christology emerges from Buddhism in Japan, where people faced the suffering of daily life in the midst of their poverty as a result of the ravages of the Second World War culminating in the bombing of Hiroshima and Nagasaki. Kitamori believed that the Bible reveals a God in pain for the sinfulness of humanity and in pain for relinquishing his only child. This relates to the basic Japanese principle of "tsurasa," the pain caused when a person suffers or dies or makes a beloved suffer or die in order to bring health and life to others – similar to God's pain-love in sending Jesus Christ in human history to suffer and die for humankind.

Though this contextual Christology was set in the context of Buddhism or was relevant to the poor,[60] it offered no concrete means to alleviate the daily suffering. As Tsutomu Shoji commented, "this sort of understanding of the Christian Gospel was largely confined to the psychological and personal level, and did not open the eyes of Christians to the social realities which had brought misery to the people."[61]

Cosmic Lord of History

Aside from the three contextual Asian Christologies that address either religiosity or poverty (cosmic Christ, liberator Jesus, and the pain-love of God), two contextual Christologies address these two pervading realities in Asia: the cosmic Lord of history and the double-baptism of Jesus. The Asian cosmic Lord of history came from M. M. Thomas's "Christ-centered humanism," a

---

59. Kazoh Kitamori, *The Theology of the Pain of God* (Louisville: WJKP, 1965).
60. This contextual Christology is a reminder to Asian Christians in nations that have a measure of success and power to not give in to triumphalism and a warning against a self-assured attitude that equates prosperity and health with divine approbation and that regards poverty and sickness as signs of a lack of faith. Simon Chan, *Grassroots Asian Theology: Thinking the Faith from the Ground Up* (Downers Grove: InterVarsity Press, 2014), 100.
61. Tsutomu Shoji, "The Church's Struggle for Freedom of Belief – An Aspect of Christian Mission," in *Living Theology in Asia*, ed. J. England (Maryknoll: Orbis, 1982), 55.

Christology whose validity is based less on its doctrinal orthodoxy than its contribution to the human "quest for a better life and for social justice."[62] Using Colossians 1 and Ephesians 1, Thomas claims that since Christ unifies creation, then Christ is present in any spirituality that moves the creation toward its goal of justice for all people. For Thomas, Jesus is the source, judge, and redeemer of the human spirituality that is at work in movements of human liberation,[63] not just within Christianity but in other religions as well.

Double Baptism of Jesus

Aloysius Pieris incorporates Asia's poverty and religiosity through his contextual Christology of Jesus's "double baptism" into "the Jordan of Asian religions and the Calvary of Asian poverty."[64] The word "baptism" describes these "two prophetic gestures" in which Jesus is immersed in the Asian reality.[65] Jesus's baptism in the Jordan of John's religiosity and that of the rural, religious poor prepared him for his second baptism on the Calvary of poverty. According to Pieris, Jesus's actions of denouncing mammon and conscientizing the poor threatened the wealthy and powerful, leading the colonizers from Rome to nail Jesus to the cross.[66]

Framing contextual Christologies within the realities of religiosity and poverty in Asia is valuable, because as a minority religion in this region we need to look beyond the four walls of the church. As we go beyond our church borders, we also need to address these two realities as we seek to make Jesus real and relevant to Asian spirituality and its quest for social flourishing and justice. The presence of Jesus in all religions, cultures, socioeconomic situations, and liberating movements can provide the bases for dialogue, inculturation, and works of liberation. However, for Asian mainline theologians, there is fear that too much stress on Jesus Christ as the one and only Savior would undermine dialogue with Asian religions, cultures, and the poor.[67]

---

62. M. M. Thomas, *Towards a Theology of Contemporary Ecumenism* (Madras, India: Christian Literature Society, 1978), 311.
63. M. M. Thomas, "The Meaning of Salvation Today – A Personal Statement," *International Review of Mission* 62 (1973): 163.
64. Aloysius Pieris, *Asian Theology*, 63.
65. Pieris, *Asian Theology*, 47.
66. Pieris, *Asian Theology*, 49. For a critique of the view of Pieris, see Levison and Pope-Levison, "Toward Ecumenical Christology," 14–15. Note also that both Thomas and Pieris have little or nothing to say about the role that religions play in the form of popular piety.
67. Peter C. Phan, ed., *The Asian Synod: Text and Commentaries* (Maryknoll: Orbis, 2015), 62.

Additional Asian Expressions of Contextualized Christologies

In addition to the framing of contextual Christologies according to religiosity and poverty, Simon Chan uses two categories of Asian Christologies: elitist (or "from above") and grassroots (or "from below") Christologies.[68] In his category of elitist Christology (which begins with the givens in the Christian tradition and then proceeds to answer the questions the Asian context poses), Chan describes how Jesus is seen as the suffering Christ (similar to Kitamori's pain-love-of-God Christology), and enlightened Christ (or a Buddha). In his grassroots Christology, he explains how Christ is called the healer and life-giver, liberator and victor, and mediator-ancestor, which are similar to prominent descriptions in African Christologies.

Christ the Healer

In the category of grassroots Christology (which begins with the questions posed by the Asian context and then proceed to ask how the Christian faith can adapt to the distinctive questions it poses), Chan describes Christ the healer, who provides for the poor another kind of liberation – spiritual liberation from fear and fatalism created by centuries of internalizing the law of karma, freedom from the fear of spirits, deliverance from demonic possession, and healing for their sickness.[69] For the grassroots, the freedom cry is answered in their personal encounter with Jesus Christ, who meets with them through Christophanies or Spirit-Christology.[70] However, a theology of healing must incorporate the understanding that accepts sickness as present reality and believes the fullness of healing at the resurrection of the body.[71]

Jesus as Victor

Moreover, Jesus is described as liberator and victor. He has defeated Satan at the cross, and subsequent to Jesus's resurrection and ascension, he continues to exercise authority in heaven and on earth as high priest at God's right hand

---

68. Chan, *Grassroots Asian Theology*, 94–117. Chan likens the categories of his contextual Christologies (elitist and grassroots) to Christology "from above" and "from below," respectively. Christology "from above" focuses on the givenness of the "text," which is the interpretive lens to view context-culture. Christology "from below" focuses on context in reshaping tradition through dialogue.
69. Chan, *Grassroots Asian Theology*, 103.
70. See Ralph Del Colle, *Christ and the Spirit: Spirit-Christology in Trinitarian Perspective* (New York: Oxford University Press, 1994).
71. Chan, *Grassroots Asian Theology*, 110.

(Matt 28:18; Heb 8:1; 10:12; 12:2). The good news of Jesus Christ is that his sacrifice on the cross has removed the appeasement of the spirits, and his continuing work as high priest assures Asian Christians that the victory over the devil is a present reality – liberation from bondage to fear and power over evil spirits. Jesus the *Christus Victor* brings to many folk religionists liberation from the fear of the spirits and fear of death. As Chan confirms, "This is why sociopolitical types of liberation theology do not quite have the impact in primal religious contexts."[72]

Jesus as Mediator-Ancestor

Jesus has been considered as our "greatest ancestor."[73] Ancestral veneration, like priestly mediation, is seen christologically. Yet despite the prevalence of ancestral veneration in Asia and the practical issues it engenders, it is seldom addressed in relation to Christology (especially among Protestants).[74] In Chinese folk religion, it is normal to use the mediation of a spiritual medium, shaman, or fortune-teller in major catastrophe (like prolonged sickness) or crucial decisions (like marriage).[75] This need for priestly mediation is not commonly explored among Asian Christian scholars, despite the post-ascension priestly ministry of Christ.

From these sets of elitist and grassroots Christologies in Asia, we see three major contrasts. First, elitist Christology tends to focus on the socioeconomic and political dimensions of life, while grassroots Christology highlights the ethnographic. Second, for elite theologians, freedom is from poverty and political oppression (seen in the Christologies of the suffering Christ and enlightened Christ), while for the grassroots theologians, liberation is physical and psychospiritual (seen in the Christologies of Jesus the healer, the victor, and ancestor-mediator). Third, the Christ of elite scholars is found in dialogue with religions, cultures, and the poor, while the Christ of grassroots scholars

---

72. Chan, *Grassroots Asian Theology*, 113.
73. Kwame Bediako, *Jesus in Africa: The Christian Gospel in African History and Experience* (Akropong-Akuapem, Ghana: Regnum Africa, 2000), 616.
74. Chan, *Grassroots Asian Theology*, 117. Chan argues for the need to explore further how the communion of the saints relate to the concept of mediator-ancestor: "Just as the traditional ancestor is believed to exist in solidarity with the living, the communion of saints includes both saints on earth and saints in heaven united in one church in Christ."
75. Ju Shi Huey, "Chinese Spirit-Mediums in Singapore: An Ethnographic Study," in *Studies in Chinese Folk Religion in Singapore and Malaysia*, ed. John Clammer (Singapore: Institute for the Study of Religions and Society, 1983), 21–24.

is encountered in Christophanies, healings, deliverance from demonic spirits, answers to prayers, and special providences.[76]

Christ as God's Face Intervening in History

Having seen contextual Christologies in Asia through the key realities of religiosity and poverty and having additional perspectives on Jesus using elitist (or "from above") and grassroots (or "from below") Christologies, we now look at the last batch of descriptions of Jesus as God's face intervening in human history.[77] Jesus has been viewed as the incarnation of God (Choan-Seng Song),[78] the avatar (Chakkarai),[79] the enactor of the acts of God (Liem Kiem

---

76. Chan, *Grassroots Asian Theology*, 126.

77. For more helpful references on contextual Christologies in Asia and beyond, see Gene L. Green, Stephen T. Pardue, and K. K. Yeo, eds., *Jesus without Borders: Christology in the Majority World* (Carlisle: Langham Global Library, 2015); Volker Küster, *The Many Faces of Jesus Christ* (Maryknoll: Orbis, 1999); Leonardo Boff and Virgil Elizondo, eds., *Any Room for Christ in Asia?* (London: SCM, 1993). For other valuable references on contextual theologies in the Majority World, see Huang Po Ho et al., *New Developments in Theology in Asia* (London: SCM, 2022); William A. Dyrness, *Learning about Theology from the Third World* (Grand Rapids: Academie, 1990); R. S. Sugirtharajah, ed., *Frontiers in Asian Christian Theology: Emerging Trends* (Maryknoll: Orbis, 1994); Douglas J. Elwood, ed., *Asian Christian Theology: Emerging Themes* (Philadelphia: Westminster, 1976); Gerald H. Anderson, ed., *Asian Voices in Christian Theology* (Maryknoll: Orbis, 1976); Emerito P. Nacpil and Douglas J. Elwood, eds., *The Human and the Holy: Asian Perspectives in Christian Theology* (Maryknoll: Orbis, 1978); A. A. Yewangoe, *Theologia Crucis in Asia: Asian Christian Views on Suffering in the Face of Overwhelming Poverty and Multifaceted Religiosity in Asia* (Amsterdam: Rodopi, 1987); Bong Rin Ro and Ruth Eshenaur, eds., *The Bible and Theology in Asian Contexts: An Evangelical Perspective on Asian Theology* (Seoul: Word of Life, 1984); and Masao Takenaka, *God Is Rice: Asian Culture and Christian Faith* (Geneva: WCC, 1986). For references for doing global theology, see Craig Ott and Harold A. Netland, eds., *Globalizing Theology: Belief and Practice in an Era of World Christianity* (Grand Rapids: Baker Academic, 2006); Jeffrey P. Greenman and Gene L. Green, eds., *Global Theology in Evangelical Perspective: Exploring the Contextual Nature of Theology and Mission* (Downers Grove: InterVarsity Press 2012); Craig Keener and M. Daniel Carroll R., eds., *Global Voices: Reading the Bible in the Majority World* (Peabody: Hendrickson, 2013); William A. Dyrness, *Invitation to Cross-Cultural Theology: Case Studies in Vernacular Theologies* (Grand Rapids: Zondervan, 1992).

78. Choan-Seng Song, "Theology of the Incarnation," in *Asian Voices in Christian Theology*, ed. Gerald H. Anderson (Maryknoll: Orbis, 1976), 145–50.

79. Vengal Chakkarai, *Jesus the Avatar* (Madras, India: Christian Literature Society, 1930). The word "avatara" (avatar) means "descent" used of the coming to earth of a god, especially Vishnu in human or other forms.

Yang),[80] the personification of the *Minjung* (people),[81] and the Dalit (outcast).[82] Through these christological expressions, Jesus is seen as the Christ who takes the side of the sufferers, who deals seriously with human problems. As a result, the sufferers will be saved, released from their suffering, and experience God's justice in a difficult world.

CONCLUDING REFLECTIONS ON THE FOURFOLD GOSPEL AND CONTEXTUAL CHRISTOLOGIES

In summary, we have surveyed the state of New Testament research on Christologies in Western Christianity through the three quests for the historical Jesus. In this survey, we noted the contextual nature of these studies, especially in initial quests describing Jesus that reflect the images of the ones who engage in the quest. We have also looked at the fourfold Gospel and have unpacked some ways that the four Gospels show their differences and commonalities (especially in the prologues of the Gospels) in presenting who Jesus is and what these distinctions and agreements imply to the respective Christologies of the Gospel writers. Moreover, we have scanned the varied expressions and examples of contextual Christologies in Asia, using the realities of religious pluralism and poverty in the region and employing elitist and grassroots Christologies.

As a way to conclude this chapter, I offer three thoughts for reflection in doing Christology for the future that seeks to read the Bible more culturally and to read the culture more biblically. These three thoughts are as follows: (1) recognizing that all Christologies are contextual; (2) holding contextual Christologies in healthy tension; and (3) exploring the potential of story and narrative in engaging Asians about the Jesus Christ found in the Bible and how he is real and how they can relate with him according to their culture and context.

Recognizing that All Christologies Are Contextual

We have noted from the beginning of this chapter that there is no one Christology explaining fully the person and work of Jesus. That is why we use

---

80. Liem Kiem Yang, "Enacting the Acts of God," *South East Asia Journal of Theology* 14, no. 2 (1973): 21–33.
81. Suh Nam Dong, "Cultural Theology, Political Theology, and *Minjung* Theology," *Bulletin of the Commission on Theological Concerns* 5, no. 6 (1984–1985): 12–16.
82. Arvind P. Nirmal, "Doing Theology from a Dalit Perspective," in *A Reader in Dalit Theology*, ed. M. E. Prabhakar (Madras: Gurukul Lutheran Theological College & Research Institute, 1990), 139–44.

the term "Christologies" to refer to the various portraits of the four Gospels and to the diverse understandings about Jesus by scholars and theologians from the West and the Majority World. Our use of "Christologies" affirms the contextual nature of those who engage in studying who Jesus is. As Veli-Matti Kärkkäinen writes, "All theologies are shaped and conditioned by their intellectual, social, psychological, and religious environments."[83]

In the four Gospels, we see the differences in the portrayal of Jesus, reflecting the unique purposes and contexts of the Gospel writers and their communities. However, we also discover that, despite the disparity in the presentation of Jesus to their audiences by the Gospel writers, there are still observable commonalities in the Gospel narratives. In fact, we highlighted these commonalities in the prologues of the four Gospels. Though we note many divergences in the gospels, we also see convergences in the rendering of the passion narratives regarding Jesus. Thus, we can consider the four Gospels as a fourfold Gospel – with four portraits and one Jesus.

Holding Contextual Christologies in Healthy Tension

How do we account for the more diverse and even contrasting portrayals of Jesus by scholars and theologians in the West and Majority World? Our answer to this question is the same: the diversity of contexts accounts for the diversity in Christologies. Such disparity in contexts further diversifies greatly, given our differences in geographical location, time period, language, ethnicity, and culture. These realities prompt us to be intentional in addressing relevant issues of time, culture, and context in our Christologies. As Kosuke Koyama exhorts, "Each society must find its own point of contact between God and its people."[84]

These points of contact between God and people in society need to be discovered, so that we can put diversities in healthy tension. Healthy tensions affirm the reality of differences in Christologies without either succumbing to the temptation to harmonize or being overwhelmed by the complexity of the diversity. Healthy tensions also enable us to engage in conversation when we interpret Christologies. As John Levison and Priscilla Pope-Levison state, "The model of interpretation is that of conversation. The interpretation engages the Bible as a conversation partner with specific questions that arise from his or

---

83. Veli-Matti Kärkkäinen, *Christology: A Global Introduction* (Grand Rapids: Baker Academic, 2003), 228.
84. Kosuke Kayama, *Water Buffalo Theology* (Maryknoll: Orbis, 1974), 86.

her context. The goal of interpretation is to allow the conversation between the Bible and its interpreters to develop a life of its own."[85]

Entering into interpretive conversations allow us to think in terms of "both/and," rather than "either/or." Instead of seeing only the value of the "text," we need to also view the value of understanding "context." Anthony Thiselton contends that the relationship between text and context is to be taken as the fusion of two horizons – a fusion that seeks to be true to the past and relevant to the present.[86] When we witness the ongoing conversation of text and context, we can put in healthy tension the following polarities: four Gospels and fourfold Gospel; differences and commonalities in the gospel narratives; Jesus of history and the Christ of Scriptures; christological titles and narrative Christology; high Christology and low Christology; elitist ("from above") Christology and grassroots ("from below") Christology. Ivor Poobalan describes the need for Christology in Asia to be both rooted (in the Bible) and responsive (to the culture).[87] We must not only be rooted or simply be responsive; we need to be both.

When we gravitate to one side of the christological tension, we need to be pushed back to see the value of the other side of the tension, if our contextual Christologies are to be deemed healthy. For example, in the Philippines, the christological image of Jesus of the suffering servant remains dominant because many Filipinos can directly identify with Jesus's intense suffering. This point of connection has prevailed for several decades to the extent that it predominates our Filipino concept of Christology. Thus, there is a need for more theological reflection on the power of God in Christ. Melba Maggay argues similarly: "There is a need to strengthen the indigenous image of God as all-powerful and de-emphasize the dominant image of Christ as forever suffering."[88] She describes further the counter-productive emphasis on the suffering of Christ this way:

---

85. John R. Levison and Priscilla Pope-Levison, "Emergent Christologies in Latin America, Asia, and Africa," *Covenant Quarterly* 52 (1994): 30.

86. Anthony C. Thiselton, *The Two Horizons: New Testament Hermeneutics and Philosophical Description with Special Reference to Heidegger, Bultmann, Gadamer, and Wittgenstein* (Grand Rapids: Eerdmans, 1980), 10–23.

87. Ivor Poobalan, "Christology in Asia: Rooted and Responsive," in *Asian Christian Theology: Evangelical Perspectives*, edited by Timoteo D. Gener and Stephen T. Pardue (Carlisle: Langham Global Library, 2019), 83.

88. Melba Maggay, *Filipino Religious Consciousness: Some Implications to Missions* (Quezon City: Institute for Studies in Asian Church and Culture, 1999), 21.

Christ pictured as wounded and always suffering, as with the Sacred Heart ringed with thorns or lying stretched and supine with a wooden cross, maybe a case of projective identification, a pain that Filipinos own as a description of their own condition. This sense of God as a bleeding heart, or worse, entombed like the Sto. Entierro, makes for a sympathetic religion, but is hardly the sort that would empower a people to rise against oppression and the forces of death and misfortune.[89]

This warning prompts us to hold the suffering Messiah image of Jesus and his *Christus Victor* picture in healthy tension.

Exploring the Value of Story and Narrative

Having seen the value of recognizing that all Christologies are contextual (whether in the fourfold Gospel, West, or Majority World) and of holding these Christologies in healthy tension, let us now look at the potential of exploring story or narrative in engaging Asians about Jesus Christ. Story and narrative are the language of the fourfold Gospel in presenting Jesus to various communities of faith. As an approach to theology, storytelling has also been seen as a viable alternative to the Western argumentation theology.

Choang-Seng Song contends that theology is the story of people expressing the passion and hope of their suffering and wrestling with God in order to understand the meaning of life. Song also argues that biblical passages are nothing but stories of God's people, and Jesus is himself a master storyteller.[90] As master storyteller, Jesus narrated stories in parables, which attracted people to listen, reflect, and respond to his invitation to reverse their thinking and behavior. Telling stories about Jesus from the fourfold Gospel can be a way to relate his person, teaching, and work to the situations, struggles, and contexts of Asians who want to make sense of life – as Jesus also helped those in his time on earth to makes sense of their lives.

Conclusion

Christology will continue to be a significant area of study and ongoing research. Christianity was born and took form in a polytheistic environment. Just as the four Gospel writers told the stories about Jesus Christ in their own

---

89. Maggay, *Filipino Religious Consciousness*, 27.
90. Choang-Seng Song, *Tell Us our Names: Story Theology from an Asian Perspective* (Maryknoll: Orbis, 1984), ix–x.

diverse contexts under Rome, so also Western and Majority World scholars and theologians have expressed Christologies in their own contexts across the world. We need to continue developing contextual Christologies in our own contexts of religious pluralism and social injustice.

Our challenge requires a continuing conversation between biblical and historical traditions and current global realities. Kärkkäinen sums up the vision for future contextual Christologies: "Doing Christian Christology is (to be) a global, intercultural exercise, transcending ecclesiastical and theological boundaries. The end result is not one Christology but a variety of rich voices, not unlike the Gospels, yet voices that share a common focus."[91] This common focus is Jesus Christ, who spoke and who continues to speak, even two thousand years after his ministry, death, and resurrection.

BIBLIOGRAPHY

Ames, William. *The Marrow of Theology*. Durham: Labyrinth, 1983.

Anderson, Gerald H., ed. *Asian Voices in Christian Theology*. Maryknoll: Orbis, 1976. Barrett, C. K. *The Gospel According to St. John*. 2nd ed. Philadelphia: Westminster, 1978.

Bauckham, Richard. "John for Readers of Mark." In *The Gospel for All*, edited by R. Bauckham, 147–51. Grand Rapids: Eerdmans, 1998.

Bediako, Kwame. *Jesus in Africa: The Christian Gospel in African History and Experience*. Akropong-Akuapem, Ghana: Regnum Africa, 2000.

Blomberg, Craig L. *Jesus and the Gospels*. Nashville: Broadman & Holman, 1997.

Bock, Darrell L. *A Theology of Luke and Acts: God's Promised Program, Realized for All Nations*. Grand Rapids: Zondervan, 2012.

Boers, Hendrikus. "Where Christology Is Real: A Survey of Recent Research on New Testament Christology." *Interpretation* 26, no. 3 (1972): 300–27.

Boff, Leonardo, and Virgil Elizondo, eds. *Any Room for Christ in Asia?* London: SCM, 1993.

Boring, M. E. "Mark 1:1–15 and the Beginning of the Gospel." *Semeia* 52 (1990): 43–91.

Brown, Colin. "Historical Quest, Quest of." *DJG* 326–40.

Brown, Raymond E. *An Introduction to New Testament Christology*. New York: Paulist, 1994.

Burridge, Richard A. *Four Gospels, One Jesus? A Symbolic Reading*. 2nd ed. London: SPCK, 2005.

---

91. Kärkkäinen, *Christology*, 229.

Burnett, Fred W. "Characterization and Reader Construction in the Gospels."
    Semeia 63 (1993): 1–26.

Capes, David B. "New Testament Christology." In *The State of New Testament
    Studies: A Survey of Recent Research*, edited by Scot McKnight and Nijay K.
    Gupta, 161–81. Grand Rapids: Baker Academic, 2019.

Center for the Study of Global Christianity. *Christianity in its Global Context,
    1970–2020: Society, Religion, and Mission*. South Hamilton: Gordon
    Conwell, 2013.

Chakkarai, Vengal. *Jesus the Avatar*. Madras, India: Christian Literature
    Society, 1930.

Chan, Simon. *Grassroots Asian Theology: Thinking the Faith from the Ground Up*.
    Downers Grove: InterVarsity Press 2014.

Cullman, Oscar. *The Christology of the New Testament*. Louisville: WJKP, 1959.

Darr, John A. *On Character Building: The Reader and the Rhetoric of
    Characterization in Luke–Acts*. Louisville: WJKP, 1992.

Del Colle, Ralph. *Christ and the Spirit: Spirit-Christology in Trinitarian Perspective*.
    New York: Oxford University Press, 1994.

Devanandan, Paul. "Called to Witness." *Ecumenical Review* 14 (1962): 155–63.

Dinkler, Michal Beth. "A New Formalist Approach to Narrative Christology:
    Returning to the Structure of the Synoptic Gospels." *HTS Theological Studies*
    73, no. 1 (2017): 1–17.

Dyrness, William A. *Invitation to Cross-Cultural Theology: Case Studies in Vernacular
    Theologies*. Grand Rapids: Zondervan, 1992.

———. *Learning about Theology from the Third World*. Grand Rapids:
    Academie, 1990.

Elwood, Douglas J., ed. *Asian Christian Theology: Emerging Themes*. Philadelphia:
    Westminster, 1976.

Funk, Robert W., Roy W. Hoover, and the Jesus Seminar. *The Five Gospels: The
    Search for the Authentic Words of Jesus*. New York: Macmillan, 1993.

Garland, David. *A Theology of Mark's Gospel: Good News about Jesus the Messiah, the
    Son of God*. Grand Rapids: Zondervan, 2015.

Green, Gene L., Stephen T. Pardue, and K. K. Yeo, eds. *Jesus without Borders:
    Christology in the Majority World*. Carlisle: Langham Global Library, 2015.

Greenman, Jeffrey P., and Gene L. Green, eds. *Global Theology in Evangelical
    Perspective: Exploring the Contextual Nature of Theology and Mission*. Downers
    Grove: InterVarsity Press 2012.

Grindheim, Sigurd. *Christology in the Synoptic Gospels: God or God's Servant*.
    London: Continuum, 2012.

Hahn, Ferdinand. *The Titles of Jesus in Christology: Their History in Early
    Christianity*. Cambridge: James Clarke, 1969.

Hooker, Morna D. "Beginnings and Endings." Pages 184–202 in *The Written Gospel*. Edited by Markus Bockmuehl and Donald A. Hagner. Cambridge: Cambridge University Press, 2005.

———. *Beginnings: Keys That Open the Gospel*. London: Trinity, 1997.

———. "'Who Can This Be?' The Christology of Mark's Gospel." In *Contours of Christianity in the New Testament*, edited by Richard N. Longenecker, 79–99. Grand Rapids: Eerdmans, 2005.

Horsley, Richard. *Jesus and the Spiral of Violence*. San Francisco: Harper & Row, 1987.

Huang, Po Ho, Daniel F. Pilario, Catherine Cornille, Stephen Van Erp, and Tran Van Doan. *New Developments in Theology in Asia*. London: SCM, 2022.

Ju, Shi Huey. "Chinese Spirit-Mediums in Singapore: An Ethnographic Study." In *Studies in Chinese Folk Religion in Singapore and Malaysia*, edited by John Clammer, 3–48. Singapore: Institute for the Study of Religions and Society, 1983.

Kärkkäinen, Veli-Matti. *Christology: A Global Introduction*. Grand Rapids: Baker Academic, 2003.

Kayama, Kosuke. *Water Buffalo Theology*. Maryknoll: Orbis, 1974.

Keener, Craig, and M. Daniel Carroll R., eds. *Global Voices: Reading the Bible in the Majority World*. Peabody: Hendrickson, 2013.

Kitamori, Kazoh. *The Theology of the Pain of God*. Louisville: WJKP, 1965.

Köstenberger, Andres J. *A Theology of John's Gospel and Letters: The Word, the Christ, the Son of God*. Grand Rapids: Zondervan, 2009.

Koyama, Kosuke. *Three Mile an Hour God*. London: SCM, 1979.

Küster, Volker. *The Many Faces of Jesus Christ*. Maryknoll: Orbis, 1999.

Kwa, Kiem-Kiok, and Samuel Ka-Chieng Law, eds. *Missions in Southeast Asia: Diversity and Unity in God's Design*. Carlisle: Langham Global Library, 2022.

Levison, John R., and Priscilla Pope-Levison. "Emergent Christologies in Latin America, Asia, and Africa." *Covenant Quarterly* 52 (1994): 29–47.

———. "Toward an Ecumenical Christology for Asia." *Missiology* 22, no. 1 (1994): 3–17.

Longenecker., Richard N. *Contours of Christianity in the New Testament*. Grand Rapids: Eerdmans, 2005.

Maggay, Melba. *Filipino Religious Consciousness: Some Implications to Missions*. Quezon City, Philippines: Institute for Studies in Asian Church and Culture, 1999.

Marshall, I. Howard. *The Origins of New Testament Christology*. Updated ed. Downers Grove: InterVarsity Press, 1990.

Matera, Frank J. *New Testament Christology*. Louisville: WJKP, 1999.

————. "Prologue as the Interpretative Key to Mark's Gospel." *JSNT* 34 (1988): 3–20.

Metzger, Bruce. *A Textual Commentary on the Greek New Testament*. Stuttgart: United Bible Societies, 1971.

Nacpil, Emerito P., and Douglas J. Elwood, eds. *The Human and the Holy: Asian Perspectives in Christian Theology*. Maryknoll: Orbis, 1978.

Nirmal, Arvind P. "Doing Theology from a Dalit Perspective." In *A Reader in Dalit Theology*, edited by M. E. Prabhakar, 139–44. Madras: Gurukul Lutheran Theological College & Research Institute, 1990.

Ott, Craig, and Harold A. Netland, eds. *Globalizing Theology: Belief and Practice in an Era of World Christianity*. Grand Rapids: Baker Academic, 2006.

Panikkar, Raimundo. *The Unknown Christ of Hinduism: Toward an Ecumenical Christophany*. Maryknoll: Orbis, 1981.

Perrin, Norman. *A Modern Pilgrimage in New Testament Christology*. Philadelphia: Fortress, 1974.

Phan, Peter. *Being Religious Interreligiously: Asian Perspectives on Interfaith Dialogue*. Maryknoll: Orbis, 2004.

————, ed. *The Asian Synod: Text and Commentaries*. Maryknoll: Orbis, 2015.

Pieris, Aloysius. *An Asian Theology of Liberation*. Maryknoll: Orbis, 1988.

Poobalan, Ivor. "Christology in Asia: Rooted and Responsive." In *Asian Christian Theology: Evangelical Perspectives*, edited by Timoteo D. Gener and Stephen T. Pardue, 83–100. Carlisle: Langham Global Library, 2019.

Pope-Levison, Priscilla, and John R. Levison. *Jesus in Global Contexts*. Louisville: WJKP, 1992.

Powell, Mark A. *What Is Narrative Criticism?* Philadelphia: Fortress, 1990.

Rayan, Samuel. "Reconceiving Theology in the Asian Context." In *Doing Theology in a Divided World*, edited by Fabella, Virginia, and Sergio Torres, 124–42. Maryknoll: Orbis, 1985.

Rhoads, David. "Narrative Criticism: Practices and Prospects." In *Characterization in the Gospel: Reconceiving Narrative Criticism*, edited by David Rhoads and Kari Syreeni, 264–85. Sheffield: Sheffield Academic Press, 1999.

Ro, Bong Rin, and Ruth Eshenaur, eds. *The Bible and Theology in Asian Contexts: An Evangelical Perspective on Asian Theology*. Seoul: Word of Life, 1984.

Sanders, E. P. *Jesus and Judaism*. London: SCM, 1985.

Santos, Narry F. "Mark 1:1–15: The Paradox of Authority and Servanthood." In *Interpreting the New Testament Text: Introduction to the Art and Science of Exegesis*, edited by Darrell Bock and Buist Fanning, 323–39. Wheaton: Crossway, 2006.

Schüssler Fiorenza, Elisabeth. *In Memory of Her*. New York: Crossroad, 1994.

Schweitzer, Albert. *The Quest of the Historical Jesus: A Critical Study of its Progress from Reimarus to Wrede*. Translated by W. Montgomery. London: Adam and Charles Black, 1910.

Shoji, Tsutomu. "The Church's Struggle for Freedom of Belief – An Aspect of Christian Mission." In *Living Theology in Asia*, edited by J. England, 49–57. Maryknoll: Orbis, 1982.

Song, Choan-Seng. *Tell Us our Names: Story Theology from an Asian Perspective*. Maryknoll: Orbis, 1984.

———. "Theology of the Incarnation." In *Asian Voices in Christian Theology*, edited by Gerald H. Anderson, 145–50. Maryknoll: Orbis, 1976.

Strauss, Mark L. "Christology and Christological Purpose in the Synoptic Gospels: A Study of Unity in Diversity." In *Reconsidering the Relationship between Biblical and Systematic Theology in the New Testament*, Edited by Benjamin Reynolds, Brian Lugioyo, and Kevin J. Vanhoozer, 41–62. Tübingen, Germany: Mohr Siebeck, 2014.

———. *Four Portraits, One Jesus: An Introduction to Jesus and the Gospels*. Grand Rapids: Zondervan, 2007.

Sugirtharajah, R. S., ed. *Frontiers in Asian Christian Theology: Emerging Trends*. Maryknoll: Orbis, 1994.

Suh, Nam Dong. "Cultural Theology, Political Theology, and *Minjung* Theology." *Bulletin of the Commission on Theological Concerns* 5, no. 6 (1984–1985): 12–16.

Takenaka, Masao. *God Is Rice: Asian Culture and Christian Faith*. Geneva: WCC, 1986.

Thiselton, Anthony C. *The Two Horizons: New Testament Hermeneutics and Philosophical Description with Special Reference to Heidegger, Bultmann, Gadamer, and Wittgenstein*. Grand Rapids: Eerdmans, 1980.

Thomas, Benjamin P. "Confronted with the Facts." In *Portraits of Global Christianity: Research and Reflections in Honor of Todd M. Johnson*, edited by Gina A. Zurlo, 163–64. Littleton: William Carey, 2023.

Thomas, M. M. "The Meaning of Salvation Today – A Personal Statement." *International Review of Mission* 62 (1973): 158–69.

———. *Towards a Theology of Contemporary Ecumenism*. Madras, India: Christian Literature Society, 1978.

Tuckett, Christopher. *Christology and the New Testament: Jesus and His Earliest Followers*. Louisville: WJKP, 2001.

Vanhoozer, Kevin J. "Christology in the West: Conversations in Europe and North America." In *Majority World Theology: Christian Doctrine in Global Context*, edited by Gene L. Green, Stephen T. Pardue, and K. K. Yeo, 116–32. Downers Grove: IVP Academic, 2020.

Vermes, Geza. *Jesus the Jew*. London: Collins, 1973.

Watson, Francis. *The Fourfold Gospel: A Theological Reading of the New Testament Portraits of Jesus*. Grand Rapids: Baker Academic, 2016.

Wickremesinghe, C. Lakshman. "Alienated Church and Signs of the Times." In *Living Theology in Asia*, edited by John C. England, 183–90. Maryknoll: Orbis, 1982.

Witherington, Ben III. "Jesus as the Alpha and Omega of New Testament Thought. In *Contours of Christianity in the New Testament*, edited by Richard N. Longenecker., 25–46. Grand Rapids: Eerdmans, 2005.

———. *Jesus the Sage*. Minneapolis: Fortress, 1994.

———. *The Jesus Quest: The Third Search for the Jew of Nazareth*. Downers Grove, IL: InterVarsity, 1995.

———. *The Many Faces of the Christ: The Christologies of the New Testament and Beyond*. New York: Crossroad, 1998.

Wright, N.T. *Jesus and the Victory of God*. London: SPCK, 1996.

Yang, Liem Kiem. "Enacting the Acts of God." *South East Asia Journal of Theology* 14, no. 2 (1973): 21–33.

Yewangoe, A. A. *Theologia Crucis in Asia: Asian Christian Views on Suffering in the Face of Overwhelming Poverty and Multifaceted Religiosity in Asia*. Amsterdam: Rodopi, 1987.

CHAPTER 2

BREAKING DOWN THE DIVIDING WALLS

The Gospel of Reconciliation/Solidarity from a Chinese Perspective

Xiaxia E. Xue

Tension, conflict, and division seem to be characteristics in the history of the church from the first century of the apostolic period. In another work, I noted that, "starting from the early church in the first century and throughout every following age, people have experienced divisions in the church."[1] The New Testament documents the tensions that already existed in the first-century Jerusalem church, such as when the Greek-speaking followers of Jesus complained against the Hebrew-speaking ones about being neglected in the daily supply of food (Acts 6:1–6), and in Paul's criticism of the divided parties in the Corinthian church (1 Cor 1–4).

Such tensions persist throughout the church's history. Thus, the great schism between the Eastern churches (based in Constantinople) and the Western churches (based in Rome) occurred around AD 1054. Various factors contributed to the break, including the political rivalry between Latin-speaking Rome and Greek-speaking Constantinople, and theological disputes (e.g. disagreement over the Nicene Creed, the procession of the Holy Spirit, the use of leavened or unleavened bread in the Eucharist, etc.).[2]

Another well-known split within the Western churches was the Protestant Reformation, which divided the Western church into Protestantism and the Roman Catholic Church in the sixteenth century. Many factors contributed to the cause of the Reformation, including tensions between the church and the political authorities, the corruption of the church institution, the influence of

---

1. Xiaxia E. Xue, "The Community as Union with Christ in the Midst of Conflict: An Ecclesiology of the Pauline Letters from a Chinese Perspective," in *The Church from Every Tribe and Tongue: Ecclesiology in the Majority World*, ed. Gene L. Green, Stephen T. Pardue, and K. K. Yeo, Majority World Theology Series (Carlisle: Langham Global Library, 2018), 114–15.
2. Alister E. McGrath, *Christianity: An Introduction*, 3rd ed. (West Sussex, UK: Wiley Blackwell, 2015), 138–39.

culture and economy, etc. These conflicts and divisions between the Protestant churches and the Roman Catholic Church led to thirty years of religious wars in which more than one million people were killed or wounded. Furthermore, within the development of the Protestant movement, there were splits over theological issues, resulting in many denominations, such as the Baptists, the Methodists, the Lutherans, the Anglicans, the Anabaptists, the Reformers, etc.

There continues to exist all kinds of conflict and tension between church leaders and lay people, and even amongst church leaders themselves or amongst lay people. I personally have experienced church divisions several times as a result of conflicting ideas over church operations. It seems that from ancient times to today, tensions and divisions in the church are unavoidable. Does this contradict the gospel of unity and solidarity, or go against the way of the Lord's church (the body of Christ)? How can we reconcile the concept of the gospel of unity with these church divisions throughout the history of Christianity? This essay will explore these issues and argue that: (1) churches share the human characteristic of tension and fragility, but the gospel of reconciliation and solidarity is revealed through tensions and divisions; and (2) underneath the divergent forces of social groups, there is an inherent value of solidarity and unity which can be manifested with the work of the Holy Spirit. The current Chinese churches, particularly in Hong Kong, will be in sight throughout this argument.

In what follows, I will offer a brief summary of some of the divisions within the contemporary Chinese church. Then, appealing to related NT passages I will illustrate how, in the midst of conflicts and divisions, the gospel of reconciliation is revealed through the work of the Holy Spirit. In this core part, I will highlight three types of conflicts and divisions and demonstrate how the Holy Spirit works amid such tensions. The essay will conclude with overall view of the work of the Spirit in bringing about unity and reconciliation in and through the church.

DIVISIONS WITHIN THE CURRENT
CHINESE CHURCH AND SOCIETY

The divisions within contemporary Chinese society and Chinese churches are complex and multifaceted. First, differences in cultural values have led to the increasing friction between those from the mainland and those from Hong Kong. Hong Kong, which is a post-colonial society, has been influenced by British cultural values and language. By contrast, the mainland Chinese live under the influence of traditional Chinese cultures and have been governed by the People's Republic of China since 1949. These different traditions and cultural values contribute to persistent divisions between residents of mainland China and Hong Kong.

An incident helps illustrate this tension. In January 2012, a child with his mother visiting from mainland China was seen eating on a Hong Kong train. Eating on public transport in Hong Kong is prohibited, which led to the child's mother and a Hong Kong man yelling at each other in their respective languages.[3] Some Hongkongers made negative judgments, stating "that's what mainlanders are like." Afterwards, a Peking University professor stated that Hongkongers were "British running dogs," which in turn caused a tremendous protest and calls for the government to stop the "infiltration" of mainlanders.[4] In addition, there was increased hatred toward new immigrants from the mainland to Hong Kong, driven by fear that they may drain public resources, such as healthcare, housing, and education. The tension between Hongkongers and mainlanders is also reflected in the church. For instance, outreach ministries from Hong Kong churches to mainland Chinese have substantially decreased due to political issues and an environment of mutual distrust.[5]

These divisions are driven in part by Hong Kong people's attitudes toward the governments of mainland China and Hong Kong. Tensions increased dramatically after the 2019 Hong Kong protests (The Anti-Extradition Law Amendment Bill Movement), particularly after the national security bill for Hong Kong was promulgated. Pro-Beijing citizens supported the Hong Kong government and police, while protesters pushed for the realization of five demands, one of which was the withdrawal of the extradition bill. There were also divisions among the protesters, with lines drawn between the moderate group and the radical group. The latter became violent by attacking police and vandalizing targets symbolizing the government (MTR, banks, etc.) or shops representing China (some pro-Beijing restaurants). The pro-Beijing citizens also attacked those radical protesters. The whole society experienced violence, suffering, and profound division.

These political disagreements were reflected in churches as well, and Christians with different political stances fought with each other. For instance,

---

3. "Mainland Visitors Eating on A Hong Kong Train Caused A Huge Fight," 23 January, 2012, https://www.businessinsider.com/mainland-visitors-eating-on-hong-kong-train-cause-a-huge-fight-2012-1.
4. See "Dogs and Locusts," *The Economist* (4 February 2012). The article can be accessed online at https://www.economist.com/china/2012/02/04/dogs-and-locusts.
5. Xue, "Community as Union with Christ," 126.

around forty young people quit their positions at the Evangelical Tung Fook Church because of disagreements with how the church leaders responded to the political turmoil. These young people wanted the church to have a voice on such political matters, speaking truth into political situations. However, the church leaders tended to keep silent on political issues in order to avoid pressure from the government. This reflects a wider division among Christians in Hong Kong, who are in at least two camps: the yellow camp (pro-democratic Christians) and the blue camp (pro-government Christians). The conflicts or confrontations among them can be seen within the churches and in all kinds of media. The COVID-19 pandemic added a new dimension of division as Christians adopted various responses to the government's vaccination mandates.

Another significant division in Hong Kong society and churches is related to the different ethnic groups in Hong Kong and mainland China. Both Hongkongers and mainlanders are Han Chinese, constituting around 92 percent of the demographic. There are also other minority groups constituting a smaller percentage of the demographic: in Hong Kong, Filipino 2.5 percent, Indonesian 2.1 percent, others 3.4 percent.[6] In mainland China, there are fifty-five minority ethnic groups, altogether constituting less than 8 percent of the population. In mainland China, the Han Chinese are found mainly on the middle and lower reaches of the Yellow River, the Yangtze River and the Pearl River valleys, and the Northeast Plain, while the fifty-five ethnic minorities are scattered over vast areas, mainly distributed in the border of areas of northeast, north, northwest and southwest China.[7] In part due to their geographic location, these groups are often economically and educationally disadvantaged and socially marginalized.

Likewise, Hong Kong Chinese communities are dominated by Cantonese speakers, while non-Cantonese speakers are in the minority and are sometimes marginalized or discriminated against as a result. As a mainlander with a heavily-accented Cantonese accent, I have already experienced discrimination several times, though it would be much greater for those who have different skin tones from the Han Chinese ethnic group. Some discriminatory terms are used to refer to people of minority ethnic groups, such as "Ah-cha" for

---

6. Home Affairs Department, "The Demographics: Ethnic Groups," https://www.had.gov.hk/rru/english/info/demographics.htm.

7. China Internet Information Center, "Fifty-six Ethnic Groups," *China Through a Lens*, http://www.china.org.cn/english/features/38107.htm.

people of Indian or South Asian descent. Hong Kong churches often have very little awareness of the need to include people of different cultures and races.

We have described the three main types of divisions within contemporary Chinese society and Chinese churches – conflicting social-cultural values; political, social and religious disagreements; and distinct ethnicities. We will now explore the key to reconciliation amidst the divisions.

THE GOSPEL OF RECONCILIATION: BREAKING DOWN THE DIVIDING WALLS

Breaking Down the Dividing Wall between Groups with Conflicting Cultural Values

Conflict between different social groups can arise from their conflicting cultural values. Contemporary Chinese people and the first-century Jews share a similar tension caused by differing cultural values, which include a hierarchy of social classes.

Hong Kong was occupied by the British in the late nineteenth century and then by the Japanese during World War II. In 1946, the British re-established civil government in Hong Kong, and thousands of Chinese people came back to Hong Kong. Under the influence of Chinese and Western cultures, Hongkongers developed multicultural values that differed from the traditional values of the Han Chinese from mainland China. For example, Hong Kong, which is a special administrative region, has its own governmental system for legal, economic and financial affairs. Democracy and freedom are more important in Hong Kong than in mainland society. As we saw earlier disparate social values have led to conflicts between Hong Kong and mainland Chinese in their encounters with one another.

This tension has similarities to the situation within first-century Judaism, where the culture of the Jewish diaspora communities bore important differences from the prevailing Jewish culture in Jerusalem. Many diaspora communities lived outside of Palestine for hundreds of years. Jews in such communities were often assimilated into the culture in which they resided while also maintaining their identity as Jews by their adherence to some key Jewish traditions.[8] Understandably, when Jews from different cultural locations joined together as a church, tensions arose.

---

8. John M. G. Barclay, *Pauline Churches and Diaspora Jews*, WUNT 2/275 (Tübingen: Mohr Siebeck, 2011), 141–55.

Social Conflict in the Book of Acts

In the first century, the Jews who were dispersed into different nations had come together to Jerusalem on the day of Pentecost (Acts 2:1–11). Many diasporic Jews may have stayed in the Palestine area after Peter's speech. They repented, were baptized in the name of Jesus Christ, and received the gift of the Holy Spirit (2:38). There were at least three thousand who became followers of Jesus (2:41–42). However, the increased number of disciples generated tensions and conflicts, especially among the Greek-speaking Jewish followers of Jesus (the "Hellenists") and the Aramaic-speaking disciples (the Hebrews) (6:1–7).[9]

On the one hand, this conflict was concerned with food distribution. The Hellenists had complained against the Hebrews that they were being neglected in the daily distribution of food (6:1). This was an instance of discrimination within the congregation, for "the Hellenistic widows were receiving less than their fair share in the overall food distribution."[10] On the other hand, the tensions and divergences between the Hellenists and the Hebrews may have also had roots in different understandings of the Torah (cf. 6:1–8:3).[11] Stephen, who shared a freer understanding of the Torah than that of the Hebrews, was persecuted in Jerusalem. According to Ulrich Luz, "At a very early date . . . the different attitude toward the Torah was a question that divided the followers of Jesus. It may be that the law-free Gentile mission was first carried on by such Greek speaking Jewish followers of Jesus from the Diaspora (11:20)."[12]

Such tensions evidently permeated in the earliest Jewish Christian communities. Many Hellenistic Jews assimilated into the local cultures, laying emphasis on Jesus's love command rather than ritual laws, such as when Paul and some other Jewish Christians in Antioch shared table fellowship with non-Jewish followers of Jesus (Gal 2:11–21).[13] By contrast, the Jewish Christians in Jerusalem were required to observe the Torah strictly. How did the first disciples handle these tensions and conflicts? How could they break down the walls amongst Jesus followers who carried different cultural heritages? Luke's description in Acts is of help here.

---

9. Lukas Vischer, Ulrich Luz, and Christian Link, *Unity of the Church in the New Testament and Today* (Grand Rapids: Eerdmans, 2010), 44.

10. Robert T. Carpenter, "Multiethnic Churches: Their Current and Potential Impact in a Time of Racial Reckoning," *Dialogismos* 6 (2022): 27–28.

11. Vischer, Luz, and Link, *Unity of the Church*, 44.

12. Vischer, Luz, and Link, *Unity of the Church*, 45.

13. Vischer, Luz, and Link, *Unity of the Church*, 46.

On the surface, "the neglect of the food distribution" issue was handled by setting up an administrative team of the seven. On a deeper level, however, it was God's work through the Holy Spirit. The chosen seven were full of the Holy Spirit, were of wisdom and had good reputation (6:3). Stephen, particularly, was "a man full of faith and the Holy Spirit" (6:5), "full of grace and power," who "did great wonders and signs among the people" (6:8); and he spoke with wisdom and the Spirit (6:10). From the repeated reference to the Holy Spirit, we can deduce that the focus of Acts was how the Holy Spirit worked to support the way the disciples dealt with the conflict. However, it is still not so clear how the Holy Spirit helped the situation.

The divergences in understandings of the Torah caused serious divisions between the Jerusalem Jewish Christians and the Hellenistic Christians. Peter's vision in Acts 10 is an example of how tensions were resolved by the work of the Holy Spirit. Where Peter adhered to the ritual law, it was the Holy Spirit who asked him to eat the so-called unclean food and to enter into the house of the uncircumcised (11:5–10, 12, 16–18). Thus, it was the Holy Spirit who reminded Peter to break through the walls between the Jews and the Gentiles. In sum, it is evident from the Acts narratives that the role of the Holy Spirit is essential to break down the barriers between different groups and their respective cultural influences.

Social Conflict in 1 Corinthians

Another instance of division, one that resulted from differences of social class, is shown in the divided parties of the Corinthian church. The conflict in the Corinthian church may have been a matter of competing statuses or positions in church, and by weighing one apostle over another.[14] As Gerd Theissen has stated, "the disagreement among different parties may be a matter of scrapping for position within the pecking order."[15] This is seen from Paul's word contrasts of "wise," "powerful," and "of noble birth," against "foolish," "weak," and "low and despised in the world" (1 Cor 1:26–27 ESV). In other words, the conflict among different groups was "a struggle for position within the congregation, carried on primarily by those of high social status."[16] The tension between them is also evident in the participation of the Lord's Supper (1 Cor 11:17–34).

---

14. David Arthur deSilva, *An Introduction to the New Testament: Contexts, Methods & Ministry Formation* (Downers Grove: IVP Academic, 2004), 565.
15. Gerd Theissen, *The Social Setting of Pauline Christianity: Essays on Corinth*, trans. John H. Schutz (Edinburgh: T&T Clark, 1982), 55.
16. Theissen, *The Social Setting of Pauline Christianity*, 56.

Some rich members in the church took part in dinner without waiting for the others;[17] other members (especially the slaves and the poor), possibly because they had to come late due to their work, had nothing "to bring to contribute to the common meal,"[18] and were left with nothing to eat (11:20–21).

How did Paul address these conflicts in the parties and build up the solidarity of the church? Paul identified himself with those in the lowest position first, stating to the Corinthians that "I came to you in weakness and in fear and in much trembling" (2:3 NIV). Then he gave an illustration of the church as a body with many members and where each individual member had its own function for the church (12:12–31). It seems that Paul was trying to break down the influence of the hierarchical classes by highlighting the equal status amongst church members in front of Christ.[19] However, could the various social classes view each other as equal? The key is in the power of the Spirit. Paul, after identifying himself with the low and the despised, turned to the work of the Spirit, indicating that his speech and proclamation were "with a demonstration of the Spirit and of power" (2:4 NIV). Later, he emphasized again that "we speak of these things in words not taught by human wisdom but taught by the Spirit" (2:13 NRSV). For Paul, people with the Spirit discern/examine (ἀνακρίνω [anakrinō]) all things (2:15), which parallels the expression that "we have the mind of Christ" (2:16 NRSV).[20] In other words, with the Spirit of God, Jesus followers are able to know what God is doing in the world.[21]

It is worth noticing that in the Lord's Supper, Paul does not explicitly refer to the Spirit. However, before his teaching about how to come together to eat and wait for one another (11:33–34), he speaks seven times of discernment (11:29–34; διακρίνω [diakrinō], κρίμα [krima], and so on), an activity specifically connected to the Spirit in 2:15. Therefore, from this perspective, we can see that through the indwelling Holy Spirit of discernment, the barriers within

17. Anthony C. Thiselton, *The First Epistle to the Corinthians: A Commentary on the Greek Text*, NIGTC (Grand Rapids: Eerdmans, 2000), 860–62. Some scholars, including Thiselton, have demonstrated from historical and archaeological evidence that the splits are related to the status of the participants.

18. Vischer, Luz, and Link, *Unity of the Church*, 87.

19. Andrew Chester, "The Pauline Communities," in *A Vision for the Church Studies in Early Christian Ecclesiology in Honour of J.P.M. Sweet*, eds. Markus Bockmuehl and Michael B. Thompson (Edinburgh: T&T Clark, 1997), 110–11.

20. Gordon D. Fee, *The First Epistle to the Corinthians*, rev. ed., NICNT (Grand Rapids: Eerdmans, 2014), 125.

21. Fee, *The First Epistle to the Corinthians*, 125. See also Siu Fung Wu, "Paul, the Spirit-People, and People on the Margins," *Australasian Pentecostal Studies* 22, vol. 2 (2021): 260–78.

the social hierarchy which separate people from different classes or groups can be removed, as long as we keep listening to the Spirit of discernment.

How might this discerning Spirit help to transform Christians in terms of bias based on social class? In 3:1–4, Paul points out that when the Corinthians lived as those of the flesh, they thought and behaved like the people of their present age, being governed by worldly concerns, and not living out lives transformed by the Spirit.[22] That is why they were divided in terms of who they belonged to (3:4). By contrast, Jesus followers, led by the Spirit, could discern that they were all working together (συνεργοί [sunergoi]) as God's servants, in God's field (θεοῦ γεώργιον [theou geōrgion]) and God's building (θεοῦ οἰκοδομή [theou oikodomē]; 3:9), because God's Spirit dwells in the midst of them (3:16). According to Fee, "the Spirit is the key, the crucial reality, for life in the new era. The presence of the Spirit, and that *alone*, marks them off as God's new people, God's temple, when assembled in Christ's name in Corinth."[23]

Breaking Down the Dividing Walls between Groups with differing Political, Social and Religious Viewpoints

Tension and conflicts that occur within churches can arise out of non-religious factors.[24] However, according to Mayer, religious conflict is even more complex:

> Conflict occurs when something is contested. When we couple religion with conflict, we might expect that what is contested is ideology or morality (i.e., belief). But this is not necessarily the case, and religious conflict is best described as a more complex phenomenon that engages a combination of contested domains, including power, personality, space or place, and group identity. These contested domains should not be confused with enabling factors or conditions, which . . . can be political, social, economic, cultural and psychological.[25]

Likewise, the divisions and conflicts within churches are often connected to political and social factors. Mayer's theory can be applied to the conflicts

---

22. Fee, *The First Epistle to the Corinthians*, 131.
23. Fee, *The First Epistle to the Corinthians*, 160.
24. Christoph W. Stenschke, "The Conflicts of Acts 1–8:3 in View of Recent Research on Religious Conflicts in Antiquity (Part One: Theoretical Issues and Contested Domains)," *EuroJTh* 26, no. 1 (2017): 15.
25. Wendy Mayer, "Religous Conflict: Definitions, Problems and Theoretical Approaches," in *Religious Conflict from Early Christianity to the Rise of Islam*, eds. Wendy Mayer, Bronwen Neil, and Christian Albrecht, Arbeiten Zur Kirchengeschichte Ser (Berlin: De Gruyter, 2013), 2–3.

of contemporary Hong Kong churches. In particular, after the Umbrella Movement in 2014 and the Anti-Extradition Law Amendment Bill Movement in 2019, Hong Kong society has increasingly been torn apart by massive destruction and violence. Similarly, churches went through arguments, fights, and splits due to differing political viewpoints. After the Anti-Extradition Movement, church circles have been divided into the "yellow camp" – those who tended to support the movement or were very concerned with social issues – and the "blue camp," who tended to support the government or did not want to talk about politics. The conflicts were so acute that some pastors came to feel they could only serve one group or the other, but could not serve them together within a single congregation.[26]

As we have already observed, similar dynamics characterized the earliest churches. In what follows, we will consider the conflict at Antioch to shed some light on how Paul dealt with such tensions. In the first-century Jerusalem church, the first Jesus followers were Jewish. For them, the Israelites were the people of God. There were generally two "different ways of viewing the status of Gentile converts with respect to Jewish believers."[27] On the one hand there were some conservative Palestinian Jews, who were the Torah-faithful Jewish Christians. Part of this group were the radical Jewish Christians, who refused "to enter a Gentile's house and to eat with them" (Acts 10:28; 11:2–3).[28] If Gentiles wanted to follow Jesus, then they must become the people of Israel, and they were required to be circumcised and to keep the commandments of the Torah.[29] On the other hand, in diaspora circles, it is hard to imagine that there could be "outright refusal of all meal fellowship with all Gentiles."[30] In other words, a good number of Jews did have contact with Gentiles and even ate with them.

However, even the Jewish Christians who had no disagreement regarding contact with Gentiles differed in how they related to Gentiles. The conflict between Peter and Paul in the Antioch incident demonstrates their differing viewpoints of table fellowship with Gentiles. We could see that the tensions

26. Christian Times, "分色牧養：一位'黃牧'之見," https://christiantimes.org.hk/Common/ Reader/News/ShowNews.jsp?Nid=160886&Pid=104&Version=0&Cid=2053&Charset=big5_ hkscs.

27. Justin Taylor, "The Jerusalem Decrees (Acts 15.20, 29 and 21.25) and the Incident at Antioch (Gal 2.11–14)," *NTS* 47, no. 3 (2001): 380.

28. Markus Bockmuehl, "Antioch and James the Just," in *James the Just and Christian Origins*, ed. Bruce Chilton and Craig A. Evans, NovTSup 98 (Leiden: Brill, 1999), 166.

29. Vischer, Luz, and Link, *Unity of the Church*, 63.

30. Bockmuehl, "Antioch and James the Just," 167.

occurred because of some political and religious concerns, not only from conflicting theological reasons.

Extensive research has already been done on the incident at Antioch (Gal 2:11–14).[31] For the sake of brevity, this essay will not get into these complex arguments, but does align with one major view that the differences between Peter and Paul are about some political or religious concerns, rather than theological reasons. The reason Peter withdrew from the open table fellowship with Gentiles is, according to Paul, because of his "fear of the men from James . . . the circumcised" (2:12).

What was Peter afraid of that led him to choose to withdraw from table fellowship with Gentiles? Peter was sent to proclaim the Lord Jesus to the Jewish people (2:9), so Peter's focus or the goal of the ministry is toward those "the circumcised." As Gibson has rightly pointed out, Peter's fear of his table-fellowship with Gentiles was because his table-fellowship "would cause Jewish believers in Judea to undergo persecution after reports reached the Jewish leadership in Jerusalem."[32] As Bockmuehl has indicated, James and his emissaries were not Judaizers (2:7–9). In fact, James's concerns for the Antioch church were primarily about political pressure. Bockmuehl therefore argues that "there is in any case enough evidence of political pressure on the Jerusalem church to suggest that the politically motivated plea for solidarity must have been at least part of the reason for James's embassy to Antioch."[33]

By contrast, Paul was indignant over Peter's action. He used a series of strong negative comments towards Peter. He rebuked Peter's behavior, saying that "he stood self-condemned," for "fear of the uncircumcised," for "hypocrisy," and for "not acting consistently with the truth of the gospel" (see 2:11–14).

Why was Paul so upset by Peter's action? It seems that Paul was more concerned about the influence of his action to the Antioch church. First, when Peter withdrew from the table fellowship with Gentiles, the other Jews and even Barnabas followed him. One can imagine how much impact Peter's action had. Not only were the other Jews "carried away," but Barnabas, who had been Paul's co-worker in the ministry of Gentiles, joined Peter too. James D. G. Dunn has rightly indicated, "That Barnabas should so act must have been a tremendous blow to Paul . . . the action of the Jewish believers as a

---

31. See Xiaxia Xue, "Mood and Ideology in Galatians 1–2," in *Romans and Galatians*, ed. Stanley E. Porter, Zachary K. Dawson, and Ryder A. Wishart, LENT (Leiden: Brill, forthcoming).
32. Jack J. Gibson, *Peter Between Jerusalem and Antioch: Peter, James and the Gentiles*, WUNT 2/345 (Tübingen: Mohr Siebeck, 2013), 262.
33. Bockmuehl, "Antioch and James the Just," 182.

whole created a wave of fervor (to maintain Jewish identity) which Barnabas could not resist."[34] From this scenario, we can infer that Paul was afraid that his ministry to Gentiles would be seriously undermined. In addition, Paul's concern was not only for his team of co-workers, but also for his responsibility toward the Gentile ministry. As Peter Richardson had put it, "before the gentile Christians in Antioch he must defend his ministry to the gentiles."[35]

In sum, both Peter and Paul had their own focuses in ministry, which caused their different responses to "the men from James." What Paul says in 1 Corinthians 9:20–23 could be applied in the context of their chosen response:

> To the Jews I became as a Jew, in order to win Jews. To those under the law I became as one under the law . . . so that I might win those under the law. To those outside the law I became as one outside the law . . . so that I might win those outside the law. To the weak I became weak, so that I might win the weak. I have become all things to all people, that I might by all means save some. I do it all for the sake of the gospel, so that I may share in its blessings. (NRSV)

It seems that their responses to "the men from James" varied because they had different concerns in their respective ministries. In other words, the tension or conflict between these two groups, represented by Peter and Paul, did not arise because of different views on the gospel, but rather on the pastoral concerns toward each group.

What is at stake here is how early Christians handled these different pastoral concerns, which generated tensions and conflicts among Christian groups. Some biblical texts reveal that Peter and Paul were reconciled to one other. In 2 Peter 3:15, Peter addresses Paul as "our beloved brother Paul" (ESV). Paul also has no difficulty to address Peter together with him, "whether Paul or Apollos or Cephas or the world or life or death or the present or the future – all are yours" (1 Cor 3:22 ESV). Also, in Galatians 2:15, Paul uses "we ourselves" (Ἡμεῖς [hēmeis]), the first word of the whole sentence, to emphasize the inclusion of Peter, and maybe other Jewish Christians (i.e., Peter, Barnabas

---

34. James D. G. Dunn, *The Epistle to the Galatians*, BNTC (Peabody: Hendrickson, 1993), 126.
35. Peter Richardson, "Pauline Inconsistency: 1 Corinthians 9:19–23 and Galatians 2:11–14," *NTS* 26, no. 3 (1980): 354–55.

and the other Jews mentioned before v. 15).[36] In the final admonitions of the Letter to Galatians, Paul sent peace and mercy to all, stressing "the Israel of God (ἐπὶ τὸν Ἰσραὴλ τοῦ θεοῦ [epi ton Israēl tou theou])."[37]

How did reconciliation occur after the conflict and after Paul's condemnations? This may shed some light on the conflicts among current Chinese churches. In light of conflicts relating to different political views among church groups, how might we perceive the gospel of the reconciliation, and whether we establish the reconciliation between opposing parties?

First, reconciliation can happen in Christ through the power of the Holy Spirit, particularly when we live according to the Spirit and produce the fruit of the Spirit (5:22–23). However, when we are controlled by our social circumstances, then we tend to live a life of fear.

Paul pointed out that Peter's (and other Jews') reaction to withdraw from table fellowship was out of fear (2:12), and Paul reprimanded this as hypocrisy. It could be that this fear made Peter overreact, or to lose sight of how his behavior affected the Gentile community of the Antioch church. External pressures from society would not have the power to divide churches except in cases where there is a connection to our inner fears.[38]

By contrast, there is a deeper trust possible in Christ, for it is "Christ who lives in me. And the life I now live in the flesh I live by faith in the Son of God, who loved me and gave himself for me" (2:20 ESV). In Christ, we may have the inner strength to face perilous circumstances because God supplies us with the Spirit and work of power among us (cf. 3:5). Through the inner strength from Christ and the Holy Spirit, divergent groups may be able to enter into each other's contexts and worldview, and see their respective concerns, with the possibility of beginning the process of true reconciliation.

Breaking Down the Dividing Walls between Divergent Ethnic Groups

Tensions arise between the divergent ethnic groups, both in contemporary China and in the first-century Jewish world. The percentage of non-Chinese

---

36. William O. Walker says, "his [Paul's] use of the 'we' is intended to associate Cephas with himself." See "Does the 'We' in Gal 2.15–17 Include Paul's Opponents?," *NTS* 49 no. 4 (2003): 565.

37. From Gal 6:16, we can see Paul's concern for the Jews, as it reads: "As for those who will follow this rule – peace be upon them, and mercy, and upon the Israel of God."

38. Parker J. Palmer, *The Courage to Teach: Exploring the Inner Landscape of a Teacher's Life* (San Francisco: Jossey-Bass, 1998), 36.

in Hong Kong is very low – around 8 percent of the population as a whole. Hong Kong society is dominated by Cantonese-speaking Chinese, most of whom may not have opportunities to interact with people of other ethnicities. In addition, most Chinese churches have been mono-cultural for decades and may not be very aware of the need to include people from different cultures into their churches. Many Chinese churches tend to be "ethnocentric," treating non-Chinese as others, or "not my people." The prejudice against non-Chinese people has become a serious obstacle for Chinese churches in participating in local cross-cultural missions. How might we break down the barriers produced by this ethnocentric ethos? In the following, Paul's personal experience of transformation and his view of the relationship between Jews and Gentiles will be explored.

Paul was a Pharisee who was zealous for the Jewish tradition and who violently persecuted the church of God (Gal 1:13–14), but whose life turned into one of proclaiming the faith he once tried to destroy among the Gentiles (1:16, 23). The turning point was Paul's vision on the Damascus Road (Acts 9:1–22), where, after encountering Jesus Christ, Paul became blind for three days (9:8–9, 22). Meanwhile, Ananias also received the vision about Paul's transformation from persecutor to chosen one, and one who would be persecuted for the sake of Jesus Christ (9:10–16). It was Ananias's prayer that helped Paul to receive his sight and become filled with the Holy Spirit (9:17). In other words, Paul's Jewish ethnocentrism was broken down and transformed because of his encounter with Jesus Christ, who provided him with the Holy Spirit, and who opened his eyes. Paul became the apostle for the Gentiles with the mission to break down the walls between Jews and Gentiles, and to include Gentiles in the people of God.

Many of Paul's Jewish contemporaries limited membership of God's people to ethnic "Israel"; that is, only Israel had privileged status in their covenant with God, and not the Gentiles.[39] According to Yee, this is a form of "'ethnocentrism' in that it is a closed ethnic religion, referring to the Jewish evaluation of other human groups (and their cultures and practices), from the own perspective of the Jews."[40] In the context of the Jew-Gentile division (Eph 2:11–12), Paul stated that Christ made peace between both groups (2:14–18). Within these five verses, "peace" is repeated four times. I agree with Andrew

---

39. Tet-Lim N. Yee, *Jews, Gentiles, and Ethnic Reconciliation: Paul's Jewish Identity and Ephesians,* SNTSMS 130 (Cambridge: Cambridge University Press, 2005), 71.
40. Yee, *Jews, Gentiles, and Ethnic Reconciliation,* 71–72.

Lincoln's comment stating that "peace" in this passage stands "primarily for the cessation of hostilities and the resulting situation of unity. It is a relational concept which presupposes the overcoming of alienation (cf. vv. 12–13) and hostility (cf. v. 15) between Gentiles and Jews."[41] Christ has broken down the dividing wall, which is the hostility between both groups (2:14). Such hostility may have been triggered by the exclusiveness of the Jewish law, which "engendered personal and social antagonisms."[42] Christ made reconciliation through the cross, through which he put hostility to death in himself (2:16) and poured out his sacrificial love toward the world so that we can bear with one another in love (4:1–6).

Yet how might the two opposing groups experience peace and begin the reconciliation process? Paul brings into view the function of the Holy Spirit. Both groups have access in one Spirit through Christ (2:18); in him both are being built together to become the dwelling place of God in the Spirit (2:22). Both Jews and Gentiles experience God as their Father and have access to him through the one Spirit. As Lincoln states, "access to God as Father through Christ and in the Spirit is the ground of the peace proclaimed to both Jews and Gentiles, but it is also true that the exercise of this new privilege by both groups in the one Spirit is the sign of the peace between them."[43] Paul's emphasis on the Spirit for establishing the unity of the church among different ethnicities is also shown in 1 Corinthians 12:13, where Paul argues that ". . . in the one Spirit we were all baptized into one body – Jews or Greeks, slaves or free – and we were all made to drink of one Spirit" (NRSV).

In sum, when he encountered Jesus Christ and was filled with the Holy Spirit, Paul was transformed from a Judaizer, zealous for the Jewish tradition, into the Lord's apostle, who proclaimed the gospel to the Gentiles. Through this encounter, Paul's Jewish ethnocentrism was broken down, and instead turns towards bridging the gap between Jews and Gentiles by encouraging their indwelling in the one Spirit. For Paul, conflicts caused by barriers of different ethnic backgrounds can be transformed through the work of the Holy Spirit. When the inner barriers of alienation are removed, reconciliation becomes possible.

---

41. Andrew T. Lincoln, *Ephesians*, WBC 42 (Waco: Word Books, 1990), 140.
42. Lincoln, *Ephesians*, 142.
43. Lincoln, *Ephesians*, 150.

A Brief Summary

From the above discussion, we can see that since the beginning of the early church in the first century through to the current age, Christians have experienced conflict and divisions in the church. These tensions and conflicts arise for all kinds of different causes, including differences in cultural values or social classes, political or social religious factors, and distinct ethnicities.

We have seen that the Holy Spirit plays a significant role in confronting conflicts and divisions among different social groups. Firstly, when the Greek-speaking and the Aramaic-speaking Jews disputed about food distribution, those who were full of faith and the Holy Spirit were chosen to handle the issue. Similarly, when facing the conflict of the Corinthian parties, the Spirit of discernment was brought into view, helping Christians to have their prejudices over social classes transformed. Secondly, regarding the Antioch conflict, Paul saw that it was Peter's inner fear that led to his "hypocritical" behavior. Paul pointed toward God as the one who provides the Spirit to strengthen believers to enter into the different contexts of others and to understand their respective concerns. Thirdly, Paul's encounter with Jesus Christ and the filling of the Holy Spirit led to his transformation from being racially prejudiced to becoming an apostle for the Gentiles. Paul also realized that it is through dwelling in the one Spirit that peace and a reconciled relationship between Jews and Gentiles may be established.

RECONCILIATION/SOLIDARITY THROUGH THE WORK OF THE HOLY SPIRIT

It should be noted that this essay does not consider the Holy Spirit as a remedy for all ills. Nor should we see conflict as always in need of elimination. Neither do we regard reconciliation or solidarity as realities that will develop overnight. However, there is significance in the way that the Holy Spirit has been brought into view whenever conflicts and tensions are spoken of. In what follows, there are points that may be worth noting for sustaining reconciliation in divided societies through spiritual formation.

First, the work of the Holy Spirit reminds Christians to see the so-called dark side of the world in new perspective. Conflict and divisions are characteristic of all communities in human history. They are features in social life alongside solidarity and unity. The Chinese symbol of yin and yang demonstrate this, where "the Chinese symbol of yang harbors a dark spot of yin, and the symbol of yin harbors a light spot of yang."[44]

In other words, there is no phenomenon of pure unity of social communities without there being an antithetical side. In fact, true solidarity may only be realized in the struggles and conflicts we experience in our social lives. As Parker J. Palmer has said,

> we must abandon the commonsense notion that the monsters we meet within ourselves are enemies to be destroyed. Instead, we must cultivate the hope that they can become companions to be embraced . . . For only our monsters know the way down to that inner place of unity and wholeness; only these creatures of the night know how to travel where there is no light.[45]

If "the monster" here could refer to the divisions, conflicts, splits etc., then we may travel with this tension and move towards unity and wholeness.

Second, when fear and political pressure produce tension and conflict among opposing groups, Paul invites us to depend on inner strength from the Spirit by our indwelling in Christ and Christ in us. Is an individual's inner strength able to transform society so as to prevent it from being torn apart? Can unjust oppression be changed by an individual's inner life of peace? Of course, it is not easy for those who are experiencing injustice. Yet regaining inner strength may be the first step. Palmer is right that "the external structures . . . would not have the power to divide us as deeply as they do if they were not rooted in one of the most compelling features of our inner landscape – fear."[46] We do not have to respond to people and the external world based on inner fears. We can choose to respond to them from our inner hope and compassion. As Paul says, "I pray that . . . he [the Father] may grant that you may be strengthened in your inner being with power through his Spirit" (Eph 3:16 NRSV).

Third, putting on our new being in union with Christ by dwelling in the Holy Spirit opens new possibilities for social life. Through the cross and the work of the Holy Spirit, it is possible to establish reconciliation and solidarity in communities full of tension and splits. As we have seen, our viewpoint

---

44. Parker J. Palmer, *The Active Life: A Spirituality of Work, Creativity, and Caring* (San Francisco: Jossey-Bass, 1990), 16.
45. Palmer, *The Active Life*, 31.
46. Palmer, *The Courage to Teach*, 36.

relating to community barriers may be transformed by our experience of God as Father through the work of the Holy Spirit.

In summary, the Holy Spirit can generate reconciliation in a divided society, and we should dwell in this reality so as to live out lives transformed by the Spirit. As Paul writes in Galatians, "the fruit of the Spirit is love, joy, peace, patience, kindness, generosity, faithfulness, gentleness, and self-control . . . If we live by the Spirit, let us also be guided by the Spirit. Let us not become conceited, competing against one another, envying one another" (5:22–26 NRSV). In the Spirit, we regard each other as equals. Every church member has his or her own function, plays their roles and supports one another (1 Cor 12:12–31), for "in the one Spirit we were all baptized into one body . . . and we were all made to drink of one Spirit" (12:13 NRSV).

Moreover, with the guidance of the Holy Spirit, we do not perceive ourselves as the victims of our social circumstances, consigned to a life of fear. Rather, we are empowered with the inner strength so as to be able to enter into each other's contexts and understand their respective concerns. In Paul's words, when we share in the Spirit, we are "of the same mind, having the same love, being in full accord and of one mind. Do nothing from selfish ambition or conceit, but in humility regard others as better than yourselves. Let each of you look not to your own interests, but to the interests of others" (Phil 2:1–4 NRSV). Further, in one Spirit, we all have access to God, so that we are citizens with the saints and members of the household of God (Eph 3:11–22). The barriers of ethnic division crumble and reconciliation becomes possible. Under the guidance of the Holy Spirit, we can find reconciliation and solidarity and live out a life of faith, hope and love.

CONCLUSION

This essay started with a brief history of division in the church, demonstrating that tensions and divisions are characteristic in church communities. In particular, divisions in the current Chinese churches, especially the Hong Kong churches, were in view. We explored the various types of the conflicts and divisions, and considered some relevant NT texts (Acts 6:1–7; 1 Cor 1–4; 11:17–34; Gal 2:11–14; Eph 2:11–21) to examine Paul's way of handling conflict. The discussion has shown that the Holy Spirit plays a key role for the gospel of reconciliation and solidarity. We observed that dwelling in the Holy Spirit helps us to be released from fear, and to receive inner peace and strength and to live out a life of faith, hope and love.

When we choose to respond to the outer world from inner peace, hope and compassion, building the reconciliation between divided groups becomes possible. In sum, this essay argues that churches share the human characteristic of tension and fragility, but that reconciliation can be revealed amid tension and division. Moreover, unity is possible amid divergences among social groups (social, political, theological, or otherwise) through the work of the Holy Spirit, who brings wholeness and solidarity into reality.

BIBLIOGRAPHY

Barclay, John M. G. *Pauline Churches and Diaspora Jews*. WUNT 2/275. Tübingen: Mohr Siebeck, 2011.

Bockmuehl, M. "Antioch and James the Just." In *James the Just and Christian Origins*, edited by Bruce Chilton and Craig A. Evans, 155–98. Leiden: Brill, 1999.

Carpenter, R. T. "Multiethnic Churches: Their Current and Potential Impact in a Time of Racial Reckoning." *Dialogismos* 6 (2022): 25–35.

Chester, A. "The Pauline Communities." In *A Vision for the Church Studies in Early Christian Ecclesiology in Honour of J. P. M. Sweet*, edited by Markus Bockmuehl and Michael B. Thompson, 105–20. Edinburgh: T&T Clark, 1997.

China Internet Information Center, "Fifty-six Ethnic Groups," *China Through a Lens*. http://www.china.org.cn/english/features/38107.htm.

Christian Times, "分色牧養：一位'黃牧'之見." https://christiantimes.org.hk/Common/Reader/News/ShowNews.jsp?Nid=160886&Pid=104&Version=0&Cid=2053&Charset=big5_hkscs.

DeSilva, D. A. *An Introduction to the New Testament: Contexts, Methods & Ministry Formation*. Downers Grove: IVP Academic, 2004.

Dunn, J. D. G. *The Epistle to the Galatians*. BNTC. Peabody: Hendrickson, 1993.

Fee, G. D. *The First Epistle to the Corinthians*. Rev. ed. NICNT. Grand Rapids: Eerdmans, 2014.

Gibson, J. J. *Peter Between Jerusalem and Antioch: Peter, James and the Gentiles*. WUNT 2/345. Tübingen: Mohr Siebeck, 2013.

Lincoln, Andrew T. *Ephesians*, WBC 42. Waco: Word Books, 1990.

Mayer, W. "Religious Conflict: Definitions, Problems and Theoretical Approaches." In *Religious Conflict from Early Christianity to the Rise of Islam*, edited by Wendy Mayer, Bronwen Neil, and Christian Albrecht, 1–19. Arbeiten Zur Kirchengeschichte Ser. Berlin: De Gruyter, 2013.

McGrath, A. E. *Christianity: An Introduction*. 3rd ed. West Sussex: Wiley Blackwell, 2015.

Ministry of Foreign Affairs of the People's Republic of China. https://www.mfa.gov.cn/ce/ceag/eng/zggk/t1064047.htm.

Palmer, P. J. *The Courage to Teach: Exploring the Inner Landscape of a Teacher's Life.* San Francisco: Jossey-Bass, 1998.

———. *The Active Life: A Spirituality of Work, Creativity, and Caring.* San Francisco: Jossey-Bass, 1990.

Richardson, P. "Pauline Inconsistency: 1 Corinthians 9:19–23 and Galatians 2:11–14." *NTS* 26, no. 3 (1980): 347–62.

Stenschke, C. W. "The Conflicts of Acts 1–8:3 in View of Recent Research on Religious Conflicts in Antiquity (Part One: Theoretical Issues and Contested Domains)." *EuroJTh* 26, no. 1 (2017): 15–31.

Taylor, J. "The Jerusalem Decrees (Acts 15.20, 29 and 21.25) and the Incident at Antioch (Gal 2.11–14)." *NTS* 47, no. 3 (2001): 372–80.

Theissen, G. *The Social Setting of Pauline Christianity: Essays on Corinth.* Translated by John H. Schutz. Edinburgh: T&T Clark, 1982.

Thiselton, A. C. *The First Epistle to the Corinthians: A Commentary on the Greek Text.* NIGTC. Grand Rapids: Eerdmans, 2000.

Vischer, L., U. Luz, and C. Link, *Unity of the Church in the New Testament and Today.* Grand Rapids: Eerdmans, 2010.

Walker, W. O. "Does the 'We' in Gal 2.15–17 Include Paul's Opponents?" *NTS* 49 no. 4 (2003): 560–65.

Wu, S. F. "Paul, the Spirit-People, and People on the Margins." *Australasian Pentecostal Studies* 22, no. 2 (2021): 260–78.

Xue, X. E. "The Community as Union with Christ in the Midst of Conflict: An Ecclesiology of the Pauline Letters from a Chinese Perspective." In *The Church from Every Tribe and Tongue: Ecclesiology in the Majority World*, edited by Gene L. Green, Stephen T. Pardue, and K. K. Yeo, 114–35. Carlisle: Langham Global Library, 2018.

———. "Mood and Ideology in Galatians 1–2." In *Romans and Galatians*, ed. Stanley E. Porter, Zachary K. Dawson, and Ryder A. Wishart, LENT. Leiden: Brill, forthcoming.

Yee, T. N. *Jews, Gentiles, and Ethnic Reconciliation: Paul's Jewish Identity and Ephesians.* SNTSMS 130. Cambridge: Cambridge University Press, 2005.

CHAPTER 3

METAPHORS OF SALVATION IN THE NEW TESTAMENT AND THEIR IMPLICATIONS IN ASIA

Johnson Thomaskutty

INTRODUCTION

The word *metaphor* can mean either "to carry over" or "to transfer, especially of the sense of one word to a different word." Ancient authors including the New Testament writers were conscious of the languages that they were using in the process of convincing their readers. The *semiotic* aspects such as *semantics* (*what* is the content in the text?), *syntactics* (*how* is the information formed within the textual framework?), and *pragmatics* (*why* the information function in a typical way in relation to the receiver?) were used by the authors to make their writings conform to the literary practices of their times. Their usage of language with the help of metaphors, imageries, symbolism, and figurative aspects enabled their readers to understand divine truths in earthly terms. The NT authors foregrounded the theme of salvation through the usage of metaphors and thus developed their ideologies in a human-friendly, interpretative, and theologically integrative manner. Metaphors in the NT thus enable a reader to connect between the earthly and the heavenly to carry over meaning above and beyond their literal and conceptual semantics for developing an idea about the unseen and ideological aspects.

As Asia is the cradle of most of the world's religions,[1] a reader can conceptualize and perceive the way metaphors are part and parcel of some of the religious texts which carry meaning beyond the existential and contextual realities. This essay attempts to decipher the following aspects through the means of historical, literary, theological, and contextual aspects: first, the historical annals through the means of metaphorical usages within the NT; second, understanding the literary and narrative dynamism of the text to see the

---

1. Judaism, Hinduism, Zoroastrianism, Buddhism, Christianity, Islam, Jainism, Sikhism, and others all have their origins in Asia.

connection between the metaphors and the soteriological aspects; and third, interpreting the metaphorical language of the NT with pragmatic implications in the Asian context.

DEFINITION OF METAPHOR AND SALVATION

A broader definition of metaphor shall throw more light on the subject matter with precision. *A Concise Dictionary of Metaphors and Similes* explains that:

> A metaphor is a figure of speech that describes a subject by assert-ing that it is, on some point of comparison, the same as another otherwise unrelated object. Metaphor is a type of analogy and is closely related to other rhetorical figures of speech that achieve their effects via association, comparison or resemblance including allegory, hyperbole, and simile.[2]

As stated above, metaphors enable a writer, reader, or interpreter to estab-lish certain levels of comparison, analogy, and association. The *Cambridge Dictionary* defines metaphor as "an expression, often found in literature that describes a person or object by referring to something that is considered to have similar characteristics to that person or object."[3] Here, metaphor is understood as a tool to interpret or understand something else by means of comparison. Murray J. Harris comments that "The open-ended potency of metaphor de-rives from its suggestiveness and the surprise it creates in the listener or reader regarding the point or points of aptness."[4] Though an objective definition of the term metaphor is a herculean task, a reader can understand that it is used as a literary tool to clarify and suggest mysterious aspects in a text.

A single metaphor can be used as per the demands of the context with multifarious meanings. Thus Christ is called a lion (Rev 5:5), because he is noble, heroic, and unconquerable; the devil is likewise called a lion, because he is roaring, rapacious, and devouring (1 Pet 5:8); wicked men and tyrants are called so (Job 4:10–11; 2 Tim 4:7), because they are fierce, outrageous, and cruel to weaker men, as the lion is to weaker creatures.[5] The potential of

---

2. *Concise Dictionary of Metaphors and Similes* (New Delhi: V&S Publishers, 2014).
3. The Cambridge Dictionary further describes metaphor as "an expression that describes a person or object by referring to something that is considered to possess similar characteristics." See https://dictionary.cambridge.org/dictionary/english/metaphor.
4. Murray J. Harris, *Slave of Christ: A New Testament Metaphor for Total Devotion to Christ*, NSBT (Downers Grove: InterVarsity Press, 1999), 20.
5. Benjamin Keach, *Preaching from the Types and Metaphors of the Bible* (London: Ravenio Books, 2014), Book 1, Part 1.

a metaphor to address various situations is brought to the foreground here. D. M. Miller provides a functional description of metaphor.[6] He argues that two lexical items of disparate meanings are linked on the basis of some form of comparison, with specific semantic implications.[7] In that sense, a metaphor is a thing, an idea, or a vehicle that enables a writer, reader, or interpreter to understand something else through comparison and association that results in semantic implications.

Asian religious traditions use several metaphors to convey the idea of salvation to attune a devotee to their conceptual and ideological framework. In the Advaitic tradition, terms such as *moksha* (liberation), *Samadhi* (one with the divine), and *paramanandam* (eternal bliss), *Brahmanubhav* (the experience of Brahman) are used to express the idea of salvation. In Buddhist traditions, concepts such as *nirvana* (extinction of suffering) and *sunyata* (emptiness) are used to express the idea of reaching the highest truth. These experiences are considered the highest points in a person's life. In Jainism, achieving *kevalya Jnana* (highest knowledge) is a unique experience in relation to the highest truth. The majority of these metaphorical expressions used in Asian religions have several semantic and ideological resemblances, even though Asian religions and Christianity are derived out of two distinct socio-religious and politico-cultural frameworks.[8] A dialogical reading of both the Indian and the NT traditions may throw important light on the similarities and differences between the two traditions.

The authors of the NT employ multiple metaphors to decipher divine ideas in human terms and convey the meaning and effects of salvation.[9] I. Howard Marshall comments, "Salvation is closely related to Jesus and his mission. It is a comprehensive term for the benefits brought by the sovereign action of God through the Messiah."[10] As divine aspects are described in earthly terms, the authors of the NT depend heavily on metaphors. Jan G. van der

---

6. D. M. Miller, *The Net of Hephaestus: A Study of Modern Criticism and Metaphysical Metaphor* (Berlin: De Gruyter, 1971), 127.

7. Jan G. van der Watt, *Family of the King: Dynamics of Metaphor in the Gospel according to John*, BibInt 47 (Leiden: Brill, 2000), 6.

8. Special thanks to Dr. John V. Mathew, Professor of Religions at The United Theological College for these insights.

9. Kar Yong Lim says, "If metaphors are part of how we think and understand reality, then they are part of how we understand ourselves and relate to others. In this respect, metaphors play a significant role in the formation of social identity." Kar Yong Lim, *Metaphors and Social Identity Formation in Paul's Letters to the Corinthians* (Eugene: Wipf & Stock, 2017), 48.

10. I. H. Marshall, "Salvation," *DJG*, 724.

Watt comments, "The message of salvation does not only stand central to virtually all the books of the New Testament, but also forms a foundation for the self-definition and identity of early Christians."[11] As a new community, the followers of Jesus had to redefine their existence in the light of the cross-events. The people of God were even expected to achieve salvation through "adventure in the sense of opposition, persecution, hesitation, but also of love, joy, peace, and a mission for God."[12] Salvation is thus a divine gift in the midst of both the pleasant and antagonistic situations of life in the world.[13]

METAPHORS OF SALVATION IN THE SYNOPTIC GOSPELS

The Synoptic Gospels contain several metaphors to convey the message of salvation with profundity. The kingdom of God or kingdom of heaven metaphor is one of the overarching semantic expressions used in the first three Gospels to express the soteriological and eschatological content.[14] The political expression "kingdom" is used in comparison to and over against the worldly kingdoms; but the ultimate purpose of the metaphor is to invite the readers toward the divine reign and the heavenly rule in the world.[15] According to C. C. Caragounis, "The term 'kingdom of God' or 'kingdom of Heaven' signifies God's sovereign, dynamic and eschatological rule. The kingdom of God lay at the heart of Jesus's teaching."[16] The aspects such as people's entry into the kingdom of God and being part of it can be understood in terms of accepting the offer of salvation as followers of God.[17]

Jesus implicitly uses the metaphor of a wedding in three places in the Synoptic Gospels: first, in a discussion of fasting (Mark 2:18–22; Matt 9:14–17; Luke 5:33–39); second, a parable about a wedding feast (Matt 22:1–14; Luke 14:16–24); and third, in a parable on the kingdom of God (Matt

---

11. Jan G. van der Watt, *Salvation in the New Testament: Perspectives on Soteriology*, SNT 121, ed. Jan G. van der Watt (Leiden: Brill, 2005), 1.

12. Van der Watt, *Salvation in the New Testament*, 1.

13. Erik Konsmo says, "Metaphors about God are necessary because without them individuals could know little or nothing about God. The same holds true for the Holy Spirit." Erik Konsmo, *The Pauline Metaphors of the Holy Spirit: The Intangible Spirit's Tangible Presence in the Life of the Christian*, StBibLit 130 (New York: Peter Lang, 2010), 23.

14. Van der Watt, *Family of the King*, 377.

15. Van der Watt, *Family of the King*, 376–78.

16. C. C. Caragounis, "Kingdom of God/Kingdom of Heaven," *DJG*, 417.

17. Bultmann has aptly remarked that the question of salvation for the Jews was directly related to the question of the coming kingdom. Rudolf Bultmann, *Gospel of St. John: A Commentary* (Philadelphia: WJKP, 1978), 94.

25:1–13).[18] While the bridegroom is with the disciples, they are celebrating the ushering of salvation in the world. It also connotes the full measure of salvation waiting for them in the future. The parable of the wedding feast indicates that salvation is accessible to all categories of people irrespective of their status and privileges.[19] In Matthew 25:1–13, the narrator makes it obvious that salvation is accessible only to those who are prepared for it. The metaphor of ten virgins elaborates this idea as five of them were entered into salvation while the other five lost their entry.[20] In all these three passages, the metaphor of a wedding is described in salvific terms.

The metaphors such as salt (5:13) and light (5:14) in the similitude of Jesus in Matthew take the attention of the reader toward the aspects of taste, purity, and preservation (salt), and straightforwardness, enlightening, and shining (light).[21] As per the Gospel narratives, these are some of the significant characteristics of a person who is being saved. In Matthew 6:19–24, the metaphor of treasures takes our attention to attentiveness to the kingdom of God.[22] The metaphors such as "narrow gate" and "broad gate" in 7:13–14 further take the attention of the reader to some of the principles of salvation.[23] The contrast between "building on the rock" and "building on the sand" points to steadfastness, stability, and endurance in the midst of trials and temptations in the world (7:24–27; Luke 6:47–49).[24] While those who are saved build on the rock, those who are doomed to destruction build on sand. This contrast is brought to the foreground through metaphorical and figurative language. The narrator uses micro-metaphors associated with the macro-metaphors to amplify the meaning and the message of the text. The sub-metaphors such as rain, streams, winds, house, and foundations allow the main metaphors to convey the message more fully.[25] The expression of ideas through several images and

18. Norbert Schnell, *The Bride of Christ – A Metaphor for the Church: Systematical Exegetical Analysis* (Zürich: LIT Verlag, 2020), 109.

19. Sebastian R. Smolarz, *Covenant and the Metaphor of Divine Marriage in Biblical Thought* (Eugene: Wipf & Stock, 2011), 162–64.

20. David W. Bennett, *Metaphors and Ministry: Biblical Images for Leaders and Followers* (Eugene: Wipf & Stock, 2004), 35–36.

21. See David W. Wead, *The Literary Devices in John's Gospel*, The Johannine Monograph Series, rev. ed. (Eugene: Wipf & Stock, 2018), 115.

22. Ernst Baasland, *Parables and Rhetoric in the Sermon on the Mount: New Approaches to a Classical Text*, WUNT 351 (Tübingen: Mohr Siebeck, 2015), 337–38.

23. Baasland, *Parables and Rhetoric in the Sermon on the Mount*, 498.

24. Bruce J. Malina and Jerome H. Neyrey, "Jesus the Witch: Witchcraft Accusations in Matthew 12," *Social-Scientific Approaches to New Testament Interpretation*, ed. David G. Horrell (Edinburgh: T&T Clark, 1999), 44–46.

25. Malina and Neyrey, "Jesus the Witch," 44–46.

metaphors equips the reader to grasp the divine aspects in anthropomorphic, physiomorphic, and sociomorphic terms.

The earthly elements are also significant for conveying heavenly truths, as the heavenly realm is incomprehensible to the ordinary human mindset. This is the reason heavenly things are conveyed in earthly terms and language. The metaphors used in Matthew such as cloth and wineskin (Matt 9:16–17; cf. Mark 2:21–22; Luke 5:36–39), sower, soil, and crop (13:1–9; cf. Mark 4:1–20; Luke 8:4–15), weeds and wheat (Matt 13:24–30), mustard seed (13:31–32; Mark 4:30–32), yeast (Matt 13:33; 16:5–12; Luke 13:20–21), hidden treasures (Matt 13:44), pearl (13:45–46), dragnet (13:47–51), house-owner (13:52),[26] sheep (18:7–14; Mark 9:43–50; Luke 15:3–7), vineyard and workers (Matt 20:1–16), barren fig tree (21:18–22; cf. 24:32–35; Mark 11:12–14, 20–26), landowner (Matt 21:33–44; Mark 12:1–12; Luke 20:9–19), wedding banquet (Matt 22:1–14; Luke 14:16–24), ten virgins (Matt 25:1–13), talents (25:14–30), and others are part of the parables of Jesus with a message about the kingdom of God and God's salvific plan for the people.[27] As a result, people with an earthly mindset and worldly ideological framework are able to understand the heavenly truths as they are expressed through earthly metaphors and parables.[28] Jesus uses metaphors as one of the key elements in his rhetoric to make his discussions conceivable to the human mindset. The Synoptic evangelists incorporate an ample number of metaphors within their narrative framework to make their dramatic discourses reader-friendly and persuasive.

Finally, there is a complex interplay between the Last Supper story in the Synoptic Gospels (Mark 14:22–25; Matt 26:26–29; Luke 22:19–20) and in 1 Corinthians 11:23–34.[29] In the narrative, the words "body" (*sōma*) and "blood" (*haima*) are metaphorically represented by loaves and wine. Jesus's statements "This is my body . . . This is my blood" establish a ritual and religious action with the help of metaphorical aspects.[30]

As we have seen, the Synoptic Gospels consistently use metaphors as tools or pointers to some conceptual and ideological aspects of salvation. The heavenly and earthly are semantically mediated through the means of multiple

---

26. Judith V. Stack, *Metaphor and the Portrayal of the Cause(s) of Sin and Evil in the Gospel of Matthew*, BibInt 182 (Leiden: Brill, 2020), 151.
27. Stack, *Metaphor and the Portrayal*, 151.
28. R. T. France, *The Gospel of Matthew*, NICNT (Grand Rapids: Eerdmans, 2007), 507–12.
29. Stephen R. Shaver, *Metaphors of Eucharistic Presence: Language, Cognition, and the Body and Blood of Christ* (Oxford: Oxford University Press, 2022), 81–90.
30. Shaver, *Metaphors of Eucharistic Presence*, 86.

and overlapping metaphors and imageries as the evangelists use metaphors in isolation and in groups to foreground certain core ideas. This aspect of the Synoptic Gospels is persuasive as readers are interlocked within the framework of the text to grasp the meaning of it.

METAPHORS FOR SALVATION IN THE FOURTH GOSPEL

The Fourth Gospel has a network of metaphors that demonstrates its soteriological framework to the reader. John is more particular than the Synoptic evangelists about the usage of metaphors and figures of speech. For example, while the Synoptic Gospels use the word *parabolē* (or "parable") for the artistic portrayals,[31] John uses the word *paroimia* (or "a figure of speech") in few occasions (10:6; 16:25, 29) and explains in detail how Jesus is a figure of salvation through protection, guidance, pasturing, and laying down his life.[32] While the Synoptic Gospels use kingdom of God or kingdom of Heaven as an overarching metaphor, John uses life or eternal life as an overarching metaphor in terms of salvation.[33] D. H. Johnson comments: "John also makes a point of stressing the idea of life as a gift from God. The Father has life in himself and has given the Son life to have in himself (5:26; cf. 1:4). The Son is the bread of life (6:35, 48) who gives life to the world by his death (6:51) and through his Spirit and words (6:63, 68)."[34]

John's emphasis is not simply reflected in terminology but also in his conceptual framework. The Synoptic evangelists demonstrate God as a king of the kingdom; hence, the followers are dynamically aligned within that system as *subjects* of the king.[35] In contrast, the Fourth Gospel refers to God as the Father of the family; hence, the followers are dynamically aligned within that system as *children* of the Father.[36] This metaphorical difference in the Fourth Gospel points to a different meaning, as John's narrative demonstrates a Father-child relationship with an emphasis on closeness, familiarity, and responsibility.

---

31. K. R. Snodgrass, "Parable," *DJG*, 591–601.
32. The word *paroimia* is used in the New Testament only five times: John 10:6; 16:25 (x2), 29; and 2 Peter 2:22. In the LXX, both *paroimia* and *parabolē* translate the Hebrew *mašal* and the Aramaic *mathla* and both have the basic meaning of "saying," "proverb,' and "riddle." See Nicholas Cachia, *The Image of the Good Shepherd as a Source for the Spirituality of the Ministerial Priesthood*, TGSS (Roma: Editrice Pontifica Universita Gregoriana, 1997), 133.
33. While kingdom of God/Heaven is a political metaphor, life/eternal life is a filial metaphor.
34. D. H. Johnson, "Life," *DJG*, 469.
35. Emphasis is mine. Caragounis, "Kingdom of God/Kingdom of Heaven," 417–30.
36. Emphasis is mine. Johnson, "Life," 469–71.

Other metaphors such as life, light, witness, darkness, glory, children, dwelling, Father, Son, and others fill the prologue of John (1:1–18) to prepare the readers to the body of the Gospel.[37] The metaphor of following is placed at the outset (1:43) and at the close (21:19, 22) of the Gospel to enclose everything in an inclusio that is much aligned within the soteriological framework of John.[38] The metaphor of dove for Holy Spirit in 1:32 further elaborates the descent of God's presence in the world below. According to Mark G. Boyer, "The dove is a metaphor for God's Spirit. It calls to mind the hovering spirit of creation in the Hebrew Bible's (Old Testament's) Book of Genesis. Out of chaos the brooding, Spirit-dove hatches order and new life."[39] The narrator uses dove as a metaphor for brooding, purity, new creation, and life. The presentation of Jesus as the Lamb of God denotes many semantic details such as sacrificial nature and victory (1:29, 36).[40]

Jesus's metaphorical interest is obvious in his utterance in the temple: "Destroy this temple, and I will raise it again in three days" (2:19). Jesus here speaks about his crucifixion.[41] The metaphorical speech of Jesus with an emphasis on salvation is further revealed through his statements on the hour (2:4; 4:21, 23; 5:25, 28; 7:6, 8; 7:30; 8:20; 12:23) and lifting up of the Son of Man (3:14; 12:32).[42] The metaphors such as birth from above (3:3), birth in water and spirit (3:5), bride, bridegroom, and friend of the bridegroom (3:27–30), water and drinking (4:10–14; 7:37–38), work (5:17; 6:29), and judgment and testimony (5:19–46) elaborates several details regarding soteriology within John's framework.[43]

In addition, the "I AM" Sayings of Jesus are filled with metaphorical aspects: bread (6:35, 41, 48); light (8:12; 9:5); gate (10:7, 9); shepherd (10:11);

---

37. Johnson Thomaskutty, *The Gospel of John: A Universalistic Reading*, Biblical Hermeneutics Rediscovered 25 (New Delhi: Christian World Imprints, 2020), 37–52.

38. Johnson Thomaskutty, "The Gospel of John," *An Asian Introduction to the New Testament*, ed. Johnson Thomaskutty (Minneapolis: Fortress Press, 2022), 145.

39. Mark G. Boyer, *Waiting in Joyful Hope: Daily Reflections for Advent and Christmas* (Mumbai: St. Paul's, 2003), 135.

40. Jasper Tang Nielsen, "The Lamb of God: The Cognitive Structure of a Johannine Metaphor," *Imagery in the Gospel of John*, WUNT 200, eds. Jörg Frey, Jan G. van der Watt, and Ruben Zimmermann (Tübingen: Mohr Siebeck, 2006), 217–58.

41. Aage Pilgaard, "The Qumran Scrolls and John's Gospel," *New Readings in John: Literary and Theological Perspectives*, eds. Johannes Nissen and Sigfred Pedersen (London: T&T Clark International, 1999), 141–42.

42. Gerry Wheaton, *The Role of Jewish Feasts in John's Gospel*, SNTSMS 162 (Cambridge: Cambridge University Press, 2015), 54.

43. Andreas J. Köstenberger, *A Theology of John's Gospel and Letters* (Grand Rapids: Zondervan, 2009), 481.

resurrection and life (11:25); way, truth and life (14:6); and vine (15:1).[44] In order to amplify the major metaphors, the narrator uses a network of related metaphors to create imagery and foreground the facts and figures with salvific emphasis.[45] The metaphor of bread in chapter 6 is amplified with other related metaphors such as eating, filling the stomach (6:26, 51, 53), hunger and thirst (6:35), and food and drink (6:55).[46] The metaphor of bread is placed within the imagery of hunger and thirst to give the reader a wider understanding. The metaphor of bread plays a significant semantic function within the extended imagery to convey a salvific message.[47]

In John 9, the metaphor of light functions in relation to a network of metaphors such as blindness, darkness (9:1), day, night (9:4), and others.[48] The metaphors such as gate and shepherd can be understood in the company of other metaphors within the imagery such as sheep, sheep pen, thief and a robber, shepherd of the sheep, watchman, stranger, pasture, hired hand, wolf, flock, and others. The idea that those who enter through the gate will be saved conveys a message of salvation, protection, and rest (10:9). Similarly, the metaphor of vine is amplified with the help of other metaphors such as gardener, cutting off, branch, bearing fruit, fruit, pruning, withering, fire, burning, and others. They convey a message together as metaphors work in networks.[49] The metaphor of family is another significant macro-metaphor within John's narrative framework that envisages the message of salvation.[50] The micro- and macro- levels of metaphors and their network are some of the significant phenomena of the Fourth Gospel that are designed to persuade the reader to attain or continue to remain in salvation.

METAPHORS FOR SALVATION IN THE PAULINE CORPUS

Like the Gospel writers, Paul adopted many metaphors from the Jewish and Greco-Roman surroundings to describe salvation. As a child of his time, he

---

44. Paul N. Anderson, *From Crisis to Christ: A Contextual Introduction to the New Testament* (Nashville: Abingdon Press, 2014), 150–52.
45. Van der Watt, *Family of the King*, vii–xxi.
46. See Susan Hylen, *Allusion and Meaning in John 6*, BZNW 137 (Berlin: Walter de Gruyter, 2005).
47. Johnson Thomaskutty, *Dialogue in the Book of Signs: A Polyvalent Analysis of John 1:19–12:50*, BibInt 136 (Leiden: Brill, 2015), 206–48.
48. Johnson Thomaskutty, "The Irony of Ability and Disability in John 9:1–41," *HTS Theologiese Studies/Theological Studies* 78, no. 1: 1–7.
49. Thomaskutty, *Dialogue in the Book of Signs*, 341–53.
50. Van der Watt, *Family of the King*, vii–xxi.

reflects the socio-political and religio-cultural realities and concepts of his world throughout his writings.[51] As in the Fourth Gospel, Paul incorporates the metaphor of "family" in Romans 8:10–25.[52] Robinson foregrounds metaphor, morality, and the spirit in 8:1–17. As Romans 8 is considered the apex of Paul's thought regarding the Spirit, the integration of metaphor, morality, and Spirit is a noticeable factor.[53] The familial metaphor of "adoption" (*huiothesia*) appears four times together in Romans and Galatians (Gal 4:5; Rom 8:15; 8:23; 9:4).[54] It is one of the significant soteriological terminologies used by Paul.

He states that salvation is not free: "you are bought with a price" (1 Cor 6:20; 7:23). Christians get a new owner, Christ. The death of Jesus functioned as legal tender to make this purchase. In Romans 3:24–25 we have justification, redemption, and place of atonement – a conflation of judicial, economic, and sacrificial imagery.[55] Finlan says, "Paul will move from one metaphor to the other, but always there is a transaction by which salvation is purchased, arranged, or ritually obtained for us."[56] Finlan further says:

> One of Paul's methods of argument was to present concepts that could be accepted by both Jews and Gentiles. The beneficial death of Jesus, interpreted with cultic metaphors, was a crucial bridging concept. The Greek tragedians had developed the idea of self-sacrifice for one's city or for a religious principle into a major literary/religious theme. The Jews spoke in their scriptures of the selfless suffering of a prophet or a religious one, bordering on self-sacrifice (in Psalm 22 and 69; Isaiah 53; Zechariah 11 and 13; Wisdom 2).[57]

By bridging the Jewish and Gentile ideas, Paul ultimately endeavored to universalize the message of salvation. To accomplish this, he used metaphors

---

51. Jan Grobbelaar and Gert Breed, eds., *Welcoming Africa's Children: Theological and Ministry Perspectives* (Durbanville, South Africa: AOSIS, 2016), 55.

52. See Bruce James Anderson, *"Family" Metaphors in Romans 8:10–25 and Their Social Context in Ancient Rome* (Auckland: University of Auckland, 1997).

53. William E. W. Robinson, *Metaphor, Morality, and the Spirit in Romans 8:1–17*, ECL (Atlanta: SBL Press, 2016), 9.

54. Erin M. Hein, *Adoption in Galatians and Romans*, BibInt 153 (Leiden: Brill, 2017), 1.

55. Stephen Finlan, *The Background and Content of Paul's Cultic Atonement Metaphors* (Atlanta: Society of Biblical Literature, 2004), 5.

56. Finlan, *The Background and Content of Paul's Cultic Atonement Metaphors*, 5.

57. Finlan, *The Background and Content of Paul's Cultic Atonement Metaphors*, 8.

as one of the significant elements in his rhetoric.[58] Kar Yong Lim comments that, "In his letters to the Corinthians, Paul skillfully uses metaphors drawn from the social reality, cultural background, and symbolic universe of his predominantly Greco-Roman audience. He also creatively employs metaphors to instruct, rebuke, and build up these communities. Not only are metaphors central to Paul's arguments, they are also a powerful tool of communication which enabled his audience to visualize things in new and different ways."[59]

In his letters to the Corinthians, Paul speaks of salvation using a variety of metaphors such as servants, working, field, building, skilled master builder, laying foundation (1 Cor 3:9–10), *paterfamilias* (4:14–15), athlete imagery (9:24–27), letter (2 Cor 3:1–3), and human body (1 Cor 12:14–18).[60] He consistently uses familial imagery to communicate the post-salvation social realities of Christians, speaking of "my brothers and sisters" (1:11; 15:58),[61] and deploying familial metaphors in other ways, such as noting that "In Christ Jesus I became your father" (4:15 NIV; see vv. 14–21; 2 Cor 6:11–13; 11:2; 12:14).[62] Similarly, he uses temple metaphors – "you are God's temple" (1 Cor 3:16 NIV) – and body metaphors, such as when he famously declares that "you are the body of Christ." In 1 Corinthians 9:19–23, he introduces himself as a slave of Christ and all.[63] The metaphor of "slave" or "slavery" as a discipleship paradigm and total devotion to God is highly emphasized throughout his works.[64] Paul's method of aligning his discourses within the local context and expounding their meanings in salvific and universalistic terms is paradigmatic for a contemporary reader.

In 1 Thessalonians, Paul uses several metaphors to convey the message of salvation. He addresses the Thessalonian congregation as siblings (1 Thess 1:4), "a powerful metaphor evoking the bonds of affection that Paul and his companions had for the Thessalonians and the ties that linked the members

---

58. Munther Isaac says, "Paul's own involvement in spreading the gospel to Gentiles . . . influenced Paul to move forward with this universalization process." Munther Isaac, *From Land to Lands, from Eden to the Renewed Earth* (Carlisle: Langham Academic, 2015), 239.

59. Lim, *Metaphors and Social Identity Formation in Paul's Letters to the Corinthians*, 3.

60. Lim, *Metaphors and Social Identity Formation in Paul's Letters to the Corinthians*, 3–4.

61. It is used one hundred and thirteen times in the undisputed Pauline letters such as Romans, 1 & 2 Corinthians, Galatians, Philippians, 1 Thessalonians, and Philemon. Lim, *Metaphors and Social Identity Formation in Paul's Letters to the Corinthians*, 53.

62. Lim, *Metaphors and Social Identity Formation in Paul's Letters to the Corinthians*, 93–94.

63. Dale B. Martin, *Slavery as Salvation: The Metaphor of Slavery in Pauline Christianity* (Eugene: Wipf & Stock, 1990), xxi.

64. Harris, *Slave of Christ: A New Testament Metaphor for Total Devotion to Christ*, 139–56.

of the community to one another."[65] In 1 Thessalonians 2:7, Paul's usage of maternal imagery is also richly evocative. To speak of a mother's endearment toward her children, he uses the term "nurse" (*trophos*), referring to a wet nurse or nursing mother. These metaphors highlight that protection, and physical, mental, and emotional care and love are all part of salvation according to Paul. Another metaphor – "walking through life" (4:1–12) can also be interpreted in terms of salvation. In Philippians 1:21–23, he uses terms from the business world to express a dilemma: "For to me, living is Christ and dying is gain [*kerdos*]," deploying common Greek terms used for profit and loss.[66] Paul's usage of metaphors is derived out of the ideas and daily practices of the Greco-Roman world. The head and body metaphor in Ephesians 5:21–33 emphasizes unity, association, and human functionality under divine authority.[67]

Finally, it is notable that Paul uses family metaphors throughout the Letter to Philemon.[68] Collins comments that:

> The crux of Paul's appeal to Philemon is that he is writing about a family matter. Philemon is not only Paul's friend and fellow evangelist, but he is also Paul's brother (Phlm 7, 20). Apphia is Paul's sister (Phlm 2). The group to whom the missive is addressed gathers in Philemon's home.[69]

Paul acknowledges Onesimus's new identity as "my child" (Phlm 10) and one "whom I have begotten while in chains" (Phlm 12).[70]

While Paul framed his soteriological concepts, he stated them in integral connectivity with his Christology, ecclesiology, and eschatology. The majority of the metaphors used in the Pauline writings either directly or indirectly link to the soteriological framework of the author. For Paul, "salvation" is a synonym for the Synoptic kingdom of God/heaven and the Johannine life/

---

65. Collins further comments, "Togetherness, interdependence, goodwill, affection, friendship, protection, glory, and honor are among the values that come to mind when people talk about family relationships." Raymond F. Collins, *The Power of Images in Paul* (Collegeville: The Liturgical Press, 2008), 12.

66. Collins, *The Power of Images in Paul*, 49.

67. See Gregory W. Dawes, *The Body in Question: Metaphor and Meaning in the Interpretation of Ephesians 5:21–33*, BibInt 30 (Leiden: Brill, 1998).

68. For more details about Pauline metaphors, see Markus Egg, "To Those Walking in the Footsteps of the Faith: Deliberate Metaphor in the Pauline Epistles," *Drawing Attention to Metaphor*, Figurative Thought and Language, eds. Camilla Di Biase-Dyson and Markus Egg (Amsterdam: John Benjamins Publishing Company, 2020), 229–62.

69. Collins, *The Power of Images in Paul*, 72.

70. Collins, *The Power of Images in Paul*, 72.

eternal life concepts. He guides his reader toward that particular experience by way of using multiple metaphors, figurative language, and imageries. The usage of metaphors enables the reader to be connected to the horizontal and the vertical realities of the divine message as both the earthly and the heavenly are part of the textual semantics.

METAPHORS FOR SALVATION IN OTHER NEW TESTAMENT WRITINGS

As in the Gospels and Pauline epistles, metaphors, images, and figurative language are part of the other writings of the NT. The Book of Acts can be considered a tale of two cities – Jerusalem and Rome. Jerusalem symbolizes the Jewish context for the genesis of Christianity; Rome can be considered the symbol of the Gentile world to which the gospel was spread out.[71] Metaphors such as light and its variant fire (2:3–4; 7:55; 9:3; 12:7; 22:6; 26:13), and prison and jails (5:18–23; 12:1–11, 12–16; 16:20–39) are used both literally and metaphorically within Acts.[72] The *Dictionary of Biblical Imagery* states, "There are approximately twenty references to prisons and ten each to gates, doors and guards. In several prison incidents Luke gives us dramatic, and even ironic images of open and closed doors."[73] The metaphorical overtones of open and closed doors indicate worldly obstacles and heavenly redemption. The forensic imageries of trial and defense as well as oratorical situations are master images in the Book of Acts.[74]

The Book of Acts uses several soteriological metaphors that take the readers to a different level of spiritual experience. For example, in Acts 2:1–4, the author uses some of the metaphors in the context of the Pentecost event. Pentecost, a counterpart to the story of Babel (Gen 11:1–9), is introduced with a sound, blowing, violent wind, filling the house, and tongues of fire. A salvific experience through the initiative of the Holy Spirit was necessitated with earthly metaphors to indicate the heavenly visitation.[75] The metaphor of disciple is used as a general term in the same way as a "disciple" and "Christian" throughout the Book of Acts (Acts 9:10, 25–26, 36; 11:26; 14:21; 15:10; 16:2;

---

71. "Acts of the Apostles," *Dictionary of Biblical Imagery*, eds. Leland Ryken, James C. Wilhoit, and Tremper Longman III (Secunderabad: Authentic, 1998), 7.
72. "Acts of the Apostles," *Dictionary of Biblical Imagery*, 8.
73. "Acts of the Apostles," *Dictionary of Biblical Imagery*, 8.
74. "Acts of the Apostles," *Dictionary of Biblical Imagery*, 8.
75. See Joanna Radwanska Williams, "'Native Speaker' as a metaphorical construct," *Metaphors for Learning: Cross-cultural Perspectives*, ed. Erich A. Berendt (Amsterdam: John Benjamin Publishing Company, 2008), 147.

21:16).[76] The Book of Acts reflects several aspects related to salvation derived out of the early Christian community's experiences.

The Letter to the Hebrews is pregnant with metaphors, imagery, and figurative language adopted mostly from the Old Testament writings. As the *Dictionary of Biblical Imagery* says, "Virtually all the images in Hebrews are associated with its extensive comparison and contrast of the Old Testament cult with the redemptive work of Christ, which supersedes it."[77] Hebrews includes several images of Christ (1:2, 5, 8; 3:1–6; 4:14), atonement (2:17; 9:6–14, 23–28; 10:1–10; 13:11–13), and salvation and apostasy (1:14; 2:15; 6:1–2, 4–5, 12; 9:15; 11:10, 13–16; 12:5–11).[78] To come to salvation is depicted with the image of drinking, as to have "been enlightened, to have tasted the heavenly gift, and have shared in the Holy Spirit, and have tasted the goodness of the word of God and the powers of the age to come" (6:4–5).[79] The cultic, priestly, and royal language of Hebrews introduces the reader to a superior savior and a superior way of salvation through the means of Christ.[80] The atoning work of Christ – a key element of Christian salvation – is depicted as "tasting death" (2:9), and Christ is described as the "forerunner" (6:20), the "pioneer of salvation" (2:10), and "pioneer and perfecter of faith" (12:2).[81]

The authors of the General Epistles also use several metaphors and images. The images in the Letter of James cluster around key themes, including the tongue (Jas 3:5–6), faith and works (2:14–17, 26), the rich and poor (1:9–11; 5:2–4), the unregenerate self and salvation, and the Christian life and hope.[82] Salvation is birth by the word of truth so that we can become first fruits of God's creatures (1:18). The author exhorts the readers to strip off dirty garments in order to welcome the implanted word that has the power to save our souls (1:21).[83] In 1 Peter, the author uses the name Israel both in literal and metaphorical senses (1 Pet 2:9–10). Metaphors such as priesthood (2:4–5, 9) and warfare (1:13; 4:1) are used within the soteriological framework of the letter.[84] The "waterless springs" and "storm-driven clouds" were forceful

---

76. David W. Bennett, *Metaphors of Ministry: Biblical Images for Leaders and Followers* (Eugene: Wipf & Stock, 1993), 110.
77. "Hebrews, Letter to the," *Dictionary of Biblical Imagery*, 374–76.
78. "Hebrews, Letter to the," *Dictionary of Biblical Imagery*, 374–76.
79. "Hebrews, Letter to the," *Dictionary of Biblical Imagery*, 375.
80. "Hebrews, Letter to the," *Dictionary of Biblical Imagery*, 375.
81. "Hebrews, Letter to the," *Dictionary of Biblical Imagery*, 375.
82. "James, Letter of," *Dictionary of Biblical Imagery*, 433–34.
83. "James, Letter of," *Dictionary of Biblical Imagery*, 434.
84. "Peter, First Letter of," *Dictionary of Biblical Imagery*, 636–38.

images for dwellers in Palestine, where water is precious and in some places a rare commodity (see 2 Pet 2:17).[85] The Fourth Gospel's image of a courtroom witness is echoed in the Johannine epistles as a powerful metaphor for salvation in 1 John (1:1–3; 4:14).[86] In the Letter of Jude, a number of images suggest the community as a household to be preserved in its integrity. Like a body, it must guard against defilement or blemish (Jude 23–24).[87] Thus, the General Epistles foreground a strong message of salvation by means of metaphors and imagery.

The Book of Revelation narrates the visions, events, and stories mostly through imagery, metaphors, and symbolical language. Mitchell G. Reddish comments about the literary genre of the book, noting that it "contains strange visions, gruesome monsters, perplexing numbers, and confusing repetitions."[88] Metaphors such as Christ as the Alpha and Omega (1:8), and the church as the golden lamp stands (1:12; 2:1) describe the connection between Christ and the church.[89] The Son of Man figure in 1:12–16 introduces a powerful image contrasted with the puny little powers of the world. Describing Rome as Babylon and as a whore is both metaphorical and symbolical. Nuptial traditions from the Roman social discourse are incorporated in the book by adopting the bride and bridegroom imagery throughout.[90] The primary image of Christ in Revelation is the slain Lamb, a reminder of the sacrificial, atoning work of Christ. Imagery and metaphors run in the book through the throne room of God, four living creatures, numbers,[91] figures,[92] seals, trumpets, bowls, last judgment, new Jerusalem, new heaven and new earth, and many others to convey a message through the envelop of apocalyptic language.[93] Revelation was written during a crisis period of the Christian community as they were undergoing severe persecution and challenges of emperor worship. The author of the book foregrounds a conflicting situation between the power structures

---

85. "Peter, Second Letter of," *Dictionary of Biblical Imagery*, 638.
86. "John, Letters of," *Dictionary of Biblical Imagery*, 457.
87. "Jude, Letter of," *Dictionary of Biblical Imagery*, 466.
88. Mitchell G. Reddish, *Revelation*, SHBC (Macon: Smyth & Helwys, 2001), 3.
89. See Fred Hansen, *The Alpha and Omega and Lampstands Metaphors: A Linguistic Theory of Metaphor as Applied to the Book of Revelation* (Nijmegen: Radboud University, 2017).
90. For more details, see Lynn R. Huber, *Like a Bride Adorned: Reading Metaphor in John's Apocalypse*, Emory Studies in Early Christianity (New York: T&T Clark International, 2007).
91. In the book, seven is a number of perfection, 666 is the number of the beast, and 144,000 is a remnant out of Israel.
92. Woman clothed with the sun, male child, beast from the earth, beast from the sea, and enormous red dragon.
93. Donald Guthrie, *New Testament Introduction*, rev. ed. (Downers Grove: InterVarsity Press, 1990), 929–85.

and the vulnerable Christians and conveys a message of salvation and hope to the community of God.

METAPHORS FOR SALVATION IN THE
NEW TESTAMENT AND IN ASIA

Asian religious scriptures include multifarious metaphorical expressions to convey the divine aspects into human terms and categories. A large number of metaphors in the New Testament writings are in several ways reminiscent to other religious metaphors.[94] Moreover, the Asian origin of the New Testament writings makes many of its metaphors more understandable for readers of this part of the world. The semiotic similarities between metaphors of the New Testament and other Asian writings demonstrate their universal significance.

According to Victor Turner, metaphors are "multivocal symbols, whole semantic systems, which bring into relation a number of ideas, images, sentiments, values, and stereotypes. Components of one system enter into dynamic relations with components of the other."[95] The relatedness between the heavenly and the earthly, Old Testament and New Testament, New Testament and its first century CE context, and New Testament and the contemporary realities can be understood through the means of proper interpretation of the metaphorical system embedded within the texts. Through metaphorical expressions, the component system of one is interspersed into the component system of the other. Mostly the New Testament metaphors are used to express the theme of human salvation and redemption amid sinfulness, death, persecution, and hopelessness. The task of the reader is to unlock the semantic domains of the text through the means analyzing the metaphorical expressions and their dynamic relationships. Asian readers of the New Testament texts can understand the textual dynamics through the symbolic interconnectedness as the texts and the contemporary contexts implicate each other for significance.

In what follows, I will explore two metaphorical aspects that make evident the connection between the New Testament's metaphors for salvation and the Asian setting. First, consider the power of fire. In Asian religious language, fire is considered as a metaphor of purity, cleansing, power, presence of the divine, and salvation and judgment. The New Testament writings align in

---

94. For more details, see Paul Chilton and Monika Kopytowska, eds., *Religion, Language, and the Human Mind* (Oxford: Oxford University Press, 2018).
95. Victor Turner, *Dramas, Fields, and Metaphors: Symbolic Action in Human Society* (Ithaca: Cornell University Press, 1974), 29.

several ways within this linguistic phenomenon. Charteris-Black says, "In literature and poetry fire is a widely accepted metaphor for describing human passions – especially those related to love and sexual desire. The transformative power of fire as a force in the physical world forms the perfect analogy for describing the transforming effect on the individual who is in love."[96] It is therefore worth noting that the transformative power of Christ, the Holy Spirit and the effects of salvation are spoken of in terms of fire in many New Testament texts (Luke 3:15–18; 24:32; Rom 12:1; Tit 2:14; 2 Pet 3:18).[97] The Book of Revelation similarly explores the theme of judgment through the usage of the metaphor fire (Rev 8:5; 14:10). Though both the New Testament writings and the other Asian religious texts emerged out of two conceptual and ideological frameworks, a serious reader can find out the dialogic links and accommodative tendencies between the writings.

In Hindu dances and art forms metaphorical descriptions were incorporated, including fire.[98] The naṭarāja image of Śiva as "Lord of the dance," posed in a circle of fire, combines beauty with energy. It is notable that in Revelation, fire is also connected to Christ's beauty and power: "His eyes were like a flame of fire" (1:14 NRSV; cf. 2:18; 19:12) and "His legs were like pillars of fire" (10:1 NRSV).[99] The same metaphor was used with several ranges of meanings and on various occasions to address different things. Though there are several resemblances between the New Testament and other religious texts with regard to the usage of metaphors, the New Testament texts mostly use them in relation to the theme of salvation and punishment.

Aside from fire, consider a second collection of metaphors: those related to a wedding. As alluded to above, the bride and bridegroom connection is used as one of the most significant soteriological metaphors in the New Testament writings. In the Fourth Gospel, Jesus is introduced as a bridegroom (John 3:28–30). Moloney comments:

---

96. Jonathan Charteris-Black, *Fire Metaphors: Discourses of Awe and Authority* (London: Bloomsbury Academic, 2017), 10.

97. Jonathan F. Bayes, *Revival, The New Testament Expectation: Is there a New Testament Theology of Revival?* (Eugene: Resource Publications, 2016), 16; also see Daniel Frayer-Griggs, *Saved through Fire: The Fiery Ordeal in New Testament Eschatology* (Eugene: Pickwick Publications, 2016), 136–38.

98. Anne-Marie Gaston, "Dance and Hinduism: A Personal Exploration," *Studying Hinduism in Practice*, ed. Hillary P. Rodrigues (Oxfordshire: Routledge, 2012), 89–100.

99. Charteris-Black says, "Its [fire's] role as a potent symbol therefore constraints its use as a metaphor because fire is an actual manifestation of Ahura Mazda." While in Hinduism fire is more metaphorical, in Zoroastrianism it is symbolical as it is the predominant expression of the sacred in daily life. See Charteris-Black, *Fire Metaphors*, 91.

> The Baptist's use of marriage imagery has two sources. The Scriptures often speak of Israel as the bride of God (cf. Isa 62:4–5; Jer 2:2; Eze 16:8; 23:4; Hos 2:21) and the Christian Church continued this imagery to speak of itself as the bride of Christ (cf. 2 Cor 11:2; Eph 5:25–27, 31–32; Rev 21:2; 22:17).[100]

The Old Testament and the New Testament writers employed bride, bridegroom, and marriage metaphors to communicate the most important aspects of salvation. Asian writings also reflect a similar tendency to use weddings as key metaphors for sacred realities. In the Hindu understanding, marriage is considered a magical-spiritual-social union.[101] The ideology of the bride-bridegroom-wedding imagery in the New Testament texts conceptually aligns well with the Shiva and Parvati relations. In both, the aspects of love, devotion, and faithfulness are symbolically integrated for human response and action.

The biblical metaphors reflect some of the socio-religious and politico-cultural realities of the Asian context. The metaphors related to family, royal aspects, priesthood, war, agriculture, business, fishing, finance and banking, and others are derived out of the core realities of the Asian people. Metaphors such as light, life, law, death, darkness, rivers, mountains, lakes, colors and others are used to indicate several social, religious, cultural, and political realities with symbolical meaning. In the process of biblical exegesis and interpretation, Asian readers can consider those connecting links as means for hermeneutical integration and crosspollination.

Lim states that "many of the metaphors used in the New Testament, particularly in the Pauline epistles, naturally appeal to Asians. These include, among others, church as a communal assembly, family, siblings, body, and temple metaphors. These metaphors should be read as addressing not simply individuals but the entire community."[102] Other metaphors such as soldier, athlete, and farmer in 2 Timothy 2:1–7 fit well within the contextual realities of the Asian people. As Gilbert Soo Hoo comments, "A metaphorical reading

---

100. Francis J. Moloney, *The Gospel of John*, SP 4 (Collegeville: The Liturgical Press, 1998), 106.

101. Maya Tiwari, "Steeped in rich cultural metaphors and spiritual symbols of the Vedas, Hindu marriage is based on the theme of magical-spiritual-social union which is intended to help ascend and energy of each partner's karma into the progressively pious content of their souls." Maya Tiwari, *Women's Power to Heal through Inner Medicine* (Poulsbo: Mother Om Media, 2012), 289.

102. Kar Yong Lim, "The New Testament and the Sociocultural and Religious Realities of the Asian Contexts," *An Asian Introduction to the New Testament*, ed. Johnson Thomaskutty (Minneapolis: Fortress Press, 2022), 10.

transports us Asian readers from the world of the text and the world behind the text to our world before the text."[103] As Lim and Hoo note, a proper understanding of the metaphors in the New Testament is possible if we dynamically connect the "behind," "in" and "in front of" the textual realities with a literary, theological and contextual emphasis. Through these dynamic involvements with the textual and the contextual worlds, a reader can perceive the text not only from the "there and then" perspectives but also from the "here and now" perspectives.

As Jesus is incarnated into the form of a human (John 1:14), he is qualified to be called *son of the soil* and *God's son schooled in nature*.[104] Jesus's accommodative nature to the flesh-and-blood realities of the world enabled him to bridge between the heavenly and the earthly in dynamic association.[105] In his discourses, Jesus uses metaphorical language to express the nature of salvation in earthly terms. Following his footprints, the apostles and the authors of the New Testament employed several metaphors rooted in the teachings of Jesus. The metaphors used in the New Testament are instrumental in understanding the heavenly aspects in earthly language. This is an encouragement for all the interpreters of the New Testament in the Asian context to create new symbolisms, metaphors and imageries to address the changing situations of the world.

In the contemporary Asian context, readers of the New Testament can create semantic bridges between the metaphors of the New Testament and the metaphors of the Asian contextual realities. This initiative of the readers shall bear more fruits in the Asian socio-religious context. As the biblical writings are mostly emerged out of the Asian realities, readers with their Asian mindset can comprehend the essence of the truths more relationally than readers from other parts of the world. One of the advantages of the Asian readers is that the expressions and metaphors of the New Testament reflect their own flora and fauna. Asian readers of the New Testament can be more creative in the process of interpreting the sacred writings in the light of the Asian realities. A reader can bring more creativity if she is able to create new metaphors as per the requirements of the new situations of the world. But that shall be done with utmost care and concentration.

---

103. Gilbert Soo Hoo, "The Letter to the Hebrews," *An Asian Introduction to the New Testament*, ed. Johnson Thomaskutty (Minneapolis: Fortress Press, 2022), 447.
104. Jesus's nature parables and complete accommodation of human culture exemplify this fact.
105. Hans Dirk van Hoogstraten, *Deep Economy: Caring for Ecology, Humanity and Religion* (Cambridge: James Clarke & Co., 2001), 2–3.

The ethical exhortations, legal codes, household aspects, farming and agricultural realities, fishing, war situations and soldier concerns, athletic imageries, teaching setting, and others in the New Testament can be attuned to the concerns of the Asian realities. Asian religions like Judaism, Hinduism, Zoroastrianism, Buddhism, Jainism, Islam, Sikhism, and Baha'i faith employ several metaphors, imageries, symbolisms, and figurative language to express the religious truths. A New Testament interpreter with an Asian background can connect her/his hermeneutical spectrum with that of the other religious metaphors to create dialogic interpretative avenues. As John's Gospel perceives the aspects of knowing, seeing, and believing are integrally connected (4:53; 6:69; 10:38; 17:8),[106] *knowing is seeing* is one of the significant expressions in some of the Buddhist traditions.[107] As the kingdom of God is a metaphor used for the building up of an ideal community in the teachings of Jesus, *Sangha* is used as a metaphor for a new community in Buddhism.[108] Thus, an Asian reader of the New Testament can make several bridges between the New Testament realities and the Asian realities through the means of the metaphorical expressions inscribed in both the traditions. In that process, a reader must perceive that New Testament metaphors are mostly soteriological in nature as they link their semantic domains directly or indirectly to the concerns of people's salvation, liberation and transformation.

CONCLUDING REMARKS

The above discussion enables us to understand the fact that metaphors and figurative language are some of the key literary components of the New Testament writings. The usage of this typical language enabled the authors to link the socio-religious and politico-cultural realities in their writings. The earthly metaphors used by Jesus and the New Testament authors are mighty weapons to elaborate and associate the mysterious knowledge in the earthly idiom. As salvation of the world is at the core of the New Testament writings, the majority of the metaphors are used with a soteriological intent.

---

106. Johnson Thomaskutty, "The Gospel of John," 144.

107. David L. McMahan says, "These metaphorical expressions all draw in different ways from various aspects of visual experience, suggesting a coherent system of metaphors for understanding knowledge in terms of seeing." David L. McMahan, *Empty Vision: Metaphor and Visionary Imagery in Mahāyāna Buddhism* (London: RoutledgeCurzon, 2002), 66.

108. See Sam Peedikayil Mathew, *Method and Message of Gautama Buddha and Jesus Christ: Explorations in Cross-scripture Hermeneutics* (Bangalore/Delhi: CISRS/ISPCK, 2020), 256–60.

The following things are important to focus on in the process of reading the New Testament with a contemporary outlook: first, the message of salvation was central to the writers of the New Testament in a context in which the common people were suffering in their socio-religious and politico-cultural world. Second, as salvation is a divine arrangement, the authors of the New Testament employed metaphors, imageries, and figurative language to explain the heavenly in earthly terms. Third, the soteriological aspects of the New Testament writings, by means of human-friendly language, persuades the people of the world to associate themselves with the heavenly paradigms. Fourth, a re-reading of the New Testament in the light of the metaphorical language embedded therein can equip the readers to understand the soteriological message of the New Testament. And fifth, as Asian religious expressions are mostly conveyed through metaphors, a reader of the New Testament can develop a dialogical reading to foreground the message of salvation with profundity. As the cross is the apex point of human salvation, readers of the New Testament in Asia and elsewhere must see the significance of metaphors in conveying the message of salvation, liberation, and transformation. As the majority of the New Testament metaphors are connected to the realities of the Asian people, Asian readers should employ contextual and dialogical interpretation of the New Testament by focusing on its metaphorical language.

BIBLIOGRAPHY

Anderson, Bruce James. *"Family" Metaphors in Romans 8:10–25 and Their Social Context in Ancient Rome*. Auckland: University of Auckland, 1997.

Anderson, Paul N. *From Crisis to Christ: A Contextual Introduction to the New Testament*. Nashville: Abingdon Press, 2014.

Baasland, Ernst. *Parables and Rhetoric in the Sermon on the Mount: New Approaches to a Classical Text*. WUNT 351. Tübingen: Mohr Siebeck, 2015.

Bayes, Jonathan F. *Revival, The New Testament Expectation: Is there a New Testament Theology of Revival?* Eugene: Resource Publications, 2016.

Bennett, David W. *Metaphors and Ministry: Biblical Images for Leaders and Followers*. Eugene: Wipf & Stock, 1993/2004.

Boyer, Mark G. *Waiting in Joyful Hope: Daily Reflections for Advent and Christmas*. Mumbai: St. Paul's, 2003.

Bultmann, Rudolf. *Gospel of St. John: A Commentary*. Philadelphia: WJKP, 1978.

Cachia, Nicholas. *The Image of the Good Shepherd as a Source for the Spirituality of the Ministerial Priesthood*. TGSS. Roma: Editrice Pontifica Universita Gregoriana, 1997.

Caragounis, C. C. "Kingdom of God/Kingdom of Heaven." *DJG* 468.

Charteris-Black, Jonathan. *Fire Metaphors: Discourses of Awe and Authority*. London: Bloomsbury Academic, 2017.

Chilton, Paul, and Monika Kopytowska, eds. *Religion, Language, and the Human Mind*. Oxford: Oxford University Press, 2018.

Collins, Raymond F. *The Power of Images in Paul*. Collegeville: The Liturgical Press, 2008.

Concise Dictionary of Metaphors and Similes. New Delhi: V&S Publishers, 2014.

Dawes, Gregory W. *The Body in Question: Metaphor and Meaning in the Interpretation of Ephesians 5:21–33*. BibInt 30. Leiden: Brill, 1998.

Egg, Markus. "To Those Walking in the Footsteps of the Faith: Deliberate Metaphor in the Pauline Epistles." In *Drawing Attention to Metaphor. Figurative Thought and Language*, edited by Camilla Di Biase-Dyson and Markus Egg, 230–62. Amsterdam: John Benjamins Publishing Company, 2020.

Finlan, Stephen. *The Background and Content of Paul's Cultic Atonement Metaphors*. Atlanta: Society of Biblical Literature, 2004.

France, R. T. *The Gospel of Matthew*. NICNT. Grand Rapids: Eerdmans, 2007.

Frayer-Griggs, Daniel. *Saved through Fire: The Fiery Ordeal in New Testament Eschatology*. Eugene: Pickwick Publications, 2016.

Gaston, Anne-Marie. "Dance and Hinduism: A Personal Exploration." Pages 89–100 in *Studying Hinduism in Practice*. Edited by Hillary P. Rodrigues. Oxfordshire: Routledge, 2012.

Grobbelaar, Jan, and Gert Breed, eds. *Welcoming Africa's Children: Theological and Ministry Perspectives*. Durbanville, South Africa: AOSIS, 2016.

Guthrie, Donald. *New Testament Introduction*. Rev. ed. Downers Grove: InterVarsity Press, 1990.

Hansen, Fred. *The Alpha and Omega and Lampstands Metaphors: A Linguistic Theory of Metaphor as Applied to the Book of Revelation*. Nijmegen: Radboud University, 2017.

Harris, Murray J. *Slave of Christ: A New Testament Metaphor for Total Devotion to Christ*. NSBT. Downers Grove: InterVarsity Press, 1999.

Hein, Erin M. *Adoption in Galatians and Romans*. BibInt 153. Leiden: Brill, 2017.

Huber, Lynn R. *Like a Bride Adorned: Reading Metaphor in John's Apocalypse*. Emory Studies in Early Christianity. New York: T&T Clark International, 2007.

Hylen, Susan. *Allusion and Meaning in John 6*. BZNW 137. Berlin: Walter de Gruyter, 2005.

Isaac, Munther. *From Land to Lands, from Eden to the Renewed Earth*. Carlisle: Langham Academic, 2015.

Johnson, D. H. "Life." *DJG* 469–71.

Keach, Benjamin. *Preaching from the Types and Metaphors of the Bible*. London: Ravenio Books, 2014.

Konsmo, Erik. *The Pauline Metaphors of the Holy Spirit: The Intangible Spirit's Tangible Presence in the Life of the Christian*. StBibLit 130. New York: Peter Lang, 2010.

Köstenberger, Andreas J. *A Theology of John's Gospel and Letters*. Grand Rapids: Zondervan, 2009.

Lim, Kar Yong. *Metaphors and Social Identity Formation in Paul's Letters to the Corinthians*. Eugene: Wipf & Stock, 2017.

————. "The New Testament and the Sociocultural and Religious Realities of the Asian Contexts." In *An Asian Introduction to the New Testament*, edited by Johnson Thomaskutty, 5–28. Minneapolis: Fortress Press, 2022.

Malina, Bruce J., and Jerome H. Neyrey. "Jesus the Witch: Witchcraft Accusations in Matthew 12." In *Social-Scientific Approaches to New Testament Interpretation*, edited by David G. Horrell, 29–68. Edinburgh: T&T Clark, 1999.

Marshall, I. H. "Salvation." *DJG* 719–24.

Martin, Dale B. *Slavery as Salvation: The Metaphor of Slavery in Pauline Christianity*. Eugene: Wipf & Stock, 1990.

Mathew, Sam Peedikayil. *Method and Message of Gautama Buddha and Jesus Christ: Explorations in Cross-scripture Hermeneutics*. Bangalore/Delhi: CISRS/ISPCK, 2020.

McMahan, David L. *Empty Vision: Metaphor and Visionary Imagery in Mahāyāna Buddhism*. London: RoutledgeCurzon, 2002.

Miller, D. M. *The Net of Hephaestus: A Study of Modern Criticism and Metaphysical Metaphor*. Berlin: De Gruyter, 1971.

Moloney, Francis J. *The Gospel of John*, SP 4. Collegeville: The Liturgical Press, 1998.

Nielsen, Jasper Tang. "The Lamb of God: The Cognitive Structure of a Johannine Metaphor." In *Imagery in the Gospel of John*, WUNT 200, edited by Jörg Frey, Jan G. van der Watt, and Ruben Zimmermann, 217–56. Tübingen: Mohr Siebeck, 2006.

Pilgaard, Aage. "The Qumran Scrolls and John's Gospel." In *New Readings in John: Literary and Theological Perspectives*, edited by Johannes Nissen and Sigfred Pedersen, 126–42. London: T&T Clark, 1999.

Reddish, Mitchell G. *Revelation*. SHBC. Macon: Smyth & Helwys, 2001.

Robinson, William E. W. *Metaphor, Morality, and the Spirit in Romans 8:1–17*. ECL. Atlanta: SBL Press, 2016.

Ryken, Leland, James C. Wilhoit, and Tremper Longman III, eds. *Dictionary of Biblical Imagery*. Secunderabad: Authentic, 2006.

Schnell, Norbert. *The Bride of Christ – A Metaphor for the Church: Systematical Exegetical Analysis*. Zürich: LIT Verlag, 2020.

Shaver, Stephen R. *Metaphors of Eucharistic Presence: Language, Cognition, and the Body and Blood of Christ*. Oxford: Oxford University Press, 2022.

Smolarz, Sebastian R. *Covenant and the Metaphor of Divine Marriage in Biblical Thought*. Eugene: Wipf & Stock, 2011.

Snodgrass, K. R. "Parable." *DJG* 591–601.

Soo Hoo, Gilbert. "The Letter to the Hebrews." In *An Asian Introduction to the New Testament* edited by Johnson Thomaskutty, 423–48. Minneapolis: Fortress Press, 2022.

Stack, Judith V. *Metaphor and the Portrayal of the Cause(s) of Sin and Evil in the Gospel of Matthew*. BibInt 182. Leiden: Brill, 2020.

Thomaskutty, Johnson. *Dialogue in the Book of Signs: A Polyvalent Analysis of John 1:19–12:50*. BibInt 136. Leiden: Brill, 2015.

———. *The Gospel of John: A Universalistic Reading*. Biblical Hermeneutics Rediscovered 25. New Delhi: Christian World Imprints, 2020.

———. "The Gospel of John." In *An Asian Introduction to the New Testament*, edited by Johnson Thomaskutty, 127–56. Minneapolis: Fortress Press, 2022.

———. "The Irony of Ability and Disability in John 9:1–41." HTS Theologiese Studies/Theological Studies 78, no.1 (2022): 1–7.

Thompson, M. M. "John, Gospel of." *DJG* 368–83.

Tiwari, Maya. *Women's Power to Heal through Inner Medicine*. Poulsbo: Mother Om Media, 2012.

Turner, Victor. *Dramas, Fields, and Metaphors: Symbolic Action in Human Society*. Ithaca: Cornell University Press, 1974.

Van der Watt, Jan G. *Family of the King: Dynamics of Metaphor in the Gospel according to John*. BibInt 47. Leiden: Brill, 2000.

———. *Salvation in the New Testament: Perspectives on Soteriology*. SNT 121. Ed. Jan G. van der Watt. Leiden: Brill, 2005.

Van Hoogstraten, Hans Dirk. *Deep Economy: Caring for Ecology, Humanity and Religion*. Cambridge: James Clarke & Co, 2001.

Wead, David W. *The Literary Devices in John's Gospel*. The Johannine Monograph Series. Rev. and exp. ed. Eugene: Wipf & Stock, 2018.

Wheaton, Gerry. *The Role of Jewish Feasts in John's Gospel*. SNTSMS 162. Cambridge: Cambridge University Press, 2015.

Williams, Joanna Radwanska. "'Native Speaker' as a metaphorical construct." In *Metaphors for Learning: Cross-cultural Perspectives*, edited by Erich A. Berendt, 139–56. Amsterdam: John Benjamin Publishing Company, 2008.

CHAPTER 4

HOLINESS IN THE NEW TESTAMENT

Its Various Expressions and Practices

Bennet Lawrence

In the early nineteenth century, the famous British missionary to India William Carey and his fellow missionaries and colleagues reported the practice of infanticides in India.[1] Many Hindu mothers were reported to have sacrificed their children in the holy river Ganges to wash their sins.[2] A mother killing her own child is a gruesome reminder of the presence of extreme practices performed to effectuate holiness in parts of Asia. Though the concepts of sin and holiness are varied across the region, the idea of living a holy life is common to almost every community across Asia.

What is holiness in the New Testament? The Greek word to be holy (*hagiazō*) means "to set apart for a holy purpose."[3] The basis for the New Testament doctrine of holiness is rooted in the Old Testament.[4] What is "holy" is set apart from the common.[5] God alone is truly holy,[6] but certain things such as sacrifices, certain places like the temple,[7] and certain people, like priests, were considered holy, as they were set apart for God. The essential reason behind the believer's call for holiness is based on the idea that God himself is holy. God is described as "holy, holy, holy" (Isa 6:3; Rev 4:8). The triple adjective for God displays his important attribute.[8] The reaction of Isaiah after seeing

---

1. Evangeline Anderson-Rajkumar, "Ministry in the Killing Fields," *Christian History* 11 (1992): 35–37.
2. Anderson-Rajkumar, "Ministry in the Killing Fields," 35–37.
3. Donald Guthrie, *New Testament Introduction*, rev. ed. (Hyderabad: Authentic, 2003), 661.
4. O. Procksch, "*hagios*," *TDNT* 1:100.
5. Clarence Craig, "Paradox of Holiness: The New Testament Doctrine of Sanctification," *Int* 6, no. 2 (1952): 147–61.
6. See Exodus 15:11; Leviticus 11:44; 19:2; 20:26; 22:32; 1 Samuel 2:2; 1 Chronicles 16:29, 35; Job 6:10; Psalms 11:4; 15:1; 22:3; 33:21; 47:8; 71:22; 77:13; 97:12; 99:5; Proverbs 9:10; Isaiah 6:3; 40:25; 43:15; 57:15; Ezekiel 36:23; 38:23; Habakkuk 1:13.
7. Burning bush (Exod 3:5); Temple (Ps 93:5; Isa 64:11; 1 Chr 29:3; Hab 2:20); Temple Mount (Ps 48:1).
8. R. C. Sproul, *The Holiness of God* (Carol Stream: Tyndale House, 1998), 21.

God exemplifies the holiness of God. He says "Woe to me! . . . I am ruined! For I am a man of unclean lips, and I live among a people of unclean lips" (6:5 NIV).

There is an analogy between God's holiness and the holiness of his people. Thus, Leviticus 19:2 says, "Be holy because I, the Lord your God, am holy." The Israelites are called by God to live a set apart life for God (Lev 17–26), and a person is considered holy when he or she obeys the laws of YHWH (Exod 19:5–6).[9] Thus, Deuteronomy 28:9 (NIV) says, "The LORD will establish you as his holy people . . . if you keep the commands of the LORD your God and walk in obedience to him." Similarly, in the prophetic books, when the people disobeyed the law, the prophets condemned them and warned them of the consequences of their sins (Isa 5:24; Ezek 22:26; Zeph 3:4).

Similarly, in the New Testament, God is identified as the holy one (1 Pet 1:15; Rev 4:8; 15:4; Luke 1:49; John 17:11). The believers are identified as holy as well (1 Cor 1:2). In the Old Testament, primarily the Jews were considered holy (Exod 19:6; Deut 7:6). As Adewuya says, "Israel's separation from the nations implies distinctiveness in terms of religion and social values and modelling God's attractive holiness to the people of the nations."[9] In Hinduism, however, Brahmins – the people from the highest caste in the hierarchy of four caste groups – are considered holier than the others.[10] The lower caste people could move up the ladder only in the next life, and only if they live a holy and pious life. In the Old Testament, however, Jewish people were called to be holy to be an example to the other nations.

In the New Testament, all believers, both Jews and the Gentiles, are identified as holy (1 Pet 2:9). In Christ, Paul says, there is no Jew nor Gentile (Gal 3:28). Thus, a major theme of the New Testament is that the Gentiles are being grafted into the holy stump of God, and so are also identified as part of this holy nation (Rom 11:17; 15:16; Eph 2:19).[11] It is Christ who made this church holy (Eph 5:26–27; Rom 15:16) and in him they are holy (Phil 1:1). Therefore, believers are called to live a holy life.

It will be a herculean task to cover all the passages that deal with holiness in the New Testament in a short chapter. Though this theme could be dealt with theologically using selected verses which deal with holiness, a coherent

9. J. Ayodeji Adewuya, *Holiness in the Letters of Paul: A Necessary Response to the Gospel* (Eugene: Cascade, 2016), 18.

10. Nancy M. Martin, "Hinduism and Holy people," *Holy People of the World: A Cross-cultural Encyclopedia*, ed. Phyllis G. Jestice, 3 vols. (Santa Barbara: ABC-CLIO, 2004), 3:368–69.

11. Procksch, "*hagios*," *TDNT* 1:106.

understanding of the theme could be attained by dealing with larger portions of texts. Therefore, this chapter will focus on the epistles to the Romans, the epistle of 1 Corinthians, and the Sermon on the Mount to elucidate the New Testament's teaching on holiness. Other relevant passages will be woven throughout as we consider not only what holiness means in the New Testament, but also how it connects with the concepts of holiness in Asia.

THE PROBLEM OF SIN AND HOLINESS
IN THE EPISTLE OF ROMANS

The concept of sin is important as a prerequisite for comprehending the significance of holy life. In Hinduism and Buddhism, the evil actions of a person could potentially take a person far away from liberation.[12] According to their beliefs, the soul (*atman*) can take thousands of rebirths (*samsara*) as it is caught in the cycle of rebirths. The ultimate goal of the soul, then, is to strive towards its release from this unending cycle, its liberation (*moksha* or *nirvana*), an equivalent to Christian salvation. The results of the sins of a person (*karma*) will make this journey longer. However, obeying the laws (*dharma*) and doing good works (good *karma*) could take the person closer to liberation (*moksha*).

In Christianity, sin is defined as "any evil action or evil motive that is in opposition with God."[13] Moreover, sin in the New Testament is seen as human spiritual disability which hinders an individual from fulfilling the standards of God.[14] While in Hinduism, a person's *karma* from previous lives could be attributed for his or her present condition, Paul attributes the reasons for the sinful state of the human beings to the sinful act of the first human beings. For Paul, sin entered the world through Adam (Rom 5:12–14; 1 Cor 15:21). Because human beings are born into sin, they continue to commit sin, which further leads them to death. As Romans 6:23 (NIV) emphatically puts it, "the wages of sin is death." This death includes physical death, spiritual death and eternal death.[15]

In Romans 1:18–32, Paul explains that because the Gentiles did not acknowledge the true God and honor him, God gave them to the futility of their hearts (1:21, 24, 26, 28). Therefore, they committed sins such as

---

12. Kandiah Sivalogathan, *Understanding Hinduism* (Gurgaon, India: Zorba Books, 2020), 83–91.
13. Millard J. Erickson, *Introducing Christian Doctrine*, 2nd ed., ed. L. Arnold Hustad (Grand Rapids: Baker, 2001), 187.
14. Erickson, *Introducing Christian Doctrine*, 189.
15. Millard J. Erickson, *Christian Theology*, 2nd ed. (Grand Rapids: Baker, 1998), 629–32.

sexual impurities and shameful acts and "every kind of wickedness" (1:29). God's wrath and death came to them because they did these things even after knowing "God's righteous decree" (1:32). Paul similarly condemns the Jewish people as sinners as well because even though they knew God's ordinances, they still committed similar sins (2:1). Therefore, for Paul, "all have sinned and fall short of the glory of God" (3:23). And for him, the only way they could be saved and made holy is through the "redemption that came through Christ Jesus" (3:24).

In Romans 3:21–31, Paul describes the aspects of justification, which gives the solution for the problem of sin. In justification, "God gives his sin-conquering righteousness to every human being through faith in Jesus Christ."[16] The sins of believers are forgiven when they put faith in Jesus Christ.[17] Moreover, they are also declared righteous, much as one is vindicated in a court of law.[18]

A story from South Asia about a king named Manu Needhi Cholan, who ruled Sri Lanka and South India during the second century BC, is famously told to exemplify the establishment of justice in past times.[19] This king was known for establishing justice; but when his son ran over a calf with his chariot, the mother cow went to the king for justice. Learning what happened to the calf, the king made the chariot run over and kill the prince to establish justice.

Here, justice is established through the sacrifice of the prince. However, in Romans, Paul says, though Jesus Christ did not commit any sins God gave him "as a propitiation by his blood" for the declaration of the believers as righteous (3:25 ESV). Through the blood of Jesus Christ, a believer, then, is identified as a holy person by God.[20] Justification is, therefore, about identifying who belongs to the people of God.[21]

---

16. Udo Schnelle, *Theology of the New Testament*, trans. M. Eugene Boring (Grand Rapids: Baker Academic, 2007), 264.

17. Anders Nygren, *Commentary on Romans*, trans. Carl C. Rasmussen (London: SCM Press, 1952), 171; Douglas J. Moo, *The Epistle to the Romans* (Grand Rapids: Eerdmans, 1996), 266.

18. George Eldon Ladd, *A Theology of the New Testament*, ed. Donald A. Hagner, rev. ed. (Grand Rapids: Eerdmans, 1993), 480; also Michael Horton, *Pilgrim Theology: Core Doctrines for Christian Disciples* (Grand Rapids: Zondervan, 2012), 291.

19. N. Sethuraman, *The Cholas: Mathematics Reconstructs the Chronology* (Kumbakonam: Sethuraman, 1977), 143.

20. Alister McGrath, *Christian Theology: An Introduction*, 6th ed. (Oxford: Wiley Blackwell, 2017), 340.

21. N. T. Wright, *Paul* (Minneapolis: Fortress, 2009), 121. Wright reminds that justification should be seen within the idea of covenant. It is about identifying who is the righteous within the covenant.

Nevertheless, the NT's conception of justification does not elucidate how a believer grows in holiness.[22] As Stott says, "To justify is to declare or pronounce righteous, not to make righteous."[23] It is about declaration and not transformation.[24] Though one's sins are forgiven before God, the believer is expected to grow in holiness after he or she is declared righteous. In the process of sanctification, the believer is expected to actively work towards holiness.[25]

Being Holy in Romans

From Romans 6 onwards, Paul describes several ways by which a believer can live a holy life. For Ridderbos, Romans 6 talks about "moral reversal" in the new life in Christ.[26] The believer now is asked to live a holy life that is significantly different from their old life. For Paul, the believer could be holy *by being dead to sin* (6:1–14). Because believers are dead to sin, they are set free from it (6:7). They are therefore exhorted to live a holy life by considering themselves dead to sin. A dead person cannot react when an aromatic bowl of biriyani is kept in front of him. Similarly, the believer is expected to be dead to sin even though temptations may be present all around.

Similarly, Paul says, the believers must be *slaves to righteousness* in order to be holy (6:15–23).[27] The believer was a slave to sin earlier (6:17); now, the believer is set free from sin, and has become a slave to righteousness (6:18). This means that the believer is now able to bring forth deeds of holiness. Whereas earlier, the believer was a slave to "impurity and to ever-increasing wickedness" (6:19), Paul says, "now that you have been set free from sin and have become slaves of God, the benefit you reap leads to holiness, and the result is eternal life" (6:22). Believers should therefore bring forth holiness in their new lives by considering themselves to be slaves to righteousness.

Further, for Paul, a person cannot be holy by merely obeying the law. The law brings the knowledge of sin (3:20) and it even increases sins (5:20).[28]

---

22. Thomas R. Schreiner, *Faith Alone – The Doctrine of Justification: What the Reformers Taught . . . and Why It Still Matters* (Grand Rapids: Zondervan, 2015), 74.
23. John Stott, *Romans: God's Good News for the World* (Downers Grove: InterVarsity Press 1994), 110.
24. Thomas R. Schreiner, *40 Questions about Christians and Biblical Law*, ed. Benjamin L. Merkle (Grand Rapids: Kregel, 2010), 118.
25. Horton, *Pilgrim Theology*, 305.
26. Herman Ridderbos, *Paul: An Outline of His Theology* (Grand Rapids: Eerdmans, 1966), 258.
27. Michael Gorman, *Participating in Christ: Explorations in Paul's Theology and Spirituality* (Grand Rapids: Baker Academic, 2019), 192.
28. Richard Longenecker, *Galatians*, WBC 41 (Grand Rapids: Zondervan, 1990), 138–39.

While believers were bound to the law before becoming Christians, they are now released from the law, just as a woman is released from her marriage when her abusive husband has died (7:3). The believer is now dead to the law (7:4). When the believer obeyed the law before becoming a Christian, "the sinful passions aroused by the law" led the person to sin more and they eventually led her to death (7:5). However, "the new way of the Spirit" released the believer from these sins and bondage so that the believer could live a holy life by the help of the Spirit [see Rom 8] (7:6).

Thus, Paul argues that though the law is holy and good (7:12) it only produced sins (7:8). This is because the law did not have the capacity to bring forth holiness because of the presence of sinful flesh (7:13–25). That is, sin dwells in the flesh (7:14), and when the law is applied to the flesh it only produced more sins (5:20; 7:8). As Craig S. Keener notes, the law "righteously teaches right from wrong, but it does not transform a person to be righteous, to undo the power of sin Adam introduced into humanity. It was 'weak' because it depended on 'flesh' to fulfill it – and flesh could never fulfil God's righteousness."[29] It is Christ by his death who brought forth righteousness to the believer. Moreover, the Holy Spirit helps the believer live a holy life by transforming the flesh to bring forth holiness (8:1–14).[30] The law is important in the journey of holiness. Therefore, the law, which could not be fulfilled by the flesh, is now finally fulfilled by the help of the Spirit so that the believer could be holy (8:4). Therefore, the Spirit plays an important role in helping the believer fulfil the law and in transforming the flesh to be holy.[31] Diagrammatically this can be explained this way:

Law + Flesh → Sins
Law + Spirit + Flesh → Holiness

---

29. Craig S. Keener, *Romans* NCC (Eugene: Cascade, 2009), 99; Thomas R. Schreiner, *Romans* BECNT (Grand Rapids: Baker Academic, 1998), 399.
30. Keener, *Romans*, 99. Stott, *Romans*, 219. Karl Barth, *A Shorter Commentary on Romans*, ed. Maico M. Michielin (Bodmin: MPG, 2007), 55.
31. Keener, *Romans*, 99. See also Arren Bennet Lawrence, *Legalistic Nomism: A Socio-Rhetorical Reading of Paul's Letter to the Galatians* (New Delhi: ISPCK, 2016), 81–82.

For Paul, sanctification is not completely the work of God as though the believer is not required to do anything for holiness (what might be called "auto-sanctification"). Neither is it purely based on human efforts (what we might call "active sanctification"). For Paul, the believer is exhorted to be holy by the help of the Spirit (what we might call "guided sanctification"). Erickson puts it this way: "while sanctification is God's work, the believer has a role as well, entailing both removal of sinfulness and development of holiness."[32] Gorman similarly explains, "there is a clear human role in the process of sanctification (6:19) or transformation (12:1–2)."[33] The believer works in the power of the Holy Spirit in this process of sanctification.

Being Holy with the Help of the Holy Spirit

This process of Spirit-empowered holiness is Paul's focus in Romans 8. There Paul explains that:

> For what the Law could not do, weak as it was through the flesh, God *did*: sending his own Son in the likeness of sinful flesh and *as an offering* for sin, he condemned sin in the flesh, so that the requirement of the law might be fulfilled in us, who do not walk according to the flesh but according to the Spirit. (8:3–4)

God sent his own Son as an offering for the sins of the humans in order to condemn the sin in the flesh and to fulfil the requirements of the law. For Paul, the law must be fulfilled in the life of the believer so that she can be holy.

Though in one sense the work of the Son has fulfilled the requirements of the law, believers are also expected to act in appropriating this fulfilment of the law.[34] The believer is exhorted by Paul to "walk according to the Spirit" in order to actualize the work of the Son in the life of the believer. Schreiner summarizes this idea as follows:

> The law itself was powerless to produce the fulfillment of the law envisioned in verse 3, not because there was any deficiency in the law per se, but because human beings under the power of the flesh are unable to practice what the law says. Those who are in Christ, however, are in a very different position. They are right in God's sight by virtue of the work of Christ on the cross. The

---

32. Erickson, *Introducing Christian Doctrine*, 327.
33. Gorman, *Participating in Christ*, 220.
34. Schreiner, *Romans*, 406.

judicial work of God in Christ is the basis by which the law can be fulfilled in their lives. *By the work and power of the Holy Spirit they are able to keep the law.*[35]

Therefore, for Paul, the fulfilment of the requirements of the law constitutes both the Son's work and believer's walking in the Spirit. The Holy Spirit, then, actively works in the life of the believer to fulfil the requirements of the law in order to be holy.[36] Consequently, the Spirit's working in power in the believer is essential for holy living.

How can the believer fulfill the requirements of the law with the help of the Spirit? The believer is expected to "walk according to the Spirit" (8:4). This involves conscious walking according to the ways of the Spirit and not according to the flesh (8:4; Gal 5:17). Believers are exhorted *to set their minds on the things of the Spirit* but not on the things of the flesh (Rom 8:5; Col 3:2). Paul says, "For the mind set on the flesh is death, but the mind set on the Spirit is life and peace" (Rom 8:6 NASB 1995; see also Gal 6:7–8). Thus, Paul argues that thinking about spiritual things will help a believer live a holy life.

In Zoroastrianism, one can be holy by having "pure thoughts, pure words, and pure deeds."[37] Similarly, in Buddhism, the first of the *Ariya Atthangika Magga* (the Noble Eightfold Path) is "right thought" which would bring forth "right understanding," which would further lead to "right speech," "right actions," "right livelihood," "right effort," "right mindfulness," and finally to "right concentration" – the state of enlightenment. In Buddhism, then, right thoughts lead a person to enlightenment (i.e., salvation in Buddhism).

Though these ideas are similar to Paul's thought, there is no divine agent who helps the person to think right thoughts. For Paul, the Spirit acts as the divine agent who empowers the believer to think rightly. This way, the believer is *in the Spirit* and not in the flesh (Rom 8:8–11).[38] When the believer dwells in the Spirit, the Spirit also dwells in the believer and works out the transformation of the believer. In this way, the believer *lives according to the Spirit* and not according to the flesh (8:12).

Further, believers must *put the deeds of the flesh to death* (8:13; Col 3:5–10). They must constantly be on guard to kill the deeds of the body when they pop

---

35. Schreiner, *Romans*, 407–8, italics added. Also James Thompson, *Moral Formation according to Paul* (Grand Rapids: Baker Academic 2011), 13.
36. Stott, *Romans*, 221–22.
37. Cited in James Bisset Pratt, *India and Its Faiths* (New York: Cosimo, 2005), 322.
38. See also 1 Corinthians 3:16 and 6:19.

up. A possible image here could be a cowboy swiftly taking his gun to shoot a target that pops up over the horizon. Similarly, when believers find a deed of the flesh rising up, they should shoot and kill it to remain holy. The Spirit will help in this regard as well (Rom 8:13). In this way, the believer must *be led* constantly by the Spirit of God to be holy (8:14).

As the Holy Spirit helps believers to be holy, he also testifies them to be the children of God (8:14). He assists believers in calling God as "Abba! Father!" (8:15; Gal 4:6), and helps them recall that they are the children of God (Rom 8:16; Heb 10:15–18). Further, the Spirit helps in their adoption as the children of God (Rom 8:16). The Spirit helps by interceding for them (8:26–28; also 1 Cor 2:10–15). Moreover, the Spirit also helps in the perfection of the believer. Paul says, "For those whom he foreknew, he also predestined . . .; and these whom he predestined, he also called; and these whom he called, he also justified; and these whom he justified, he also glorified" (Rom 8:30 NASB). Hence, the Spirit assists in the perfection of the believer.

Holiness, Suffering and Glorification

Regarding glorification, Paul says in Romans 5:2–4 (ESV), "we rejoice in *hope of the glory of God*. Not only that, but we rejoice in our sufferings, knowing that suffering produces endurance, and endurance produces character, and character produces hope." For Paul, the believer's glorification is ensured through suffering.

Suffering is common in Asia, as poverty, persecution, injustice, sickness, lack of facilities to alleviate the standard of life are prevalently present. According to United Nations University, more than 420 million people are still in poverty in Asia.[39] Persecution is also widely found in Asia as religious intolerance is found in Communist China, Hindu majority India, Islamic countries in the Middle East, and in Vietnam, Sri Lanka, etc. It is also said that one in three Christians face persecution in Asia.[40] Against this backdrop, Romans reminds us that suffering produces holiness, which further leads the believer to glorification.

In Romans 8, Paul displays how the Spirit helps a believer to be holy. This could be called "pneumatic nomism," that is, the fulfilment of the law

---

39. UNU-WIDER, "A snapshot of poverty and inequality in Asia," WIDER Research Brief, *UNU-WIDER* 2020, no. 2, April 2020, https://tinyurl.com/2p8utcn3.
40. "One in Three Christians Face Persecution in Asia, Report Finds," *The Guardian*, 16 Jan 2019, https://tinyurl.com/58d4zvtd.

(nomism) by the help of the Spirit (*pneuma*). Paul, then, may be expected to continue his explanation on how the believer could be holy by loving one another as he has done in the Book of Galatians (after 5:12). However, Paul takes a digression to discuss the status of the Jews in Romans 9–11.[41] From Romans 12 onwards, however, Paul describes loving one another as the other way of being holy.

Be Holy by Loving One Another

Romans 12:1 picks up where Romans 8 leaves off. That is, Paul describes a process in which we fulfil the law through holy living in the power of the Spirit. Thus, Paul writes, "Do not conform to the pattern of this world, but *be transformed* by the renewing of your mind" (Rom 12:2 NIV). Further, in Romans 12:3–8, Paul asks the Roman church leaders to give opportunity to all believers in using their gifts in the church. In Romans 12:9–21, he exhorts them to do good to all. In 13:1–7, he asks the believers to submit to the governing authorities. In 13:8–14, he instructs the believers to be holy by loving one another. In 14:1–15:13, he exhorts the majority to accept the weak brethren and accommodate them. Loving one another is the strong theme that unites all these passages. Moreover, 13:8–14 shows Paul's exhortation on fulfilling the law by loving one another, which is similar to Paul's teaching on fulfilling the law by the Spirit (Rom 8). We can call this "agapal nomism," fulfilling the law (nomism) by loving one another (*agapal*).

In Romans 13:8 (ESV), Paul says, "the one who loves another has fulfilled the law." For him, the law must be fulfilled in the life of the believer. Paul explains it further by using a few laws from the Ten Commandments such as, "You shall not commit adultery, you shall not murder, you shall not steal, and you shall not covet" (13:9). For him, all these commandments are fulfilled by loving one another.[42] For Paul, the believer could live a holy life by fulfilling the laws through loving one another (Rom 13:10). Paul structures the Book of Romans to show how a person could live a holy life by the help of the Spirit and by loving others, as he has done also in Galatians. There, he exhorts the recipients about justification by faith in Jesus Christ from 1:1–5:12. After 5:13, he shows how a person can be holy by loving one another and by the help of the Spirit.

---

41. C. H. Dodd, *The Epistle to the Romans* (London: Hodder & Stoughton, 1932), 148. Against this view see Krister Stendahl, *Paul Among Jews and Gentiles* (Fortress Press, 1976), 4.
42. Thompson, *Moral Formation According to Paul,* 124.

Galatians 5:13–15 Fulfil the law by loving others
> Galatians 5:16–26 Be holy by the help of the Spirit

Galatians 6:1–6 Be holy by loving others
> Galatians 6:7–8 Be holy by the help of the Spirit

Galatians 6:9–10 Be holy by loving others

Thus, both in Romans and in Galatians, Paul demonstrates that a believer is judicially made holy before God, and is expected to live in the power of the Spirit by loving one another to live a holy life.

HOLINESS IN 1 CORINTHIANS

Aside from Romans, 1 Corinthians is another NT letter that deals with holiness extensively. In the letter's introduction, the Corinthian believers are "called to be holy" (1 Cor 1:2). Corinthian believers are "sanctified in Christ" (1:2) and they were washed and made holy (6:11).[43] And so, they cannot live in the sins of the past (6:9–11).[44] Thus, Paul expected the believers of Corinth to live a holy life.[45] Nonetheless, when the situational reality was quite different from the expected holiness Paul used letters as a means of building the holiness of the church.[46]

Unity in Diversity (1:10–4:21)

We learn in the first chapter that Paul heard from Chloe's household that there were divisions among them (1:11–12).[47] For Paul, there should be no divisions among the believers, as they should be "united with same mind and thought" (1:10). Wright says disunity is one of the sins Paul wrote against frequently.[48] He addresses similar issues in Philippians 2:1–4, where he says humility is the key to establish unity in the church. Similarly, he says here that the Corinthian believers should not see themselves as wise or kings or rich (4:8; also 1:26) nor should they judge others.[49] They should not be puffed up

---

43. Luke Timothy Johnson, *The Writings of the New Testament: An Interpretation* (Bangalore: Theological Publication in India, 2009), 298.
44. Scot McKnight, *Pastor Paul: Nurturing a Culture of Christoformity in the Church* (Grand Rapids: Brazos, 2019), 192.
45. Johnson, *The Writings of the New Testament*, 302.
46. Thompson, *Moral Formation According to Paul*, 3.
47. Guthrie, *New Testament Introduction*, 460–61; Johnson, *The Writings of the New Testament*, 298; Johnson, *The Writings of the New Testament*, 302.
48. N. T. Wright, *Interpreting Paul: Essays on the Apostle and His Letters* (London: SPCK, 2020).
49. Johnson, *The Writings of the New Testament*, 299.

(4:6) but they should be humble and strive towards unity.[50] According to Paul, humility allows the believer to avoid the sin of disunity and to contribute to the holiness of the church.

Incest and Spiritual Purity of the Church (5:1–13)

In 1 Corinthians 5:1–13, Paul writes against a man who was sleeping with his father's wife (5:1). Though sexual immorality and prostitution were common in the Greco-Roman world, the wider culture found incest detestable (*Institutes* I.63; *Pro Cluentio* 5.27; Catullus 88–91). For Paul, this sin will not only affect that believer, but it may destroy the whole church (5:6–8). Therefore, he exhorted the believers to remove this man (5:2, 7, 13) and discipline him so that the purity of the church could be preserved. The collective holiness of the church is important for Paul.

African scholar Adewuya notes that "the biblical perspective on Christian living, and particularly on holiness must begin with the notion of the holy people of God who are in covenant relationship with God and not primarily the solitary individual in her relationship to God."[51] While most Asians are by disposition non-confrontational,[52] Asians share with African cultures and the New Testament writers a high value on the role of the community.[53] For this reason, even when it is difficult, believers must strive to preserve the purity and holiness of the church by confronting serious and unrepented sin.

Lawsuits and Concern for the Weak (6:1–11)

In 1 Corinthians 6:1–11, Paul exhorts the believers not to take their lawsuits to the courts, but asks them to resolve their disputes in the church. Private arbitration was a common method of solving the disputes in Roman world.[54] Though courts were also available for addressing disputes, many powerful

---

50. Robert H. Gundry, *A Survey of the New Testament* (Manila: OMF Literature, 1994), 362.
51. J. Ayodeji Adewuya, *Holiness and Community in 2 Cor 6:14–7:1: Paul's View of Communal Holiness in the Corinthian Correspondence*, StBibLit 40 (New York: Peter Lang, 2001), 168–69.
52. Tseen-Ling Khoo, *Banana Bending: Asian-Australian and Asian-Canadian Literatures* (Hong Kong: Hong Kong University Press, 2003), 188; Yan Xia, "Introduction to Chinese Youth: Commentary," *Chinese Youth in Transition*, eds. Jieying Xi, Yunxiao Sun and Jing Jian Xiao (Hampshire: Ashgate, 2006), 102.
53. Greg Sheridan, *Asian Values Western Dreams: Understanding the New Asia* (St Leonards: Allen & Unwin, 1999), 104; Victor T. King, *The Sociology of Southeast Asia: Transformations in a Developing Region* (Honolulu: University of Hawaii Press, 2008), 152.
54. Arren Bennet Lawrence, "Standing against Injustice: Reading 1 Corinthians 6:1–11 in Context," *JAET* 25, no. 1 (2022): 44.

people used the courts to extort money from the weak and the poor.[55] A powerful person may possibly abuse a weak person by taking him to court. For Paul, abusing a weak person or excusing injustice is sinful. Corruption is prevalent in some cultures in Asia,[56] and especially in these contexts, the church should stand against corruption and injustice to establish holiness in church and society.

In this section, Paul also exhorts the church not to be involved in sins such as swindling. Paul says, "Neither the sexually immoral nor idolaters nor adulterers nor men who have sex with men nor thieves nor the greedy nor drunkards nor slanderers nor *swindlers* will inherit the kingdom of God" (6:9–10 NIV). The holiness of the believers is so important to Paul that he goes on to warn that if they continue in these sins, they will not inherit the kingdom of God (6:10).

Prostitution, Sexual Immorality and Sexual Purity (6:12–7:40)

Prostitution was common in the Greco-Roman world (Seneca, *Dialogi* 12.16.3; Plutarch, *Brutus* 46; *Moralia* 144 E–F; Juvenal, *Satires* 4.1–20; Aulus Gellius, *Attic Nights* 5.11.2). Even if it was socially acceptable, Paul urges believers in Christ to "flee sexual immorality" (6:18). His argument for pursuing sexual purity is rooted in the reality that a believer is a member of Christ (6:15) and has been bought with a price (6:20). If these things are the case, Paul argued, the church must remain holy by avoiding prostitution and sexual immorality.

Sexual perversion and pornography are common in the present era. For Paul, as the body is the temple of the Holy Spirit, so also the believer should not indulge in sexual immorality (6:19). Moreover, in chapter 7, Paul exhorts the married people to fulfil their conjugal rights to their spouse so as to avoid sexual immorality (7:1–7). Though Paul would prefer that his unmarried readers remain single, he suggests that they should get married if they are tempted towards sexual immorality (7:25–38). Sexual purity, then, is important for Paul.

In many Asian religions, holiness is connected with visiting holy places such as temples, churches, rivers, holy mountains, etc. Pilgrimages are a

---

55. Ptolemaeus, "Petition to the Epistrategus P. Marcius Crispus," *P. Mich. inv.* 255, https://quod.lib.umich.edu/a/apis/x-1602.
56. Domenic Sculli, "Culture and Level of Industrialization as Determinants of Corruption in Asia," *Fighting Corruption in Asia: Causes, Effects and Remedies*, ed. John Kidd and Frank Jurgen Richter (New Jersey: World Scientific, 2003), 203–20.

common aspect of Hinduism (called *tirtha*) and Islam (*hajj*), and these journeys are often understood to make a person holy (*Skanda Purana* 1.2.13.10). In ancient Hindu texts, bathing places such as holy rivers were considered to be places for washing away of sins.[57] Today, many Hindus visit holy rivers and other holy places to wash their sins and to purify themselves.[58] However, it is striking that the New Testament never suggests that Christians visit any holy place to become holy. Holiness is not associated with any location or geographical feature. Anyone from anywhere can be made holy by having faith in God and by the help of the Holy Spirit. The believer's body is holy as it is the temple of the Holy Spirit and because she is bought with a price (6:20).

Holiness and Food Offered to Idols (8:1–11:1)

In 1 Corinthians 8:1–11:1, Paul agreed with the strong believers of Corinth that they could eat the food offered to the idols, because idols do not have any spiritual significance (8:4–6). The "idol is nothing" according to Paul (8:4). Therefore, the food offered to idols is neutral, and eating that food is not sin. However, Paul cautions them about eating this food as this could become a stumbling block for the weak believers (8:9). When a weak believer sees the strong person eating this food in the temple s/he may be emboldened to eat that food. And when he does so, Paul says, it may become a sin for him, as the weak believer may be eating it against his conscience which considers eating food offered to the idols as sin. Therefore, that which is not sin may become sin as it causes others to sin against their conscience (8:12).[59]

Imitation and Holiness

In 1 Corinthians 8:13 (NIV) Paul said, "I will never eat meat again" so as to not be a hinderance for others. In 11:1, he says, "Follow my example, as I follow the example of Christ" (also 1 Thess 1:6). By imitating Christ (Phil 2:5) and by imitating Paul, the believer could remain holy.[60] In Philippians 3:17 (ESV), he gives himself as an example to follow, "Brothers, join in imitating me." Further he says, "keep your eyes on those who walk according to the example you have in us." For Paul, the church can live a holy life by following good examples around them. As an intern would follow a potter or a craftsman

---

57. Gautama 19.14; Baudhayana 3.10.12; Vashishta Dharma Sutra 22.12; Vayu Purana 77.125; Brahman Purana 25.4 – 6).
58. Ashok Mishra, *Hinduism: Ritual, Reason and Beyond* (Mumbai: StoryMirror, 2019), 243.
59. Andrew Murray, *The School of Obedience* (Chicago: Fleming H. Revell, 1899), 101.
60. See also Hebrew 13:7; 1 Timothy 4:12; 2 Timothy 3:7.

to learn the skills, a believer should follow good examples around them in the journey towards holiness.[61]

JESUS, HOLINESS AND THE SERMON ON THE MOUNT

In the Gospels, Jesus frequently exhorts the disciples to live a holy life. Jesus's teaching on holiness is especially clear in the Sermon on the Mount, making it an ideal case study for our purposes in this chapter. In Matthew's account of the beatitudes, Jesus states that the spiritually poor are blessed as they will inherit the kingdom of God (5:3). The disciples who hunger and thirst for righteousness will be filled (5:6). In addition, they are expected to be pure in heart (5:8). The disciples are expected to be perfect as the Father is perfect (5:48). This perfection is expected to be emulated by fulfilling the law as Christ himself did not come to abolish the law but to fulfill it (5:17).[62] Jesus expected the disciples to be perfect by loving others (5:43–47),[63] a message that resounds in Paul's teachings as well. Among the six antitheses, Jesus's teachings on murder and adultery need distinct attention.

Murder vs. Anger

In 5:21–26, Jesus addresses the problem of murder and he teaches the disciples how to be holy by avoiding murder. The Old Testament law taught the disciples that God's people should not commit murder (Exod 20:13; Deut 5:17). Anger is the root cause of murder and so by avoiding anger the disciples are expected to preserve their holiness (5:22).[64] Manson says, "The point of the antithesis [comparison] lies in the contrast between the outward act, of which an earthly court can take cognizance, and the inward disposition."[65]

Here we see a pattern that is typical of the Sermon on the Mount: Jesus goes beyond the external actions to deal with the internal attitudes that bring forth holiness. For the sake of holiness, he commands his disciples to go beyond modifying their actions to the point of altering bad attitudes.

---

61. Gerald F. Hawthorne, *Philippians*, WBC 43 (Waco: Word, 1983), 162.

62. See Arren Bennet Lawrence, *Comparative Characterization in the Sermon on the Mount: Characterization of the Ideal Disciple* (Eugene: Wipf & Stock, 2017), 139–64.

63. Charles Quarles, *Sermon on The Mount: Restoring Christ's Message to the Modern Church* (Nashville: B&H Academic, 2011), 169.

64. Donald A. Hagner, *Matthew 1–13*, WBC 33a (Dallas: Word, 1997), 116.

65. T. W. Manson, *The Sayings of Jesus* (London: SCM, 1949), 155.

Adultery vs. Lust

Jesus exhorted in Matthew 5:27–30 that the disciples must avoid lust so as to obey the law that commands to avoid adultery (Exod 20:14; Deut 5:18). Lust is the root cause of adultery and the disciples must avoid lust to remain holy.[66] Sexual promiscuity is a major problem of the present world. Use of pornography has increased considerably globally, including in our region. Children and adolescents are widely exposed to pornography due to the wider availability of gadgets and internet. Research conducted across Asia suggests that a significant percentage of adolescents are exposed to pornography at a young age: to highlight only a few examples, 50 percent of Koreans experience this;[67] 41 percent of youth in Hong Kong;[68] and 37 percent of young people in Taiwan.[69] In light of this, the disciples of Jesus must follow his teaching and must avoid lustful thoughts to remain holy. Here Paul and Jesus speak with one voice, declaring that transforming the thoughts of a person is important for the disciple to maintain holiness.

External Holiness vs. Internal Attitudes

Jesus frequently spoke against Pharisaic hypocrisy. In Matthew 6, Jesus exhorts the disciples not to be like the Pharisees who practiced their acts of piety ostentatiously. The Pharisees gave alms (6:1–4), prayed (6:5–6), and fasted ostentatiously (6:16–18). Yet Jesus called them "whitewashed tombs, which look beautiful on the outside but on the inside are full of the bones of the dead and everything unclean" (23:27 NIV). He also said that they tend to concentrate primarily on external appearances rather than internal attitudes (23:5). Similarly, in some forms of Christianity in Asia, close attention is paid to dress codes, removing jewels, etc. as the forms of display of piety and holiness. For Jesus, internal attitudes are important and so he asked the disciples to practice the acts of piety privately (6:1–18) and to concentrate on internal attitudes to maintain holiness. Jesus's teachings on holiness reiterate the NT emphasis on living a holy life. The believer in Jesus Christ and the follower of the NT is expected to live a holy life.

---

66. Daniel J. Harrington, *The Gospel of Matthew*, SP 1 (Collegeville: Liturgical Press, 1991), 87.
67. T. G. Ko and E. S. Yang, "Research on the Adolescents' Usage Patterns on the Internet Adult Sites," *Korean Journal of Physical Education* 46, no. 4 (2007): 305–15.
68. S. To, S. S. Ngai, and S. I. Kan, "Direct and Mediating Effects of Accessing Sexually Explicit Online Materials on Hong Kong Adolescents' Attitude, Knowledge and Behavior Relating to Sex," *Children and Youth Services Review* 34 (2012): 2156–63.
69. V. Lo and R. Wei, "Exposure to Internet Pornography and Taiwanese Adolescents' Sexual Attitudes and Behavior," *Journal of Broadcasting & Electronic Media* 49, no. 2 (2005): 221–37.

CONCLUSION

Holiness is an important theme integral to NT teaching; clearly, God has called all believers to live a holy life (2 Tim 1:9). To understand the NT perspective on holiness, this chapter carefully considered the articulation of holiness set out in the Book of Romans and Jesus's teaching in the Gospels. In the Book of Romans, believers are not only exhorted to pursue holiness but are also informed that they have the Holy Spirit to empower them in their quest for holiness. Furthermore, in Romans chapters 12 to 15, the apostle Paul illustrates how believers can lead lives marked by holiness through their love for one another within their community. Similarly, Jesus's teachings in the Sermon on the Mount emphasize the importance of internal attributes in leading a holy life. In a context where many turn to temples, sacred sites, and rituals for a promise of holiness, the NT vision is refreshingly clear. Rather than seeking holiness through these human efforts, the NT calls us to enjoy the enablement of the Holy Spirit to live out the gospel's call to be a part of "God's chosen people, holy and dearly loved" (Col 3:12 NIV).

BIBLIOGRAPHY

Adewuya, J. Ayodeji. *Holiness and Community in 2 Cor 6:14–7:1: Paul's View of Communal Holiness in the Corinthian Correspondence*. StBibLit 40. New York: Peter Lang, 2001.

———. *Holiness in the Letters of Paul: A Necessary Response to the Gospel*. Eugene: Cascade, 2016.

Anderson-Rajkumar, Evangeline. "Ministry in the Killing Fields." *Christian History* 11 (1992): 31–37.

Barth, Karl. *A Shorter Commentary on Romans*. Edited by Maico M. Michielin. Bodmin: MPG, 2007.

Craig, Clarence. "Paradox of Holiness: The New Testament Doctrine of Sanctification." *Int* 6, no. 2 (1952): 147–61.

Dodd, C. H. *The Epistle to the Romans*. London: Hodder and Stoughton, 1932.

Erickson, Millard J. *Christian Theology*. 2nd ed. Grand Rapids: Baker, 1998.

———. *Introducing Christian Doctrine*. 2nd ed. Edited by L. Arnold Hustad. Grand Rapids: Baker, 2001.

Gorman, Michael. *Participating in Christ: Explorations in Paul's Theology and Spirituality*. Grand Rapids: Baker Academic, 2019.

Gundry, Robert H. *A Survey of the New Testament*. Manila: OMF Literature, 1994.

Guthrie, Donald. *New Testament Introduction*. Rev. ed. Hyderabad: Authentic, 2003.

Hagner, Donald A. *Matthew 1–13*. WBC 33a. Dallas: Word, 1997.

Harrington, Daniel J. *The Gospel of Matthew*. SP 1. Collegeville: Liturgical Press, 1991.

Hawthorne, Gerald F. *Philippians*. WBC 43. Waco: Word, 1983.

Horton, Michael. *Pilgrim Theology: Core Doctrines for Christian Disciples*. Grand Rapids: Zondervan, 2012.

Johnson, Luke Timothy. *The Writings of the New Testament: An Interpretation*. Bangalore: Theological Publication in India, 2009.

Keener, Craig S. *Romans*. NCC. Eugene: Cascade, 2009.

Khoo, Tseen-Ling. *Banana Bending: Asian-Australian and Asian-Canadian Literatures*. Hong Kong: Hong Kong University Press, 2003.

King, Victor T. *The Sociology of Southeast Asia: Transformations in a Developing Region*. Honolulu: University of Hawaii Press, 2008.

Kittel, Gerhard, and Gerhard Friedrich, eds. *Theological Dictionary of the New Testament*. Translated by Geoffrey W. Bromiley. 10 vols. Grand Rapids: Eerdmans, 1964–1976.

Ko, T. G., and E. S. Yang. "Research on the Adolescents' Usage Patterns on the Internet Adult Sites." *Korean Journal of Physical Education* 46, no. 4 (2007): 305–15.

Ladd, George Eldon. *A Theology of the New Testament*. Edited by Donald A. Hagner. Rev. ed. Grand Rapids: Eerdmans, 1993.

Lawrence, Arren Bennet. *Comparative Characterization in the Sermon on the Mount: Characterization of the Ideal Disciple*. Eugene: Wipf & Stock, 2017.

———. *Legalistic Nomism: A Socio-Rhetorical Reading of Paul's Letter to the Galatians*. New Delhi: ISPCK, 2016.

Lawrence, Bennet. "Standing against Injustice: Reading 1 Corinthians 6:1–11 in Context." *JAET* 25, no. 1 (2022): 33–52.

Lo, V., and R. Wei. "Exposure to Internet Pornography and Taiwanese Adolescents' Sexual Attitudes and Behavior." *Journal of Broadcasting & Electronic Media* 49, no. 2 (2005): 221–37.

Longenecker, Richard. *Galatians*. WBC 41. Grand Rapids: Zondervan, 1990.

Manson, T. W. *The Sayings of Jesus*. London: SCM, 1949.

Martin, Nancy M. "Hinduism and Holy People." *Holy People of the World: A Cross-cultural Encyclopedia*. Edited by Phyllis G. Jestice. 3 vols. Santa Barbara: ABC-CLIO, 2004. 3:367–71.

McGrath, Alister. *Christian Theology: An Introduction*. 6th ed. Oxford: Wiley Blackwell, 2017.

McKnight, Scot. *Pastor Paul: Nurturing a Culture of Christoformity in the Church*. Grand Rapids: Brazos, 2019.

Mishra, Ashok. *Hinduism: Ritual, Reason and Beyond*. Mumbai: StoryMirror, 2019.

Moo, Douglas J. *The Epistle to the Romans*. Grand Rapids: Eerdmans, 1996.

Murray, Andrew. *The School of Obedience*. Chicago: Fleming H. Revell, 1899.

Nygren, Anders. *Commentary on Romans.* Translated by Carl C. Rasmussen. London: SCM Press, 1952.

Pratt, James Bisset. *India and Its Faith.* New York: Cosimo, 2005.

Quarles, Charles. *Sermon on The Mount: Restoring Christ's Message to the Modern Church.* Nashville: B&H Academic, 2011.

Ridderbos, Herman. *Paul: An Outline of His Theology.* Grand Rapids: Eerdmans, 1966.

Schnelle, Udo. *Theology of the New Testament.* Translated by M. Eugene Boring. Grand Rapids: Baker Academic, 2007.

Schreiner, Thomas. *40 Questions about Christians and Biblical Law.* Edited by Benjamin L. Merkle. Grand Rapids: Kregel, 2010.

———. *Faith Alone – The Doctrine of Justification: What the Reformers Taught . . . and Why It Still Matters.* Grand Rapids: Zondervan, 2015.

———. *Romans.* BECNT. Grand Rapids: Baker Academic, 1998.

Sculli, Domenic. "Culture and Level of Industrialization as Determinants of Corruption in Asia." In *Fighting Corruption in Asia: Causes, Effects and Remedies,* edited by John Kidd and Frank Jurgen Richter, 203–20. New Jersey: World Scientific, 2003.

Sethuraman, N. *The Cholas: Mathematics Reconstructs the Chronology.* Kumbakonam: Sethuraman, 1977.

Sheridan, Greg. *Asian Values Western Dreams: Understanding the New Asia.* St Leonards: Allen & Unwin, 1999.

Sivalogathan, Kandiah. *Understanding Hinduism.* Gurgaon, India: Zorba Books, 2020.

Sproul, R. C. *The Holiness of God.* Carol Stream: Tyndale House, 1998.

Stendahl, Krister. *Paul Among Jews and Gentiles.* Fortress Press, 1976.

Stott, John. *Romans: God's Good News for the World.* Downers Grove: InterVarsity Press, 1994.

Thompson, James. *Moral Formation According to Paul.* Grand Rapids: Baker Academic, 2011.

To, S., S. S. Ngai, and S. I. Kan. "Direct and Mediating Effects of Accessing Sexually Explicit Online Materials on Hong Kong Adolescents' Attitude, Knowledge and Behavior Relating to Sex." *Children and Youth Services Review* 34 (2012): 2156–63.

Wright, N. T. *Interpreting Paul: Essays on the Apostle and His Letters.* London: SPCK, 2020.

———. *Paul.* Minneapolis: Fortress, 2009.

Xia, Yan. "Introduction to Chinese Youth: Commentary." In *Chinese Youth in Transition,* edited by Jieying Xi, Yunxiao Sun, and Jing Jian Xiao, 80–96. Hampshire: Ashgate, 2006.

CHAPTER 5

THE HOUSEHOLD OF GOD

Gender Dynamics, Biblical Ethics, and Asian Ideals

Joyce Wai-Lan Sun

INTRODUCTION

This essay reflects on the New Testament teachings on gender (i.e., men and women) relations. The topic deserves renewed attention because the New Testament is often viewed as contributing to the constant marginalization and discrimination of women. The teaching for wives to submit to their husbands together with Paul's apparent prohibition of women exercising authority over men in the church both seem to portray women as permanently inferior to men.

Feminist interpreters have long complained of women being silenced, denigrated, or made invisible in biblical narratives. Many of them see the Bible as merely a product of patriarchy and androcentric (i.e., male-centered) in nature. Those with a more radical stance further reject the Bible as hopelessly oppressive in its present form and seek for a reconstruction of biblical history.[1] One prominent example is Elisabeth Schüssler Fiorenza, who asserts that "Biblical texts are not verbally inspired revelation," but are only "historical formulations within the context of a religious community."[2] Schüssler Fiorenza therefore adopts what she calls a model of "feminist critical hermeneutics," with a view to reconstruct and to reclaim biblical history as women's own history.[3] As David Scholer summarizes, Schüssler Fiorenza's four-stage hermeneutic includes, among others "(1) the hermeneutic of suspicion, which questions all androcentric and patriarchal texts; and (2) the hermeneutic of proclamation,

---

1. For a comprehensive survey of the different typologies of feminist hermeneutics, see David M. Scholer, "Feminist Hermeneutics and Evangelical Biblical Interpretation," *Evangelical Review of Theology* 15, no. 4 (1991): 307–10.
2. Elisabeth Schüssler Fiorenza, *In Memory of Her: A Feminist Theological Reconstruction of Christian Origin* (London: SCM Press, 1983), xv.
3. Schüssler Fiorenza, *In Memory of Her*, 29.

which takes the texts that are supportive of women and proclaims them."[4] Although such critical feminist approaches to the Bible can be a good reminder for traditional interpreters to beware of their own hermeneutical stances and biases, it also betrays substantial distance from the commitment of evangelicals to the authority of the whole Bible as the inspired revelatory word of God and the final arbiter of truth.

Due to limitation of space, this essay intends to focus only on the gender debate among evangelicals and their different understandings of the relevant New Testament texts. On the one side are those traditionalist interpreters who opt for a literal understanding of the New Testament texts and regard them as timeless principles applicable for all time, including our modern situations. This group of interpreters describe their own stance as "complementarian,"[5] but others prefer to call them "traditionalists," "hierarchicalists," "patriarchalist" or simply "male leadership perspective."[6] For complementarians, men and women, due to God's creation order, have intrinsic differences and, thus, distinctive gender roles. According to a plain reading of the Bible, such gender roles necessarily mean male leadership and female subordination.[7] In other words, men are born to lead, and women born to be subordinate whether at home, in the church or sometimes even in society, regardless of gifts and talents. As Cherith Nordling points out, such so-called biblical manhood and womanhood "are biological categories that include divinely ordained gender roles."[8] While claiming to recognize the equality in "being and status" between women and men, the complementarians insist that women are having different (and subordinating) roles and functions from men.[9]

At the other end of the debate is another group of evangelical interpreters whose stance is labeled "complementarity without hierarchy,"[10] "bibli-

---

4. Scholer, "Feminist Hermeneutics and Evangelical Biblical Interpretation," 309–10.
5. John Piper and Wayne Grudem, eds., *Recovering Biblical Manhood & Womanhood: A Response to Evangelical Feminism* (Wheaton: Crossway Books, 1991).
6. See Rebecca Merrill Groothuis, "'Equal in Being, Unequal in Role': Exploring the Logic of Woman's Subordination," in *Discovering Biblical Equality: Complementarity without Hierarchy*, eds. Ronald W. Pierce and Rebecca Merrill Groothuis (Downers Grove: InterVarsity Press, 2004), 301–33; Cherith Fee Nordling, "Gender," in *The Oxford Handbook of Evangelical Theology*, ed. Gerald R. McDermott (Oxford: Oxford University Press, 2010), 503.
7. See John Piper, "A Vision of Biblical Complementarity: Manhood and Womanhood Defined According to the Bible," in *Recovering Biblical Manhood & Womanhood*, 52–54.
8. Nordling, "Gender," 503.
9. For a critique of the logical efficacy of such stance, see Groothuis, "Equal in Being, Unequal in Role," 301–33.
10. Pierce and Groothuis, eds., *Discovering Biblical Equality: Complementarity without Hierarchy*.

cal equality," "egalitarianism," and "evangelical feminism." While upholding the authority of the Bible and recognizing the intrinsic difference between men and women, these interpreters seek to uncover the biblical support for gender equality. As Ronald Pierce and Rebecca Merrill Groothuis asserts, "Egalitarianism recognizes patterns of authority in the family, church and society . . . but rejects the notion that any office, ministry or opportunity should be denied anyone on the grounds of gender alone."[11] Similar to the complementarians, biblical egalitarians also proceed with rigorous investigation of the Bible. Where they differ is that they take the literary and historical contexts of the relevant texts and the overall spirit of the whole Bible as suggesting a movement towards equal gender roles. Hints and nuances left by the biblical authors are underlined and understood as opening an avenue for further development and transformation in the modern-day context.

There are Asian evangelical interpreters, however, who do not prefer to use the terminology of "equality" or "egalitarianism" to describe male and female relationships.[12] Nor do they necessarily embrace a rigid hierarchical structure of "authority and subordination" for men and women. In the following sections, we will first consider the major issues involved in the evangelical gender debate and the different interpretations of the disputed New Testament texts among interpreters. The last section will attempt to transcend the "hierarchical roles" and "equality" polemic by recovering an ideal "interdependence model" for Asian men and women relations. It seeks to demonstrate that such an "interdependence model" is what the New Testament is most likely reflecting and, at the same time, most suitable for the Asian context.

MEN AND WOMEN IN THE FAMILY

One storm center of the evangelical gender debate is the three so-called household codes in the New Testament; namely, Ephesians 5:21–6:9; Colossians 3:18–4:1; 1 Peter 2:18–3:7. These passages expressly teach Christian wives to submit themselves to their husbands (Eph 5:22; Col 3:18; 1 Pet 3:1), and in the cases of Ephesians and Colossians, as what is fitting for Christian living "in and to the Lord." The Ephesian Household Code further provides the

---

11. Ronald W. Pierce and Rebecca Merrill Groothuis, "Introduction" in *Discovering Biblical Equality*, 13.
12. For example, Sakhi Athyal, "Women in Mission," *ATA Journal* 1, no. 2 (1993): 50–69; Simon Chan, "Evangelical theology in Asian context," in *The Cambridge Companion to Evangelical Theology*, eds. Timothy Larsen and Daniel J. Treier (Cambridge, NY: Cambridge University Press, 2007), 229.

theological basis for the submission of wives as that "the husband is the head of the wife" just as "Christ is the head of the church" (Eph 5:23).

For complementarians such as George Knight III, this comparison of "the headship of the husband over the wife" to "the headship of Christ over the church" essentially renders the husband "as one who has authority and is the leader."[13] Earlier on, James B. Hurley proposed that a wife "is to continue to live a godly life even with an abusive pagan husband . . . the suffering wife of an unbeliever is called by God, even in her painful situation, faithfully and to demonstrate the obedient love of the church for Christ by her submissive love for her husband (5:22–24; 1 Pet 3:4–6)."[14]

Interpreters who adopt a different stance from the complementarians and Hurley generally prefer to put the biblical household codes back in their historical contexts. It is commonly recognized that in the Greco-Roman world, women usually married in their teens and men in their thirties or later. A man could already "function socially and economically" when he got married, while a woman married when "she was still a girl who had never even been allowed to answer a knock at the front door of her home."[15] In addition to the fact that formal education was usually reserved for men, it is no surprise that women were generally viewed as inferior to men, and sometimes no more than chattels or possession to their husbands.

David Balch, in his comprehensive examination of contemporaneous Greek philosophical literature, also concludes that the New Testament pattern of subordination in the household was in fact something commonly found outside Judaism and Christianity.[16] Balch's finding in effect renders any claim of women's subordination (and men's leadership) to be "divinely instituted"[17] doubtful. Instead, Paul was only following the social convention of his time, and for the sake of Christian witness, when he exhorted the wives to submit to their husbands. As Yusak Budi Setyawan observes, in Greek philosophical teachings, "Man was believed as 'soul' and woman 'body,' accordingly the man

---

13. George W. Knight III, "Husbands and Wives as Analogues of Christ and the Church: Ephesians 5:21–33 and Colossians 3:18–19," in *Recovering Biblical Manhood & Womanhood: A Response to Evangelical Feminism*, 170.
14. James B. Hurley, *Man & Woman in Biblical Perspective: A Study in Role Relationships and Authority* (Leicester: Inter-Varsity Press, 1981), 154.
15. Scholer, "Feminist Hermeneutics and Evangelical Biblical Interpretation," 315–16.
16. David L. Balch, *Let Wives Be Submissive: The Domestic Code in 1 Peter*, SBLMS 26 (Atlanta: Scholars Press, 1981).
17. See Knight, "Husbands and Wives as Analogues of Christ and the Church," 170–71.

should control the woman since the soul controls the body."[18] The use of the household code in Ephesians 5:21–33 was only for Christians "to prove themselves as an entity that does not threaten harmony of a larger community."[19] Howard Marshall also remarks that Paul "did not know any other form than the patriarchal structure."[20] The position of authority of husbands was simply "assumed"[21] rather than validated as divinely appointed.

Indeed, there are certain elements in the Ephesian household code that would be surprising to Greco-Roman eyes.[22] In the commonly accepted original Greek text (NA[28]), there is no verb in Ephesians 5:22. The verbal idea of the submission (*hupotassō*) of wives comes from verse 21, in which all believers are exhorted to "submit to one another." Whether one regards 5:21 to be a transition or a governing principle of the household code proper in 5:22–6:9, the submission of wives in verse 22 must necessarily be understood in the light of verse 21 from which its verbal idea derives. As verse 21 is teaching "mutual submission" among believers, it is natural to expect similar mutual submission to happen between the Christian husband and wife as well.

What is important to note for the purpose of this essay is that this Pauline idea of "mutual submission" necessarily defies any rigid structure of "authority and subordination" as ordinarily connoted by the idea of "submission."[23] A formal mechanical structure of "hierarchy" or "equality" between men and women was simply not in Paul's mind when making his teachings. Nor was he interested in formulating who should have the final say at all times and in all respects in the marriage,[24] or whether both husband and wife should have an equal number of opportunities to make final decisions in day to day living.[25]

In fact, Paul has not expressly exhorted husbands to lead or to exercise their authorities over the wives in the household code. What husbands are urged to do is rather to "love" their wives (5:25; see also Col 3:19), which was

---

18. Yusak Budi Setyawan, "Be Subject to Your Husband as You are to the Lord" in Ephesians 5:21–33 – Illuminated by an Indonesian (Javanese)," *AsJT* 21, no. 1 (2007): 54–55.
19. Setyawan, "Be Subject to Your Husband as You are to the Lord," 61.
20. I. Howard Marshall, "Mutual Love and Submission in Marriage: Colossians 3:18–19 and Ephesians 5:21–33," in *Discovering Biblical Equality: Complementarity without Hierarchy*, 204.
21. Marshall, "Mutual Love and Submission in Marriage," 187.
22. Since the wives-and-husbands pair in the Colossian household code is much shorter and its main points are also covered in the Ephesian one, it is sufficient for this essay to focus on the Ephesian household code due to space consideration and for simplicity's sake.
23. See also Brian Wintle and Ken Gnanakan, *Ephesians*, Asia Bible Commentary Series (Singapore: Asia Theological Association, 2006), 174–75.
24. *Contra* Knight, "Husbands and Wives as Analogues of Christ and the Church," 170.
25. *Contra* Pierce and Groothuis, "Introduction," 17.

unthinkable in the Greco-Roman world. The intensity of the love expected from husbands is underlined as analogous to the self-sacrificial love of Christ (Eph 5:25). As George Knight III also acknowledges, *hupotassō* ("submit") when applied to wives denotes "submission in the sense of voluntary yielding in love."[26] Mutuality and reciprocity, rather than a rigid power structure, is once again seen to be Paul's ideal form of men and women's relationship in marriage.

It is also against this backdrop of "mutuality of love" that Paul's idea of the headship of husbands over their wives (5:28–29) should be understood. While presumably aware of the Greco-Roman concept of a husband's headship as "authority" and "control," Paul emphasizes that husbands are to love their wives as their own bodies (i.e., himself). As Brian Wintle and Ken Gnanakan observe, Paul is advocating "pragmatic self-interest" for the husbands.[27] Idicheria Ninan also remarks, "The husband and wife are inseparable, for the head cannot live without the body."[28] Just as wives need to depend on their husbands socially and economically especially in the Greco-Roman culture,[29] husbands are also dependent on their wives' well-being for their own interest. Being of the same "one flesh" (5:31; cf. Gen 2:24), the cherishing and nourishment received by the wives from their husbands (Eph 5:29) is, at the same time, cherishing and nourishment for the husbands themselves.

Paul's ideal for Christian relationship in a marriage is best reflected in his last words for the Ephesian household code: every man is to love his wife as himself, while the wife is to respect her husband (5:33). For Paul, the relationship of husbands and wives is about mutual service and reciprocal giving up of one's own interest *for the other*, rather than asserting one's authority and right *over and against the other*.

Such a tenet of self-giving and consideration *for the other* is also at the core of the Petrine household code with regard to the husband-and-wife relationship (1 Pet 3:1–7). Here, Christian submission of wives (*hupotassō*, 3:1) is directed to unbelieving Gentile husbands. It must be remembered that wives were supposed to follow the religion of their husbands according to the Greco-Roman culture. The Roman moral philosopher Plutarch actually

---

26. Knight, "Husbands and Wives as Analogues of Christ and the Church," 168.
27. Wintle and Gnanakan, *Ephesians*, 185.
28. Idicheria Ninan, "Ephesians," in *South Asia Bible Commentary*, ed. Brian Wintle (Rajasthan: Open Door Publications, 2015), 1645.
29. For the metaphor of "body and head" to denote the dependence of wives on the husbands for living and supporting, see Gordon D. Fee, "Praying and Prophesying in the Assemblies: 1 Corinthians 11:2–16," 142–60, in *Discovering Biblical Equality: Complementarity without Hierarchy*, 154; Marshall, "Mutual Love and Submission in Marriage," 199.

teaches, "Wherefore it is becoming for a wife to worship and to know only the gods that her husband believes in, and to shut the front door tight upon all queer rituals and outlandish superstitions."[30]

It is in the light of possible tensions created by the wives adopting their own Christian religion that they are taught to voluntarily submit themselves to their husbands.[31] Although Wayne Grudem strenuously asserts that such submission is to "affirm her husband as leader,"[32] the precise reason given in the biblical text itself is to "win over" (kerdēthēsontai, 3:1) her unbelieving husband to the Christian faith. Rather than the one being led, the wife is encouraged to be "the leader of the husband" in the matter of his religion!

Although Christian wives need to be cautious not to appear subversive to the surrounding social order and to minimize tension within the unbelieving household,[33] neither are they taught to stifle themselves into mere passive submission. They have to disobey their husbands on one major point: to retain their own religious faith, despite adverse comments or rebukes. They are not to be frightened by any intimidation (3:6), but to "stand fast" in the grace of God (5:12).[34] All these in essence render the wife an independent moral agent before her husband, with free will to choose how to conduct her own Christian way of life in the unbelieving household.

Such a transformative and liberative overtone is even more notable in the Petrine exhortation to Christian husbands (3:7). These husbands could expect their wives to follow their Christian religion. Just as the Greco-Roman culture regarded women as "the weaker sex" (3:7 NIV), it also recognizes women as the "weaker partner." However, such weakness on the part of the wives is no longer taken as the basis for the hegemony of husbands and control, but on the contrary, for their "being considerate" when living with their wives.

Particularly noteworthy for the purpose of this essay is that husbands are further instructed to treat their wives with "respect" (literally "honor," timēn),

---

30. Plutarch, *Moralia* 140D (Babbit, LCL).
31. For a more detailed elaboration of the household tensions and dishonor to the husbands that may result from the refusal of Christian wives to worship the household gods, see Joyce Wai-Lan Sun, *This is True Grace; The Shaping of Social Behavioural Instructions by Theology in 1 Peter* (Carlisle: Langham Academic, 2016), 92–93.
32. Wayne Grudem, "Wives Like Sarah, and the Husbands Who Honor Them: 1 Peter 3:1–7," in *Recovering Biblical Manhood & Womanhood: A Response to Evangelical Feminism*, 196.
33. See Peter H. Davids, "A Silent Witness in Marriage: 1 Peter 3:1–7," in *Discovering Biblical Equality: Complementarity without Hierarchy*, 234.
34. For "grace" to mean "salvation" in 1 Peter 5:12, see also 1:10, 13; 3:7. See also Sun, *This is True Grace*, 14.

the reason being that wives are their "co-heirs of the grace (i.e., salvation) of life" (*sugklēronomois charistos zōēs*). Having been born again (*anagennēsas*) through the resurrection of Jesus Christ (1:3), the relationship between Christian husbands and wives is not the same as ordinary men and women. Both of them, Christian husbands and wives, are at the same time the children of God (cf. "obedient children," 1:14). They have the same destiny of inheriting the eschatological salvation to be realized in the last time (1:5).

This understanding of husband-wife relation as "co-heirs" is hardly hierarchical or structural, but mutual and interdependent. Just as wives are dependent on their husbands for consideration and honor as the weaker partner, husbands are also dependent on their wives' receiving proper consideration and honor to maintain their own relationship with God. Neglecting thoughtful consideration and honor to their wives as co-heirs of God's grace actually hinders the men's prayers to God (3:7). Just as theology and ethics cannot be separated, the ontological beings of men and women are also inseparable from their conduct in daily life.[35]

Therefore, although New Testament writers were working within the current patriarchal social and familial order, they were not endorsing, nor thereby "sanctifying" such order as "divinely instituted." They were ready to transform and to "christianize"[36] the existing structure to reflect and to embody God's grace and salvation, as well as Christ's self-sacrificing love for his people. The relationship between men and women is not spoken of in terms of "hierarchical roles" or "power structures," but God's kingdom value of "fraternal love," "justice" and "mutual interdependence." If the submission of slaves taught in the household codes could be adjusted with the ultimate abolition of slavery after the biblical times, it is also possible for the teaching on women's subordination to be transformed to embody God's continuous redemptive and liberative act in history.

MEN AND WOMEN IN THE CHURCH

Just like the New Testament household codes, the debate over women's teaching or exercising authority continues to haunt the church. The crucial question lies in whether Paul's teachings should be taken as timeless principles,

---

35. *Contra* the egalitarian perception of men and women as "equal in being but hierarchical in roles."

36. See also Greg W. Forbes and Jason J. F. Lim, *1 Peter*, Asia Bible Commentary Series (Singapore: Asia Theological Association, 2006), 80–81.

applicable for all times and in all situations. Before looking at the disputed texts (in 1 Corinthians and 1 Timothy), we can first examine how Paul addresses the women who worked with him in his churches. This can help to clarify whether Paul would possibly intend to exclude women permanently as a class from leading and teaching in the church.

The prominent piece of evidence is Paul's greetings in Romans 16:1–16. Here, Paul puts Phoebe first on his long name list and commends her to the Roman church (16:1–2). She was called a *deacon* and the benefactor of many people, including Paul himself. Many interpreters take the view that Phoebe was in fact the bearer of this letter to the Roman church on behalf of Paul.[37] She was clearly no mere ordinary helper, but a prominent figure in the Christian community.

As for Paul's greeting list itself, it is observed that "at least five of the nine women Paul greets were ministry colleagues."[38] Among them was Priscilla, whose name is often placed before her husband Aquila (16:3; Acts 18:18–26). This would have surprised many people in Greco-Roman society if not for Priscilla's own importance. Acts 18:24–26 indeed records that Priscilla did join in to explain the Christian faith to Apollos (a man!). Together with the fact that Priscilla was singled out by Paul from the Ephesian church to send his greetings in 2 Timothy 4:19, she was most probably one of those women who took part in the teaching and leading in Paul's churches.

In addition, Paul also mentions one Junia (*Iounia*, Rom 16:7) which is a feminine name in Greek. Paul even describes her as "outstanding among the *apostles*" (cf. 1 Cor 4:6–9; 9:5–6; 15:6–7; Gal 1:19). As an "apostle," Junia surely had certain teaching and leading authority, which in fact received Paul's affirmation and commendation. In any event,[39] Paul repeatedly addresses these female co-workers as his "benefactor(s)" (Phoebe, Rom 16:2), "co-worker" (Priscilla, Rom 16:3) and "fellow prisoner (*sunaichmalōtos*)" (Junia, 16:7). Nowhere does he express any disapproval or reservation to their prominent roles in the church. On the contrary, Paul expresses his dependence on them for provisions, for sharing his works, and companionship in sufferings. While

---

37. See Richard N. Longenecker, *The Epistle to the Romans*, NIGTC (Grand Rapids: Eerdmans 2016), 1064–65.

38. Linda L. Belleville, "Women Leaders in the Bible," in *Discovering Biblical Equality: Complementarity without Hierarchy*, 116.

39. Due to space consideration, this essay can only raise some prominent examples. For a more comprehensive discussion, see Waldemar Kowalski, "The Role of Women in Ministry: Is There a Disconnect between Pauline Practice and Pauline Instruction?" *AsJT* 21, no. 1 (2007): 54–55.

Waldemar Kowalski insightfully asks, Is there a disconnect between Pauline practice and Pauline instruction?,"[40] the answer most probably is "No."

Bearing in mind Paul's general acceptance and even appreciation of women occupying prominent roles in the church, we now proceed to consider his controversial teaching in 1 Timothy 2:11–15. Here, Paul notoriously requests women to "learn in quietness and full submission" (verse 11) and declares, "I do not permit a woman to teach or to assume authority over a man" (verse 12). He then draws upon the creation narrative in Genesis 2 and 3, especially Eve's transgression, to support his command (1 Tim 2:13–14).

For the complementarians and other traditionalist interpreters, 1 Timothy 2:11–15 permanently prohibits women from teaching or having authority over men. Douglas Moo contends that Paul is restricting all women from "preaching" and "teaching of Bible and doctrine in the church, in colleges and seminaries" to all men.[41] Even the position of "deacons" in many modern local churches should be denied to women.[42] Paul Barnett likewise suggests that under 1 Timothy 2:11–15, women's pastoral, didactic and sacramental ministry should only be conducted under the leadership of a senior teacher in "specialist, single sex congregations."[43]

Other interpreters, on the other hand, seek to understand Paul's intention from the historical context of 1 Timothy as whole. It is notable that Paul mentions both at the beginning and at the end of the letter that certain persons were teaching false doctrines (*heterodidaskaleō*, 1 Tim 1:3; 6:3). These false teachers apparently were causing ongoing controversies and frictions in the Ephesian church (1 Tim 1:4, 20; 6:4–5). Adding to the crisis was the presence of a group of widows (women) in the church who had "turned away to follow Satan," – the false teachers (5:15).[44] They went about from house to house, "saying things they ought not to" (5:13), probably for the purpose of promoting the false teachings.

It is against this backdrop of disorder and controversies that 1 Timothy 2 deals with the order and proper attitude of men and women in public worships. While men were exhorted to stop their anger and disputing during prayers

---

40. Kowalski, "The Role of Women in Ministry," 147–70.
41. Douglas Moo, "What Does it Mean Not to Teach or Have Authority Over Man?: 1 Timothy 2:11–15," in *Recovering Biblical Manhood & Womanhood: A Response to Evangelical Feminism*, 185–86.
42. Moo, "What Does it Mean Not to Teach or Have Authority Over Man?," 187.
43. Paul W. Barnett, "Wives and Women's Ministry (1 Timothy 2:11–15)," *Evangelical Review of Theology* 15, no. 4 (1991): 334.
44. For Satan to be the source of false teachings in Ephesus, see 1 Timothy 4:1.

(2:8), women were requested not to interrupt or usurp the teaching and the authority of those properly appointed to such position, who were usually men in the Greco-Roman world (2:12). Women in these special circumstances needed to learn quietly, rather than attempting to propagate disruptive false teachings during public gatherings.[45]

The occasional nature of 1 Timothy helps to clarify Paul's purpose for resorting to the creation story in 1 Timothy 2:13–14. Verse 14 provides a hint that Paul's focus is on Eve's deception into disobedience, and not on her taking up any leadership role over Adam (cf. 2 Cor 11:3). The shift from "Eve" to "the woman" is also notable. The crux of Paul's analogy seems to be that while "Adam was formed first, then Eve" (verse 13), it was however "the woman" who was first deceived (verse 14). This was precisely the situation in the Ephesian church that women (and not men) were the ones being deceived by false teachings (cf. 1 Tim 4:1). They should therefore meanwhile learn, but not teach or exercise authority. This is far from saying that women should be similarly excluded from teaching and exercising authority over men for all times and in all places.

As Ephesians 5:31 demonstrates, the creation narrative in Genesis is nowhere understood in the New Testament as instituting a hierarchical role-relationship or endowing Adam with authority over Eve. Man and woman are simply to be "one flesh." This is what 1 Corinthians 11:11–12 likewise underscores, "woman is not independent of man, nor is man." Just as "woman came from man, so also man is born of woman." As Finny Philip succinctly comments, "In Christ men and women should live in mutual interdependence."[46]

It is in the light of this gender interdependence in the Lord that Paul's teaching on head covering (11:2–16) should be understood. Although traditionalist interpreters often rely on men's headship over women (11:3) as biblical support for men's leadership and women's submissiveness,[47] women are in fact allowed to lead prayers and to proclaim God's words (prophesize) in church gatherings with the presence of male participants (11:5).

---

45. For a more detailed discussion on the situational nature of 1 Timothy 2:11–15, see Paul Trebilco and Simon Rae, *1 Timothy*, Asia Bible Commentary Series (Singapore: Asia Theological Association, 2006), 45–48.

46. Finny Philip, "1 Corinthians," *South Asia Bible Commentary*, ed., Brain Wintle (Rajasthan: Open Door Publications, 2015), 1555–84, 1574.

47. E.g. Thomas R. Schreiner, "Head Coverings, Prophecies and the Trinity: 1 Corinthians 11:2–16," in *Recovering Biblical Manhood & Womanhood: A Response to Evangelical Feminism*, 124–39.

While it cannot be denied that "headship" denotes certain pre-eminence on the part of men,[48] what Paul exactly means by "covering head" is not hinted at in the text. Any attempted explanation must remain speculative.[49] It is noticeable however, that improper head covering, which probably had implications for gender distinctions, were not underlined as "sinful," but "dishonoring" (*kataischunō*, 11:4, 5; *atimia*, 11:14) and "disgraceful" (*aischros*, 11:6). Paul's objection to the absence of women's head coverings during public prayer and prophesizing were socially based on the contemporary Mediterranean honor and shame culture, rather than theologically on any divinely instituted gender roles hierarchy.

If there is any implication for modern day application, Paul's concern in 11:2–16 is on proper order and conduct in church gatherings. Both men and women are exhorted to avoid socially objectionable behavior which may subject themselves and others to shame and disgrace, and thereby put the whole church into disrepute.[50] The creation narrative recalled in 11:8–9 somehow betrays man's "dependency" on woman for his "glory" (11:7), which can turn out to be social "shame/dishonor" (11:5) due to woman (his wife)'s improper behavior. The mutuality and interdependence within the Pauline configuration of male headship is aptly captured by David deSilva when he remarks, "female honor is embedded in male honor in naming the husband as the 'head' of the wife, who is incorporated conceptually into his 'body.'"[51]

ASIAN MEN AND WOMEN IN THE HOUSEHOLD OF GOD

After a general survey of the modern evangelical gender debate and the New Testament texts in dispute, this section reflects on how the New Testament may best be applied to the Asian context. As Timoteo Gener asserts, "God's project in the world is the revelation of the triune God's great love, shown in . . . redemption (from sin, evil, and death) and community, and the inbreaking of God's kingdom and the new creation."[52] What we look for is a

---

48. Proposals put forth in the past include "authority," "source" on the part of men, and "dependence" on the part of women.

49. Note the variety of explanations given in previous scholarly works.

50. This concern for proper order and propriety in the church is probably also in Paul's mind when he asks women to keep silent in 1 Cor 14:34–35, see Craig S. Keener, "Learning in the Assemblies: 1 Corinthians 14:34–35," in *Discovering Biblical Equality*, 164, 171.

51. David A. deSilva, *Honor, Patronage, Kinship & Purity: Unlocking New Testament Culture* (Downers Grove, IL: InterVarsity Press, 2000), 34.

52. Timoteo D. Gener, "Divine Revelation and the Practice of Asian Theology," in *Asian Christian Theology*, ed. Timoteo D. Gener (Carlisle: Langham Global Library, 2019), 20.

model of men and women's relationship that is both embedded in the New Testament witnesses and, at the same time, demonstrative of God's loving and redemptive reign in Asia. The question that needs to be considered is, "What is the proper way of life for Asian men and women as God's kingdom people in his household?"

To answer this question, the first thing one needs to bear in mind is that, besides God's eternal revelatory word, the New Testament is also a product of history. All its books, including Paul's letters, were written in concrete time and space, with specific situations and particular circumstances needed to be addressed. The intended meaning of the writers must be understood in the light of their own assumed social structures and presuppositions from two thousand years ago, before we are able to explore how the voices of these writers should continue to be heard in modern day context.

On the other hand, as Gordon Fee judiciously observes, "an interpreter always brings to a text a considerable amount of cultural baggage and personal bias."[53] The concerns and emphasis of interpreters in the West are not necessarily the same as in the East. While evangelical interpreters, especially in North America, framed their gender debate in terms of power structures, i.e., "hierarchical gender roles" vs. "equality," Asian interpreters have the liberty not to follow the same line when engaging the gender question. We are in our own position to locate unique points of contact between ancient biblical texts and the Asian reality, and to devise a proper biblical model of Christian living that is best in tune with the Asian cultural context and thought forms.

It is commonly recognized that many Asian societies are still marked by patriarchal and hierarchical structures that constantly subject women to an inferior position. The Association for Theological Education in South East Asia reported in 2008 that:

> The rising cases of violence against women and children, as well as issues aimed directly at marginalizing women from mainstream activities, the evident gender deficit in organizations and institutions, and the circumvention of women's quest for equal rights and opportunities have become a growing concern in Asia. Often times the oppression of women in Asia is reinforced by Asian cultures and religions.[54]

---

53. Gordon D. Fee, "Hermeneutics and the Gender Debate," 365.
54. Association for Theological Education in South East Asia, "Guidelines for Doing Theologies in Asia," *International Bulletin of Missionary Research*, 32, no. 2 (2008): 77.

At home, stories are being told about how wives are victimized and abused due to general expectations for them to be dependent and to submit to the authority of the husbands. Women under traditional Confucian influence, for example, are often expected to adopt the "three obedience" (三從, *sān cóng*) including "to obey the husband after marriage" (出嫁從夫, *chūjià cóng fū*). Gemma Tulud Cruz tells us that, "This low status is reflected in the various forms of gendered violence that continue to plague Asian women."[55]

In Asian churches and in the mission fields, it is in fact widely acknowledged that women are making substantial contributions and discharging essential responsibilities. Many of them have already received proper theological training and demonstrated no less commitment to ministry.[56] However, this group of equipped kingdom workers are constantly deprived of the opportunities to use their gifts to lead, to preach and even to teach, only because of their sex as women. Ordination for ministry is even more remote for women in many places.

In view of all these, putting emphasis on women's submission and men's headship in the New Testament could only fortify the already highly hierarchical social structure and aggravate the tragic situation of many Asian women at home. Many gifted and well-trained Christian women will continue to be excluded from church leadership and teaching roles simply because they are women. If the New Testament writers chose to write within the existing patriarchal social structure only for the sake of Christian witness, and in order not to appear subversive to the current social order, Christian witness in Asia nowadays actually demands the sanction of any abuse and discrimination against women. As a matter of fact, the education standard of Asian women has generally been elevated. Many countries already have laws to protect women from discrimination, especially in relation to employment opportunities. Insisting on stifling women to inferior and submissive roles may only jeopardize the church's public witness and reputation.[57] The church should, rather, constantly locate the redemptive and liberating voice in the New Testament texts, and discern how the New Testament writers were seeking to transform

---

55. Gemma Tulud Cruz, "Christianity and the Cause of Asian Women," *The Oxford Handbook of Christianity in Asia*, ed. Felix Wilfred (New York: Oxford University Press, 2014), 304.

56. Jessy Jaison, "The Vital Mission of Theological Schools to their Women Constituency," *JAET* 16, nos. 1–2 (2008): 84.

57. It has indeed been observed that "the role of women in the church is worse than in secular society." See Cruz, "Christianity and the Cause of Asian Women," 307.

and to correct the injustice, systemic sin and malpractice permeating in current culture.

At the same time, "communal harmony and solidarity" is still very much treasured in many Asian societies. The Western feminist and egalitarian discourses on gender equality of rights and decision making may sound individualistic and destructive to proper social order to many Asian ears. As Sakhi Athyal observes, "The men and women of Asia are family and community oriented, and this means that they do not want to lose their relational identity. They have always tried to keep in mind the well-being and happiness of others in the process seeking their own liberation."[58]

Asian discourses on gender relations should therefore transcend the polemics between "hierarchical gender roles" and "equality" often found in Western debate and look for a model of Christian living that is not expressed in terms of power relations and self-assertion. Power seeking and asserting of rights should not have any place in the household of God, whether at home or in the church. It is proposed in this essay that "mutual interdependence" is the ideal form of men and women relations that is repeatedly emphasized in the New Testament,[59] and, at the same time, embedded in the Asian soil.

By "mutual interdependence," both men and women are not interested in seeking rights and authority over the other, nor do they care who has the last word for everything. Christian men and women recognize that they need each other to make themselves whole as fully human, male and female respectively. This is what happened in the creation story of Adam and Eve in the Book of Genesis. Although it is true that Eve did come from Adam's rib (Gen 2:21–23; cf. 1 Cor 11:8), it is equally true that God saw it "not good for the man to be alone" so that Eve was made a helper "who corresponds to him" (Gen 2:18 NET). Just as Eve could not be human without Adam, Adam also could not be fully human without Eve. Both man and woman need the other to be complete as one flesh (2:24; cf. Eph 5:31).

As discussed in the above sections, such mutual interdependence within the one flesh is what Paul most probably wants to emphasize when he compares the husband to the head of his wife (5:23; 1 Cor 11:3). While not

---

58. Athyal, "Women in Mission," 54.

59. Although the complementarians claim that they also recognize the beauty of mutual interdependence between men and women (see John Piper and Wayne Grudem, "Preface," in *Recovering Biblical Manhood & Womanhood: A Response to Evangelical Feminism*, xiv), it is difficult to see how such mutuality can happen if one party persistently stresses to have authority over the other.

appearing as a threat to proper social order, the liberation of the wives is not expressed in terms of equality in everything with the husbands, but is found in the self-sacrificial love of husbands as that of Christ (Eph 5:25), and as the head loves its own body (5:29). Even when the wife is willing to submit, a loving and self-sacrificing husband will hardly impose his own will upon the wife regardless of her wish, not to say treat her as an object of abuse or exploitation.[60] A husband's well-being as the head is the same as and, indeed, dependent on the well-being of the wife as the body. The honor of the husband as the head is also the same as and dependent on the honor of the wife as the body (1 Cor 11:5, 7).

Likewise, for Paul, the whole church congregation, whether men or women, are potential candidates to receive the gifts of the Holy Spirit, "each of you has a hymn, or a word of instruction, a revelation, a tongue or an interpretation" (14:26; compare 12:1–11). Both need each other to build up the church as the body of Christ. Nowhere in the New Testament can we find Paul expressly requesting men to lead or to exercise authority over women in the church.[61] What we can find is that "God has placed the parts in the body, every one of them, just as he wanted them to be" (12:18 NIV). No one in the body of Christ can say "I do not need you" and even the weaker parts of the body are indispensable (12:21–22). Although men and women are born with different traits and certain type of ministries may be more suitable for one gender than the other, no role or office in the church or in the mission field should be reserved for one sex merely by birth. Each man and woman should be able to share God's kingdom works as partners in accordance with his/her calling, and with full use of his/her spiritual gifts, and expertise.

Such truly biblical mutual interdependence can also find its resonance in Chinese culture. According to traditional Chinese thought, the female principle (Yin) and the male principle (Yang) work together to bring about the harmony of the whole cosmos and nature. The wholeness and well-being of one's life also depends on the balance and the harmonious co-working of Yin and Yang.[62] The perceived partnership and mutual interdependence between Yin and Yang is well expressed in a Chinese saying, "Female (Yin) alone does not grow. Male (Yang) only does not survive" (孤陰不長，獨陽不生; *gū yin*

---

60. See also Marshall, "Mutual Love and Submission in Marriage," 194.
61. See also Fee, "Hermeneutics and the Gender Debate," 374.
62. For a more detailed introduction to the workings of Yin and Yang in Chinese cosmology, see Archie C. Lee, "Feminist Critique of the Bible and Female Principle in Culture," *AsJT* 10 (1996): 246–47.

bù cháng, dú yáng bù shēng). Similar vision for the cooperation of the female and male forces in maintaining the balance of the world and nature may also be found in other Asian cultures and may serve to provide the momentum for transformation in line with the biblical ideal of men and women relationships.

FINAL REFLECTION

In his Letter to the Galatians, Paul reminds Christians that since we are all "one" in Christ, "There is neither Jew nor Gentile . . . nor is there male and female" (Gal 3:28 NIV). Such oneness in Christ does not mean that there is no longer any distinction between men and women, but that any barriers and power structures imposed by secular culture on gender relations are now removed in Christ.

As God's newly formed people brought about by the gospel, Christian men and women as "heirs together of the grace of life" (1 Pet 3:7 NKJV) should have the vison and temperament to transcend the old way of hungering for authority, power, status and rights that characterizes the surrounding culture. The question is not how to assert one's entitled authority and rights, but how to live out the kingdom values of sacrificial love, humility, fraternity, and righteousness in the household of God at home and in the church. Maybe this is how the New Testament texts should be faithfully applied to govern men and women relations today.

BIBLIOGRAPHY

Association for Theological Education in South East Asia. "Guidelines for Doing Theologies in Asia." *International Bulletin of Missionary Research* 32, no. 2 (2008): 77–80.

Athyal, Sakhi. "Women in Mission," *ATA Journal* 1, no. 2 (1993): 50–69.

Balch, David. *Let Wives Be Submissive: The Domestic Code in 1 Peter*, SBLMS 26. Atlanta: Scholars Press, 1981.

Barnett, Paul W. "Wives and Women's Ministry (1 Timothy 2:11–15)." *Evangelical Review of Theology* 15, no. 4 (1991): 23–32.

Belleville, Linda L. "Women Leaders in the Bible." In *Discovering Biblical Equality: Complementarity without Hierarchy*, edited by Ronald W. Pierce, Rebecca Merrill Groothuis, and Gordon D. Fee, 110–25. Downers Grove: InterVarsity Press, 2005.

Chan, Simon. "Evangelical theology in Asian context." In *The Cambridge Companion to Evangelical Theology*, edited by Timothy Larsen and Daniel J. Treier, 225–40. Cambridge: Cambridge University Press, 2007.

Cruz, Gemma Tulud. "Christianity and the Cause of Asian Women." In *The Oxford Handbook of Christianity in Asia*, edited by Felix Wilfred, 302–14. New York: Oxford University Press, 2014.

Davids, Peter H. "A Silent Witness in Marriage: 1 Peter 3:1–7." In *Discovering Biblical Equality: Complementarity without Hierarchy*, edited by Ronald W. Pierce, Rebecca Merrill Groothuis, and Gordon D. Fee, 224–38. Downers Grove: InterVarsity Press, 2005.

DeSilva, David A. *Honor, Patronage, Kinship & Purity: Unlocking New Testament Culture.* Downers Grove: InterVarsity Press, 2000.

Fee, Gordon D. "Praying and Prophesying in the Assemblies: 1 Corinthians 11:2–16." In *Discovering Biblical Equality: Complementarity without Hierarchy*, edited by Ronald W. Pierce, Rebecca Merrill Groothuis, and Gordon D. Fee, 142–60. Downers Grove: InterVarsity Press, 2005.

———. "Hermeneutics and the Gender Debate." In *Discovering Biblical Equality*, edited by Ronald W. Pierce, Rebecca Merrill Groothuis, and Gordon D. Fee, 364–81. Downers Grove: InterVarsity Press, 2005.

Forbes, Greg W., and Jason J. F. Lim. *1 Peter.* Asia Bible Commentary Series. Singapore: Asia Theological Association, 2006.

Gener, Timoteo D. "Divine Revelation and the Practice of Asian Theology." In *Asian Christian Theology*, edited by Timoteo D. Gener, 13–37. Carlisle: Langham Global Library, 2019.

Grudem, Wayne. "Wives Like Sarah, and the Husbands Who Honor Them: 1 Peter 3:1–7." In *Recovering Biblical Manhood & Womanhood: A Response to Evangelical Feminism*, edited by John Piper and Wayne Grudem, 194–208. Wheaton: Crossway, 1991.

Hurley, James B. *Man & Woman in Biblical Perspective: A Study in Role Relationships and Authority.* Leicester: Inter-Varsity Press, 1981.

Jaison, Jessy. "The Vital Mission of Theological Schools to their Women Constituency." *JAET* 16, nos. 1–2 (2008): 82–97.

Keener, Craig S. "Learning in the Assemblies: 1 Corinthians 14:34–35." In *Discovering Biblical Equality*, edited by Ronald W. Pierce, Rebecca Merrill Groothuis, and Gordon D. Fee, 161–71. InterVarsity Press, 2005.

Kowalski, Waldemar. "The Role of Women in Ministry: Is There a Disconnect between Pauline Practice and Pauline Instruction?" *AsJT* 21, no. 1 (2007): 147–70.

Lee, Archie C. "Feminist Critique of the Bible and Female Principle in Culture." *AsJT* 10 (1996): 240–52.

Longenecker, Richard N. *The Epistle to the Romans.* NIGTC. Grand Rapids: Eerdmans, 2016.

Marshall, Howard. "Mutual Love and Submission in Marriage: Colossians 3:18–19 and Ephesians 5:21–33." In *Discovering Biblical Equality: Complementarity without Hierarchy*, edited by Ronald W. Pierce, Rebecca Merrill Groothuis, and Gordon D. Fee, 186–204. InterVarsity Press, 2005.

Moo, Douglas. "What Does it Mean Not to Teach or Have Authority Over Man?: 1 Timothy 2:11–15." In *Recovering Biblical Manhood & Womanhood: A Response to Evangelical Feminism*. Edited by John Piper and Wayne Grudem, 179–93. Wheaton: Crossway Books, 1991.

Ninan, Idicheria. "Ephesians." In *South Asia Bible Commentary*, edited by Brian Wintle, 1631–47. Rajasthan: Open Door Publications, 2015.

Nordling, Cherith Fee. "Gender." In *The Oxford Handbook of Evangelical Theology*, edited by Gerald R. McDermott, 497–511. Oxford: Oxford University Press, 2010.

Philip, Finny. "1 Corinthians." In *South Asia Bible Commentary*. Edited by Brian Wintle, 1555–84. Rajasthan: Open Door Publications, 2015.

Pierce, Ronald W., and Rebecca Merrill Groothuis. *Discovering Biblical Equality: Complementarity without Hierarchy*. Downers Grove: InterVarsity Press, 2004.

Piper, John, and Wayne Grudem, eds. *Recovering Biblical Manhood & Womanhood: A Response to Evangelical Feminism*. Wheaton: Crossway Books, 1991.

Plutarch. *Moralia*. Translated by Frank Cole Babbitt. LCL 222. London: William Heinemann, 1957.

Scholer, David M. "Feminist Hermeneutics and Evangelical Biblical Interpretation." *Evangelical Review of Theology* 15, no. 4 (1991): 305–20.

Schüssler Fiorenza, Elisabeth. *In Memory of Her: A Feminist Theological Reconstruction of Christian Origin*. London: SCM Press, 1983.

Setyawan, Yusak Budi. "'Be Subject to Your Husband as You are to the Lord' in Ephesians 5:21–33 – Illuminated by an Indonesian (Javanese)," *AsJT* 21, no. 1 (2007): 50–68.

Sun, Joyce Wai-Lan. *This is True Grace; The Shaping of Social Behavioural Instructions by Theology in 1 Peter*. Carlisle: Langham Academic, 2016.

Trebilco, Paul, and Simon Rae. *1 Timothy*. Asia Bible Commentary Series. Singapore: Asia Theological Association, 2006.

Wintle, Brian, and Ken Gnanakan. *Ephesians*. Asia Bible Commentary Series. Singapore: Asia Theological Association, 2006.

CHAPTER 6

THE HOPE OF GLORY

New Testament Vision and a Hope for Asian Christians

Siang-Nuan Leong

We are living in extremely difficult times. Nations struggled to prevent economic fallout from lockdowns and closed borders due to the COVID-19 pandemic. Families and livelihoods were very affected. Global economic outlook, food security, and world peace are all threatened by volatile political relationships, and protectionist nationalistic agendas. The drawn-out Russian invasion of Ukraine and the more recent Israel-Hamas war have added to the bleak outlook. As such, biblical reflection on hope in the *eschaton* ("the last days") is more pertinent than ever, especially its significance for the here-and-now. A survey on the state of the question below reveals the need for a separate treatment on the biblical theology of hope of glory. Themes expressed with connection to glorious hope in the New Testament are collected. Attention is also given to metaphors and contexts of the biblical passages in the interpretive process. Finally, the significance of the themes for the present day are explored.

IMPORTANT EARLY DEVELOPMENTS

Jürgen Moltmann gave prominence to the last things in his vast theological work. He does not prefer eschatology to be defined as theology of "the last things," but rather as reflection on the advent of God in this world through Jesus Christ. Jesus's death and resurrection act as promise of a new creation.[1] In his view the kingdom of God is already here in the *eschaton* in the hope of what is to come.[2] Moltmann's theology interacts with the Bible, and so straddles the boundary between biblical theology and systematic theology.

---

1. Jürgen Moltmann, *The Coming of God: Christian Eschatology*, trans. Margaret Kohl (London: SCM Press, 1996), 22–23.
2. Jürgen Moltmann, *The Theology of Hope: On the Ground and the Implications of a Christian Eschatology*, trans. James W. Leitch (Minneapolis: Fortress Press, 1993), 223.

Works on eschatological hope that draw solely from the approach of biblical theology are few. Bauckham and Hart's *Hope against Hope: Christian Eschatology at the Turn of the Millennium* crosses multiple disciplines.[3] Various essays discuss eschatological themes from the New Testament, the significance of these themes for a better world, and the nature of apocalyptic language and depictions. It is important to think through the nature of the biblical texts when doing biblical theology.

Phelan's *Essential Eschatology: Our Present and Future Hope* highlights the issues that demoralize the world, and yet instils a biblical framework of hope for the reader to do serious reflection on eschatological themes in the Bible.[4] While Phelan's discussion is driven by issues where hope is needed, I will start with the New Testament concept of "hope of glory" and allow the text to interact with issues today. Meanwhile, Jonathan Menn offers a comprehensive treatment of the millennial rule, the second coming, antichrist, rapture and the Book of Revelation for the general reader.[5] This essay will focus on the central concepts that the New Testament emphasizes in relation to the hope of glory.

Among Asian scholars, Roland Chia's *Hope for the World*[6] starts with a biblical theology of hope, and subsequently ventures into interdisciplinary discussion and theological dialogue with other systematic theologians. In an essay, "Eschatology and Hope in Asia," in a compendium on *Asian Christian Theology*,[7] Roland Chia highlights the threat of terrorism, divergences in poverty and wealth, and various religious outlooks in Asia. Chia has done a commendable job of making clear the socio-religious distinctions in the Asian context.

ESCHATOLOGICAL HOPE OF GLORY
IN THE NEW TESTAMENT

The process of arriving at biblical theology in this essay will be akin to Grant Osborne's method: to first make sense of the data in the biblical text through the process of exegesis, then to arrive at an "overall scriptural unity behind

---

3. Richard Bauckham and Trevor Hart, *Hope against Hope: Christian Eschatology at the Turn of the Millennium* (Grand Rapids: Eerdmans, 1999), 72–210.
4. John E. Phelan Jr., *Essential Eschatology: Our Present and Future Hope* (Downers Grove: InterVarsity Press, 2013).
5. Jonathan Menn, *Biblical Eschatology* (Eugene, Oregon: Resource Publications), 2013.
6. Roland Chia, *Hope for the World: The Christian Vision*, Global Christian Library (Carlisle: Langham Global Library, 2012).
7. Timoteo D. Gener and Stephen T. Pardue, eds., *Asian Christian Theology* (Carlisle: Langham Global Library, 2019).

one's interpretation of individual passages," ultimately allowing us to derive theological themes.[8] A further step here is to understand the significance of the themes for the addressees of the New Testament books in view, and then to use this to inform reflection for the present-day. As Asia is a vast and diverse region, one can only highlight issues in particular places and allow the readers to make connections with similar situations elsewhere.

The outpouring of the Holy Spirit on the disciples of Jesus at Pentecost, and the subsequent workings of the Holy Spirit indicate that "the last days" prophesied in Joel 2:28–32 have arrived. The ministry of Jesus was an indication of the onset of the eschatological timeframe, as Hebrews 1:2 (NIV) indicates: "but in these last days he has spoken to us by his Son." Thus, it can be said that Jesus ushered in the eschatological timeframe, and the subsequent writings in the New Testament are all relevant for eschatology. I will draw upon passages which contain the concept of the "hope of glory" within this scope.

Hope of Glory: Overcoming Sin and Death

Romans 8:18–25 in its literary context speaks in metaphorical terms of the hope of being liberated from sin (8:9–17) and "decay" (*phthoras*, or death; cf. 7:10–11) into "the glorious freedom of the children of God." The text explains that the believer was once "sold as a slave" to sin, and could only live to please its master, the sinful nature (7:14–20; 8:12). But under the adoption process, the Spirit of God acts as the "witness" to God's will of adoption (*huiothesias*, 8:15–16), as part of the metaphorical play of the legal process.[9]

The process will culminate in the redemption of the enslaved body (Rom 8:23). At that point in time, the redeemed who were originally "slaves," metaphorically speaking, experience the "glorious freedom" of undeserved slaves as sons of God.[10] In the Greco-Roman world, slaves who become freedman were not welcomed as co-heirs with biological sons. Adoption took place normally

---

8. Grant R. Osborne, *The Hermeneutical Spiral: A Comprehensive Introduction to Biblical Interpretation*, rev. ed. (Downers Grove: IVP Academic, 2006), 350.

9. In the Greco-Roman world, witnesses were sometimes involved in the making of wills, and the awarding of the inheritance. Hugh Lindsay, "Adoption in Greek Law: Some Comparisons with the Roman World," *Newcastle Law Review* 3, no. 2 (1999): 99–100. By contrast, in the metaphorical depiction in Ephesians, the Spirit acts as the "deposit" for process of the redemption of God's people and awarding them their inheritance (Eph 1:14). In the ancient Roman world, a deposit was paid by the adopter to the court as a compensation for any eventual revocation of adoption (Hugh Lindsay, *Adoption in the Roman World* [Cambridge: Cambridge University Press, 2009], 40).

10. Michael Peppard, "Adopted and Begotten Sons of God: Paul and John on Divine Sonship," *CBQ* 73, no. 1 (2011): 96–97.

in a childless family for the purpose of continuing the family line.[11] Here, the adopted son shares in the inheritance of God together with Jesus, God's firstborn (8:18–27). God's magnanimous treatment of "slaves" accentuates the "glory that will be revealed" in the adopted son (8:18). At this point in time, the hope of glory is realized.

In spiritual terms, such a "glorious freedom" for the emancipated is set in the literary context of liberation from suffering, and decay or death (*phthoras*, Rom 8:21–23; see also 7:17 and 8:28–39). This "glorious freedom" reflects the glorious grace of God towards the slaves in the act of emancipation and adoption.

From Paul's discourse in Romans chapters 6–7, we learn that the emancipation, and subsequent adoption as sons, aims to break the subordination of the created being to sin and death, with the help of the Holy Spirit. The Spirit enables the mortal bodies to receive life as well. This refers to a future resurrection from the dead, as the hope depicted here is realized in another plane of existence (8:19–21).

Ramsey Michaels observes the tension in the in-between stage of adoption before the redemption of the body at resurrection.[12] In the Roman practice, the adoptee is usually handed over (sold) to an intermediary, effecting the transaction. Subsequently, the adoptee is returned to his natural father. This happens twice. It is only at the third time of handing over the son to the adopter that the legal right (*potestas*) of the biological father over his son is broken and the adoption effected.[13] In the meantime, the Spirit helps the believer to overcome the weakness of sinful nature (8:26), as they choose to "live according to the Spirit," while "putting to death the misdeeds of the body" (8:13). In this way,

---

11. Marcin Kowalski, "The Brokerage of the Spirit in Romans 8," *CBQ* 80 (2018): 651. This work mines the Greco-Roman framework to illuminate the metaphor of the Spirit's role in the adoption process. Even though the parallels between a broker and the Spirit do not seem too compelling, this work illustrates the Greco-Roman system as framework to understand the metaphors in Romans. Without such a lens, it is difficult to interpret the many figurative details in Paul's argument. Along a similar approach, see also Robert Brian Lewis, *Paul's "Spirit of Adoption" in its Roman Imperial Context*, LNTS (London: T&T Clark, 2018).

12. J. Ramsey Michaels, "The Redemption of our Body," in *Romans & the People of God*, eds. Sven K. Soderlund and N. T. Wright (Grand Rapids: Eerdmans, 1999), 100. Michaels has delivered an in-depth study on the text of Romans 8:19–22.

13. James M. Scott, *Adoption as Sons of God: An Exegetical Investigation into the Background of* ΥΙΟΘΕΣΙΑ *in the Pauline Corpus*, WUNT 2/48 (Tübingen: Mohr Siebeck, 1992), 12.

the adopted son can live a life that is worthy of his new family as a son of God (8:9–14).[14] There is a great indebtedness on the part of the adoptee.

In 2 Corinthians, resurrection of the body is also couched in metaphorical terms. In 5:1–10, when the "earthly tent" is destroyed, the believer is to be clothed with a "heavenly dwelling" or "eternal house" (5:1–4 NIV). The Spirit of God becomes the "deposit" guaranteeing inheritance of the heavenly dwelling for believers (5:5). Paul speaks earlier on of his desire to be away from the body and to be with the Lord in response to the persecution that he and his fellow co-workers are facing (4:7–12, 16–18). The certainty of the resurrection of believers is built on the historical fact of Jesus's resurrection (4:14).

Paul's teaching on the resurrection of the body receives more attention in 1 Corinthians 15. There, Paul is arguing for the reality of bodily resurrection in a bid to stem the wrong perspective of his readers, who were living a lifestyle of merry-making, feasting, and mixing with bad company, thinking there is no resurrection (15:12, 32–34). It is likely that Paul is responding to a kind of popular philosophy, such as Epicureanism. One needs to be careful not to adopt the hedonistic lifestyle as though there is no afterlife.[15]

Theological Implications

What theological reflections can we draw from the hope of glory in Romans 8? In the period of the already-but-not-yet, the eschatological passages call the believer to live on a different moral plane than that of the world. This is the focal point of the teaching in Romans chapters 6–8. Romans 12:1–2, which begins the section of exhortation on Christian living (12–15) applies the earlier point on setting the mind on what the Spirit desires (8:5), and in this way not conforming to "the pattern of the world."

Throughout our region, conservative Asian values are fast eroding and being consumed by the popular culture. For instance, there has been a "sexual revolution" in China in the post-Mao era to undo the de-sexualization (or sexual repression) in the time of Chairman Mao. This revolution is characterized by a departure from the Confucian or Taoist outlook on sex for procreation and

---

14. Trevor J. Burke, "Adoption and the Spirit in Romans 8," *EvQ* 70, no. 4 (1998): 319–20. For the Spirit's role in allowing believers to overcome sin and death in the message of Romans, see L. Ann Jervis, "The Spirit Brings Christ's Life to Live," in *Reading Paul's Letter to the Romans*, ed. Jerry L. Sumney, RBS 73 (Atlanta: Society of Biblical Literature, 2012), 144–48.

15. See Graham Tomlin, "Christians and Epicureans in 1 Corinthians," *JSNT* 68 (1997): 51–72. 1 Thess 4:13–18 also writes about the resurrection of the body. This will be covered under the second coming of Jesus below.

social order.[16] Even the website of Chinese Communist Party features female nudity.[17] In some contexts in China, it has become normal to gift business partners or clients with sexual services today, not just with huge banquets and other benefits. It is not uncommon for people in China to consider offering sexual services to advance one's prospect in business. The female body is often viewed as a commodity to gain income and security.[18]

Studies indicate that the majority of the Chinese public approves of pre-marital sex. A higher percentage say they would approve if there was love between the sexual partners.[19] A study based on a national survey of sexual behavior in the year 2000 indicates 30–50 percent of women and men in their twenties and thirties have engaged in premarital sex.[20] There is also widespread acceptance of extra-marital relationships, more so by men than women.[21] Even so, a national study shows a rapid increase in the prevalence of multiple sex partners (MSP) among women, with a jump from 8.1 percent in 2000 to 29.6 percent in 2006. Those who are cohabiting with another partner are three times more likely to report MSP than those who are single.[22]

In South Korea, another country rooted in Confucian values, women are facing the threat of voyeurism even in their own bedrooms, not to mention the prevalence of spy-cams installed in hotels, changing rooms, and toilets.[23] Footage feeds the fantasies of voyeurs, and brings in substantial income when

---

16. Weijun Zheng et al., "Detraditionalisation and Attitudes to Sex outside Marriage in China," *Culture, Health and Sexuality* 13, no. 5 (2011): 497–511, see 497.
17. Everett Yuehong Zhang, "China's Sexual Revolution," in *Deep China: The Moral Life of the Person, What Anthropology and Psychiatry Tell us about China Today*, ed. Arthur Kleinman, et al. (Berkeley; Los Angeles; London: University of California Press, 2011): 132–34, 162. Zhang provides vivid ethnographical records of the situation in China.
18. Harriet Zundofer, "Men, Women, Money, and Morality: The Development of China's Sexual Economy," *Feminist Economics* 22, no. 2 (2015): 6–8.
19. Zheng et al., "Detraditionalisation and attitudes to sex outside marriage in China," 506.
20. William L. Parish, Edward O. Laumann, and Sanyu A. Mojola, "Sexual Behavior in China: Trends and Comparisons," in *Population and Development Review* 33 no. 4 (2007): 743–44.
21. In the study conducted by Zheng et al., only 61 percent were opposed to extra-marital relationship. Zheng et al., "Detraditionalisation and attitudes to sex outside marriage in China," 506.
22. Yingying Huang, Kumi Smith, and Suiming Pan, "Changes and Correlates in Multiple Sexual Partnerships among Chinese Adult Women – Population-based Surveys in 2000 and 2006," *AIDS Care: Psychological and Socio-medical Aspects of AIDS/HIV*, no. 23, Sup 1 (2011): 100, https://doi.org/10.1080/09540121.2010.516350.
23. "'My Life is not your Porn': digital sex crimes in South Korea," Human Rights Watch, June 2021, https://www.hrw.org/sites/default/files/media_2021/06/southkorea0621_web_1_0.pdf. Aldrin M. Peñamora, "The Way of the Cross and the Good Life," in *Asian Christian Ethics: Evangelical Perspectives*, eds., Aldrin M. Peñamora and Bernard K. Wong (Carlisle: Langham Global Library, 2022), 165–90.

sold. A whole cyber sexual economy is driving the trend. The floodgates of the sexual revolution are open in two countries with traditional Asian roots.

Clearly, the loosening of sexual mores and the treatment of sex as a commodity for gain contradict the principle of respect for the person. In total contrast to the self-seeking contemporary culture, God's grant of sonship to slaves in Romans reveals the magnanimity and abundance of his grace toward all people. In God's redemptive work, the slave becomes a co-heir with the natural son (Christ, Rom 8:17) – something frowned upon in the Greco-Roman world. This testifies to the kind of love and respect God exhibits and calls for in his creatures. Thus, in the Christian view of romantic relationships, sexual engagement serves the purpose of edifying and expressing love to the other. This alternative view stands in stark contrast to the cultural norms, which emphasize satisfying lustful desires or material pursuits through multiple sex partners and harmful practices.

Similarly, the New Testament casts a hopeful vision for those who struggle against the temptations of lust and slavery to sin. Paul describes his own frustration with "this body that is subject to death," which in its literary context refers to the sinful nature in the body that results in death (7:13). Importantly, Paul sounds a note of hope, reminding us that "The Spirit helps us with our weakness" (8:26 NIV). Thus, Christians who struggle with lust can overcome sinful desires by walking according to the Holy Spirit. Christians should also note the importance of cultivating virtues in Paul's writings (e.g. the "fruit of the Spirit" in Gal 5:22), which bears similarity in certain ways with Confucian teaching, in which virtues also take center stage.[24] Yet the difference between Christian and Confucian view of morality is the presence of an external agent – the Holy Spirit – who helps a believer in his or her weaknesses. This is the key point. As we see in Ephesians 5:3–20, the Spirit counteracts deeds of darkness by being filled with the Spirit and encouraging one another with spiritual songs. The redemptive role of God through Jesus Christ provides the basis of a right relationship with God and with others. A redemptive role is not present in the "heaven" (*tian*) of Confucian thought.[25]

LGBTQ issues are now pervasive in once conservative Asian societies. Taiwan legalized the permanent union of same-sex partners in May 2019, short

---

24. Philip J. Ivanhoe, "Virtue Ethics and the Chinese Confucian Tradition," in *Virtue Ethics and Confucianism*, ed. Stephen Angle and Michael Slote (New York: Routledge Taylor and Francis Group, 2013), 28–46.
25. Aldrin M. Peñamora, "The Way of the Cross and the Good Life," 175.

of applying the term "marriage" to such union.[26] The Singapore government passed a bill to repeal a law criminalizing gay sexual acts. This was after prolonged advocacy from LGBTQ supporters and counteracting responses from the Christian community. At the same time, protection against legal challenge will be put in place for defining "marriage" as between one man and one woman.[27] Churches are increasingly faced with the need to serve those suffering sexual identity issues, but churches remain inhibited out of fear.[28] What would Jesus do? Jesus dines with "sinners," acknowledging their need for healing and repentance (Luke 5:31–34). It takes faith in the power of the Holy Spirit for churches to open doors and bring about restoration. The Christian community has been seen as perpetrators of hatred against the LGBTQ community. This calls for helpful communication between both communities.[29]

Hope of Glory: Inclusion of the Gentiles into the Faith Community

In Pauline and Lukan works, the inclusion of the Gentiles or the marginalized in the faith community is a major theme. Paul writes in his epistle to the Ephesians about the hope of inheritance as God's adopted sons – both Jews and Gentiles – and of the glory that is being ascribed to God for his magnanimity and generosity in lavishing such grace not only on the Jews but also on the Gentiles (Eph 1:3–14). The main concern in Ephesians is the unity of Jews and Gentiles in the faith community (1:3–4:16). Long-standing animosity and a deep divide between the two people groups are reflected in the epistle: a wall of hostility exists; the Gentiles are stigmatized as the "uncircumcised" and seen as an alien group separated from God and the faith community. Paul explains that Christ has abolished the Jewish law to achieve the unity of the Jews and Gentiles in a faith community (2:14–18). Importantly, he couches the inclusion of the Gentiles in terms of their hope of redemption and inheriting of

---

26. Shang-Jen Chen, "Homosexuality in Twenty-First Century Asia," in *Asian Christian Ethics: Evangelical Perspectives*, eds Aldrin M. Peñamora and Bernard K. Wong (Carlisle: Langham Global Library, 2022), 249.

27. Yan Han Goh, "Singapore Passes Laws to Decriminalise Gay Sex, Protect Definition of Marriage against Legal Challenge," *Straits Times*, 29 November 2022, https://www.channelnewsasia.com/singapore/singapore-passes-laws-decriminalise-gay-sex-protect-definition-marriage-against-legal-challenge-3108996.

28. National Council of Churches in Singapore, *A Christian Response to Homosexuality* (Singapore: Genesis Books, 2004), 82–97; Shang-Jen Chen, "Homosexuality in Twenty-First Century Asia," 243–51.

29. Lisa Blankenship, *Changing the Subject: A Theory of Rhetorical Empathy* (Logan, UT: Utah State University Press, 2019), 83–102.

God's possessions (1:3–14).[30] As a result of this eschatological work, "glorious praise" is due God (1:6).

A similar idea occurs in Romans 11:11–32. Gentiles are grafted onto the olive tree after its original branches (representing the people of Israel) are broken off due to their unbelief. Paul's exhortation to the faith community in Rome concerns mutual acceptance between Jews and Gentiles (14:1–15:13). Since all have sinned and fallen short of God's glory (2:1–29; 3:9–20), justification by faith is the way forward (3:21–31).

Such is the theological basis for mutual acceptance between people groups. For those being justified by faith, their "boasting" (*kauchaomai*) is in the "hope of God's glory" (5:2), as opposed to those who "boast" (*kauchaomai*) in the Jewish law (2:23). The Jewish law should not bring about division in the Christian community. God's call to both Jew and Gentile brings full glory to God (9:23–26). Paul praises God for his great mercy of accepting both people groups in a doxology (11:33–36; cf. 11:25–32).

The inclusion of all people groups in God's salvific grace is likewise an important theme in the writings of Luke. His Gospel depicts Jesus Christ coming for the poor, oppressed and lowly (4:18–19). There is a certain reversal to the status of the poor and the despised, *vis-à-vis* the rich and powerful (Luke 6:20–27; 16:1–31; 18:1–30; 19:1–10). The Book of Acts emphases the inclusion of the Gentiles into the faith community. No doubt, there are different views on the purpose of Acts,[31] but the narrative clearly emphasizes this theme.[32] In Jesus's last instructions to his disciples, he promised God's empowerment to those who bear witness about Jesus to the ends of the world (Acts 1:2, 8). Subsequently, the gospel of Jesus is preached in an ever-widening geographic circle, under the leading of the Holy Spirit (13:1–3; 16:6–10). The outpouring of the Holy Spirit at Pentecost serves the purpose of preaching Jesus to people who come from far and wide (2:1–11). The quote from Joel 2:28–32 is applied to show that in the "last days" (Acts 2:17), God's Spirit is given to people of all backgrounds, and "everyone who calls on the name of the Lord will be saved." In the subsequent narrative, there is a recurring motif of the Holy Spirit being given to Gentiles, sometimes with similar outward

---

30. Ephesians 1:14 could be interpreted with the metaphorical framework of adopted sons freed from slavery and awaiting the possession of their inheritance.

31. Craig S. Keener, *Acts: An Exegetical Commentary*, 4 vols. (Grand Rapids: Baker Academic, 2012), 1:435–58.

32. Christoph W. Stenschke, *Luke's Portrait of Gentiles Prior to Their Coming to Faith*, WUNT 2/108 (Tübingen: Mohr Siebeck, 1999), 34.

manifestations as with the Jews at Pentecost. These outward manifestations are meant to publicize God's acceptance of different people groups (8:19; 10:44–48; 15:8; 19:6).

In Acts, Peter (10:1–11:18) and Paul (chs. 13–28) each play a crucial role in breaking through the Jewish-Gentile barrier. Luke narrates two meetings at the Jerusalem church endorsing the acceptance of Gentiles into the faith community without first forcing them to become Jews through circumcision and Jewish observances (chs. 11 and 15). In line with Jesus's opening instruction and promise in Acts 1:8, the book ends on the note of the obtuseness of the Jews (citing Isa 6:9–10), and God's salvation being preached to the Gentiles instead (Acts 28:25–28). Even though the inclusion of the Gentiles is not couched in the language of "hope" nor of "glory" in Acts, the narrative clearly celebrates the inclusion of the Gentiles as a glorious revelation of God's eschatological plan. This is akin to the unveiling of the "mystery" in Ephesians 3:1–6 (see also 1:9), whereby God's glorious grace to both Jews and Gentiles is revealed (1:11–14). A similar idea is presented in the Revelation, whereby the worshipping community consists of peoples of all nations and languages (Rev 7:9; cf. 21:23–24).

Theological Implications

As with the marginalization of those deemed unfit for God's kingdom by the religious upper class and the Jewish society in Jesus's times, here is discrimination and oppression of the *shudra* caste, the lowest of the castes, and the "untouchables," the outcasts, in India. This is a deep-seated humanitarian issue. The efforts of Gandhi and other activists may not have arrived at longstanding effects, since social injustices in relation to the caste system remain.[33]

It so happens that the social situation of the *dalits* mirrors that of the outcasts of the Jewish society in the Greco-Roman world, in the times of Jesus and his apostles. Both in the worldview of the Indian caste system and in Judaism, there is an emphasis on ritual purity and birth.[34] Spatially, Gentile regions were perceived as unclean. Jews would avoid entering the homes of Gentiles for fear of contracting uncleanness. Jews sharing meals with Gentiles was unthinkable because of the ritual uncleanness of the food Gentiles consume. Gentiles were

---

33. Nishikant Kolge, *Gandhi Against Caste* (New Delhi: Oxford University Press, 2017), 206–7.
34. Hyam Maccoby, *Ritual and Morality: The Ritual Purity System and its Place in Judaism* (Cambridge: Cambridge University Press, 1999), 10.

not allowed beyond the outer courts of the Jewish temple. One could contract uncleanness by touching them.[35]

Similarly, the untouchables in India cannot eat or be with other castes in the same school, stay in the same dwelling, nor use the same wells. The jobs they do are restricted to the menial and dirty. Those who touch them contract uncleanness and need to be ritually purified. Even their shadows are deemed to defile.[36] In some parts of India, *dalits* are still not allowed to enter the Hindu temple. They are made to remain somewhere at the steps leading up to it, despite legislative battles being fought on the issue.[37] The various castes advocate and practice endogamy to prevent their birth heritage from mixing.[38] The *dalits* are considered to be under some kind of "curse" because of their "caste body," and they could not escape their lowly position. It is said that such a stigma could not even be cast off by dying with separate burial grounds marked out for them.[39]

Like the *dalits*, the Gentiles were deemed to be under the curse of a Judaistic religious order, since they could not fulfil the righteous requirements of the law; they did not have the Jewish law in the first place! However, Jesus Christ gave his body in exchange, and bore the curse of the law, so that the judgment of the law on the Gentiles was abrogated (Gal 3:10–14; Eph 2:14–15). The Gentiles were set free from their demeaning status and declared to be of one faith community with the Jewish brothers and with equal rights before God (2:17–22). In the Book of Acts, the power of the Holy Spirit ensured that Jesus was preached to the "ends of the earth," and signified God's acceptance of the non-Jews through external manifestations of the Spirit. They became co-heirs with the Jews under the glorious grace of God (3:6; cf. 1:3–14), so that there is neither Jew nor Gentile in Jesus Christ (Gal 3:28–29).

Deep-seated divides of class and race, such as the age-old caste divide in the Indian society, often involve religious, political, and economic considerations.[40]

---

35. Jerome H. Neyrey, "The Idea of Purity in Mark's Gospel," *Semeia* 35 (1986): 91–128.

36. Sujay Biswas, "A re-reading of Gandhi's and Ambedkar's Emancipatory Discourses for Social Action against Untouchability," *Community Development Journal* (2023): 190.

37. Suratha Kumar Malik, "Dalit and the Historiography of Temple Entry Movements in India: Mapping Social Exclusion and Cultural Subjugation," *Contemporary Voice of Dalit* (2022): 10–12.

38. J. Bheemaiah, "Dialectics of Caste Culture: A Social Crisis in Indian Nation," in *Social Science and Humanity: International Proceedings of Economics Development and Research*, vol. 5, part 2, ed. Feng Tao (Singapore: IACSIT Press, 2011), 454–56.

39. Anupama Rao, *The Caste Question: Dalits and the Politics of Modern India* (Berkeley: University of California Press, 2009), 268.

40. See Rao, *The Caste Question*.

Unconditional acceptance, regardless of background, is accorded in Jesus Christ (3:28). Despite best efforts by pastors or missionaries, caste rigidities continue to plague some Christian churches in India, such as needing to hold separate worship services or use separate communion cups for different classes.[41] In this, we are reminded of the effort of apostle Paul in bringing peace to the Jewish and Gentile Christians in the churches of Rome and Ephesus.

The coming together of different castes, of Muslims and Hindus for weekly worship and yearly meal "for everyone, without distinction of caste, creed or community" was achieved at the Christukula Ashram in Tirupattur, Tamil Nadu.[42] The history of mission work in India had seen mass movement conversions of the lowest castes, and especially the casteless in the late colonial era.[43] Understanding and navigating such a foreign culture were not without difficulties to missionaries.[44]

Myanmar is also seeing a deep-seated fragmentation of society along ethno-religious fault lines, especially in terms of the crisis of the Rohingya Muslims, who live in the Rakhine state. The Rohingyas speak a dialect of Bengali and bear Muslim names. In contrast, the majority of the Myanmar's population speak the Burmese language and are Buddhists. The military junta plays to the sentiment of antagonism and disdain towards the Rohingyas. Through legislation and constitutional changes, the Rohingyas have been stripped of legal status of residence in the country and have become stateless.[45] Clashes erupted between the Arakan Rohingya Salvation Army (ARSA) and the junta military.[46] Executions, rape, and other abuses against the Rohingya population were reported. At least seven hundred thousand Rohingyas had fled to Bangladesh after a brutal "clearance operation" in August 2017.[47] The

---

41. Nigel Ajay Kumar, "Renewed Action for Age-Old Concerns," in *Asian Christian Ethics: Evangelical Perspectives* (Carlisle: Langham Global Library, 2022), 289.

42. Babu Immanuel, *Acts of the Apostles: An Exegetical and Contextual Commentary*, India Commentary on the New Testament (Minneapolis: Fortress Press, 2016), 56.

43. Laura Dudley Jenkins, *Religious Freedom and Mass Conversion in India*, Pennsylvania Studies in Human Rights (Philadelphia: University of Pennsylvania Press, 2019), 33–35.

44. A particular narrative blamed colonial powers and missionaries of having contributed to the caste divide, see Kumar, "Renewed Action for Age-Old Concerns," 278–82.

45. Jobair Alam, "The Current Rohingya Crisis in Myanmar in Historical Perspective," *Journal of Muslim Minority Affairs* 39, no. 1 (2019): 17–18.

46. Albert Eleanor and Lindsay Maizland, "The Rohingya Crisis," Council on Foreign Relations, 23 January 2020, https://www.cfr.org/backgrounder/rohingya-crisis.

47. Alam, "The Current Rohingya Crisis in Myanmar in Historical Perspective," 1.

military was believed to have razed villages, torn down buildings and bulldozed abandoned villages.[48]

What would be Jesus's response to the treatment of the Rohingya population? We see Jesus serving the marginalized and those despised by Jewish legalists of his time. He subverted the privileged mentality of the wealthy and religious self-righteous; he elevated the status of the lowly in the kingdom of God. Long sections in the Gospel of Luke are dedicated to this (see above). What role should Christian communities play? Where work remains for Christian communities, the Holy Spirit will continue to bring transformation with the same will and power today as in Acts. The heart of God has not changed in between the first and the twenty-first century.

Hope of Glory: Suffering, Persecution, and the Glorious Kingdom

Any discussion of eschatological hope is not complete without a discussion of the heavenly city. Revelation 21 reveals the holy city Jerusalem, the bride of the Lamb, representing the ultimate community of God, composed of those who remained faithful. The author John reiterates the need for Jesus-followers to remain faithful in face of persecution (2:3, 9–10; 13:9–10; 6:9–11). John was himself put in exile on the island of Patmos for the faith (1:9). The reality of persecution is depicted in the visions of Revelation (13; 17:6). They also depict a full reversal of lowly and persecuted status of the faithful at the fulfilment of God's kingdom.

Martyred souls at the altar (6:9–11; 19:1–8) will reign with Christ in the millennial kingdom (20:4–6) and their place in the glorious New Jerusalem is secured (20:6). Those martyred had refused imperial worship and had not compromised their faith to protect their lives or to survive economically (20:4).[49] The churches in Asia Minor to whom the letter is addressed were facing pressure from the imperial cult of the ruling dynasty in the nineties of the first century CE. They were also warned not to affiliate with the Jewish

---

48. "Myanmar: Remaking Rakhine State," Amnesty International, 12 March 2018, https://www.amnesty.org/en/documents/asa16/8018/2018/en/.
49. For the "mark of the beast," see Siang-Nuan Leong, "Windows to the Polemics against the So-Called Jews and Jezebel in Revelation: Insights from historical and co(n)textual analysis" (PhD thesis, University of Edinburgh, 2009), 129–58, https://era.ed.ac.uk/handle/1842/4453.

synagogue community as a cover for their monotheistic faith, as this amounted to defecting to the camp of Satan.[50]

In a similar vein to the overcomers in Revelation, what the patriarchs in Hebrews 11 hoped for (11:1) would culminate in an unshakable kingdom (12:28). Here in Hebrews, the "heavenly Jerusalem," is the "church of the firstborn" and "spirits of righteous man made perfect" (12:23). In Revelation, the "bride" descending from heaven represents the righteous Jesus-followers (19:7–8; 21:2). The foundations and gates of the city are symbolic of God's people (21:12–14). In both books, the metaphorical depiction aims to define who the inheritors of God's kingdom are. Both books call for readers to persevere in the faith in face of challenges as they await the glorious end (Heb 10:21–39; Rev 13:10; 14:12). The authors warn of a very different end for those who continue to live in sin or choose to apostatize (Heb 6:4–6; 12:4–6, 14–17; 13:4–6; Rev 2–3; 14:7–12; 18:4).

In his exposition of justification by faith, Paul touches on perseverance in suffering, and right Christian living in relation to "the hope of the glory of God" (Rom 5:2–3). He pits the self-righteousness and boasts of those relying on the Jewish law (2:23; 3:27; cf. 2:1, 17–29) against the God-centeredness of those trusting and rejoicing in God's grace and mercy for justification (4:1–5; 4:13–5:8). Perseverance in godly character despite opposition and human weakness is rooted in a steadfast hope in God's love and faithfulness.

Moreover, Paul reminds his readers that God will not disappoint those who trust in him (5:1–11). "The glory of God" in Romans 5:2 speaks of God's immense love, grace, and mercy through the salvific act of Jesus Christ (chs. 4–5, esp. 5:5–8, 12–21). This constitutes the basis of a believer's hope (4:20; 5:11; 6:4).[51]

The coming of Jesus is couched in various images in Revelation, such as on a cloud (1:7; 14:14–16) or as a warrior coming like a thief (16:15–16). The

---

50. Revelation 2:9 could reflect those who took cover with the synagogue. They could have accused Christians as proof of their loyalty to the Judaistic community. Jesus has given the church an open door. Some defectors, who seem to have prior ties with Jesus and the church, would eventually return and admit their mistake (3:9). They would never leave the New Jerusalem (again), being immovable pillars there (3:12).

The position of the mark of the beast possibly corresponds to the way Jewish sects outside mainstream Judaism wore the *tefillin* (cf. Mishnah Megillah 4.8). See Leong, "Windows to the Polemics against the So-Called Jews and Jezebel in Revelation," 128–58.

51. In context, the "glory of God" (*tēs dochēs tou theou*, 5:2) reads as an "attributed genitive." Paul focusses on God's attributes, which could sustain a believer through faith challenges. For "attributed genitive," see Daniel B. Wallace, *Greek Grammar Beyond the Basics: An Exegetical Syntax of the New Testament* (Grand Rapids: Zondervan, 1996), 89.

text warns Christians to keep their clothes on, and not be naked and shamed at the time of Jesus's return. This is a call to believers to watch their deeds.[52] The detail of Jesus coming on a cloud and as a thief also occurs in 1 Thessalonians (4:16–17; 5:1–4). That text similarly encourages good Christian living (5:4–9). In 1 Thessalonians, the term *parousia* (2:19; 3:13; 4:15; 5:23), used for the coming of Jesus, is used in the context of an imperial or divine visit of a king or deity to a city. Middleton sees such a metaphorical schema: the herald sounding the trumpet, the city sending a delegation to receive the dignitary outside the city, and accompanying him back to the city, where he is welcomed by the population (cf. 4:15–17).[53] The images of Jesus coming as a warrior and thief act to spur backslidden Christians to return to the words of Jesus.[54]

While the visions in Revelation lead up to the establishment of the rule of God and the Lamb in the new heaven and earth, the Gospels concentrate on the timeframe of Jesus's first coming and the faith communities of the first century. Nonetheless, both corpuses concentrate on kingdom ethics for the present time.

One key attribute of discipleship is self-denial. This corresponds to the kind of Messiah Jesus is, especially his death on the cross. The Gospel of Mark highlights the ambition of the twelve disciples for power.[55] Mark juxtaposes Jesus's forecasting of his impending humiliation and death, and how his disciples vied for high positions among themselves, in anticipation of his assumption of power (Mark 9:30–37; 10:32–45). Jesus reminds them repeatedly that his purpose is to die a redemptive death for many (10:45;

---

52. Revelation has a way of using clothes and nakedness to refer to the deeds of Christians (cf. Rev 3:2–4; 3:15, 18).

53. Hence, J. Richard Middleton does not see it suitable to extend this description into a teaching of the concept of the "rapture" (*A New Heaven and a New Earth: Reclaiming Biblical Eschatology* [Grand Rapids: Baker Academic, 2014], 222).

As for the Book of Revelation, I find it difficult to determine which point in time believers are literally caught up into the mid-air to meet up with Jesus Christ, like in 1 Thessalonians, and so it is not appropriate to base any concept of rapture on Revelation due to its prevalent use of imagery.

54. See echoes to the battle in the admonishments to the churches in Asia Minor: the double-edged sword (Rev 3:12–13, 16; cf. 19:15); Jesus coming like a thief (3:3; cf. 16:15) and the admonishments about the proper attire, symbolic of the righteous deeds (3:4–5; 16:15; 20:14; cf. 19:8).

We see the emphasis on keeping the words of Jesus (22:7, 12) as the purpose for broaching the topic of Jesus's return. In fact, the battle was fought with the double-edged sword (19:15 and 1:16), the "Word of God" (19:13; cf. Heb 4:12). The enemy camp consists of a false prophet (Rev 19:20)! It is a battle concerning faithful adherence to God's word.

55. Peter, who wanted to stop Jesus from going to the cross, was called "Satan" (Mark 8:29–33). Another disciple took out his sword to defend Jesus (14:47).

14:22–24) and he declares that his disciples should likewise carry the cross (8:34–38). Jesus prepared his disciples for persecution (13:11–13; 14:27). The Markan phenomenon of the "Messianic secret" likely highlights a non-political messiahship.[56] Mark does not shy away from the topic of suffering, and the ending reads like a tragedy of failed discipleship in the face of opposition (16:8). Similar ideas can be found in the other Gospels. It is without a doubt that Jesus's kingdom will one day manifest in power, but the faith community here and now is reminded to take on the perspective of beatitudes: blessed are the poor in spirit and the persecuted (Matt 5:3, 10).

Apocalyptic literature is often birthed out of a situation of persecution or oppression. Developments would eventually culminate with a state of victory and bliss for God's people (e.g. Rev 12–13 vs 20–21; 6:9–11 vs 7:9–17). The image of the luxurious heavenly city is an encouragement and reward to those who chose poverty and suffering to remain true to the commands of Jesus. The images of victory in battle and the millennial rule, likewise, compensate for the persecution endured on earth (2:9–10 vs 2:11).[57] In contrast, those who assimilate into corrupted culture of this world to get rich will lose it all in eternity (2:14–15 vs 2:16; 14:9–11). Apocalyptic rhetoric provides believers a reversal of the suffering and bring hope from the perspective of the end.[58] This is meant to strengthen the resolve for believers to hang on to their faith (14:12).

Theological Reflection

The challenge to the church today, as with the Jewish community in the New Testament era, is a self-centredness mentality. Unlike the boast of self-justification based on fulfilling the Jewish law, Christian circles today are challenged by an antinomian attitude of disregarding God's commands. This comes from a desire to assimilate with the ways of the world. The notion of hyper-grace does away with kingdom ethics and the need for repentance on the part of

---

56. Jesus's glory and exalted status can only be proclaimed after his death and resurrection (Mark 9:1–13, esp. 1–3, 7, 9, 12–13). The Jesus in Mark often prevented the proclamation of his exalted identity and power (1:23–25; 3:11–12; 7:35–36). But he was fine with it being made known publicly except in Gentile lands (5:18–20), where the notion of a Messiah is inconsequential.

57. Those who are a part of the first resurrection (the millennial rule), will not be a part of the second death (Rev 20:6).

58. Khiok-khng Yeo, "An Eschatological View of History in the New Testament: Messianic and Millenarian Hope," *AsJT* 15, no. 1 (2001): 48.

believers.[59] Along similar lines, the popular prosperity gospel can sound as inviting.[60] However, self-denial and enduring persecution are part-and-parcel of kingdom ethics. God calls the faith community to self-denial, to set herself apart from the values of the world.

The other challenge is the threat of persecution. Southeast Asia has been a hotbed for terrorist groups for many years.[61] After the end of the potential ISIS caliphate in Iraq and Syria, and a stop to the Malawi siege in the Philippines, terrorist groups are going online, even a virtual Caliphate for ISIS, fighting an ideological war, and expanding receptivity to their causes.[62] In some pockets of southeast Asia, there is increasing receptivity to militant Islamist perspectives. From time to time, there have been attacks on targets claimed by various Jihadist groups.[63]

A Christian in turbulent times must be prepared to face the threat of life or suffering under anti-Christian political systems. Revelation warns of defecting to another religion to seek protection or relief. The perspective of the glorious end for the martyrs helps the Christian to endure and seek hope in the future kingdom of God.

CONCLUSION

This essay has highlighted three themes that surface in the New Testament in relation to the "hope of glory." These themes cast light on key issues in Asia today. First, we see that God's redemptive grace and the power of the Holy Spirit can transform lives by freeing us from slavery to sin. Where frustration remains, the believer can look forward to resurrection, as a fulfilment of the process of the adoption as God's children, where there will be total freedom from the sinful desires of the body. In a sexually charged and confused culture, God's children can live rightly. Second, as God has extended his glorious grace and mercy to people of all backgrounds, all peoples can hope to be heirs of

---

59. Andrew Christian Nelson, "Hyper Grace Theology: A Definition and Systematisation" (PhD thesis, University of Aberdeen, 2021), 20–150, https://ethos.bl.uk/OrderDetails.do?uin=uk. bl.ethos.844811.

60. Kate Bowler, *Blessed: A History of the American Prosperity Gospel* (Oxford: New York: Oxford University Press, 2013).

61. Zachary Abuza, *Militant Islam in Southeast Asia: Crucible of Terror* (Colorado: Lynne Rieneer Publishers, 2003), 4.

62. Angelica Habulan et al., "Southeast Asia: Philippines, Indonesia, Malaysia, Myanmar, Thailand, Singapore, Online Extremism," *Counter Terrorist Trends and Analyses*, 10, no. 1, Annual Threat Assessment (2018): 25–28. For virtual caliphate, see 7, 16.

63. Abuza, *Militant Islam in Southeast Asia*, 1–188. The book outlines the growth and activities of Jihadist movements in Southeast Asia, particularly in Philippines, Malaysia, and Indonesia.

God. There is a levelling between all peoples in Christ. This has implications for how the Christian community lives this alongside oppressed people groups, such as the *dalits*. Lastly, the threat of terrorism and persecution is more acute in some places than in others. Even in peaceful times, living out kingdom ethics would mean self-denial and refusing the temptations of worldly wealth and power.

As apocalyptic notions loom in face of wars, moral degradation, and social oppression exacerbates, the glorious day of perfection draws nearer. There and then, the whole salvific community would be completely revealed (Rom 8:18–25). It is now for Christians to seize the opportunity to live out, as much as is possible, a semblance of the beauty that is to come, so that all can see and desire to be part of the new heaven and earth (Rev 21). The themes of "hope of glory" in the New Testament speak of the potential in Christians to make a difference, strengthened by the indwelling power of the Holy Spirit.

BIBLIOGRAPHY

Abuza, Zachary. *Militant Islam in Southeast Asia: Crucible of Terror*. Colorado: Lynne Rieneer Publishers, 2003.

Alam, Jobair. "The Current Rohingya Crisis in Myanmar in Historical Perspective." *Journal of Muslim Minority Affairs* 39, no. 1 (2019): 1–25.

Amnesty International. "Myanmar: Remaking Rakhine State." 12 March 2018. https://www.amnesty.org/en/documents/asa16/8018/2018/en/.

Bauckham, Richard, and Trevor Hart. *Hope against Hope: Christian Eschatology at the Turn of the Millennium*. Grand Rapids: Eerdmans, 1999.

Bheemaiah, J. "Dialectics of Caste Culture: A Social Crisis in Indian Nation." In *Social Science and Humanity: International Proceedings of Economics Development and Research*, vol. 5, part 2, edited by Feng Tao, 454–58. Singapore: IACSIT Press, 2011.

Biswas, Sujay. "A re-reading of Gandhi's and Ambedkar's Emancipatory Discourses for Social Action against Untouchability." *Community Development Journal* 58, no. 2 (2023): 188–205.

Blankenship, Lisa. *Changing the Subject: A Theory of Rhetorical Empathy*. Logan: Utah State University Press, 2019.

Bowler, Kate. *Blessed: A History of the American Prosperity Gospel*. Oxford; New York: Oxford University Press, 2013.

Burke, Trevor J. "Adoption and the Spirit in Romans 8." *EvQ* 70, no. 4 (1998): 311–24.

Chen, Shang-Jen. "Homosexuality in Twenty-First Century Asia." In *Asian Christian Ethics: Evangelical Perspectives*, edited by Aldrin M. Peñamora and Bernard K. Wong, 243–51. Carlisle: Langham Global Library, 2022.

Chia, Roland. *Hope for the World: The Christian Vision*. Global Christian Library. Carlisle: Langham Global Library, 2012.

Eleanor, Albert, and Lindsay Maizland, "The Rohingya Crisis." Council on Foreign Relations, 23 January 2020. https://www.cfr.org/backgrounder/rohingya-crisis.

Feal, Greg. "Apocalyptic Thought, Conspiracism and Jihad in Indonesia." *Contemporary Southeast Asia*, 41, no. 1. Special Issue, *Militant Islam in Southeast Asia: New Insights into Jihad in Indonesia, Malaysia and the Philippines* (2019): 63–85.

Goh, Yan Han. "Singapore Passes Laws to Decriminalise Gay Sex, Protect Definition of Marriage against Legal Challenge." *Straits Times*, 29 November 2022.

Habulan, Angelica et al. "Southeast Asia: Philippines, Indonesia, Malaysia, Myanmar, Thailand, Singapore, Online Extremism." *Counter Terrorist Trends and Analyses* 10, no. 1 (2018): 7–30.

Huang, Yingying, Kumi Smith, and Suiming Pan. "Changes and Correlates in Multiple Sexual Partnerships among Chinese Adult Women – Population-based Surveys in 2000 and 2006." *AIDS Care: Psychological and Socio-medical Aspects of AIDS/HIV*, no. 23, Sup. 1 (2011): 96–104.

Human Rights Watch. "'My Life is not your Porn': digital sex crimes in South Korea." June 2021. https://www.hrw.org/sites/default/files/media_2021/06/southkorea0621_web_1_0.pdf.

Immanuel, Babu. *Acts of the Apostles: An Exegetical and Contextual Commentary*. India Commentary on the New Testament. Minneapolis: Fortress Press, 2016.

Ivanhoe, Philip J. "Virtue Ethics and the Chinese Confucian Tradition." In *Virtue Ethics and Confucianism*, edited by Stephen Angle, and Michael Slote, 28–46. New York: Routledge Taylor and Francis Group, 2013.

Jenkins, Laura Dudley. *Religious Freedom and Mass Conversion in India*. Pennsylvania Studies in Human Rights. Philadelphia: University of Pennsylvania Press, 2019.

Jervis, L. Ann. "The Spirit brings Christ's Life to Live." In *Reading Paul's Letter to the Romans*, edited by Jerry L. Sumney, 139–56. RBS 73. Atlanta: Society of Biblical Literature, 2012.

Keener, Craig S. *Acts: An Exegetical Commentary*. 4 vols. Grand Rapids: Baker Academic, 2012.

Kolge, Nishikant. *Gandhi against Caste*. New Delhi: Oxford University Press, 2017.

Kowalski, Marcin. "The Brokerage of the Spirit in Romans 8." *CBQ* 80 (2018): 636–54.

Kumar, Nigel Ajay. "Renewed Action for Age-Old Concerns." In *Asian Christian Ethics: Evangelical Perspectives*, edited by Aldrin M. Peñamora and Bernard K. Wong, 275–99. Carlisle: Langham Global Library, 2022.

Leong, Siang-Nuan. "Windows to the Polemics against the So-Called Jews and Jezebel in Revelation: Insights from historical and co(n)textual analysis." PhD thesis. University of Edinburgh, 2009.

Lewis, Robert Brian. *Paul's "Spirit of Adoption" in its Roman Imperial Context.* LNTS. London: T&T Clark, 2018.

Lindsay, Hugh. "Adoption in Greek Law: Some Comparisons with the Roman World." *Newcastle Law Review* 3, no. 2 (1999): 91–110.

———. *Adoption in the Roman World.* Cambridge: Cambridge University Press, 2009.

Maccoby, Hyam. *Ritual and Morality: The Ritual Purity System and its Place in Judaism.* Cambridge: Cambridge University Press, 1999.

Malik, Suratha Kumar. "Dalit and the Historiography of Temple Entry Movements in India: Mapping Social Exclusion and Cultural Subjugation." *Contemporary Voice of Dalit* (2022): 1–14.

Menn, Jonathan. *Biblical Eschatology.* Eugene, Oregon: Resource Publications, 2013.

Michaels, J. Ramsey. "The Redemption of our Body," In *Romans & the People of God*, edited by Sven K. Soderlund, and N. T. Wright, 92–114. Grand Rapids: Eerdmans, 1999.

Middleton, J. Richard. *A New Heaven and a New Earth: Reclaiming Biblical Eschatology.* Grand Rapids: Baker Academic, 2014.

Moltmann, Jürgen. *The Theology of Hope: On the Ground and the Implications of a Christian Eschatology.* Translated by James W. Leitch. Minneapolis: Fortress Press, 1993.

———. *The Coming of God: Christian Eschatology.* Translated by Margaret Kohl. Minneapolis: Fortress Press, 1996.

National Council of Churches in Singapore. *A Christian Response to Homosexuality.* Singapore: Genesis Books, 2004.

Nelson, Andrew Christian. "Hyper Grace Theology: A Definition and Systematisation." PhD thesis. University of Aberdeen, 2021.

Neyrey, Jerome H. "The Idea of Purity in Mark's Gospel." *Semeia* 35 (1986): 91–128.

Osborne, Grant R. *The Hermeneutical Spiral: A Comprehensive Introduction to Biblical Interpretation.* Revised and expanded. Downers Grove: IVP Academic, 2006.

Parish, William L., Edward O. Laumann, and Sanyu A. Mojola. "Sexual Behavior in China: Trends and Comparisons." *Population and Development Review* 33, no. 4 (2007): 729–56.

Peñamora, Aldrin M. "The Way of the Cross and the Good Life." In *Asian Christian Ethics: Evangelical Perspectives*, edited by Aldrin M. Peñamora and Bernard K. Wong, 165–90. Carlisle: Langham Global Library, 2022.

Peppard, Michael. "Adopted and Begotten Sons of God: Paul and John on Divine Sonship." *CBQ* 73, no. 1 (2011): 92–110.

Phelan Jr., John E. *Essential Eschatology: Our Present and Future Hope.* Downers Grove, Illinois: InterVarsity Press, 2013.

Rao, Anupama. *The Caste Question: Dalits and the Politics of Modern India.* Berkeley: University of California Press, 2009.

Scott, James M. *Adoption as Sons of God: An Exegetical Investigation into the Background of* ΥΙΟΘΕΣΙΑ *in the Pauline Corpus.* WUNT 2/48. Tübingen: Mohr Siebeck, 1992.

Stenschke, Christoph W. *Luke's Portrait of Gentiles Prior to Their Coming to Faith.* WUNT 2/108. Tübingen: Mohr Siebeck, 1999.

Tirumurti, T. S. "Letter dated 25 May 2022 from the Chair of the Security Council Committee established pursuant to resolution 1988 (2011) addressed to the President of the Security Council." United Nations Security Council, May 26, 2022.

Tomlin, Graham. "Christians and Epicureans in 1 Corinthians." *JSNT* 68 (1997): 51–72.

Wallace, Daniel B. *Greek Grammar Beyond the Basics: An Exegetical Syntax of the New Testament.* Grand Rapids: Zondervan, 1996.

Yeo, Khiok-khng. "An Eschatological View of History in the New Testament: Messianic and Millenarian Hope." *AsJT* 15, no. 1 (2001): 38–51.

Zhang, Everett Yuehong. "China's Sexual Revolution." Pages 106–51 in *Deep China: The Moral Life of the Person, what Anthropology and Psychiatry tell us about China today.* Edited by Arthur Kleinman et al. Berkeley; Los Angeles; London: University of California Press, 2011.

Zheng, Weijun et al. "Detraditionalisation and Attitudes to Sex outside Marriage in China." *Culture, Health and Sexuality* 13, no. 5 (2011): 497–511.

Zundofer, Harriet. "Men, Women, Money, and Morality: The Development of China's Sexual Economy." *Feminist Economics* 22, no. 2 (2015): 1–23.

CHAPTER 7

LIBERTY FOR THE CAPTIVES AND GOOD NEWS FOR THE POOR

Thawng Ceu Hnin

INTRODUCTION

Pope Francis states, "Poverty is precisely at the heart of the Gospel. If we were to remove poverty from the Gospel, people would understand nothing about Jesus's message."[1] The issue of wealth and poverty is not something new. As Helen Rhee writes, "The issue of wealth and poverty for the Christian faith is as ancient as the original Jesus movement and reaches farther back to ancient Israelite thought and practices reflected in the Hebrew Scriptures."[2] It was a major issue during the biblical era and is still a significant social and economic issue today. According to the World Bank, over three hundred and twenty million people in Asia live in extreme poverty, with hundreds of millions living on less than $2.15 per day (178.57 INR). Hunger is a significant issue in Asia, with low-quality, deficient food essential for survival and growth.[3] In such times, how can we proclaim liberty for the captives and good news for the poor? How does the Bible address and relate to our realities?

This chapter considers the NT teachings on poverty and wealth. Specifically, we consider the causes of poverty in the NT, the identity of the poor, and Jesus's response to poverty. As we move along, we will also consider the NT portrayal of the rich and the church's responsibilities toward the poor inside and outside its walls. Finally, the chapter will briefly note the similarities and differences between the NT view – as seen in the teachings of Jesus, Paul, and James in particular – and the teachings of local Asian religious traditions. As we will see, Asian Christians are mandated to demonstrate our faith's distinctive

---

1. Carol Glatz, "Pope Francis: Concern for Sign of Gospel, Not Red Flag of Communism," *Catholic News Service*, 16 June 2015, https://www.ncronline.org/blogs/francis-chronicles/pope-francis-concern-poor-sign-gospel-not-red-flag-communism.
2. Helen Rhee, *Wealth and Poverty in Early Christianity* (Minneapolis: Fortress, 2017), ix.
3. Samuel Kofi Tetteh Baah et al., "September 2023 global poverty update from the World Bank: new data on poverty during the pandemic in Asia," https://blogs.worldbank.org/en/opendata/september-2023-global-poverty-update-world-bank-new-data-poverty-during-pandemic-asia.

vision for caring for the poor. However, we must first consider the causes of poverty in the Greco-Roman world of the NT.

CAUSES OF POVERTY IN THE BIBLICAL WORLD

Most people living in the Roman provinces were materially poor. We encounter these groups of people frequently in the life and ministry of Jesus. According to Christopher J. H. Wright, there are three significant causes of poverty in the OT. The first cause was "natural causes."[4] Natural disasters such as earthquakes, invasions of locusts, and drought devastated a "local economy." Secondly, "laziness" causes poverty. This sapiential teaching pervades the Book of Proverbs (e.g. 10:4; 21:5). Thirdly, the primary cause of poverty is "oppression."[5] This suggests that the rich become more prosperous by exploiting the poor. This "oppressive exploitation" takes sundry forms in the OT; for example, exploitation of the socially, economically, and ethically weak, misuse of power (corruption of political leaders), and judicial corruption.[6]

In the NT, the causes of poverty are attributed to oppression (e.g. Jas 2:6; 5:16), laziness (2 Thess 3:11–12), extravagance (e.g. Luke 15:11–24), natural disaster (e.g. Acts 16:26),[7] premature death, overpopulation,[8] and civil wars. For instance, when Vespasian captured Tarichea (AD 67 in Galilee), the homeless people, fugitives, rebels, and criminals were assassinated, jailed, or marketed because he thought these people were lethal political threats to the *Pax Romana* (Roman Peace). The repeated wars have caused economic, political, and religious instabilities.[9] Finally, one can also include taxation in the list. Gamaliel II said, "By four things does the empire exist: by its tolls, bathhouses, theatres, and crop taxes."[10] During the first century AD, taxation was the principal source of income for the Roman Empire, even though the

---

4. Christopher J. H. Wright, *Old Testament Ethics for the People of God* (Downers Grove: IVP Academic, 2004), 169.
5. Wright, *Old Testament Ethics*, 170.
6. Wright, *Old Testament Ethics*, 171–72.
7. Craig S. Keener, *The IVP Bible Background Commentary: New Testament* (Downers Grove: IVP Academic, 2014), 372.
8. While there seems to be no New Testament data addressing the issue of high population, Gildas Hamel argues that overpopulation was a major cause of poverty during the first century CE, especially in urban cities. See *Poverty and Charity in Roman Palestine: First Three Centuries C.E.*, NES 23 (Los Angeles: University of California Press, 1990), 159.
9. Luise Schottroff and Wolfgang Stegemann, *Jesus and the Hope of the Poor*, trans. Matthew J. O'Connell (New York: Orbis Books, 1986), 16.
10. Judah Goldin, trans., *The Fathers According to Rabbi Nathan*, Yale Judaica Series X (New Haven: Yale University Press, 1955), 116.

empire had accumulated immense wealth through its conquests.[11] Joachim Jeremias notes, "The state asserted its rights mainly through levying taxes."[12] The collected taxes were utilized to sustain and support Roman military activities.[13] Two taxes were regularly collected: *tributum soli* (land tax) and *tributum capitis* (poll tax). The former denotes taxes collected from land, houses, slaves, and ships within Roman provinces.[14] It was a tax on "agricultural produce" paid by those who used the land.[15] The latter refers to a "poll" or "head tax" levied on "men aged fourteen to sixty-five, and women twelve to sixty-five."[16] In addition, there were also taxes like requisitions, market tax, and tithes.[17] Because of these reasons, most of the Palestinian populace lived in poverty.

THE POOR IN THE SYNOPTIC GOSPELS

In the Gospel of Mark, the word poor (*ptōchos*) occurs only five times (10:21; 12:42–43; 14:5, 7). This does not mean that Mark has no other references for the poor. A careful reading of the Gospel shows various indirect references to and concerns for the poor in the Markan language. Thomas Hanks, for instance, indicates indirect references to poverty: the lifestyles of John the Baptist (1:6; 6:17, 27) and Jesus (6:3; 11:12; 14:65; 15:15, 19), the voluntary deprivation of the disciples (1:18, 20; 2:23–25; 6:8–9, 36–37; 9:41; 10:28–31), and the socioeconomic level of the crowds and their environment as reflected in Jesus's teaching (2:21 – the use of old, mended clothes; 5:2–3, 5; 7:11–13; 8:1–2; 12:1–2).[18]

As in Mark, *ptōchos* occurs in five places in the Gospel of Matthew (5:3; 11:5; 19:21; 26:9, 11). Despite minimal references to the poor, Matthew's concerns for the poor are also seen in the importance he gives to "almsgiving" (6:1–4) and in his "fierce denunciation of oppression" (23:1–36).[19] In 5:3–5,

---

11. James S. Jeffers, *The Greco-Roman World of the New Testament Era: Exploring the Background of Early Christianity* (Downers Grove: IVP Academic, 1999), 143.
12. Joachim Jeremias, *Jerusalem in the Time of Jesus*, trans. F. H. and C. H. Cave (Philadelphia, PA: Fortress, 1969), 124.
13. David J. Downs, "Economics, Taxes, and Tithes," in *The World of the New Testament: Cultural, Social, and Historical Contexts*, ed., Joel B. Green and Lee Martin McDonald (Grand Rapids: Baker Academic, 2013), 163.
14. Jeffers, *The Greco-Roman World*, 143.
15. Everett Ferguson, *Backgrounds of Early Christianity* (Grand Rapids: Eerdmans, 1993), 87.
16. Jeffers, *The Greco-Roman World*, 143.
17. Neyrey, "Who is Poor in the New Testament," n.p.
18. Thomas Hanks, "Poor, Poverty," *ABD* 5:416.
19. Hanks, "Poor, Poverty," *ABD* 5:417.

the poor are ranked with those who hunger, thirst and mourn. In 11:4–5, the Matthean poor comprise the blind, lame, lepers, deaf, and the dead.

Luke uses several Greek terms for poor, such as *endeēs, penichros, ptōchos*, and *chreia*. Of the four, *ptōchos* is the most crucial term for Luke. It occurs ten times (4:18; 6:20; 7:22; 16:20, 22; 14:13, 21; 18:22; 19:8; 21:3). The Lukan text shows his more profound concern for the poor. Who are the poor for Luke? The poor, for Luke, are those people who are imprisoned, blind, oppressed (4:18), widows (2:37; 7:12; 18:3–5; 21:2–3), lepers (5:12–13; 7:22; 17:12); lame (7:22), and the crowd (e.g. 4:30; 5:19). Similarly, Mark Allan Powell suggests that the poor and marginalized in Luke comprise the sick, differently-abled, slaves, lepers, shepherds, prostitutes, tax-collectors, Samaritans, gentiles, foreigners, refugees, children, the elderly, widows and women, the blind, and the beggars.[20] In Luke, the poor are also "the pious poor of the Hebrew Scriptures who are exploited, in part because of their association with God," says Darrell L. Bock.[21]

Jesus himself was materially poor. The synoptists agree that Jesus was from a low-income family. At his birth, his parents could not afford an inn (2:1–21). When performing the Mosaic purificatory rites, his parents could get only "a pair of doves or two young pigeons" (2:22–24 NIV). In the OT sacrificial system, if a person was materially poor and unable to afford a lamb, he may offer "two turtledoves" or "two young pigeons" (e.g. Lev 5:7; 12:8). Jesus, by profession, was a carpenter.

Moreover, Jesus was designated "the carpenter's son" or the "carpenter" (Matt 13:55; Mark 6:3 NIV). Carpentry as an occupational designation may refer to either the "building profession" or "cabinet-maker."[22] In either case, a carpenter was a "wage-earning day laborer."[23] Jesus and his disciples were not professional beggars but were "barely avoiding utter poverty."[24] The early church fathers also confirmed that Jesus came from an impoverished family. For instance, John Chrysostom highlights Jesus's humble beginnings and the importance of selecting disciples from disadvantaged backgrounds. Jesus chose impoverished individuals and built his table and clothes from everyday items. He traveled by foot, often becoming tired, and sat alone on the ground,

20. Mark Allan Powell, *What are They Saying about Luke* (New York: Paulist, 1989), 91.
21. Darrell L. Bock, *A Theology of Luke's Gospel and Acts* (Grand Rapids: Zondervan, 2011), 355.
22. Wolfgang Stegemann, *The Gospel and the Poor*, trans. Dietlinde Elliott (Philadelphia: Fortress, 1984), 24.
23. Stegemann, *The Gospel and the Poor*, 24.
24. Stegemann, *The Gospel and the Poor*, 24.

sometimes in the mountains or by the well, conversing with a Samaritan woman. His humble nature is a beacon of hope for those who wish to follow Jesus (*Homily on Matthew 20:29–30*, LXVI.2).

The Rich and Poor in Jesus's Teaching

Jesus customarily associated and dined with the poor, who were disregarded by society and exploited by the rich. Wolfgang Stegemann states, "The movement within Judaism in Palestine associated with the name of Jesus was a movement *of the poor for the poor.*"[25] Growing up in rural Galilee and from a low-income family, Jesus truly understood the pain of poverty. He encountered people who were materially, spiritually, and socially poor. The ensuing considers Jesus's attitude toward the accumulation of wealth.

Jesus and Materialism

The Cambridge English Dictionary defines materialism as "the belief that having money and possessions is the most important thing in life."[26] In light of this definition, we may pose the following questions. Is wealth accumulation unbiblical? Is a believer sinful if s/he owns a staggering amount of money? How did Jesus respond to it?

In the OT and second temple periods, material possessions were not considered sinful. From the beginning, God ordained humans to rule and have authority over the rest of creation. The material blessing and abundance of the Garden of Eden were created and intended for humans to enjoy.[27] God promised his people that absolute obedience to his word would bring good fortune (Deut 6:1–3).[28] Moses, for instance, warned the Israelites that they should never think their wealth came from their power and might (8:17). The Israelites were to remember that God was the ultimate source of their wealth (8:18). God commanded the rich through Moses that they were to stretch out their hands to the poor in the land (15:11) and seek justice for the poor because an act of generosity towards the poor is pleasing in the sight of God and brought divine blessing (Prov 19:17). In contrast, the love of money and

---

25. Stegemann, *The Gospel and the Poor*, 24.
26. The Cambridge English Dictionary, https://dictionary.cambridge.org/dictionary/english/materialism.
27. Craig L. Blomberg, *Neither Poverty nor Riches: A Biblical Theology of Material Possessions*, NSBT (England: Apollos, 1999), 34.
28. Ronald J. Sider, *Rich Christians in an Age of Hunger: Moving from Affluence to Generosity* (Dallas: Word Publishing, 1997), 101.

greediness for unjust gain was strictly prohibited and condemned (e.g. 1:19; Ps 62:10). There was severe destruction for those who placed their trust upon their wealth and possessions (Prov 11:28a).

In the NT, Jesus vehemently condemned the excessive love of money. In the synoptic Gospels, the rich young man asked Jesus a soteriological question: "Teacher, what good deed must I do to have eternal life?" (Matt 19:16 ESV; cf. Mark 10:17; Luke 18:18). Jesus replied to him with quotations from the OT commandments (e.g. Exod 20:2–17; Deut 5:6–21) and told the young man to sell his wealth and give to the poor for eternal treasure, causing him great sorrow as he had many possessions (Matt 19:21–22). Jesus's command calls for the "action of dispossession"[29] of wealth. His wealth hinders them from entering the kingdom of God. Similarly, Jesus, in the parable of the sower (13:1–23; Mark 4:1–20; Luke 8:4–15), speaks about four different soils upon which the seeds fell: the road, rocky ground, thorns, and good soil. He explains that the seeds that fell among the thorns represent those who hear the word, but because of their worry about the world, the deceitfulness of riches, and the pleasures of life, they remain unfruitful (Matt 13:22; Mark 4:19; Luke 8:14). Thus, Jesus's message is that the "distraction of material possessions in this life" is an obstacle to true discipleship.[30] Luke is highly pessimistic toward the sinful attitudes of the rich. The rich are shown as having unfortunate situations because they have already enjoyed everything on earth (11:41; 12:13–34; 16:1–13, 19–31; 18:18–30; 19:1–10).

Does this mean that all the rich will never inherit the kingdom of God? In Luke 19:1–10, we read the story of Zacchaeus, an economically prosperous chief tax-gatherer. This story represents the soteriological fact that "salvation is possible only by an act of God."[31] Zacchaeus suffered from social status poverty because of his profession. He worked directly for the Roman imperial state.[32] Economically, he was rich, but the people considered him a sinner, *hamartōlos* (19:2, 7). When he met Jesus, Zacchaeus was willing to renounce half of his possessions and give back as much as four times to those whom he cheated (19:8). His acts went beyond the requirement of Jewish taxes and levies.[33] This is the climax of Jesus's mission when he says he came to save sinners. Zacchaeus,

---

29. Thomas E. Schmidt, *Hostility to Wealth in the Synoptic Gospels*, JSNTSup 15 (Sheffield: Sheffield Academic, 1987), 112.

30. Blomberg, *Neither Poverty nor Riches*, 115.

31. Schmidt, *Hostility to Wealth in the Synoptic Gospels*, 159.

32. David H. Sick, "Zacchaeus as the Rich Host of Classical Satire," *BibInt* 24 (2016), 231.

33. Blomberg, *Neither Poverty nor Riches*, 141.

the sinner, meets the savior and becomes the saved. From a human point of view, the economically rich cannot enter the kingdom of God. Nevertheless, what is impossible with humans is possible with God. Zacchaeus's coming to Jesus means repenting from "his complicity in social injustice"[34] and embracing and living a new lifestyle.

Most Christians in Asian countries are converts from economically and socially disadvantaged backgrounds. For instance, it is said that about 90 percent of Pakistani Christians are Dalits from the *Chuhra* or *Mazhabi* Sikh groups.[35] *Chuhra* Sikhs are social outcasts who live across Pakistan and India.[36] If Saint Thomas's tradition is historically accurate, Thomas's stay in India extended from AD 52 to AD 72.[37] At his demise, the tradition reports that there were 6,850 Brahmans, 2,800 Kshatriyas, 3,750 Vaishyas, and 4,250 Shudras, coming to more than 17,480 souls.[38] However, today, most converts belong to lower castes. They identify with Scheduled Castes (Dalits), Scheduled Tribes, or backward classes.[39] Christian converts in India are disproportionately located in the South and some in the North East. In Myanmar, the Christian population constitutes 8.2 percent, most of whom are minorities who face significant discrimination.[40] In Indonesia, 87 percent of the people are Muslims, and 9.5 percent are Christians, who are minorities.[41] The majority of Asian Christians are not wealthy. As they are poor economically, their hearts are wide open to the message of the gospel of Jesus Christ. These Asian religious statistics show that it is challenging for the rich and the high castes to enter the kingdom of God, as it was in the time of Jesus.

---

34. Sider, *Rich Christians in an Age of Hunger*, 185.
35. Shreehari Paliath, "Why India Needs More Reliable Data on Dalit Christians and Muslims," 16 March 2021, https://scroll.in/article/989608/why-india-needs-more-reliable-data-on-dalit-christians-and-muslims.
36. Avinash Kumar and Surinder S. Jodhka, "Internal Classification of Scheduled Castes: the Punjab Story," *Economic and Political Weekly* 42, no. 43 (2007), n.p., https://www.epw.in/journal/2007/43/commentary/internal-classification-scheduled-castes-punjab-story.html.
37. Johnson Thomaskutty, *Saint Thomas the Apostle: New Testament, Apocrypha, and Historical Traditions*, JCTS 25 (London: T&T Clark, 2018), 186.
38. Robert Eric Frykenberg, *Christianity in India: From Beginnings to the Present* (Oxford: Oxford University Press, 2008), 100.
39. Ariana Monique Salazar, "8 Key Findings about Christians in India," *Pew Research Center*, 12 July 2021, https://www.pewresearch.org/fact-tank/2021/07/12/8-key-findings-about-christians-in-india/.
40. Elizabeth Koepping, "India, Pakistan, Bangladesh, Burma/Myanmar," in *Christianities in Asia*, ed. Peter C. Phan (Malden: Wiley-Blackwell, 2011): 9–44.
41. John Prior, "Indonesia," in *Christianities in Asia*, ed. Peter C. Phan (Malden: Wiley-Blackwell, 2011), 61–75.

Jesus and the Poor

Jesus states the purpose of his mission in Luke 4:18–19:

> The Spirit of the Lord is upon me because he anointed me to bring good news to the poor; he has sent me to proclaim liberty to the captives and recovery of sight to the blind, to send away those who have been oppressed in liberty, to proclaim the favorable year of the Lord.

The poor are the recipients of the Gospel. Jesus quotes these two verses from Isaiah 61:1–2 and 58:6.[42] Luke, however, has omitted two phrases from Isaiah: "to heal the broken-hearted" (61:1c NKJV) and "the day of vengeance of our God" (61:2b NKJV).[43] By quoting Isaiah, Luke presents the continuity of salvation history from the old to the new. In Isaiah, it was a prophetic announcement announced to the exilic returnees. However, Luke turns it into a "prediction," and its fulfillment is found in the "person, words, and deeds of Jesus of Nazareth."[44] In the following, we will briefly consider Luke's concern for the poor.

An Indian NT scholar, Arren Bennet Lawrence, has carefully crafted and showcased Luke's concern for the poor.[45] For example, Mary's *Magnificat* (Luke 1:46–55) shows Luke's concern for the poor. Mary praises God for bringing down the rulers from their thrones, lifting the humble, and filling the hungry with good things (1:52–53a). In contrast, the rich are sent away empty (1:53b).[46] Luke here reverses the social status of the rich and the poor. In Sermon on the Plain (6:20–26), Luke again focuses on the poor. He says, "Blessed are you who are poor" (6:20). The poor mentioned here are literally poor.[47] Luke here echoes the pious poor of the OT who were marginalized because of their association with God. In the OT, God's special care is given to the

---

42. Thomas E. Phillips, *Reading Issues of Wealth and Poverty in Luke-Acts* (Lewiston: Edwin Mellen, 2001), 96.

43. Joseph A. Fitzmyer, *The Gospel According to Luke: I–IX*, AB 28 (New York: Doubleday, 1981), 532.

44. Fitzmyer, *The Gospel According to Luke: I–IX*, 529.

45. See Arren Bennet Lawrence, "Messianic Imagination of the Poor in the Gospel of Luke," in *Towards an Integral Theology: Festschrift in Honour of Bishop Dr. M. Ezra Sargunam's 80th Birthday*, ed., Samuel Jayakumar and J. A. David Onesimu (New Delhi: Christian World Imprints, 2018), 15–37.

46. Lawrence, "Messianic Imagination," 18; Ben Witherington III, *Jesus & Money* (London: SPCK, 2010), 93.

47. Some scholars argue that the poor mentioned in Sermon on the Plain are spiritually poor. For instance, see R. H. Stein, *Luke*, NAC 24 (Nashville, TN: Broadman & Holman Publishers, 2001), 200. However, I would rather argue that they are literally poor. Alfred Plummer rightly

weak and socially afflicted (e.g. Deut 10:17–18; Pss 10:17–18; 68:5–6; 76:9; 146:7–10) who were anticipating future divine intervention (e.g. Ps 132:15; Ezek 34:15–16, 28; Isa 35:5–6; 61:1–2). Nevertheless, in Luke's Gospel, the future is realized in the present, and the poor have the good news preached to them. In other words, though the disciples were poor, they possessed the kingdom of God both now and then.

When the crowd asked John the Baptist about how they should demonstrate repentance and avoid the coming judgment, the Baptist said, "Whoever has two tunics is to share with him who has none, and whoever has food is to do likewise" (Luke 3:11; cf. Matt 3:7–10).[48] Here, the Lukan thrust is on sharing with the poor. In the same way, the tax collectors asked, "Teacher, what shall we do?" (3:12 ESV). The Baptist said to them, "Collect no more than you are authorized to do" (3:13 ESV). Likewise, the soldiers asked the same question. The Baptist replied to them, saying, "Do not extort money from anyone by threats or by false accusation and be content with your wages" (3:14 ESV). The Baptist's teaching reflects a society of justice in which everyone is equally treated and the poor are uplifted. In Luke 6:34–36, the evangelist again demonstrates his concern for the poor. Jesus's teaching in this section is the opposite of the teaching of his society. The society Jesus lived in says what is lent must be returned.

In contrast, Jesus teaches that one must lend even if the lendee cannot repay (6:35). In 12:33, Luke re-emphasizes his concern for the needy. The evangelist writes, "Sell your possessions and give to charity; make yourselves money belts which do not wear out, an unfailing treasure in heaven, where no thief comes near, nor moth destroys" (NASB). In the Matthean version (6:19–21), the expression "Sell your possessions and give to the needy" is not found. However, Luke added, "Sell your possessions and give to the needy." Adding this phrase is crucial to Luke's concern for the poor.

In Luke 7, John the Baptist sent a group of men to inquire whether Jesus is the expected Messiah of the OT or if they are to hope for another (7:20). In response to this inquiry, Jesus draws three Isaianic passages (Isa 35:5–6; 29:18–19; 61:1). Luke says, "the poor have the good news preached to them" (7:22c). The good news is that the blind see, the lame walk, the lepers are

---

said, "We have no right to supply τῷ πνεύματι from Mt. It is actual poverty that is here meant." *Luke: A Critical and Exegetical Commentary on the Gospel According to S. Luke* (London: T&T Clark, 1896), 180.

48. Witherington, *Jesus & Money*, 93.

cleansed, the deaf hear, and the dead are raised. Except for Matthew specifying Jesus as the speaker, Luke's words are identical to those of 11:4–6. Luke portrays Jesus as the beneficent Lord, while the poor are portrayed as the benefactors.[49] This verse repeats the theme of 4:18: the proclamation of good news to the poor.

As we see, Luke believes that "in Jesus's deeds, the time of salvation heralded by Isaiah has dawned."[50] Thus, according to Luke 7:22–23, Jesus, as an eschatological prophet, announces the arrival of the future era of salvation.[51] The poor are the special recipients of God's eschatological deliverance, and as Lawrence notes, "Jesus's Messianic identity is related to his Messianic imagination of the poor and sick."[52] Hence, preaching good news to the poor is not *a* mission of Jesus but *the* mission of Jesus.

THE RICH AND THE POOR IN PAUL

Although the theme of wealth and poverty are common in intertestamental Jewish wisdom literature, contemporary Greco-Roman literature, Synoptic Gospels, and James, Paul scarcely emphasizes the subject of riches, and the only detailed attention is 1 Timothy 6:6–10, and 17–19.[53] However, he does show concern for poor Christians, mentioning them in several letters (e.g. Gal 2:10; Rom 15:26; 1 Cor 13:3; 2 Cor 8:9; 9:9). For example, one of the problems Paul addresses at the church of Corinth is the growing tension between the rich and poor Christians. The rich had sufficient food, drink, and houses (11:21–22). The poor had nothing (11:22).[54] The rich consumed food and drink before the poor arrived. When the poor arrived, they had little or nothing to eat. In so doing, the rich were preserving "class distinctions characteristic of secular society."[55]

Thus, Paul uses the sacrament to establish social justice and equality. The rich are urged not to consider the poor second-class citizens in the church and society. For instance, in 12:13, Paul states, "For by one Spirit we were all baptized into one body, whether Jews or Greeks, whether slaves or free, and we

---

49. Joel B. Green, *The Gospel of Luke*, NICNT (Grand Rapids: Eerdmans, 1997), 296.
50. John Nolland, *Luke 1–9:20*, WBC 35A (Dallas: Word Books, 1989), 330.
51. I. Howard Marshall, *The Gospel of Luke: A Commentary on the Greek Text*, NIGTC (Leicester: Paternoster, 1978), 292.
52. Lawrence, "Messianic Imagination," 30.
53. T. E. Schmidt, "Riches and Poverty," in *DPL*, 826.
54. James D. G. Dunn, *The Theology of Paul the Apostle* (Grand Rapids: Eerdmans, 1998), 609.
55. Thomas R. Schreiner, *New Testament Theology: Magnifying God in Christ* (Grand Rapids: Baker Academic, 2008), 731.

were all made to drink of one Spirit" (NASB; see also Col 3:11). In Galatians 3:28, he reaffirms and says, "There is neither Jew nor Greek, there is neither slave nor free, there is no male and female; for you are all one in Christ Jesus" (NASB). Paul's dictum (the equality of all humans) is counter-cultural and anti-patriarchal. The ancient society was a society or government ruled or controlled only by men. For example, in the familial hierarchy of antiquity, the father, the head of the family, has supreme authority over his wife/wives, children, housemaids, and domestic slaves. Against this cultural stigma, Paul commands, "Masters, treat your bondservants justly and fairly, knowing that you also have a Master in heaven" (Col 4:1 ESV; see also Eph 6:9). No other ancient literature speaks of the masters treating their slaves with justice. Slaves were considered objects bought and sold at the slave markets.

In contrast, Paul commands the masters to treat their slaves with justice because they have their Master in heaven. Although he did not eradicate the ancient practice of slavery and the Roman familial pyramid, he revitalized the master-slave relationship by presenting Christ as the supreme Master of all. In this way, Paul gives importance to the equality of humankind. The Christian community that Paul has in mind is a community of difference rather than distance. He does not encourage Christians to segregate themselves from the rest of the world and inhabit the wilderness like the Qumran community. Instead, the Christians are exhorted to be *a* community of difference within *the* pagan community. Paul commands Christians to treat everyone equally regardless of economic status (rich or poor), social status (honored or shamed), and religious status (Judaic leaders or the people of the land).

In 1 Timothy 6:6–10, Paul speaks about godliness with contentment. Contentment in Stoic philosophy denotes a state of "independent of external circumstances"[56] or "self-sufficiency."[57] It is possible that Paul borrowed the Stoic concept of contentment and then Christianized and used it to refer to "an attitude of mind independent of externals and dependent only on God."[58] When one is reliant on externals, the externals take the place of God, which is equivalent to idolatry.

Paul then addresses those who want to get rich (1 Tim 6:9). He mentions three pitfalls in which these people get entangled: temptation, trap, and

---

56. T. D. Lea and H. P. Griffin, *1, 2 Timothy, Titus*, NAC 34 (Nashville: Broadman & Holman, 2001), 167.

57. G. W. Knight III, *The Pastoral Epistles: A Commentary on the Greek Text*, NIGTC (Grand Rapids: Eerdmans, 1992), 253.

58. Lea and Griffin, *1, 2 Timothy, Titus*, 167.

foolish and harmful desires. Having mentioned three pitfalls, in verse 10, he warns them with a maxim: "For the love of money is a root of all sorts of evil" (NASB). This adage is common in ancient literature. For instance, Diogenes of Sinope said, "The love of money is the mother city of all evils" (*Diogenes Laertius* 6.50).[59] Paul cites a traditional proverb because it speaks a timeless truth and strengthens his argument. Here, he does not condemn money but the love of money. It is a sin because it replaces God. Whatever replaces the place of God is idolatrous. The love of money can be overcome by letting the Holy Spirit take control of our lives. God is not blind to our needs and not deaf to our voices of petitions. Christians must seek God's kingdom and righteousness first, and he knows the rest (Matt 6:33).

THE RICH AND THE POOR IN JAMES

James appears to be a prophet who advocates for an egalitarian community. He is even called a "New Testament Amos."[60] In his epistle, James addresses the twelve tribes in Diaspora (1:1), the lowly brother and the rich (1:9–11), the rich and the poor (2:1–7), the killer (4:2), the tradesmen (4:13–17), and the large estate owners (5:1–6). Like Jesus, James attacks the rich and their mindset towards the poor. In 2:1–7, James addresses the issue of partiality in the church through his notion of sin.[61] For James, sin is often a social affair. James Riley Strange notes, "Sin *in James* is an offense that one community member commits against another."[62] In other words, those who disrespect the poor in the church and society, those who neglect to clothe, give shelter, and feed the destitute members of the church, sin (2:9).[63] The rich neglected and dishonored the poor in the community. Their acts caused James to write the statement: "Listen, my beloved brethren: did not God choose the poor of this world *to be* rich in faith and heirs of the kingdom which He promised to those who love Him?" (2:5 NASB). James, like Paul, echoes Jesus's statement: "Blessed are the poor in spirit, for theirs is the kingdom of heaven (Matt 5:3).[64]

---

59. M. Dibelius and H. Conzelmann, *The Pastoral Epistles: A Commentary on the Pastoral Epistles*, trans. Philip Buttolph and Adela Yarbro (Philadelphia: Fortress, 1972), 85.
60. William M. Tillman, "Social Justice in the Epistle of James: A New Testament Amos," *RevExp* 108 (2011): 417–27.
61. James Riley Strange, *The Moral World of James: Setting the Epistle in its Greco-Roman and Judaic Environments*, StBibLit 136 (New York: Peter Lang, 2010), 23.
62. Strange, *The Moral World of James*, 23. Italics mine.
63. Strange, *The Moral World of James*, 23.
64. Andrew Chester and Ralph P. Martin, *The Theology of the Letters of James, Peter, and Jude* (Cambridge: Cambridge University Press, 1999), 7.

In 2:5, James explains the poor with three conjoined terms: poor by the world's standard, rich in faith, and heirs of the kingdom.[65] For him, the poor can refer to "someone of devalued social means and status, someone in destitute or near-destitute circumstances, who has failed to maintain his standing in society and has fallen to a marginal position in the social order."[66] Or it can also refer to the class of "pious and humble people who put their trust in God for redemption and not in material wealth."[67] The rich oppressed them. However, God chose and sided with them.

This does not mean that the poor automatically belong to God.[68] They must be rich in faith. Rich in faith means "the extent of loyalty and commitment to God."[69] James shows that a person's social conditions did not affect God's choice. Instead, he is setting "God's concern in contrast to the lack of concern shown by the rich."[70] Favor is shown to the rich while the poor are subjected to insult. This is partiality and unacceptable because, for James, all humans are made in the likeness of God, regardless of a person's social status (3:9).

In 5:1–6, James condemns and utters a prophetic denunciation of the ruthless rich.[71] The addressees are the traveling merchants or pagans who do not necessarily profess to be members of the Christian community.[72] They were "abusive landowners who have padded their profits by withholding their workers' wages"[73] and were indicted for exploitative luxury (v. 5).[74] It is a self-centered use of resources.[75] For James, withholding or failing to pay the daily wages of the poor workers is a grave sin, and it leads the sinners to death (1:15). This idea echoes Paul's statement in Rom 6:23a: "For the wages of sin is death" (NASB). Unless they repent from their sin, the day of the Lord will bring death to them.

---

65. David H. Edgar, *Has God Not Chosen the Poor? The Social Setting of the Epistle of James* (Sheffield: Sheffield Academic Press, 2001), 112.

66. Edgar, *Has God Not Chosen the Poor?* 112.

67. R. P. Martin, *James*, WBC 48 (Dallas: Word, 2002), 65.

68. Schreiner, *New Testament Theology*, 598.

69. Edgar, *Has God Not Chosen the Poor?* 113.

70. Donald Guthrie, *New Testament Theology* (Downers Grove: InterVarsity Press, 1981), 146.

71. M. Dibelius and H. Greeven, *James: A Commentary on the Epistle of James*, trans. Michael A. Williams (Philadelphia: Fortress, 1976), 235; Edgar, *Has God Not Chosen the Poor?* 199.

72. Martin, *James*, 172; Edgar, *Has God Not Chosen the Poor?* 148.

73. Strange, *The Moral World of James*, 36.

74. Edgar, *Has God Not Chosen the Poor?* 204.

75. Todd Scacewater, "The Dynamic and Righteous Use of Wealth in James 5:1–6," *Journal of Markets and Morality* 20, no. 2 (2017): 236.

The theological and ethical perspectives of Jesus, Paul, and James provide a powerful message to twenty-first-century Christianity. Today, we witness how the underprivileged are abused in church and society. Some Christian leaders are afraid to challenge affluent Christians who oppress the poor since doing so will jeopardize the church's resources. On the other side, some Christians are incredibly wealthy in lip service but never reach out to the impoverished in the church or society. Poor workers are denied their rightful wages. The growth of wealth by evil means likewise plagues our culture and the world. With these kinds of abuses, we see a rise in moral deterioration in our rapacious culture. The morally deteriorating Christian society must take challenges from the teachings of Jesus, Paul, and James and transform our community into a community of justice in which everyone is looked at through the eyes of God.

THE PROPER USE OF WEALTH

The biblical teaching on properly using one's wealth does not originate in the New Testament but in the Old Testament. In Deuteronomy 15:7–8, 11, God says to the people of Israel,

> If there is a poor man with you, one of your brothers, in any of your towns in your land which the LORD your God is giving you, you shall not harden your heart, nor close your hand from your poor brother; but you shall freely open your hand to him, and shall generously lend him sufficient for his need *in* whatever he lacks. For the poor will never cease *to be* in the land; therefore, I command you, saying, "You shall freely open your hand to your brother, to your needy and poor in your land." (NASB)

Caring for the poor or almsgiving was a sacred obligation in the Israelite religious traditions. The book of the Covenant (Exod 20:22–23:19) displays a

> sabbatical year for debt servitude (21:2), grants the poor the produce of the land in the fallow year (23:10–11), and forbids the exploitation of the poor (22:22–27) and perversion of justice against them (23:6).[76]

The rich are not to oppress the poor, the Levites (Deut 14:27), resident aliens (Exod 23:9), and widows and orphans (Deut 24:17–18) because they are

---

76. Helen Rhee, *Loving the Poor, Saving the Rich: Wealth, Poverty, and Early Christian Formation* (Grand Rapids: Baker Academic, 2012), 27.

landless and helpless.[77] The one who gives alms offers a thank offering (Sirach 35:2).[78] The NT writers continue the OT teaching on sharing one's possessions with the poor.

In the parable of the rich young man, as mentioned earlier, Jesus told him to sell his goods. His command does not end there. He adds, "Give to the poor" (Mark 10:21; Matt 19:21; Luke 18:22). Again, Jesus says, in Luke 12:33, "sell your possessions and give to charity." This refers to "alms." In Luke's Gospel, "alms refer to charity directed to non-Christians."[79] Almsgiving is essential because the beggars depend on it.[80] It could be given and received through food, clothes, and money.[81] These synoptic data indicate how the rich can adequately use their wealth. In sharing with the poor, they store treasures in heaven, and no one can steal heavenly treasures (Matt 6:19–20; cf. Luke 12:21).

In his teaching on the proper use of wealth, Paul echoes Jesus's teaching. In Paul's understanding, the poor are the appropriate recipients of Christian liberality. In 1 Timothy 6:18, Paul told Timothy that the rich are to be rich in good works – generously sharing their wealth with the poor. In so doing, the rich are storing up treasure for the future (v. 19). This concept again echoes Jesus's teaching about storing one's treasure in heaven. For Paul, all a person has is a gift from God, and by giving to the poor, s/he imitates God (2 Cor 9:9; Acts 14:17). A person is truly wealthy when she distributes her wealth generously. By distributing liberally, she demonstrates the love of God. This idea is vividly expressed in 2 Corinthians 8:9, in which Paul sets Christ as the example of giving generously. He urges the Corinthians to be generous in giving because Christ, though rich, became poor for the sake of others.[82] In 2 Corinthians 8, Paul also sets the churches in Macedonia as the epitome of generous givers so that the Corinthian Christians would imitate them. In addition, for Paul, to give means having fellowship. In Romans 15:26, Paul expresses that the Macedonians and Achaians were pleased to fellowship with the poor saints in Jerusalem by sharing what they had in common.

Contemporary Christians can imitate the example of first-century Christians who are responsible for the poor. The churches Paul mentioned were willing to share their possessions with the poor saints in Jerusalem. They

---

77. Rhee, *Loving the Poor, Saving the Rich*, 28.
78. Neyrey, "Who is Poor in the New Testament," n. p.
79. Schottroff and Stegemann, *Jesus and the Hope of the Poor*, 109.
80. Stegemann, *The Gospel and the Poor*, 16.
81. Stegemann, *The Gospel and the Poor*, 18.
82. Guthrie, *New Testament Theology*, 667.

were in severe poverty in Jerusalem. This poverty could have been caused by (1) the pilgrims going to Jerusalem burdening the communities, (2) famine (Acts 11:27–30), and (3) economic persecutions (cf. Jas 1:9; 2:6–7; 5:1–6). Whatever the underlying reasons, one thing is sure: Jerusalem churches were poor and needed financial aid.[83] Paul took full responsibility for meeting their needs. For him, the physical well-being of the believers was also important along with their spiritual well-being, i.e., the holistic well-being of the believers.

In 1:27, James gives his definition of pure and undefiled religion. He says, "Pure and undefiled religion in the sight of *our* God and Father is this: to visit orphans and widows in their distress, *and* to keep oneself unstained by the world" (NASB 1995).[84] In this context, the verb "to visit" means "to care for," i.e., to care for the orphans and widows in their distress. James's language, "visiting the orphans and widows," echoes the OT piety (e.g. Isa 1:10–17; 58:6–7; Zech 7:10) and Jesus's teachings (Matt 25:35–45; Mark 12:40; Luke 18:2–8).[85] Orphans and widows are put together because they represent two social classes open to exploitation.[86] Thus, for James, meeting the needs of the orphans and widows is an act of sincere worship and a public demonstration of Christian spirituality. If we truly fear God, we will genuinely care for the poor in our respective societies. In the words of Jesus, it is about loving God and loving neighbors.

Many Christian leaders and pastors are enthusiastic about building and erecting magnificent megachurches. Church construction costs millions of rupees, and it has become a competition to some extent. Money is collected from church members on a monthly or yearly basis. Attending megachurches is a source of pride for many people. In this sense, I am not hostile to Christian leaders who lead the most prominent churches. However, there is one question we must always keep in mind. Are the basic needs of the poor members of the church being met? I do not intend to generalize that all megachurches in India and Asia are ignoring the basic needs of poor Christians. At the same time, there are instances where the basic needs of the poor are blatantly ignored, at least in my experience and neighborhood. As leaders build megachurches, we must also build the lives of the poor because the true church is not the visible structure but the believers. Paul sets himself as one of the best examples for

---

83. S. McKnight, "Collections for the Saints," in *DPL*, 144.
84. Rudolf Bultmann, *Theology of the New Testament*, trans. Kendrick Grobel (New York: Charles Scribner's Sons, 1951), 115.
85. Edgar, *Has God Not Chosen the Poor?* 166; Dibelius and Greeven, *James*, 121.
86. Martin, *James*, 52.

us to imitate. He was a good fundraiser, not for himself, but for those needing food and shelter. Many Christian leaders today are adept at raising funds for themselves or building kingdoms. Paul exhorts us to give generously to the poor. By sharing generously, we imitate God, express his love, and store treasure in heaven.

THE RIGHT USE OF WEALTH IN ASIAN RELIGIOUS TRADITIONS

So far, we have derived a biblical understanding of proper wealth management from the preceding discussion. As we have seen, biblical traditions strongly affirm that everything we have is a gracious gift from God. These material gifts are to be used as determined by the giver. We saw from Jesus's, Paul's, and James's teachings that the command of the faith is to give generously to the poor, an expression of God's unending love for non-Christians. We imitate God by giving without expecting anything in return.

This idea of sharing with the poor is profoundly relevant in our context. We have poor people in our respective churches, and our call is to meet their needs. In addition, extending our hands to the poor outside the church is also a biblical mandate. James reminds us that failure to care for the poor, orphans, and widows is a sin. Dishonoring the poor is a sin. Withholding the wages of daily workers is a sin, and the consequence of sin is death. These ideas convey a single message: we are genuinely wealthy only when we give generously.

Aspects of these biblical understandings of giving are also found in other Asian religious traditions. The concept of almsgiving, in particular, is common in Asian religious teachings. For instance, in Thai Buddhism, charity is a means to gain merit.[87] Interestingly, Buddhism does not seek publicity for charity. Generosity is one of Buddhism's Perfections (*paramitas*), but to be perfect, one must be selfless, without expectation of reward or praise. This concept of secrecy in giving resembles Jesus's teaching. Jesus taught the disciples that when they give to the poor, they should not shout about it but rather keep it secret so that God, who sees it in secret, will reward them (Matt 6:3–4). In Myanmar, the country where I grew up, Buddhist devotees are encouraged to give alms to monks, nuns, and temples, with the promise that doing so will bring merit to the divers. Such merit is construed as spiritual maturity, and developing the selfless intention of doing good for others leads to enlightenment.

---

87. Panya Namsanga, "The Concept of Charity in Buddhism Philosophy," *JIBS* 7, no. 2 (2016): 72.

In Islam, the word charity is derived from the Arabic word *ṣadaqah*. The word means "righteousness" and is a noble or voluntary act of giving by a person to others that is sanctified for the sake of Allah in various forms and ways.[88] Muslims believe that properties and wealth are not rewards for their good deeds but "a free grace of God delivered as a trust charge, *amanat*."[89] The Islamic religious tradition says that a portion of the wealth of the rich belongs to the needy. Surah 51.19 of the Qur'an reads, "And in their wealth, the beggar and the outcast had due share." Similarly, Surah 70.22–25 reads, "The (righteous) worshippers (are those) who are steadfast in prayer and in whose wealth there is a right acknowledged for the beggar and the destitute."[90] Islam teaches that charitable giving is a means of spiritual purification, a tool for constructing socioeconomic sustainability, and a means for social reforms that result in the well-being of an individual and society in this world and hereafter.[91]

Dana (giving) in Hinduism is an essential part of one's *dharma* (religious duty).[92] *Bhagavadgita* speaks of three types of giving: a gift without any expectation of appreciation or reward, a reluctant gift, and a gift without regard for the recipient's feelings and at the wrong time (17.20–22).[93] *Anna dana*, sharing food with others, is one of the most familiar forms of giving, and all sections of Indian society practice it.[94]

In Confucianism, *shi* denotes giving. It is an act of compassion offered for the sake of others. When a person of *ren* (benevolence) sees a widow or widower, an orphan or an aged person, the poor or the beggar who is neglected, s/he extends a helping hand.[95] Every Confucian must have this attitude when giving: "Remember what you received; forget what you gave."[96]

The concept of charity in Taoism (a.k.a. Daoism) is likewise of interest. It teaches and promotes three charitable principles manifested by the earth:

---

88. Salwa Amirah Awang et al., "The Concept of Charity in Islam: An Analysis of the Verses of Quran and Hadith," *Journal of Usuluddin* 45, no. 1 (2017): 141–72.
89. Edmund Weber, "Charity of Religions with Special Reference to Hinduism, Islam, and Christianity: An Interreligious Perspective," *JRC* 213 (2016): 4.
90. Weber, "Charity of Religions," 4.
91. Awang et al., "The Concept of Charity in Islam," 142.
92. R. S. Sugirtharajah, "Traditions of Giving in Hinduism," *Alliance Magazine*, 1 September 2001, https://www.alliancemagazine.org/feature/traditions-of-giving-in-hinduism/.
93. Sugirtharajah, "Traditions of Giving in Hinduism," n.p. Notably, there is some overlap here with Jesus's teaching in Matthew 6:1–4.
94. Sugirtharajah, "Traditions of Giving in Hinduism," n.p.
95. Lai Pan-chiu and Peter Lee, "Traditions of Giving in Confucianism," *Alliance Magazine*, 1 March 2002, https://www.alliancemagazine.org/analysis/traditions-of-giving-in-confucianism/.
96. Lai and Lee, "Traditions of Giving in Confucianism," n.p.

generating without claim, nurturing without ownership, and facilitating based on altruistic love with no intention of control.[97] Together, these principles mean that when one does charitable work, one must generate resources without claiming ownership, nurture the poor without claiming ownership, and perform charitable work out of love. These principles once again echo Jesus's teaching, namely, the attitude one must have when giving to the poor. Furthermore, three Daoist treasures are considered to be central to the spirit of charity and the heart of compassion: the *Ci* (kindness or parental love), the *Jian* (simplicity, frugality, thriftiness), and the *Bugan wei tianxia xian* (not leading the world).[98] *Ci* will ensure that the charitable work is done gently, kindly, and compassionately. *Jian* will ensure that the greedy heart is reduced. *Bugan wei tianxia xian* will instill caution and respect in human hearts, ensuring that Daoist charity is carried out as widely as possible to benefit all beings under heaven.[99]

While charity is practiced in all Asian religious scriptures and traditions, the concept of charity in Christianity is distinctive. In the Christian faith, caring for the poor is both a mandate and a symbol of faith. We do not give to the poor and needy to be saved. We give because we have been saved and are God's children. For Christians, God is the ultimate giver, and he demonstrated his generosity by giving his only son, Jesus Christ. Thus, by giving, we imitate him and reveal who God is to the world. Hence, genuine charity is missional.

CONCLUSION

The above study helps us understand that the early Christian community comprised various social and economic strata, i.e., the rich and the poor. The poor in the NT are the sick, the differently-abled (e.g. lame, blind, deaf – they are poor because they could not earn or make money), slaves, lepers, shepherds, prostitutes, tax collectors, Samaritans, Gentiles, foreigners, refugees, children, the elderly, widows, and women, the blind, the beggars, and the pious poor (e.g. association of the disciples with Jesus causes social oppression). For these people, the message of good news has come. Jesus brought holistic liberation to these people through speaking, touching, dining, and

---

97. Yanxia Zhao, "The Spirit of Charity and Compassion in Daoist Religion," *Sociology and Anthropology* 3, no. 2 (2015): 122–35.
98. Zhao, "The Spirit of Charity," 128.
99. Zhao, "The Spirit of Charity," 128–29.

healing. Furthermore, the message of Jesus is repeated by Paul and James for their respective communities.

In contrast, the rich are often criticized and condemned for their unwillingness to distribute to the needy and for their oppression and marginalization of the poor. The biblical teaching is that wealth should never be used to exploit the poor. Instead, it should be used to empower the poor. For Christians, riches should never be our social status marker. Instead, we should find our identity in God. Thus, Jesus, Paul, and James condemn the rich and their trust in possession, preventing them from entering the kingdom of God. The readers are beseeched to establish a Christian community of love in which they love, help, and care for one another. Christians are not called to establish a distance community but rather a different community. In giving liberally, we imitate God, our Creator, and demonstrate his love to the world. A Christian is wealthy only when she shares liberally with the poor and needy.

BIBLIOGRAPHY

Awang, Salwa Amirah, Fidlizan Muhammad, Joni Tamkin Borhan, and Mohammad Taqiuddin Mohamad. "The Concept of Charity in Islam: An Analysis of the Verses of Quran and Hadith." *Journal of Usuluddin* 45, no. 1 (2017): 141–72.

Baah, Samuel Kofi Tetteh, R. Andres Castaneda Aguilar, Carolina Diaz-Bonilla, Tony Fujs, Christoph Lakner, Minh Cong Nguyen, and Martha Vireros. "September 2023 global poverty update from the World Bank: new data on poverty during the pandemic in Asia." https://blogs.worldbank.org/en/opendata/september-2023-global-poverty-update-world-bank-new-data-poverty-during-pandemic-asia.

Blomberg, Craig L. *Neither Poverty nor Riches: A Biblical Theology of Material Possessions.* NSBT. England: Apollos, 1999.

Bock, Darrell L. *A Theology of Luke's Gospel and Acts.* Grand Rapids: Zondervan, 2011.

Bowen, Deborah C. "Blessed are the Poor in Spirit: Imagining Excellence Otherwise." *International Journal of Christianity & Education* 14, no. 1 (2012): 7–17.

Bultmann, Rudolf. *Theology of the New Testament.* Translated by Kendrick Grobel. New York: Charles Scribner's Sons, 1951.

Chester, Andrew, and Ralph P. Martin. *The Theology of the Letters of James, Peter, and Jude.* Cambridge: Cambridge University Press, 1999.

Chrysostom, John. *Homilies on the Gospel of St. Matthew: Part I: Homilies 1–25.* Translated by George Prevost. New Jersey: Gorgias Press, 1843, 2011.

Dibelius, M. and H. Conzelmann. *The Pastoral Epistles: A Commentary on the Pastoral Epistles*. Translated by Philip Buttolph and Adela Yarbro. Philadelphia: Fortress, 1972.

———. and H. Greeven. *James: A Commentary on the Epistle of James*. Translated by Michael A. Williams. Philadelphia: Fortress, 1976.

Downs, David J. "Economics, Taxes, and Tithes." In *The World of the New Testament: Cultural, Social, and Historical Contexts*, edited by Joel B. Green and Lee Martin McDonald, 156–68. Grand Rapids: Baker Academic, 2013.

Dunn, James D. G. *The Theology of Paul the Apostle*. Grand Rapids: Eerdmans, 1998.

Edgar, David H. *Has God Not Chosen the Poor? The Social Setting of the Epistle of James*. JSNTSup 206. Sheffield: Sheffield Academic Press, 2001.

Ferguson, Everett. *Backgrounds of Early Christianity*. Grand Rapids: Eerdmans, 1993.

Fitzmyer, Joseph A. *The Gospel According to Luke: I–IX*. AB 28. New York: Doubleday, 1981.

Friesen, Steven J. "Poverty in Pauline Studies: Beyond the So-called New Consensus." *JSNT* 26, no. 3 (2004): 323–61.

Frykenberg, Robert Eric. *Christianity in India: From Beginnings to the Present*. Oxford: Oxford University Press, 2008.

Glatz, Carol. "Pope Francis: Concern for Sign of Gospel, Not Red Flag of Communism." *Catholic News Service*, 16 June 2015. https://www.ncronline.org/blogs/francis-chronicles/pope-francis-concern-poor-sign-gospel-not-red-flag-communism.

Green, Joel B. *The Gospel of Luke*. NICNT. Grand Rapids: Eerdmans, 1997.

Guthrie, Donald. *New Testament Theology*. Downers Grove: InterVarsity Press, 1981.

Hamel, Gildas. *Poverty and Charity in Roman Palestine: First Three Centuries C.E.* NES 23. Los Angeles: University of California Press, 1990.

Jeffers, James S. *The Greco-Roman World of the New Testament Era: Exploring the Background of Early Christianity*. Downers Grove: IVP Academic, 1999.

Jeremias, Joachim. *Jerusalem in the Time of Jesus*. Translated by F. H. and C. H. Cave. Philadelphia: Fortress, 1969.

Johnson, Luke Timothy. *Sharing Possessions: What Faith Demands*. Grand Rapids: Eerdmans, 2011.

Keener, Craig S. *The IVP Bible Background Commentary: New Testament*. Downers Grove: IVP Academic, 2014.

Knight III, G.W. *The Pastoral Epistles: A Commentary on the Greek Text*. NIGTC. Grand Rapids: Eerdmans, 1992.

Koepping, Elizabeth. "India, Pakistan, Bangladesh, Burma/Myanmar." Pages 9–42 in *Christianities in Asia*. Edited by Peter C. Phan. Malden: Wiley-Blackwell, 2011.

Krishan, Y. "Buddhism and Caste System." *East and West* 48, nos. 1–2 (1998): 41–55.

Kumar, Avinash, and Surinder S. Jodhka. "Internal Classification of Scheduled Castes: the Punjab Story." *Economic and Political Weekly* 42, no. 43 (2007). https://www.epw.in/journal/2007/43/commentary/internal-classification-scheduled-castes-punjab-story.html.

Laertius, Diogenes. *Lives of Eminent Philosophers*. Translated by R.D . Hicks. London: William Heinemann, 1925.

Lai, Pan-chiu, and Peter Lee. "Traditions of Giving in Confucianism." *Alliance Magazine*, 1 March 2002. https://www.alliancemagazine.org/analysis/traditions-of-giving-in-confucianism/.

Lawrence, Arren Bennet. "Messianic Imagination of the Poor in the Gospel of Luke." In *Towards an Integral Theology: Festschrift in Honour of Bishop Dr. M. Ezra Sargunam's 80th Birthday*, edited by Samuel Jayakumar and J. A. David Onesimu, 15-37. New Delhi: Christian World Imprints, 2018.

Lea, T. D., and H. P. Griffin. *1, 2 Timothy, Titus*. NAC 34. Nashville, TN: Broadman & Holman, 2001.

Lim, Kar Yong. "The New Testament and the Sociocultural and Religious Realities of the Asian Contexts." In *An Asian Introduction to the New Testament*, edited by Johnson Thomaskutty, 5–27. Minneapolis: Fortress, 2022.

Malina, Bruce J. "Wealth and Poverty in the New Testament and its World." *Int* 41, no. 4 (1987): 354–67.

Marshall, I. Howard. *The Gospel of Luke: A Commentary on the Greek Text*. NIGTC. England: Paternoster, 1978.

McKnight, S. "Collections for the Saints." *DPL*, 143–47.

Namsanga, Panya. "The Concept of Charity in Buddhism Philosophy." *JIBS* 7, no. 2 (2016): 66–77.

Nolland, John. *Luke 1–9:20*. WBC 35A. Dallas: Word Books, 1989.

Paliath, Shreehari. "Why India Needs More Reliable Data on Dalit Christians and Muslims," 16 March 2021. https://scroll.in/article/989608/why-india-needs-more-reliable-data-on-dalit-christians-and-muslims.

Phillips, Thomas E. *Reading Issues of Wealth and Poverty in Luke-Acts*. Lewiston, ID: Edwin Mellen, 2001.

Plummer, A. *Luke: A Critical and Exegetical Commentary on the Gospel According to S. Luke*. London: T&T Clark, 1896.

Powell, Mark Allan. *What are They Saying about Luke?* New York: Paulist, 1989.

Prior, John. "Indonesia." In *Christianities in Asia*, edited by Peter C. Phan, 61–75. Malden: Wiley-Blackwell, 2011.

Rhee, Helen. *Wealth and Poverty in Early Christianity*. Minneapolis: Fortress, 2017.

———. *Loving the Poor, Saving the Rich: Wealth, Poverty, and Early Christian Formation*. Grand Rapids: Baker Academic, 2012.

Salazar, Ariana Monique. "8 Key Findings about Christians in India." *Pew Research Center* (12 July 2021). https://www.pewresearch.org/fact-tank/2021/07/12/8-key-findings-about-christians-in-india/.

Scacewater, Todd. "The Dynamic and Righteous Use of Wealth in James 5:1–6." *Journal of Markets and Morality* 20, no. 2 (2017): 227–42.

Schmidt, T. E. "Riches and Poverty." *DPL* 826–27.

———. *Hostility to Wealth in the Synoptic Gospels*. JSNTSup 15. England: Sheffield Academic Press, 1987.

Schottroff, Luise, and Wolfgang Stegemann. *Jesus and the Hope of the Poor*. Translated by Matthew J. O'Connell. New York: Orbis Books, 1986.

Schreiner, Thomas R. *New Testament Theology: Magnifying God in Christ*. Grand Rapids: Baker Academic, 2008.

Sick, David H. "Zacchaeus as the Rich Host of Classical Satire." *BibInt* 24 (2016): 229–44.

Sider, Ronald J. *Rich Christians in an Age of Hunger: Moving from Affluence to Generosity*. Dallas: Word Publishing, 1997.

Stegemann, Wolfgang. *The Gospel and the Poor*. Translated by Dietlinde Elliott. Philadelphia: Fortress, 1984.

Stein, R. H. *Luke*. NAC 24. Nashville: Broadman & Holman Publishers, 2001.

Strange, James Riley. *The Moral World of James: Setting the Epistle in its Greco-Roman and Judaic Environments*. StBibLit 136. New York: Peter Lang, 2010.

Sugirtharajah, R. Sharada. "Traditions of Giving in Hinduism." *Alliance Magazine*, 1 September 2001. https://www.alliancemagazine.org/feature/traditions-of-giving-in-hinduism/.

The Fathers According to Rabbi Nathan. Translated by Judah Goldin. Yale Judaica Series X. New Haven: Yale University Press, 1955.

Thomaskutty, Johnson. *Saint Thomas the Apostle: New Testament, Apocrypha, and Historical Traditions*. JCTS 25. London: T&T Clark, 2018.

Tillman, William M. "Social Justice in the Epistle of James: A New Testament Amos." *RevExp* 108 (2011): 417–27.

Weber, Edmund. "Charity of Religions with Special Reference to Hinduism, Islam, and Christianity: An Interreligious Perspective." *JRC* 213 (2016): 1–12.

Witherington III, Ben. *Jesus & Money*. London: SPCK, 2010.

Wright, Christopher J. H. *Old Testament Ethics for the People of God*. Downers Grove: IVP Academic, 2004.

Zhao, Yanxia. "The Spirit of Charity and Compassion in Daoist Religion." *Sociology and Anthropology* 3, no. 2 (2015): 122–35.

CHAPTER 8

RECONCILIATION AND JUSTICE

A Study of Samaria and Spatial
Perspective in Luke-Acts

Kazuhiko Yamazaki-Ransom

INTRODUCTION

I have been invited to participate in the annual Christian Forum for Reconciliation in Northeast Asia, hosted by the Northeast Asia Reconciliation Initiative (NARI), since 2019.[1] At this forum, Christians from various denominational backgrounds, nationalities (South Korea, Mainland China, Hong Kong, Taiwan, Japan, the U.S., and Canada), races, ages and genders get together. Each year we spend several days together to study, discuss, eat, laugh, cry, pray, and worship God. These are things which should not come naturally for such a group, considering the enormous historical, political, and social problems existing among the groups that are present. But when we just spend time together, something happens.

In 2019 we got together on Jeju Island in Korea and took a pilgrimage to the historic site of the Jeju April 3rd massacre in 1948, in which about one tenth of the islanders were killed by the Korean government. Through such a journey – both physically and symbolically – with this diverse group of people, I felt myself *decentralized*: decentering my own denominational, national, geographical, and cultural identity. And I began to focus on what unites us despite the great diversity among us – the sovereign lordship of Jesus Christ. It was a *spatial* experience: a new kind of space was created through the gathering of Christians from diverse backgrounds.

Since various kinds of social relationships are inseparably tied to space, the issue of social justice has a spatial dimension. The transformation from

---

1. For more about NARI, visit https://neareconciliation.com/. Due to the COVID-19 crisis the annual forums of 2020 and 2021 were held solely online, and in 2022 it was hybrid, but they were still a beneficial means of thirdspace creation nonetheless.

injustice to justice is accompanied by a change in people's perception of and engagement with space. How is this understood in terms of the kingdom of God? In this chapter, we will propose a fresh reading of Luke's narrative about Samaria and Samaritans, informed by recent developments in spatial theory, and explore its significance in the contemporary situation in Asia.

THE "SPATIAL TURN" IN BIBLICAL STUDIES

What is space? The general everyday definition of the term would be something like "a limited extent in one, two, or three dimensions," "an extent set apart or available," or "the distance from other people or things that a person needs in order to remain comfortable."[2] In other words, space is considered as some kind of container in which things exist. However, in the last century people have begun to see space as something more than just a neutral background or stage for human activities. Through the works by Henri Lefebvre, David Harvey, Edward Soja, and others, people increasingly have come to see space as socially produced or constructed.[3]

Based on Lefebvre's spatial theory, Soja posits three kinds of space. *Firstspace* is a "perceived space" related to the experience of the objective, material world. *Secondspace* is a theoretical, "conceived space" produced through subjective ideas about space.[4] Soja's idea of *thirdspace* goes beyond the dualism of firstspace and secondspace: it is a "lived space," which is simultaneously real and imagined and more.[5] Thirdspace has the potential for social transformation, creating "counterspace" for the existing social order.[6] In the case of my experience at the beginning of this essay, the physical volcanic island of Jeju is a firstspace. The secondspace is Jeju Special Autonomous Province, one of South Korea's administrative divisions, known as a popular holiday destination but which also has grave historical memories of massacre and social division

---

2. Merriam Webster Online, s.v. "space (n)," https://www.merriam-webster.com/dictionary/space.
3. See Henri Lefebvre, *The Production of Space*, trans. Donald Nicholson-Smith (Malden: Wiley-Blackwell, 1992); David Harvey, *The Condition of Postmodernity: An Enquiry into the Origins of Cultural Change* (Oxford: Wiley-Blackwell, 1992); and Edward W. Soja, *Thirdspace: Journeys to Los Angeles and Other Real-and-Imagined Places* (Cambridge, MA: Blackwell, 1996).
4. See Soja, *Thirdspace*, 10.
5. Soja, *Thirdspace*, 10–11. This type of three-part scheme is common among the spatial theories of Lefebvre, Harvey and Soja, as summarized in Matthew Sleeman, *Geography and the Ascension Narrative in Acts* (Cambridge: Cambridge University Press, 2013), 43.
6. See Soja, *Thirdspace*, 68.

attached to it. The thirdspace is Jeju as a place of reconciliation and unity under the heavenly lordship of Jesus Christ.[7]

The concept of thirdspace has significant implications for the discussion of systemic and social evil. If space is socially constructed, such space is inseparably connected with existing social relations. As Soja states, "[T]he social and the spatial are dialectically intertwined, mutually (and often problematically) formative and consequential."[8] Different perspectives on space reflect different social interests and agendas.[9] Thus, creating a new kind of space has a potentially liberating impact against systemic social evil of a society.

This so-called "spatial turn" described above has had a great impact on various human and social sciences, and biblical studies is no exception.[10] In Lukan studies, scholarly approaches to Luke-Acts have been predominantly temporal/historical, as it is typically reflected in the title of Hans Conzelmann's classic work, *Die Mitte der Zeit*.[11] However, a spatial approach to Luke's two-volume work began to appear in recent years. For example, Moxnes discusses the spatial understanding of the kingdom of God in Luke's Gospel, using Harvey's spatial theory.[12]

Probably the most extensive discussion of the spatial interpretation of Luke-Acts is that of Matthew Sleeman, who discusses the significance of the ascension in Acts, applying Soja's spatial theory. Sleeman argues that Christ, who ascended to heaven physically (namely, firstspatially) and thus absent from

---

7. Another somewhat recent social example would be George Floyd Square in Minneapolis, U.S.A., officially renamed in 2022 after George Floyd, an African American murdered by a white police officer in 2020. The physical intersection of 38th and Chicago in Minneapolis being the firstspace, the secondspace being the location marked by systemic racism and violence, and the thirdspace being the commemorative square as a touchstone for the entire Black Lives Matter movement.

8. Edward W. Soja, *Seeking Spatial Justice* (Minneapolis: University of Minnesota Press, 2010), 18.

9. As Edward Said states, "Just as none of us is outside or beyond geography, none of us is completely free from the struggle over geography. That struggle is complex and interesting because it is not only about soldiers and cannons but also about ideas, about forms, about images and imaginings." Edward W. Said, *Culture and Imperialism* (New York: Knopf, 1993), 7.

10. See Eric C. Stewart, "New Testament Space/Spatiality," *BTB* 42, no. 3 (2012): 139–50 and the bibliography attached to the article.

11. Literally, "the center of time." English translation is Hans Conzelmann, *The Theology of St. Luke*, trans. Geoffrey Buswell (New York: Harper & Row, 1960).

12. Halvor Moxnes, "Kingdom Takes Place: Transformations of Place and Power in the Kingdom of God in the Gospel of Luke," in *Social Scientific Models for Interpreting the Bible: Essays by the Context Group in Honor of Bruce J. Malina*, ed. John J. Pilch, BibInt 53 (Leiden: Brill, 2001), 176–209. Moxnes also discusses Jesus's Galilean ministry from spatial perspective in *Putting Jesus in His Place: A Radical Vision of Household and Kingdom* (Louisville: WJKP, 2003).

the earth, nevertheless guides the early church's ministry on earth throughout the narrative of Acts. That, he states, is Christ's sovereign work of transforming earthly spaces thirdspatially against their competing secondspatial significances. Space in Acts, thus, is more than just a neutral background for the story but plays a more active role. Sleeman argues that, by adding a spatial dimension to the traditional historical/temporal readings, a more comprehensive narrative understanding becomes possible. Luke was not only the first historian of the church, but also "the first Christian geographer."[13]

THE KINGDOM OF GOD IN SPATIAL PERSPECTIVE

The central message of Jesus's good news was the kingdom of God.[14] In Luke-Acts, Jesus proclaims "the good news of the kingdom of God" (Luke 4:43), and the disciples proclaim Jesus and the kingdom of God (Acts 8:12; 28:31). The modern scholarship of the NT concept of the kingdom of God started by understanding it as God's eschatological reign revealed in history, as opposed to the ahistorical, ethical understanding of the kingdom by the nineteenth-century liberal theologians.[15] As is seen in the emphasis on eschatology, the kingdom of God was often understood from a temporal point of view. This is clear from the enduring scholarly influence of Gustaf Dalman's understanding of the kingdom as God's "rule" as opposed to his "territory."[16]

Towards the end of the twentieth century, however, some scholars began to approach the kingdom of God from a spatial perspective. According to Moxnes, the "kingdom of God" that Jesus proclaimed was a new, alternative "space" to the existing spaces constructed by social order, the Roman imperial domination, the cosmic rule of Satan, etc. in Palestine and especially in Galilee. Moxnes understands the Lukan concept of the kingdom of God as "spaces of representation" that present a different way to structure "material practices."[17] It is "a vision of a liberated space that challenges the socio-political structure

---

13. Sleeman, *Geography*, 264.
14. For example, see Mark 1:14–15.
15. See Norio Yamaguchi, *"Kami no Okoku" wo Motomete: Kindai Iko no Kenkyushi* [In Search of the "Kingdom of God": Research History Since the Modern Period], rev. ed. (Tokyo: Yobel, 2021), 27.
16. Yamaguchi, *"Kami no Okoku,"* 34. Criticizing the understanding of the kingdom as "rule" since Dalman, Schüssler Fiorenza refuses to translate the Greek term *basileia*, and emphasizes the territorial dimension of *basileia*. See Elisabeth Schüssler Fiorenza, *Jesus: Miriam's Child, Sophia's Prophet: Critical Issues in Feminist Christology*, 2nd ed. (London: Bloomsbury, 2015), 98–99.
17. Moxnes, "Kingdom Takes Place," 191.

of society."[18] Using Soja's terminology, the kingdom of God can be understood as "thirdspace" that transforms the existing social structure.[19]

In the discussion below I will discuss Luke's portrayal of Samaritans in his two-volume work in light of the spatial perspective. For Luke, the reconciliation between Jews and Samaritans plays an important role in the coming of God's kingdom and the restoration of biblical Israel.

SAMARITANS IN LUKE-ACTS

Among the synoptic evangelists, Luke shows distinct interest in Samaria and Samaritans. Mark makes no mention of Samaria or Samaritans, and Matthew makes only one mention, where Jesus tells his disciples, "Do not go among the Gentiles or enter any town of the Samaritans" (Matt 10:5). He does not describe any activity of Jesus in Samaria.

In Luke-Acts, however, Samaria and Samaritans appear repeatedly. The term "Samaritan (*Samaritēs*)" appears in Luke 9:52; 10:33; 17:16; Acts 8:25, and "Samaria (*Samareia*)" appears in Acts 17:11; also in 1:8; 8:1, 5, 9, 14; 9:31; 15:3. Jesus travels through Samaria, interacts with Samaritans, and tells a story about a Samaritan. After Jesus ascends to heaven, his disciples go to Samaria to proclaim the good news.

All references to Samaria or Samaritans in Luke's Gospel are found in the so-called "travel narrative" which describes Jesus's trip from Galilee to Jerusalem (9:51–19:27). This trip is described in all of the synoptic Gospels. In Matthew and Mark, Jesus goes to Jerusalem via Perea ("the other side of the Jordan"), thus avoiding Samaria (Matt 19:1; cf. Mark 10:1), while in Luke Jesus enters Samaria (Luke 9:52). One scholar even went so far as to describe the Lukan travel narrative as Jesus's "Samaritan ministry."[20]

Samaria and the Restoration of Israel

Thus, Samaria clearly plays an important role in Luke-Acts. Why is this? To answer this question, we must turn our attention to the entire narrative framework of Luke-Acts. The key text is Acts 1:8: "But you will receive power when the Holy Spirit comes on you; and you will be my witnesses in Jerusalem, and in all Judea and Samaria, and to the ends of the earth" (NIV). In this passage

---

18. Moxnes, "Kingdom Takes Place," 192.
19. See Sleeman, *Geography*, 79. Although Moxnes depends on Harvey's spatial theory, his argument is similar to that of Sleeman, who depends mainly on Soja.
20. See Morton Enslin, "The Samaritan Ministry and Mission," *HUCA* 51 (1980): 29–38.

Jesus commands his disciples to become his witnesses right before his ascension into heaven. Here Jesus provides a three-part program of mission: (1) in Jerusalem, (2) in all Judea and Samaria, and (3) to the ends of the earth. This is not just a description of the gospel's geographic expansion, but it reflects the theological program of the Isaianic new exodus. Each stage of the above program signifies, respectively, (1) the dawn of salvation upon Jerusalem, (2) the reconstitution and reunification of Israel, and (3) the inclusion of the Gentiles within the people of God.[21] In Soja's terminology, Jesus's words not only specify the geographic territories in which the disciples proclaim the gospel (firstspace), but also state the significance of these territories from the divine perspective (secondspace), and further prepare the realization of the kingdom of God which the disciples actually experience and live out (thirdspace).[22]

In light of the narrative unity of Luke-Acts, Jesus's words in Acts 1:8 not only provide a missionary program in Acts, but also function as a key to understanding the narrative of the Gospel. The reason Samaria is emphasized in Luke's Gospel, and especially in the travel narrative, is because Jesus's trip from Galilee to Jerusalem signifies the restoration of the nation of Israel.[23] As the Davidic Messiah, Jesus came to become king of Israel, but that "Israel" includes not only Jews but also Samaritans.[24] Furthermore, the restoration of Israel has to do not only with the community of "Israelites" as the people of God, but also with the geographic spheres in which they live and the space produced there, because the commandment of Jesus is given in spatial expression.

Thus, Samaria is important for Luke in terms of the restoration of Israel.[25] Samaritans are part of Israel, the people of God, and the ministry in Samaria was an important mission the early church inherited from Jesus.[26] Only after

---

21. David W. Pao, *Acts and Isaianic New Exodus*, WUNT 2/130 (Tübingen: Mohr Siebeck, 2000), 93–95.
22. See Sleeman, *Geography*, 71–72.
23. Jeannine K. Brown and Kazuhiko Yamazaki-Ransom, "The Parable of the Good Samaritan and the Narrative Portrayal of Samaritans in Luke-Acts," *JTI* 15 (2021): 233–46.
24. See, for example, Acts 13:23. It is important to note Luke's reference to the twelve tribes of Israel (Luke 22:30; Acts 26:7) and to all Israel (Acts 2:36; 4:10), where clearly non-Jewish "Israelites" are also in view.
25. See David Ravens, *Luke and the Restoration of Israel*, JSNTSup 119 (Sheffield: Sheffield Academic, 1995), 72–106.
26. In the past, the ethnic differences and animosity between Jews and Samaritans in first century Palestine have often been overemphasized, but recent studies show that the relationship between these two groups was actually more nuanced than is often thought. This has significant implications for the interpretation of such passages as the "Parable of the Good Samaritan" in Luke 10. See Matthew Chalmers, "Rethinking Luke 10: The Parable of the Good Samaritan Israelite," *JBL* 139 (2020): 543–66.

this restoration of Israel was complete was the mission to the Gentiles ready to be carried out.

Jesus's Rejection in Samaria (Luke 9)

I will now turn to a specific passage in Luke's Gospel and attempt to offer a spatial reading of it:

> As the time approached for him to be taken up to heaven, Jesus resolutely set out for Jerusalem. And he sent messengers on ahead, who went into a Samaritan village to get things ready for him; but the people there did not welcome him, because he was heading for Jerusalem. When the disciples James and John saw this, they asked, "Lord, do you want us to call fire down from heaven to destroy them?" But Jesus turned and rebuked them. Then he and his disciples went to another village. (Luke 9:51–56 NIV)

There is a major narrative break in Luke's Gospel in 9:51: in the first half of the Gospel Jesus ministers in Galilee, but here he sets out for Jerusalem, where he will be crucified. At the beginning of the long travel narrative (Luke 9:51–19:27) is this episode of Jesus being rejected by a Samaritan village. This passage also includes the first reference to Samaritans (or, for that matter, Samaria) in Luke-Acts.

As stated above, in Matthew and Mark Jesus goes from Galilee to Jerusalem via Perea, avoiding Samaria. But in Luke Jesus goes right into Samaria. Conzelmann insists that after being rejected in the Samaritan village, Jesus avoided Samaria and went directly to Judea. According to Conzelmann, Luke's knowledge of Palestinian geography was so limited that he thought that Galilee and Judea existed next to each other, while Samaria lay alongside both.[27] Regardless of the accuracy of Luke's geographic knowledge, the importance of Samaria in Luke's travel narrative is obvious. Luke intentionally portrays Jesus as traveling to Jerusalem via Samaria.[28]

---

27. Conzelmann, *Theology*, 66, 69. However, this is doubtful because, if Conzelmann is right, Jesus in Luke could have gone to Jerusalem without ever visiting Samaria. See Jacob Jervell, *Luke and the People of God: A New Look at Luke-Acts* (Minneapolis: Augsburg, 1972), 120.

28. Jervell, *Luke and the People of God*, 121; Ravens, *Restoration*, 77–78. Sleeman (*Geography*, 32–33) criticizes Conzelmann, stating that his limited understanding of geography as merely locational markers is outdated in the modern standard of the discipline. Sleeman laments that Conzelmann's inadequate knowledge of modern geography is illustrative rather than unique in biblical studies.

Samaria lay between Galilee and Judea, so if one wished to take the shortest route from Galilee to Jerusalem, the natural choice was to go directly southward through Samaria. In fact, many Galileans used to make pilgrimage to Jerusalem through Samaria.[29] Thus Jesus and his disciples attempted to enter a certain village in Samaria (Luke 9:52), but this was more than just a movement in firstspace, a space physically perceived, for the villagers refused to let Jesus stay there (v. 53).

This incident can be understood from the perspective of spatial theory. The reason Jesus was rejected was because he had no place in the village as a secondspace of Samaritans. Luke explains that the Samaritans rejected Jesus "because he was heading for Jerusalem" (v. 53). Jesus and his disciples were on their pilgrimage to Jerusalem to celebrate Passover, but this was problematic for the Samaritans, because there was a controversy between Jews and Samaritans over the proper place of worship.[30] For Jews the only proper place for worshipping Yahweh was Jerusalem and its temple, but Samaritans insisted that Mt. Gerizim was the proper place of worship.[31] For Samaritans, their village belonged to the spatial order created around the sanctuary on Mt. Gerizim. This secondspace reflects certain social relationships, and the Samaritans decided whom to welcome and whom to reject. But Jesus (so they thought) had a different secondspatial understanding, with Jerusalem at its center. Therefore, Samaritans deemed him a threat to their spatial order, and so they rejected him. Thus, space is not a fixed entity with a singular significance, but it is always changing, with different spatial understandings competing with each other.

However, this secondspace is not the final space. The possibility of a thirdspace is open. The thirdspace is a "space of representation" which challenges the physical use of the existing space (firstspace) and its representation (secondspace), and points to an ideal space with new meanings and possibilities. Moxnes calls thirdspaces "imagined places."[32]

However, there is more than one possibility of such thirdspace. Luke first describes the disciples' expectation of thirdspace, which is expressed in their words: "Lord, do you want us to call fire down from heaven to destroy them?" (v. 54). Here they refer to the OT story of Elijah destroying with heavenly fire

---

29. See Josephus, *Jewish Antiquities* 20.6.1 §118.
30. Luke's explanation would have been incomprehensible for those who lacked knowledge of the controversy. See Ravens, *Restoration*, 82; Jervell, *Luke and the People of God*, 116.
31. See John 4:20.
32. See Moxnes, *Putting Jesus in His Place*, 14, although here Moxnes refers to the spatial concepts of Lefebvre and Harvey which correspond to Soja's thirdspace.

the people sent from the king of Samaria (2 Kgs 1:10, 12). In that narrative, the Northern Kingdom and its capital city of Samaria were ruled by the evil king Ahaziah, defiled by idolatry, and deserved divine judgment. Regardless of whether James and John actually had the power to call down fire from heaven, it is clear that in their eyes the Samaritan village whose inhabitants rejected Jesus deserved a similar judgment. With such a thirdspatial understanding, the disciples wished to challenge the secondspace of the Samaritans and transform it violently.

However, Jesus rebukes them (Luke 9:55), which means that he refused to create a thirdspace in Samaria in their way. What kind of thirdspace, then, did Jesus wish to create? It would eventually be revealed as Samaria as part of the restored Israel together with Judea, as expressed in Jesus's words "in all Judea and Samaria" in Acts 1:8, but at this point in the narrative Luke does not yet say that. They just "went to another village" (Luke 9:56).[33]

Spatial Transformation of Samaria in Luke-Acts

Within the entire narrative framework of Luke-Acts, the negative portrayal of Samaritans in Luke 9 is rather exceptional. The fact is that Luke's initial negative portrayal of Samaritans should not be understood as reflecting the author's negative view of Samaritans. It should rather be seen as setting the stage for Jesus's project of restoring Israel by uniting Judea and Samaria.

Quite a contrasting scene is recorded in Acts 8, in which Philip's ministry in Samaria is a great success. In the Gospel, Samaritans "did not receive (ouk edexanto)" Jesus (Luke 9:53, my translation), but now Samaria "has received (dedektai)" the word of God (Acts 8:14, my translation). Thus, initial Samaritan rejection in the Gospel prepares for Samaritan mission and reception in Acts.[34] What happened between these events?

In Luke's narrative, there are not many instances where Jesus and his disciples actually interact with Samaritans in Samaria.[35] After being rejected by the Samaritan village, Jesus tells the story of the "Good Samaritan" in a parable (Luke 10:25–37), in which the Samaritan is portrayed as a model

---

33. Conzelmann (*Theology*, 65–66) thinks that after this incident Jesus avoided Samaria, but nothing in the text indicates that. The fact that Jesus and his disciples had assumed the possibility of staying in Samaria indicates that the rejection this time is not a normal response for the Samaritans.

34. Sasagu Arai, *Shito Gyoden* [The Acts of the Apostles], vol. 2, Gendai Shinyaku Chukai Zensho (Tokyo: Shinkyo, 2014), 69, 72, 74.

35. In Acts 9:31 and 15:3, the existence of churches in Samaria is briefly indicated.

Israelite who is obedient to the law of neighborly love (Lev 19:18).[36] Jesus also praises the faith of a Samaritan leper (Luke 17:11–19). In these episodes, both Samaritans – one a fictional character and the other a real person – are portrayed positively, but they are individuals outside of the land of Samaria.[37]

However, Jesus's reference to Samaria in Acts 1:8 has obvious geographical implications. The disciples are commanded to become witnesses of Jesus "in all Judea and Samaria" (*en pasē tē Ioudaia kai Samareia*). Thus, Jesus's vision of the restoration of Israel, including both Judea and Samaria, is presented in spatial terms. The next time Samaria is mentioned in the narrative is in Acts 8 which describes an event in a Samaritan town.

Thus, the spatial status of Samaria has an important turning point in Acts 1:8. Jesus here gives a new spatial significance to Samaria in this passage. This spatial understanding of Samaria is different both from that of the Samaritans who rejected Jesus in Luke 9, and from that of the disciples enraged by their rejection. Their antagonistic reactions were based on their different understandings of the proper place of worship. After Jesus's resurrection, however, there was a significant change in the situation.

Why was there such a change in the narrative? Here Sleeman's study of the ascension in Acts provides a key. Sleeman argues that Jesus's ascension into heaven has a spatial significance in the narrative of Luke-Acts. Ascension does not mean his absence from the earth. It is rather "*the* moment of spatial realignment" in which all spaces on earth are restructured around the ascended Christ who rules from his heavenly throne.[38] The space of the church's mission in the Acts narrative is ordered from the heavenly perspective centering around Christ. It is important to note that Christ's commissioning of the disciples (Acts 1:8) appears immediately before his ascension (v. 9), which means that the geographic expansion of this mission must be understood in light of his ascension.[39]

---

36. See Brown and Yamazaki-Ransom, "Good Samaritan," 245. The main point of the parable is not, as is often told, to teach a universal ethic, but to show that Samaritans are also part of the biblical people of God, Israel, which is to be restored. It is suggestive that the Samaritan in the parable is travelling in Judea (Luke 10:33). He comes to a place where he does not belong and demonstrates an ideal way of living out neighborly love which leads to eternal life, thus pointing to the possibility of a new kind of spatiality.

37. Jesus met the Samaritan leper when he was travelling "along the border between Samaria and Galilee" (Luke 17:11). It was in that "liminal space" that the Samaritan leper – a doubly marginalized, borderline person – was able to come to Jesus. See John T. Carroll, *Luke: A Commentary*, NTL (Louisville: WJKP, 2012), 343–44.

38. Sleeman, *Geography*, 80; emphasis in original.

39. See Sleeman, *Geography*, 33–34, 58–59, 66–67.

A key point in this process is the decentralization of Jerusalem and especially of its temple. It is widely known that Luke's Gospel has a centripetal movement around Jerusalem: its narrative begins with a temple scene (Luke 1:5–22) and closes with another temple scene (24:52–53). In contrast, many argue that there is a centrifugal movement away from Jerusalem, with the temple continuing to play the central role. However, Sleeman objects to this line of interpretation, arguing that the spatial center of the Acts narrative is no longer the earthly temple, but the ascended Jesus on his heavenly throne. The central status of Jerusalem is now relativized, which is clearly seen in Stephen's critique of the temple in Acts 7.

This has significant implications for the issue of Samaria in Luke-Acts, because, as stated above, one reason for Jewish-Samaritan antagonism was their disagreement over the proper place of worship. The Samaritans did not receive Jesus because he was going to participate in the Passover celebration in Jerusalem (Luke 9:53). Furthermore, Jesus calls the Samaritan leper a "foreigner" (*allogenēs*) (17:18), an expression that was on the Jerusalem temple inscription which warned non-Jews not to enter.[40] Thus, the reconciliation and unification of Jews and Samaritans remained impossible as long as the Jews kept privileging Jerusalem over Mt. Gerizim. Their secondspaces were mutually irreconcilable.

However, Jesus's ascension relativizes the centrality of Jerusalem, thus creating space for Samaritans to accept the good news about him. God's presence and work are no longer bound to Jerusalem and its temple. Their center is neither Jerusalem nor Mt. Gerizim, but Jesus on his heavenly throne, and so Samaritans are now able to participate in this new spatial order on equal footing with the Jews. Such decentralization of the Jerusalem temple is clear in Stephen's speech (Acts 7:48–50), and it is no coincidence that this speech is placed right before the narrative of the Samaritan mission (Acts 8).

By analyzing the plot development in Luke-Acts, it becomes clear that the spatial status of Samaria changes within the narrative. The reason there is no explicit mission to Samaria in the Gospel of Luke after the rejection in chapter 9 – even though there are good reasons to think that Luke considers Samaritans

---

40. Chalmers, "Rethinking," 564; also noted in BDAG, s.v. *allogenēs*. Luke normally uses *ethnē* to refer to Gentiles, but *allogenēs* appears only here in the New Testament. In this episode, after healing ten lepers Jesus tells them to show themselves to the priests (Luke 17:14). Unable to go to the Jerusalem temple, the Samaritan returned to Jesus and praised God (vv. 15–16). Here Jesus is functioning as an alternative temple. See David W. Pao, *Lujia Fuyin* [Gospel of Luke], 2nd ed., 2 vols., Tien Dao Bible Commentary (Hong Kong: Tien Dao, 2017), 2:189.

as part of biblical Israel – is because in the Gospel the decentralization of the Jerusalem temple through Jesus's passion, resurrection, and ascension has yet to happen. However, even in the Gospel the vision of restoring Israel by including Samaritans is repeatedly presented to the reader, paving the way to the coming Samaritan mission. Luke's portrayal of Samaria can be summarized as follows:

Luke 9:51–56	Rejection in Samaria	Samaritans reject Jesus
Luke 10:25–37	Parable of the Good Samaritan	Samaritan in a parable
Luke 17:11–19	Samaritan leper	Samaritan in a liminal space
Acts 1:8	Samaria in Jesus's missionary program	Vision of restoring Israel
Acts 1:9–11	Ascension of Jesus	Jesus's rule from his heavenly throne begins
Acts 7	Stephen's speech	Decentralization of Jerusalem temple
Acts 8	Mission to Samaria	Samaritans accept the gospel
Acts 9:31; 15:3	Churches in Samaria	Restored Israel

Thus, the "space" of Samaria in Luke-Acts goes through a transformation through the ministry of Jesus and the disciples. Luke presents that there are conflicting secondspatial understandings of Samaria at the beginning of Jesus's journey to Jerusalem. The difference between the Samaritans' Gerizim-centered secondspace and the Jews' Jerusalem-centered secondspace produced a conflict when these two groups met, but Jesus presents an alternative thirdspatial vision of Judea and Samaria, united not around the Jerusalem temple – which would mean the subjugation of the Samaritans to the Jews – but around himself. This vision is realized in Acts by Jesus ascending to his heavenly throne and guiding the church's mission through the Holy Spirit.

Spatial Significances of Samaria in Luke-Acts

The above survey of Samaria in Luke-Acts provides some significant implications for our understanding of the Bible, Christian mission, and social justice.

First, space is important. Space is more than just a geographic expansion, a value-neutral stage, in which human activities (including Christian ministries) take place. Space reflects existing social relationships and in turn affects these relationships. Space is both physical and imaginative, multi-layered and constantly changing. Without denying the importance of the historical perspective in biblical interpretation, adding a spatial perspective will produce a richer reading of the Bible. For example, the coming of the kingdom of God on earth can (and should) be seen as producing new thirdspaces in specific geographical locations, transforming both actual physical structures and practices (firstspace) and their ideological representation (secondspace).

Second, spatiality is closely related to the issue of social justice.[41] This is no different in the Bible. If the kingdom of God is a manifestation of God's kingly rule on earth, it must challenge the existing unjust society and transform it into a just society, and such a transformation must also be realized, among other ways, in spatial terms. Regarding Samaritans, they were marginalized in the Jewish worldview and sometimes even demonized.[42] This is revealed in the disciples' angry response when Jesus was rejected by Samaritan villagers (Luke 9:54). This marginalization is simultaneously theological and spatial: the marginalization of Samaria is theologically justified by the centrality of the Jerusalem temple. As we saw above, the non-Jews, including not only the Gentiles but also the Samaritans, were prohibited from participating in the worship of God in the temple. Samaritans, on the other hand, insisted that the proper place of worship was Mt. Gerizim. Even though these two peoples worshipped the same God of Israel, they could not reconcile with each other, because they were living in different secondspaces in Israel. Thus, the split in the people of Israel as the people of God was a *spatial* problem, based on different secondspatial representations of the promised land.

Jesus solved this problem, through his death, resurrection, and ascension, not by subordinating Samaria to Judah and Mt. Gerizim to Jerusalem but by creating an alternative center for the people of God: his heavenly throne. Only through this decentralization of Jerusalem and its temple were Jews and Samaritans able to be reconciled to each other. Thus, in a sense, the Jerusalem temple was to the Jewish-Samaritan relationship what circumcision was to the Jewish-Gentile relationship: a barrier to the unity of the people of God. By creating a thirdspace of the restored Israel – and indeed the whole world – centering around his heavenly throne, Jesus guides the church's mission to transform all spaces on earth.[43]

---

41. See Soja, *Seeking Social Justice*.
42. See John 8:48.
43. This should not be understood as a mere spiritualization of concrete spatiality. For Luke, Jesus's heavenly throne is a concrete space that organizes all spaces of the world.

The temple plays an especially important role in this regard. Jerusalem and its temple play a central role in much of the biblical narrative and theology as the locus of the divine presence on earth and among God's people. At the same time, the corruption of temple authority and the subsequent divine judgment upon it has also been a subject of both the OT and NT. In Jesus's days, the temple became, especially to the poor Jews, a symbol of economic oppression by the rich elites, and Jesus pronounced judgment upon the temple for this reason.[44]

Furthermore, the temple was also a symbol of Jewish ethnocentrism, denying access to the divine presence to not only Gentiles but also to Samaritans, who were counted among "foreigners" by Jews (cf. Luke 17:18). Thus, the temple was a symbol of the inner division of the people of Israel. Green argues that the temple became the "culture center" that segregated Jews from non-Jews, stating that "far from serving as a sacred place for the worship of God by Gentiles (and Samaritans), the temple functions as a segregating force, symbolizing socio-religious demarcations between insider and outsider."[45] Green argues that for Luke, Jesus's critique of the temple does not entail its immediate destruction: the temple continues to play an important role even in Acts. However, its segregating symbolic function must be neutralized: "Rather than serving as the gathering point for all peoples under Yahweh, it has now become the point-of-departure for the mission to all peoples."[46]

The temple's segregating function was not just about its physical zoning: different areas of the temple precinct excluded different classes of people such as non-Jews, Jewish women, Jewish men who were not priests, etc. For Jews, the temple was also the center of their spatial order of all the earth, placing differing degrees of value on different geographic areas as well as those of the peoples inhabiting those areas. This could be the basis for various kinds of injustice, including theological, social, racial, and economical. Thus, the land of Samaria and the Samaritans were degraded in the Jewish worldview.[47] On the other hand, this brought about negative reactions from Samaritans, such as the Samaritan villagers' rejecting Jesus (Luke 9:53). Thus, the symbolic

44. See N. T. Wright, *Jesus and the Victory of God* (Minneapolis: Fortress, 1997), 412; Yamaguchi, *"Kami no Okoku,"* 98–104.

45. Joel B. Green, "The Demise of the Temple as 'Culture Center' in Luke-Acts: An Exploration of the Rending of the Temple Veil (Luke 23.44–49)," *RB* 101 (1994): 512.

46. Green, "The Demise of the Temple," 512. See also Nickolas A. Fox, *The Hermeneutics of Social Identity in Luke-Acts* (Eugene: Pickwick, 2021), 136.

47. This point is most explicit in John 4:9 and 8:48, but also assumed in Luke 9:54 and the parable of the Good Samaritan in Luke 10.

centrality of the temple affected social relationships and structures in various places far from Jerusalem.

It can be safely assumed that such social tension would have created various kinds of social injustice. It is widely known that Luke had a strong interest in and sympathy for the marginalized people in Jewish society such as women, children, the poor and the sick.[48] Samaritans were also among those marginalized people, and thus could be considered as the victims of Jewish segregation. The fact that Luke refers to churches in Samaria on equal footing with those in Judea and Galilee (Acts 9:31) may indicate that such segregation was – at least symbolically – resolved in the early Christian mission.

Third, this spatial transformation is a complex and multifaceted process. As discussed above, the change does not occur overnight after Jesus's ascension. The process had begun long before that event.[49] Jesus and his disciples engage with Samaria and Samaritans in various places and occasions, using various methods. It requires bold envisioning, creative imagination (like telling parables), and active and patient engagement with the people. At the same time, we should not forget that this transformation is based on the sovereign authority of the resurrected Christ and is driven by the power of the Holy Spirit.[50]

CHRISTIAN MISSION, RECONCILIATION, AND SPATIAL JUSTICE IN TODAY'S ASIA

One of the insights of contemporary spatial theory is that space is not a fixed entity but is diverse, multi-layered, and constantly changing. Massey argues that space is the ever-changing locus of the meeting between different narratives.[51] If this is true, then the Christian mission as mediating the kingdom of God on earth should not be understood as a standardized, universal model. Rather, its expression can vary according to the different indigenous cultures where the mission takes place and will change as time goes by. This can be a response to the age-old problem of the contextualization of Western Christianity

---

48. See Joel B. Green, *The Theology of the Gospel of Luke*, New Testament Theology (Cambridge: Cambridge University Press, 1995), 84–94.

49. Jesus's symbolic use of the number twelve for the apostles (Luke 6:13) alludes to the twelve tribes of Israel. Luke repeatedly refers to all people of Israel and its twelve tribes in his two-volume works. See Luke 22:30; Acts 2:36; 4:10; 13:24; 26:7. Furthermore, the prophet Anna, who welcomes the infant Jesus, is said to be of the northern tribe of Asher (Luke 2:36). All these indicate that for Luke the restoration of Israel involves all twelve tribes, not just Judah.

50. In Acts 1:8, Jesus implies that the unity of Judea and Samaria is possible when the disciples are empowered by the Holy Spirit.

51. See Doreen B. Massey, *For Space* (London: SAGE, 2005), 71.

in non-Western areas, including in Asian countries. Furthermore, the process of bringing the thirdspace of God's kingdom on earth will never cease; it requires a constant engagement by the church, and it must keep changing in accordance with the changing world.

In contemporary Asia, as in any other part of the world, cases of social injustice abound.[52] It has been noted that such social injustice has a spatial dimension: it is a spatial injustice. One example of seeking spatial justice is the environmental justice movement, which fights against "the tendency for poor and minority populations . . . to suffer disproportionally from air and water pollution and the siting of hazardous or toxic facilities."[53] These people's suffering is directly connected to the areas they inhabit. Another example is the existence of underprivileged neighborhoods of ethnic minorities, such as Korean towns in Japan, which have been the target of various kinds of inequalities and discrimination throughout history. What should be a proper Christian response to such social realities?

The answer is not simple. The above study of Luke-Acts sheds light on only a small part of the entire Bible. Even within this limited scope, the examples of Luke-Acts should not be treated as fixed models for spatial justice. The historical backgrounds of the Jewish-Samaritan relationship in Luke-Acts are vastly different from those in contemporary Asia, and even here the concrete situations vary from place to place. Nevertheless, we may glean some hints for contemporary Christian strategies for spatial justice.

First, firstspace engagement is crucial. Spatial transformation is not limited to the realm of firstspace, but it certainly involves it as an essential part. In Luke-Acts, Jesus and his disciples physically travel to Samaria and engage with the people living there. In doing so, they directly experience the spatial reality there. It may not always be a positive, pleasant experience. In fact, Jesus experienced a harsh rejection (Luke 9). But this is a necessary beginning stage for reconciliation and social transformation. Eventually, the early church conducted a successful mission in Samaria and "there was great joy in that city" (Acts 8:8 NIV).

Second, however, spatial transformation can also happen – or begin – outside the firstspace boundaries of a given area. Jesus engaged with a Samaritan leper in a border area between Galilee and Samaria (Luke 17). There he not

---

52. Soja (*Seeking Spatial Justice*, 40–41) gives the example of Israeli-occupied Palestine as a case of spatial injustice.
53. Soja, *Seeking Spatial Justice*, 52.

only physically healed his skin disease but also socially restored him into his community – this healing has much more significance. The leper's restoration and his worshipping before Jesus are both symbolic acts. They transform the rivaling secondspaces of Jews and Samaritans, with Jerusalem and Mt. Gerizim at their centers, respectively, into a new thirdspatial order of a restored Israel that includes both Judea and Samaria, centered around Jesus's living presence. Such a thing is possible precisely because space is not limited to a physical firstspace, but it also includes second and thirdspatial dimensions that are socially produced.

In contemporary Asia, too, even one symbolic act of an individual outside of the given geographic area could have the potential for a spatial transformation for reconciliation and social justice in that area. For example, there are many Korean churches in various Japanese cities. Some believers may live in Korean towns but the churches may be outside of these areas. If the Japanese churches build good relationships with the Korean churches in the neighborhood, it may raise the awareness of Japanese Christians of the social injustice in the Korean towns, and may help them to take some concrete actions.

Third, and related to the previous point, such a symbolic act could also take the form of a fictional, creative narrative. The parable of the Good Samaritan (Luke 10) is a great example of this. Jesus's powerful story was aimed to challenge the Jewish secondspace of their ethnocentrism, centered around Jerusalem and its temple and thus robbing the Samaritans of their rightful status within the people of God. It is a pity that too often this parable is interpreted as merely a nice moral story teaching individual ethics. In contemporary Asian settings, more of such transformative stories – both actual testimonies and creative fiction – need to be told to reorder unjust spaces. And this needs to be done in uniquely Asian ways so these stories touch the hearts of the Asian people.

Finally, the foundation of all of this is the centrality of Jesus Christ. In the worldview of the NT, all space is ordered centered around the risen Christ on his heavenly throne.[54] In contemporary Asia, we should always be careful not to create any "center" in our spatial order other than Jesus Christ, be it an ethnic group, class, gender, geographic territory, institution, building, individual, or anything else. Such "centers" will eventually create social imbalance and

---

54. This "heaven" may be variously represented in our modern cosmology. The New Testament was written with the worldview of the people of that particular point in history. No matter how we represent "heaven" today, the point is clear: Jesus Christ, who is the risen king over all the world, is the center of all spaces of this world, including Asia.

injustice. In our Christian mission in Asia, Christocentric thirdspace should take precedence over any other thirdspace claims: there is an ongoing "conflict of geographies, a clash of ways to view the world."[55]

This Christocentric emphasis, however, does not mean uniformity. As Sleeman states,

> This humbling of earthly space does not seek to obliterate difference, since heavenly allegiance does not require earthly uniformity and indeed defies it as masking earthly thirdspace claims. Ascension geography instead maintains a vision for multiple and pluriform believer-spaces nevertheless unified by allegiance beyond themselves.[56]

Thus, there is an ample "space" for Asian churches to promote reconciliation and social justice in uniquely Asian ways by which they are transforming the spaces they are inhabiting and engaging. It is our urgent task to discover the many other ways we can bring about this heavenly thirdspace in our firstspace corner of this world.

BIBLIOGRAPHY

Arai, Sasagu. *Shito Gyoden* [The Acts of the Apostles], vol. 2. Gendai Shinyaku Chukai Zensho. Tokyo: Shinkyo, 2014.

Brown, Jeannine K. and Kazuhiko Yamazaki-Ransom. "The Parable of the Good Samaritan and the Narrative Portrayal of Samaritans in Luke-Acts." *JTI* 15 (2021): 233–46.

Carroll, John T. *Luke: A Commentary.* NTL. Louisville: WJKP, 2012.

Chalmers, Matthew. "Rethinking Luke 10: The Parable of the Good Samaritan Israelite." *JBL* 139 (2020): 543–66.

Conzelmann, Hans. *The Theology of St. Luke.* Translated by Geoffrey Buswell. New York: Harper & Row, 1960.

Enslin, Morton. "The Samaritan Ministry and Mission." *HUCA* 51 (1980): 29–38.

Fox, Nickolas A. *The Hermeneutics of Social Identity in Luke-Acts.* Eugene: Pickwick, 2021.

Green, Joel B. "The Demise of the Temple as 'Culture Center' in Luke-Acts: An Exploration of the Rending of the Temple Veil (Luke 23.44–49)." *RB* 101 (1994): 495–515.

---

55. Sleeman, *Geography*, 54.
56. Sleeman, *Geography*, 261.

———. *The Theology of the Gospel of Luke.* New Testament Theology. Cambridge: Cambridge University Press, 1995.

Harvey, David. *The Condition of Postmodernity: An Enquiry into the Origins of Cultural Change.* Oxford: Wiley-Blackwell, 1992.

Jervell, Jacob. *Luke and the People of God: A New Look at Luke-Acts.* Minneapolis: Augsburg, 1972.

Josephus. *Jewish Antiquities, Volume IX: Book 20.* Translated by Louis H. Feldman. LCL 456. Cambridge: Harvard University Press, 1965.

Lefebvre, Henri. *The Production of Space.* Translated by Donald Nicholson-Smith. Malden: Wiley-Blackwell, 1992.

Massey, Doreen B. *For Space.* London: SAGE, 2005.

Moxnes, Halvor. "Kingdom Takes Place: Transformations of Place and Power in the Kingdom of God in the Gospel of Luke." In *Social Scientific Models for Interpreting the Bible: Essays by the Context Group in Honor of Bruce J. Malina,* edited by John J. Pilch, 176–209, BibInt 53. Leiden: Brill, 2001.

———. *Putting Jesus in His Place: A Radical Vision of Household and Kingdom.* Louisville: WJKP, 2003.

Pao, David W. *Acts and Isaianic New Exodus.* WUNT 2/130. Tübingen: Mohr-Siebeck, 2000.

———. *Lujia Fuyin* [Gospel of Luke]. 2nd ed. 2 volumes. Tien Dao Bible Commentary. Hong Kong: Tien Dao, 2017.

Ravens, David. *Luke and the Restoration of Israel.* JSNTSup 119. Sheffield: Sheffield Academic, 1995.

Said, Edward W. *Culture and Imperialism.* New York: Knopf, 1993.

Schüssler Fiorenza, Elisabeth. *Jesus: Miriam's Child, Sophia's Prophet: Critical Issues in Feminist Christology.* 2nd ed. London: Bloomsbury, 2015.

Sleeman, Matthew. *Geography and the Ascension Narrative in Acts.* Cambridge: Cambridge University Press, 2013.

Soja, Edward W. *Thirdspace: Journeys to Los Angeles and Other Real-and-Imagined Places.* Cambridge: Blackwell, 1996.

———. *Seeking Spatial Justice.* Minneapolis: University of Minnesota Press, 2010.

Stewart, Eric C. "New Testament Space/Spatiality." *BTB* 42, no. 3 (2012): 139–50.

Wright, N. T. *Jesus and the Victory of God.* Minneapolis: Fortress, 1997.

Yamaguchi, Norio. *"Kami no Okoku" wo Motomete: Kindai Iko no Kenkyushi* [In Search of the "Kingdom of God": Research History Since the Modern Period]. Rev. ed. Tokyo: Yobel, 2021.

CHAPTER 9

HONORING ELDERS, LIVING AND DEAD

Redeeming Filial Piety for Contemporary Christians

Steven S. H. Chang

INTRODUCTION

In recent years, one of the most disturbing trends in South Korea is the rising rate of suicides among the elderly, now reportedly the highest among developed countries. Two correlated trends directly contribute to the suicide crisis. On the one hand, more elderly are living in poverty. A staggering 45.7 percent of the elderly population live in poverty, which is the highest of any age bracket in South Korea, and a far higher percentage of the general population than in any other developed country.[1] On the other hand, more elderly are living alone. Census reports show that almost a third of all households in Korea are made up of just one person living alone, which is a sharp rise. Over a quarter of those single-person households are those of age sixty-five and older. This means that more than three out of every ten elderly persons live alone.[2] With the median age of South Koreans continuing to rise, this crisis will not go away any time soon.

Society observers routinely attribute the terrible plight of the elderly to the ominous decline of Confucian filial piety (*hyo* in Korean; *xiao* in Chinese). Often considered the bedrock of Korean society, Confucian filial piety became foundational after the turmoil of the final days of the Goryeo Dynasty (918–1392) which led to an "unprecedented political discourse on man

---

1. Kim Jaewon, "No Country for Old Koreans: Moon Faces Senior Poverty Crisis," *Nikkei Asia*, 29 January 2019, https://asia.nikkei.com/Spotlight/Asia-Insight/No-country-for-old-Koreans-Moon-faces-senior-poverty-crisis.
2. "35% of the Elderly Reported to Live Alone," *The Dong-A Ilbo*, 30 September 2021, https://www.donga.com/en/article/all/20210930/2953390/1.

and society."[3] For the next five hundred years of the Joseon Dynasty (1392–1910), Confucianism transformed society through the family and filial piety.[4] However, Korea experienced several traumatic developments in the twentieth century: Japanese colonization (1910–1945), the Korean War (1950–1953), post-war poverty and reconstruction (1960s), rapid industrialization and economic development (1970–80s), and the struggle for democratization (1980–90s). Today's elderly of South Korea have lived through most or all of these developments, and indeed, have borne most of the burden. Yet they are the generation left behind by those same changes. The decline of Confucian filial piety means that the elderly today may be unfortunately the last generation to care for their parents but also the first generation not to receive such support from their own children. Other Asian contexts undoubtedly face similar challenges. It is critical, then, for the churches of Korea and Asia to respond compassionately and biblically to this issue.

In response, this essay seeks to understand biblically and contextually what "honor your elders" means for Asian evangelical Christians. In East Asian countries, Confucian filial piety is an embedded reality that expresses itself first in family relations and then extends into the larger society. When considering the New Testament (NT) vision of honoring elders, Asian Christians cannot help but start from this culture of embedded filial piety passed down to us through generations of ancestors. Thus, this essay intentionally seeks to interpret the NT data through the virtue of Confucian filial piety while endeavoring to remain faithful to the biblical text and its authority for Asian evangelical Christians. In the process, there will inevitably be a comparison of the values and viewpoints between Confucian filial piety and the NT vision of honoring elders. Because Confucian filial piety and Asian cultures more generally honor not only living elders but also those who have died, this essay will consider the question of ancestor veneration and how the NT might help inform this

---

3. Chung-Hyun Baik, "Some Influences of Confucianism on Korean Christian Family Life: Confucian? Christian? Or Confucian-Christian?" *Theology Today* 76, no. 3 (2019): 244, citing Martina Deuchler, *The Confucian Transformation of Korea: A Study of Society and Ideology* (Cambridge: Harvard, 1992), 27.

4. ShinHyung Seong makes a helpful distinction between earlier "primitive" Confucianism which idealized hierarchy as functional, based on human relatedness, and later Confucianism which tended to view hierarchy ontologically, as fixed in society, giving way to abuse and oppression. The readings of Confucian filial piety from Confucius's texts below are more idealized and thus from primitive Confucianism more than its later developments ("'Honor Your Father and Your Mother' Confucius and Jesus on Filial Obligations," in *Asian Christian Ethics: Evangelical Perspectives*, ed. A. M. Peñamora and B. K. Wong [Carlisle: Langham Global Library, 2022], 65–66, 75–76).

challenging issue. The essay will conclude with a summary description of the NT vision of honoring elders, living and dead.

FROM KOREAN-CONFUCIAN FILIAL PIETY TO THE NEW TESTAMENT

Confucian filial piety suggests that any person older than oneself is to be respected, and parents and ancestors especially should be revered. For this reason, one of the first questions a Korean may ask when a relationship goes beyond social formalities is age. Based on the answer, one may decide to emphasize or do away with honorific address. Once rank is determined by age, then other social expectations follow. Generally, the older are to take care of (feed, give advice, help advance, etc.) the younger while the younger are to respect the older.

In the Korean context, Confucian filial piety is a deeply embedded reality. Jung Sun Oh claims, "Korea is the most Confucianized country in all of East Asia, more than mainland China, Taiwan, Hong Kong or Japan."[5] Further, Oh proposes that while "Confucians are a striking minority" at only 0.2 percent of the Korean population, the reality is that large portions of those claiming the major religious affiliations, Buddhist, Protestant, and Catholic, and of those claiming no religious affiliation, are in fact Confucians.[6] As an embedded reality, Confucian filial piety is more a part of the underlying culture than it is about intentional devotion to religious or moral principles.[7]

Though embedded in the culture, Confucian filial piety is indeed declining in Korea. One ordinary example is that only a decade or two ago, it was common for younger people to give up their seats on the subway or bus to older persons, but today it is far less common. Even some forty years ago, Bong Ho Son noted several reasons for filial piety's decline in Korea: (1) the state does not promote Confucianism as it had in the Joseon era; (2) its Chinese origin goes against the nationalistic trends of Korean identity and culture; (3) increasing secularization in the Korean education system and worldview; (4) disintegration of traditional structures and estrangement of the younger generations toward rituals of the past; (5) Christian influence on society that

---

5. Jung Sun Oh, "A Hermeneutics of Korean Theology of Filial Piety: A Global Theology," *AsJT* 24, no. 2 (2010): 330.
6. Oh, "Hermeneutics of Korean Theology," 330.
7. "Embeddedness" is an important concept in the social sciences and socio-economic studies, and it basically suggests that some human activities are embedded in institutions and structures not normally related to those activities.

rejects Confucian rituals like ancestor worship.[8] Forty years on, Korean society continues to shed Confucian filial piety, accelerated by rapid transformation through technology and globalization, but also by the significant growth of Protestant Christianity since the early 1980s. Because of this decline and its causes, Christians have both an opportunity and an obligation to provide a compelling biblical alternative to Confucian filial piety.

At the same time, Korean Christianity itself has been deeply influenced by Confucian values embedded in Korean culture. Chung-Hyun Baik contends that Confucianism is the "most influential religion and culture for the Korean church."[9] Thus, in a more nuanced understanding of the Korean context, Confucianism and Christianity mix and influence one another, resulting in fluidity. Consequently, filial piety is a hybrid formation for Korean Christians, making it hard to tell whether it is Christian or Confucian. I recall hearing Korean pastors preach about obeying parents, but then appealing to Korean culture more than the Bible. In light of this, the current task of understanding the honor of elders in the NT must intentionally account for Confucian filial piety as a contextual hermeneutic. In other words, Confucian filial piety embedded in Korean culture supplies the perspectives and categories for understanding how the NT envisions honoring elders.

FAMILY AND HONOR AS POINTS OF CONTACT

Two points of contact are important for this study of honoring elders in the NT. The first point of contact is that the honor of elders begins and ends with the concept of the family. The Korean-Confucian culture, the NT world, and NT Christianity all organize their communities as a family and see the family as a microcosm of the state or the larger community. Confucius and his followers as well as the Romans basically regarded their society as a large family.[10] Thus, in both the Confucian and Roman worlds, family ties, or more precisely family loyalties, were of utmost importance. The NT church was highly influenced

---

8. Bong Ho Son, "Socio-Philosophical Background for Change of Attitude toward Ancestor Worship," in *Christian Alternatives to Ancestor Practices*, ed. Bong Rin Ro (Seoul: Asia Theological Association, 1985), 235–46; also, Bong Ho Son, "Ancestor Worship: From the Perspective of Modernization," in *Ancestor Worship and Christianity in Korea*, ed. J. Y. Lee, Studies in Asian Thought and Religion 8 (Lampeter: Edwin Mellen, 1988), 61–71.
9. Baik, "Some Influences of Confucianism," 195–96.
10. Affinity between Korean kingdoms of the past and the Roman empire would be even greater and include the veneration of the emperor/ruler as head of the family. Interestingly, this family system is still operative in Japan today with its emperor.

by both Jewish and Greco-Roman ideals of the family from which a fictive family of God was theologized and ritualized.

In Confucian culture, the key relationship of the family was between father and son, and the father was to be strictly revered and obeyed. In the Roman world, too, the father of the household as *paterfamilias* (the father or male head of the family) was revered and gave order to the relationships as the leader of his family (notably, the household codes in Eph 5/Col 3 which are ordered around this figure). In the NT, the fictive Christ family is ordered around God as father and all his children are sisters and brothers, and the Son of Heaven (to borrow a Confucian term) is the most filial older Brother. The family then becomes a critical fictive notion for ordering the world in all three contexts.

In the NT Christ movement, the physical and fictive families are interconnected and fluid (for example, "church that meets in your house," Rom 16:5). And yet, when loyalties and responsibilities are parsed, believers are clearly exhorted to take care of blood relatives first before caring for the Christ family or those in the world.[11] Thus, kinship responsibility radiates outward from blood family to the fictive Christ family and then to the universal human family. Similarly, family loyalties in Confucian culture begin with the father-son relationship and radiate outward to mother and siblings, extended family, and then to the state. The individual exists for the family and the family becomes the main source of identity (thus, Korean names begin with the family name), and loyalty and solidarity with the family, whether physical (*gajok* in Korean) or fictive (*sikgu*), must be constantly affirmed. The collective family then play the role of caring for the welfare of its members, forming a safety network. Thus, when one member of the family "makes it" economically, the security of the entire family is upgraded.

The second point of contact is that the honor of elders is a part of the larger culture of honor and shame. Both the world of the NT and Asian cultures today value honor and shame, especially when connected to the family. Kar Yong Lim notes this strong resemblance, "[The] Asian social environment of honor and shame is not too far removed from the world of the Bible; it has deep affinities with the biblical world."[12] This affinity gives a hermeneutical advantage to Asian readers. In honor-shame cultures, the dynamic between

---

11. See discussion below, especially on 1 Timothy 5:4–8.
12. K. Y. Lim, "The New Testament and the Sociocultural and Religious Realities of the Asian Contexts," in *An Asian Introduction to the New Testament*, ed. J. Thomaskutty (Minneapolis: Fortress, 2022), 10.

the individual and the group is fundamental, often displaying interdependence. The honor of the individual is based on the honor of the group, and vice versa. When one member "makes it," the status of the family also goes up. Accordingly, honoring elders is about family honor and not simply about honor accorded to one individual. Those of Asian cultures understand the collective nature of honor, where honoring elders brings not only honor to the family and ethnic group but also honor to oneself as a member of that group. In this way, honoring elders is a form of self-respect.

Because of the collective nature of honor in the NT world, honor for elders was embedded in other ascriptions of honor, namely for leaders and patrons. This fluid interplay between the honor for older persons and the honor for leaders is evident in calls to honor the leaders of the church (fictive Christ family) and the governing authorities of society (fictive human family). In addition, the honor of elders is also embedded in calls for propriety in other relationships, namely in the brotherhood of the church or in the husband-wife and master-slave relationships, and even how believers are to treat all people. In these cases, a closer look at age as a factor in the ascription of honor will reveal how believers were to honor their elders. Considering these two points of contact, the next sections will describe the NT vision of honoring elders as parents, older siblings, leaders, emissaries, and ancestors.

HONORING ELDERS AS PARENTS AND OLDER SIBLINGS

The first elders to be honored are one's parents and honoring elders should resemble honoring one's parents. In 1 Timothy 5:1–2, Paul advises Timothy not to rebuke harshly an older man "but exhort him as if he were your father" (*hōs patera*, 5:1) and similarly, "older women as mothers" (*hōs mēteras*, 5:2). He ties the treatment of elders in the church (fictive Christ family) with the treatment of one's parents (physical blood family).

In Confucian filial piety, honoring elders begins with honoring parents.[13] A Korean elder once told me that human beings are unique among all creatures in that we are the only ones who take care of parents and not just our children. Indeed, Confucius measures the nobility of human beings by filial piety in the *Xiaojing* (*Classic of Filial Piety*):

---

13. See S. H. Seong, "'Honor Your Father and Your Mother' Confucius and Jesus on Filial Obligations," cited above, for a comparison of Confucian and Christian views of honoring parents.

Of all the creatures in the world, the human being is the most noble. In human conduct there is nothing more important than family reverence (*xiao*, filial piety); in family reverence there is nothing more important than venerating one's father.[14]

As "the root of humanity,"[15] reverence toward one's parents is what it means to be human and so filial piety amounts to knowing one's origin and nature.

Knowing one's roots as grounded in one's parents is also important in the NT. Paul's insistence in 1 Timothy 5:8 on providing for "one's own" (*tōn idiōn*), especially "of the household" (*oikeiōn*), clearly refers to widowed mothers and grandmothers who are blood relatives. He uses the same words, *ton idion oikon*, to distinguish two classes of widows, those with children (and grandchildren!) and those "left all alone" (5:4–5). The responsibility for "one's own" family by physical birth reflects the fifth commandment, "Honor your father and your mother" (Exod 20:12; Deut 5:16). Paul affirms the fifth commandment in the household code of Ephesians (Eph 6:2). Jesus likewise affirms this commandment when he criticizes the Jewish leaders for breaking it for the sake of tradition (Mark 7:9–13; Matt 15:1–9). The teaching of this commandment is to honor primarily those who gave physical birth to you.

How one shows honor to parents has many similarities between the NT and Confucian filial piety. Firstly, honoring parents entails obedience. In exhorting, "Children, obey (*hypakouō*) your parents in the Lord, for this is right" (Eph 6:1), Paul connects parental honoring with following their instructions.[16] And he lists "disobedience to parents" among the vices that characterize sinners (Rom 1:30; 2 Tim 3:2). The writer of Hebrews speaks of earthly fathers who "discipline" sons, presumably for disobedience in the "struggle against sin," and the respect accorded to such fathers (Heb 12:9). Confucian filial piety also emphasizes obedience. When asked about filial piety, Confucius simply replies, "Never disobey." When asked of its meaning, he replies, "When your parents are alive, serve them according to ritual."[17] By "ritual" (*li*), he means

---

14. *Xiaojing* ch. 9. Cited from Henry Rosemont, Jr., and Roger T. Ames, *The Chinese Classic of Family Reverence: A Philosophical Translation of the* Xiaojing (Honolulu: University of Hawaii Press, 2009), 85, 110. All translations of the *Xiaojing* are cited from this source which prefers "family reverence" for *xiao*, normally "filial piety" in older translations.
15. *The Analects* 1.2. Cited from Michael Nylan, ed., *The Analects: The Simon Leys Translation, Interpretations* (New York: W. W. Norton & Company, 2014); all translations are from this source.
16. BDAG, s.v. *hypakouō*; *hypakouō* means "to follow instructions, obey, follow, be subject to."
17. *Analects* 2.5.

propriety in actions, which primarily means obedience to show personal loyalty. While in Ephesians 6:1, Paul appeals to what is "right" (*dikaios*), that is, a general sense of what people know to be fitting,[18] he extends it to "Children, obey your parents *in everything*" (*kata panta*) in Colossians 3:20. The latter suggests a more radical personal loyalty, similar to what Confucian filial piety teaches. One well-known exchange records that Confucius defined "men of integrity" as "a father covers up for his son, a son covers up for his father."[19] In Confucian culture, "uprightness" may be defined as personal loyalty toward family, especially to parents.[20] While the NT would not affirm the same view of "uprightness," it nevertheless promotes obedience to parents as a demonstration of a deep personal loyalty.

Secondly, honoring parents entails service and (financial) support. In Jesus's criticism of the Jewish leaders in Mark 7:9–13/Matthew 15:1–9, the issue was a withholding of financial support by some adult Jewish sons toward their parents based on "Corban" (offering devoted to God). Jesus considers the traditional practice as a breach of the fifth commandment and affirms the financial support of one's parents as its fulfillment. Similarly, in 1 Timothy 5:3, Paul calls on the church in Ephesus to "honor widows who are truly widows" (1 Tim 5:3 ESV), a subset of the "older women," by which he means widows should be provided for (see also Acts 6:1–6). In 1 Timothy 5:4, he assumes financial support of widows by their children and even grandchildren as normal and prior to the support of these widows by the church. Paul harshly criticizes male relatives who do not provide for widows in their own household (1 Tim 5:4, 8) because they had a legal obligation to provide for widows whose dowries were passed on to them at the death of the husbands.[21] In such cases, "worse than an unbeliever" (5:8) would be a just characterization.

Confucian filial piety likewise affirms financial support by children, but the service goes beyond this life:

> When their parents are alive they are served with love (*ai*) and
> respect (*jing*) and when they are deceased they are served with

---

18. Andrew T. Lincoln, *Ephesians*, WBC 42 (Dallas: Word, 1990), 403.

19. *Analects* 13.18.

20. Lee Dian Rainey, *Confucius and Confucianism: The Essentials* (Chichester: Wiley-Blackwell, 2010), 25–26.

21. Bruce W. Winter, *Seek the Welfare of the City: Christians as Benefactors and Citizens* (Grand Rapids: Eerdmans, 1994), 70. M. I. Finley, "The Elderly in Classical Antiquity," *Greece & Rome* 28, no. 2 (1981): 167, notes, "The law everywhere . . . required sons to provide for the support of their parents and grandparents."

grief and sorrow. This is the basic duty being discharged by the living, the fulfilling of the appropriate obligations (*yi*) between the living and the dead, and the consummation of service filial children owe their parents.[22]

For older children, "appropriate obligations" for deceased parents through financial means is only an extension of the support to elderly parents while alive. A filial son might resort to menial work and even indentured servitude to support his parents.[23]

What is more, the filial support is a debt repaid to one's parents. The "appropriate obligations" to be paid to deceased parents was a "service filial children owe their parents." The honor of parents in Confucian filial piety is a debt of gratitude for one's life.[24] That Paul calls for a "repaying" (*apodidōmi*) to one's parents in 1 Timothy 5:4 suggests he also has a reciprocal obligation in mind, the kind found in other human relationships of the time (e.g. patron-client relations). The NT language of *timē*, "manifestation of esteem, honor, reverence,"[25] considers honor a "possession" or even "price" and "money" (Acts 4:34; 5:2–3), making it a matter of reciprocity. In the Septuagint (LXX), *timaō* is used for the honor shown to parents (Exod 20:12; Deut 5:16) as well as to the elderly (Lev 19:32). In the social world of the NT, the competition for honor assumes that it is a commodity of exchange. The honor of parents and elders, then, is a payment in gratitude for their direct or indirect benevolence to the next generation.

Thirdly, honoring parents entails an attitude of respect and affection. It goes without saying that honoring assumes an internal attitude of reverence. In the NT, honor is often associated with love. For example, in Romans 12:10, Paul connects the "love" and "brotherly affection" for one another with "showing honor." In 1 Peter 2:17, Peter speaks of "love for the brotherhood" in between "honor" for everyone and the emperor. In his exchange with the rich young man in Matthew's account (Matt 19:16–22), Jesus curiously pairs the fifth commandment alongside the summary command, "You shall love your neighbor as yourself" (Lev 19:18), after listing the sixth through the ninth commandments (Matt 19:18–19; compare Mark 19:10; Luke 18:20), giving

---

22. *Xiaojing* ch. 18.
23. Keith N. Knapp, "Reverent Caring: The Parent-son Relationship in Early Medieval Tales of Filial Offspring," in *Filial Piety in Chinese Thought and History*, ed. Alan K. L. Chen and Sor-hoon Tan (London: RoutledgeCurzon, 2004), 55.
24. Rainey, *Confucius and Confucianism*, 25.
25. BDAG, s.v. *timē*.

it a "position of gravitas."[26] Hence, the NT vision of honor takes for granted an inner attitude of respect and affection.

Confucian filial piety also assumes the attitudes of respect and affection, but to the point that service and support are nullified without the inner attitude. Confucius thinks that without "respect," there is no difference between feeding parents and feeding animals. He teaches, "It is the attitude that matters. If young people merely offer their services when there is work to do, or let their elders drink and eat when there is wine and food, how could this ever pass as filial piety?"[27] The priority is given to the attitude of respect more than the acts of service. Clearly, action without the right attitude is a breach of filial piety.[28] Confucian filial piety is also said to begin with the natural love that children have for their parents.[29] And without such love, the acts of service and support are rendered meaningless.

Beyond parents, Confucian filial piety extends to other family members, particularly to older brothers, and then to leaders and rulers of the nation, eventually reaching to all elders.

> The Master said, "It is only because exemplary persons (*junzi*) serve their parents with family reverence that this same feeling can be extended to their lord as loyalty (*zhong*). It is only because they serve their elder brother with deference (*ti*) that this same feeling can be extended to all elders as compliance (*shun*)."[30]

Embedded in the family system and the loyalty to rulers, filial piety is foundational to social order. In this way, "all elders" are to be shown the "same feeling" of filial piety first shown to parents. Accordingly, the honor of elders is not limited to parents alone, but also to older members of one's family and ultimately to the leaders of society.

Of the five primary human relationships of Confucian thought,[31] one is between older and younger brothers. This relationship alone seems to isolate

---

26. Diane G. Chen, "Filial Piety and Radical Discipleship in Matthew," in *T&T Clark Handbook of Asian American Biblical Hermeneutics*, eds. U. Y. Kim and S. A. Yang (London: T&T Clark, 2019), 342.

27. *Analects* 2.7–8.

28. Rainey, *Confucius and Confucianism*, 25, writes, "Confucius was very much concerned with the neglect of parents, especially when they became older and were no longer influential and active in the family's affairs."

29. Rainey, *Confucius and Confucianism*, 25.

30. *Xiaojing* ch. 14.

31. The Five Relationships are ruler-minister, father-son, husband-wife, older-younger brother, friend-friend. See Wei-Ming Tu, "Probing the 'Three Bonds' and 'Five Relationships' in

age as the differentiating factor that commands respect. Hence, the idea of "brotherhood" retains a strong sense of hierarchy. Western interpretations of "brotherhood" in NT Christianity tend to think of egalitarian relations with little sense of hierarchy. However, age was a factor in the actual relations between siblings in the church as it was in the relationships of the household (husband-wife, master-slave).[32] So, Paul gives instruction to "older" persons and "younger" persons in the church (1 Tim 5:1–2; Tit 2:2–3) and instructs Timothy to treat "younger men as brothers" (*hōs adelphous*) and "younger women as sisters" (*hōs adelphas*). Age difference should not be overlooked in the understanding of "brothers" and "sisters." Since Paul is drawing on the family metaphor (as fathers and mothers), he may very well be thinking of the relational obligations inherent in sibling hierarchy (as brothers and sisters). His assumption is that the older members of the Christ family are responsible for the younger members, and on the flip side, the younger members should respect their elder siblings. This is the exchange between older and younger, similar to the parent-child reciprocity, that both Confucian culture and the NT vision recognize.

A good NT example of sibling exchange may be found in the Parable of the Lost Son in Luke 15. The complex relationships in the family between the father and two sons when untangled reveal that the key relationship between the older and younger brothers may be the main point of the parable. The relationship between the two brothers is almost nonexistent, but reading between the lines, one notices that both brothers neglect their sibling duties. On the one hand, the younger does not respect his older brother (not to mention his father!) when asking for his share of the inheritance first and leaving his older brother to care for their father alone. He demands the reward of filial piety but passes its responsibility to his older brother.

The older brother, on the other hand, neglects his responsibility to his younger brother in that he neither stops him from offending their father nor from leaving with his father's inheritance. Further, the older brother has failed as a filial son to his father in that he does not understand his father's pain. If he had, he would go find his lost brother and bring him back to his

---

Confucian Humanism," in *Confucianism and the Family*, eds. W. H. Slote and G. A. DeVos (Albany: SUNY, 1998), 121–36.

32. Husbands were between 10 to 15 years older than their wives, and many wives were married off as young teenagers. Slaves too were undoubtedly younger as they either did not live as long, due to the rigors of servile life, or were sold when no longer useful. See Finley, "The Elderly in Classical Antiquity," 159, 166–67.

father. So, the older brother has failed both his brother and his father. The point of the parable is that unlike the Jewish leaders (15:2), Jesus is both the filial Son to his Father and the responsible older Brother who eats with tax collectors and sinners (15:1) so that he might bring the lost siblings back to the family (19:10).

HONORING ELDERS AS LEADERS AND EMISSARIES

Confucian filial piety extends loyalty beyond the immediate and extended family to leaders and rulers. The reason why Korean rulers of the Joseon era summarily adopted Neo-Confucian ideals was to reform an ailing and politically unstable society in the final days of the Goryeo era.[33] This political purpose appears to be foundational to Confucian filial piety. Thus, one of Confucius's disciples explicates, "A man who respects his parents and elders would hardly be inclined to defy his superiors. A man who is not inclined to defy his superiors will never foment a rebellion."[34]

In the NT, honoring elders is also embedded in the honor for leaders. For example, it is well known that in the Roman world, the emperor was the "father of the country" (*Pater Patriae*) and in many ways, the empire was considered the household (*familia*) of the emperor.[35] Thus, Peter's exhortation to "honor the emperor" (1 Pet 2:17) ties in with the honor of parents and elders. Further, the title of "elder" was a common leadership position in various communities. "Elders" were leaders among the Jewish people (Matt 26:3; Luke 7:3; Acts 4:8), likely reflecting the "elders of Israel" in the Old Testament, and among the early church communities, both in Jerusalem (11:30) and in other churches (14:23). "Elder" (*presbyteros*) can refer both to an older man (1 Tim 5:1) and to a leader in the church (5:17). Hence, the honor of elders is linked to the honor of leaders in the NT world and leadership is connected to mature age.

In Confucian filial piety, the leader or ruler himself models its values and excellence. In the *Xiaojing*, the "Son of Heaven (*tian*)" sets the example: "The Emperor who loves (*ai*) his own parents would not presume to hate the

---

33. Baik, "Some Influences of Confucianism," 243–47, bases his understanding of Confucian influence in Korean history on Deuchler, *The Confucian Transformation of Korea*. Cf. however John Duncan, "The Korean Adoption of Neo-Confucianism: The Social Context," in *Confucianism and the Family*, eds. W. H. Slote and G. A. DeVos (Albany: SUNY, 1998), 75–90.
34. *Analects* 1.2.
35. David A. deSilva, *Honor, Patronage, Kinship & Purity: Unlocking New Testament Culture* (Downers Grove: InterVarsity Press 2000), 195. "Father" was a title of great respect, applied widely to leaders in Jewish and Greco-Roman settings. See also Craig S. Keener, "Family and Household," *DNTB*, 356–57.

parents of others; he who respects (*jing*) his own parents would not presume to be rude to the parents of others."[36] The ruler is the ideal filial son which makes him a model for the ordinary citizen and worthy of emulation. In the NT, elders and fathers who occupy positions of leadership are often exhorted to be models. In 1 Peter 5:1–3, Peter appeals to "the elders" (*presbyteros*) to be "examples to the flock" as shepherds by "watching over them" and "not lording it over" them. In Titus 2:2, Paul exhorts older men (*presbytēs*) to be characterized as "sober-minded, dignified, self-controlled, sound in faith, in love, and in steadfastness." While the last of the four urges soundness or "health" (important for older people!) in the Christian triad (faith, hope, love), the first three have wider appeal as qualities "for venerable older men in Roman culture."[37] In particular, "dignified" (*semnos*) has the sense of "worthy of respect"[38] and acting honorably as to set an example. Similarly, the well-known qualifications of elders as overseers in 1 Timothy 3:1–7 and Titus 1:5–9 are lists of virtues that parallel what ancient moralists suggest are honorable qualities for leadership. Of particular importance, the elder-leader was to "manage his own household well, with all dignity keeping his children submissive" (1 Tim 3:4). That the household was a microcosm of the larger Christian community is assumed, and so the elder-leader should be honorable (and honored) in all ways, even in his own household. Finally, the honor of elders as leaders in the community also extends to leaders of the state. The sometimes uncomfortable exhortation to honor Roman rulers in the NT (Rom 13:1–7; 1 Pet 2:13–17) should be understood in this larger interplay between honoring elders of one's family and "elders" of the state. The honor of elders and leaders flows naturally back and forth.

In addition, the flow of honor moves from heaven to earth as elders and leaders serve as emissaries of God. Paul's use of *presbeuō* ("ambassador," 2 Cor 5:20; also Eph 6:20) is a noteworthy play on old age. The verb can mean "to be the older or the eldest" but in the NT generally means to "be an ambassador/envoy."[39] Embedded here is the idea of old age serving as leader in the role of representative for someone or a state. His use in 2 Corinthians 5:20 has this connotation of representative in connection to the ministry of reconciliation. However, the use in Ephesians 6:20 may relate to Paul's seniority or old age (see

---

36. *Xiaojing* ch. 2.
37. Craig S. Keener, *The IVP Bible Background Commentary: New Testament*, 2nd ed. (Downers Grove: InterVarsity Press, 2014), 628.
38. BDAG, s.v. *semnos*.
39. Günther Bornkamm, "*presbus, presbuteros, ktl*," *TDNT* 6:681; BDAG, s.v. *presbeuō*.

Phlm 9). As representative of Christ and God, Paul hoped to gain a hearing and a modicum of (elderly?) respect from his audience.

A puzzling aspect of Confucian filial piety is the nature and role of "heaven" (*tian*). Scholars agree that "heaven" in Confucian thought is difficult to pin down. In relation to filial piety, it appears that heaven plays the role of higher authority and accountability. In the *Xiaojing*, to call the emperor the "Son of Heaven (*tian*)" may suggest the idea of heaven's guidance and approval when he models filial piety for the people. Lee Dian Rainey notes, "Filial piety acts as a tie between heaven and earth, not only because when one serves one's parents one serves heaven, but also because 'Filial piety is as the constant in heaven, as rightness on earth, and the path of human beings.'"[40] As "tie" between heaven and earth, filial piety may be considered a heavenly quality that humans may manifest on earth. In this way, the "Son of Heaven" is an emissary who sets heaven's example on earth.[41] The "enlightened kings" who practice filial piety have "served the heavens (*tian*)." The result was that "the gods and spirits sent down their blessings upon them."[42] Blessings of prosperity and long life promised in connection to the fifth commandment (Eph 6:3; Exod 20:12) seem to fit well with Confucian notions. It is difficult to think of "blessings" without the thought of rewards and ultimately accountability.[43]

In the NT, it is not heaven but a personal God who animates filial piety through creation.[44] Thus, Paul bows his knees (in good filial piety) to the "Father (*patēr*), from whom every family (*patria*) in heaven and on earth is named . . ." (Eph 3:14–15). The imagery, likely based on the Roman emperor's honorific title as *Pater Patriae*, portrays God as Father of all human families. For Paul, the honor of God as Parent of the human family takes precedence over the emperor who is "father of the country." A rich biblical theology of creation lies behind this picture. The implication is that the honor of God as Creator forms the basis of honoring parents, elders, and leaders. What is more, every parent, elder, or leader in some way reflects the Creator God, as *the*

---

40. Rainey, *Confucius and Confucianism*, 29, quoting from the *Xiaojing* ch. 2.

41. Khiok-Khng Yeo, "The Rhetorical Hermeneutic of 1 Corinthians 8 and Chinese Ancestor Worship," *BibInt* 2, no. 3 (1994): 303, thinks that Confucius envisioned familial values (filial piety) as actually transcendental values, and parents ought to be honored as "mediators of God."

42. *Xiaojing* ch. 16.

43. Oh, "Hermeneutics of Korean Theology," 341–43, suggests that Koreans have a strong sense of heaven's will and resulting blessings if heeded.

44. Daniel Qin, "Confucian Filial Piety and the Fifth Commandment: A Fulfillment Approach," *Asian Journal of Pentecostal Studies* 16, no. 1 (2013): 153–54, see the Confucian idea of "heaven" as basically humanistic.

Parent, Elder, or Leader. In this way, every elder is an emissary of the Creator God, and thus, deserves respect in that role.

Further, the NT affirms the honor of elders as emissaries of God's glory. When human beings exchange God's glory (*doxa*) for idolatrous images (*eikōn*) in Romans 1:23, this sin leads to other vices, including disobedience to parents (Rom 1:30), and all fall short of the glory of the Creator (3:23). Idolatry nullifies the Creator's glory because human beings are created in God's image to reflect his glory, but glory is also reflected in the relationship of creation, male and female, the heart of family order (so, the husband as the image [*eikōn*] and glory [*doxa*] of God in 1 Cor 11:7). Every parent and elder, then, as representative images of God's glory, deserve honor as God's emissaries. What is more, in 1 Timothy 5:4, the verb *eusebeō* is used "to show uncommon reverence or respect"[45] to widows, which Paul says should be expressed in financial support. Extrabiblical uses of *eusebeia* (piety) refer to noble actions both toward God and toward others, especially relatives (parents) and state leaders, that respects the ordering of family and state.[46] When NT writers consider piety (*eusebeia*) a Christian virtue, they have in mind a reverence for God that expresses itself in brotherly affection for others (2 Pet 1:6). To honor elders with respect and affection is to give glory to God.

HONORING ELDERS AS ANCESTORS OF FAITH

Confucian filial piety teaches that parents must be honored not only when alive but also "when they are deceased they are served with grief and sorrow." For Confucius, this is the "consummation of service" that children owe to their parents.[47] The prescriptions in the *Xiaojing* are elaborate: proper grief and sorrow, ritualized symbols and actions, mourning for three years and continuous offerings to the deceased. Korean expressions of this Confucian practice formed the pinnacle of filial piety with the traditional *chesa* (ancestral tablet and table of food), as part of the ancestral rites several times a year.[48] In

---

45. BDAG, s.v. *eusebeō*.

46. Werner Foerster, "*sebomai, sebazomai, ktl*," *TDNT* 7:176–78.

47. *Xiaojing* ch. 18. Also, *Analects* 2.5 reads, "When your parents are alive, serve them according to ritual. When they die, bury them according to ritual, make sacrifices to them according to ritual."

48. *Charye* ceremony on Lunar New Year and *Chuseok* (Harvest moon), *sije* ceremony four times a year for each season, and *kije* on the anniversary of day of death of the ancestors, for up to four generations. See Paul Mantae Kim, "The Ancestral Rite in Korea: Its Significance and Contextualization from an Evangelical Perspective," *International Journal of Frontier Missiology* 32, no. 3 (2015): 117–27, for detailed explanation of Korean practices.

addition, the Korean practices were influenced by ancient shamanism, giving them a distinctively spiritual character by which ancestral spirits are called upon as mediators.[49]

In the Roman world, ancestor worship was likewise common, complete with social and civic support, and ritual offerings of food and wine to the dead who were venerated as to gods. Elaborate memorial events were staged at burial sites by family members at great expense, but evidence shows that families of lesser means also served their dead ancestors. As Ramsay MacMullen notes, "Ancestor worship was for everyone, everywhere."[50] In addition, the imperial cult venerated emperors as gods, similar to other gods found in the Roman world, but it also venerated the emperor as part of the family religion of the *genius* (ancestor spirit), taking on the form of an ancestral cult. David deSilva notes, "Each family performed rites honoring its *genius*, the guardian spirit of the head of the household, and its *lar*, the spirit of the family's founding ancestor."[51] In light of these realities in the NT world, the first Christian communities must have grappled with ancestral veneration. The evidence of the early Christian centuries shows that it was indeed widely known and sanctioned as part of the veneration of martyrs and saints.[52]

Yet, despite the ubiquity of ancestral veneration in its context, the NT itself is largely silent about such practices with little evidence of any interaction with or veneration of the dead. Biblical examples of necromancy and mediums are always forbidden (Lev 19:31; 20:6, 27; 1 Sam 28:3, 7; 1 Chr 10:13–14). In the NT, the story of Lazarus and the rich man in Luke 16:19–31 may leave room for the dead to visit with or speak to the living, but in the end, the visit of the dead, if possible at all, is made useless since the living can "hear" the Scriptures instead (16:29–31). Further, the baptism for the dead in 1 Corinthians 15:29 is a notorious Pauline crux of which Western commentators tend to settle for a practice that saw unbelievers asking for and receiving baptism in order to be reunited with their believing dead ancestors.[53] Whatever the practice was,

49. Deok Won Ahn, "Liturgical Encounter: A Comparison among the Celebration of All Saints, Ancestor Worship, and *Chudo Yebae*," *Theology and Praxis* 37 (2013): 113–16.
50. Ramsay MacMullen, "The End of Ancestor Worship: Affect and Class," *Historia: Zeitschrift für Alte Geschichte* 63, no. 4 (2014): 493.
51. David A. deSilva, "Ruler Cult," *DNTB*, 1026–30.
52. MacMullen, "The End of Ancestor Worship," 494–513; also R. MacMullen, "Christian Ancestor Worship in Rome," *JBL* 129, no. 3 (2010): 597–613; Hae Jung Park, "All Saints Worship: Possible or not in a Korean Protestant Context?," *Theology and Praxis* 45 (2015): 51–55.
53. E.g. Anthony C. Thiselton, *The First Epistle to the Corinthians*, NIGTC (Grand Rapids: Eerdmans, 2000), 1248. This explanation is precisely the opposite of why most Asian Christians,

it affirms the desire to connect with dead ancestors through baptism but does not seem to require veneration of the dead, nor any interaction by the living with the dead.

Moreover, grieving over the death of believing loved ones in 1 Thessalonians 4:13–18 emphasizes resurrection hope over grieving "like the rest of mankind, who have no hope" (v. 13). Given its pervasiveness at the time, it is likely that the grieving "like the rest" involved some form of ancestor cult. Yet, Paul's response does not acknowledge any such practice by believers. He simply points to the hope of being reunited with dead believers when the Lord returns. The silence of the NT seems to suggest that unlike Korean-Confucian filial piety, the NT vision of honoring parents and elders does not condone veneration after death.

Needless to say, ancestor worship has long been an issue for the Christians and churches of Asia. For Asian evangelicals, still worth reading is the publication of the 1983 ATA "Consultation on the Christian Responses to Ancestor Practices" which includes perspectives from China, Japan, Korea, Taiwan, Malaysia, and Thailand.[54] The contributions in general toe the standard evangelical line that when ancestral practices encroach on the worship of God, then the practices must be rejected because the first and second commandments cannot be broken in order to keep Asian expressions of the fifth commandment.

In Korean history, the confrontations over ancestor worship led to mass persecutions of Catholics in the late 1700s to 1800s and upwards of some ten thousand deaths.[55] As latecomers to Korea when Confucian norms had weakened considerably, Protestants fared better when they, like the early Catholics, rejected ancestral practices as idolatry. This hard line largely remains the evangelical position in Korea to this day and those who have tried to push the

---

who are usually the first believers in their family line, find it desirable to pray for their dead grandmother or embrace a form of second chance theory, based on a particular reading of 1 Peter 3:19; 4:6. For a detailed discussion on second chance theory, see Hirokatsu Yoshihara, "A Study of 1 Peter 3:18b–20a and 4:6: A Response to the Notion of Christ's Postmortem Evangelism to the Un-evangelized, a View Recently Advocated in Japan, Part 1" and "Part 2," *Asian Journal of Pentecostal Studies* 20, no. 2 (2017): 183–97, 199–217.

54. Bong Rin Ro, ed., *Christian Alternatives to Ancestor Practices* (Seoul: Asia Theological Association, 1985). Some articles by Korean contributors were published in another monograph, Jung Young Lee, ed., *Ancestor Worship and Christianity in Korea*, Studies in Asian Thought and Religion 8 (Lampeter: Edwin Mellen, 1988).

55. Kim Myung-Hyuk, "Historical Analysis of Ancestor Worship in the Korean Church," in *Christian Alternatives to Ancestor Practices*, 165–68.

envelope have been emphatically rejected.[56] At the same time, the average member in the Korean church is forced to rethink how they relate to family members during holidays and memorial days when ancestors are venerated. Especially children and wives of unbelieving fathers and husbands find it difficult to refuse participation and would often rather choose to go through the motions without "worshipping" the ancestor as an idol.

There have been some noteworthy discussions on ancestor worship by Asian evangelicals. ShinHyung Seong suggests that while both Confucianism and Christianity have attached "religious connotations" to filial piety, they are expressed differently.[57] Confucian filial piety expresses religiosity through ancestor worship while Christian filial piety expresses religiosity through obeying God's command as an act of discipleship. This is because the foundational difference is that Confucianism is humanistic while Christianity is theistic. Wonsuk Ma parses out "three types of ancestor veneration" in three motifs: the religious, the cultural/ethical, and the political motifs.[58] The religious type is "ancestor worship" while the cultural/ethical type, Ma labels as "ancestor veneration." And the political type combines ancestor veneration with emperor worship. The distinguishing of types reminds us that ancestor veneration in Asia is a complex, multifaceted practice that requires a multidimensional response, depending on the type.

Encouraging fresh responses to ancestor worship among Asian evangelicals, Simon Chan contends for an Asian evangelical ecclesiology that takes "full cognizance of the importance of the family,"[59] in which the communion of saints includes not only the living believers but also deceased ones. Suggesting that Asian evangelicals draw more from rich Christian traditions of the past, Chan pleads for "concrete ritual acts" that demonstrate how Asian Christians honor their dead. To apply to the issue of ancestor worship, K. K. Yeo unpacks an "interpathic" approach to eating meat sacrificed to idols in 1 Corinthians 8

---

56. Kim, "Historical Analysis of Ancestor Worship," 170–73, recounts a well-remembered instance when Rev. Yonggi Cho of the famed Yoido Full Gospel Church preached a sermon, condoning the participation of Christians in ancestral practice since deceased parents are simply people, not idols, and serving them with affectionate remembrance is simply honoring them (by the 5th commandment). There was widespread condemnation by his evangelical peers.

57. S. H. Seong, "'Honor Your Father and Your Mother' Confucius and Jesus on Filial Obligations," 74.

58. Wonsuk Ma, "Three Types of Ancestor Veneration in Asia: An Anthropological Analysis," *JAM* 4, no. 2 (2002): 201–15. Kim, "The Ancestral Rite in Korea," cited above, suggests another set of three motifs of ancestor veneration: religious, social, and psychological.

59. Simon Chan, "Toward an Asian Evangelical Ecclesiology," in *Asian Christian Theology: Evangelical Perspectives*, ed. T. D. Gener and S. T. Pardue (Carlisle: Langham Global Library, 2019), 145.

in which Paul temporarily shares the Corinthians' assumptions, beliefs, and values, both cognitively and affectively experiencing what they thought and felt about meat sacrificed to idols. In so doing, Paul avoids prohibition and turning an ethical response into a legalistic obligation, but rather recognizes the needs of the weak for greater knowledge and of the strong for more love. By refusing to give an absolute "yes" or "no" answer, according to Yeo, Paul establishes a "deliberative, community discourse," which shows that he values the process more than the answer.[60]

Korean scholars have already begun to draw on parallels from Christian tradition. Deok Weon Ahn compares the tradition of All Saints celebration with Korean ancestor worship, which is influenced by Confucian filial piety and Korean shamanism, and suggests that the Korean church's *chudo yebae* (memorial service) "inculturates" both tradition and indigenous practice as a "dynamic expression of the faith of God's people."[61] Hae Jung Park traces the development of the cult of the saints, starting with the veneration of martyrs, beginning with Jesus and Stephen in the NT, and wonders why such a veneration cannot inform Korean Protestant practices of memorial services, including a reaffirmation of the communion of the saints and supplementing the Eucharist to the memorial service for the dead.[62] Sungmu Lee contends that the Christian Eucharist and the Korean-Confucian *chesa* share similarities and that the latter can inform and add new richness to the practice of the Eucharist itself.[63] It appears that the Korean church continues to develop the *chumoyeshik*, the worship ceremony commemorating the memory of a deceased loved one that most Protestant denominations now endorse.

In light of these contributions, the NT's silence on the matter of ancestor veneration must be reconsidered. The silence may suggest that ancestor veneration was a difficult issue for the first believers who were surrounded by such practices, in much the same way that it is for Asian Christians today. For the early Christ movement to address such a large-scale, deep-seated practice certainly had the potential to provoke conflict, persecution, and even widespread martyrdom. A similar large-scale issue was slavery, which the first Christians only address tangentially (see 1 Cor 7:21; Phlm 16). From this perspective, there may have been a strategic purpose to the silence, similar to the way many

---

60. Yeo, "The Rhetorical Hermeneutic of 1 Corinthians 8," 17.
61. Ahn, "Liturgical Encounter," 123.
62. Park, "All Saints Worship," cited above.
63. Sungmu Lee, "The Eucharist and the Confucian *Chesa* (Ancestor Rite)," *Worship* 82, no. 4 (2008): 323–38.

Korean denominations do not have an official stance on member participation in family ancestral rites. The NT authors, while seeking to balance the tension between knowledge and love, may not have wanted to give a one-size-fits-all solution to the ancestral veneration issue, similar to the issue of food sacrificed to idols.[64] Rather, they may have wanted the gospel to speak into the issue more subtly. In other words, believers would come to understand through the gospel that their belief in Christ's death and resurrection satisfied the need for ancestor veneration as they fully grasped their union with even deceased believers in and through Christ.[65]

In the NT vision, the honor of God the Father and his filial Son forms the foundation of honoring elders, and so the nature of God and why he sent his Son must factor into any response to ancestor veneration. If God as Creator is the first Father, then every ancestor points us back in some sense to God's parenthood. The genealogies of the Bible remind us of this truth. In the NT, the genealogy of Jesus in Luke 3:23–38 traces back to God, not only because he is the Son of God, but also because every human being is a son or daughter of God when traced back far enough. What is more, the genealogy of Jesus in Matthew 1:17 shows respectable ancestors (Abraham, David) but also many disreputable ones (Judah and Tamar, Rahab, many bad people).

In honoring God as our first Ancestor, we can also honor every ancestor, whether believer or unbeliever. In addition, when we consider why God sent his Son, we must understand that Jesus came to redeem a new family for God with children "born of God" by faith (John 1:12–13). This fictive family is a new creation, and it incorporates believers from the past, as Hebrews 11 reminds us. In this fictive family across time, the honor of elders should be extended to the *ancestors of faith*, recognizing God's redemptive purposes through them.[66]

While writing this essay, I spent precious time with my dying father, a firm believer in Christ, and discovered something about my grandfather whom I

---

64. See discussion on Yeo, "The Rhetorical Hermeneutic of 1 Corinthians 8," above.

65. In view of Chan, "Toward an Asian Evangelical Ecclesiology," cited above, I wonder if the first Christians had a robust-enough ecclesiology that understood well, perhaps better than evangelicals today, that communion with deceased believers was on-going in Christ, and so at least partially satisfying the need for the practice of ancestor veneration. Although interesting to speculate, this would not satisfactorily explain the silence, I would think, especially when considering deceased unbelievers.

66. Paul's mention of "ancestors" (*progonos*) in the context of giving thanks to God in 2 Timothy 1:3 as he remembers Timothy in prayer suggests that he understood the important influence of ancestors on him and his service to God.

never knew because he passed away when dad was a teenager. While his family was living as North Korean refugees in the South after the war, my father was "forced" to go to church by my grandfather who interestingly, by all family accounts, was not a confessing believer. My father speculates that grandfather escorted him to church every Sunday so that his most rebellious son (of four brothers) would not turn to gangsterism.

When asked about his most cherished memory of grandfather, my father shared about being at an outdoor Christian (evangelistic?) event as a boy and being harshly scolded by my grandfather for not singing along with the congregation. When my father turned to look at my grandfather, he remembers him being in tears and wondering why, given that older Korean men do not shed tears easily. Hearing this story, I wondered if my ancestor was a believer after all. And yet, regardless of his faith status, I was led to give thanks to God for my grandfather, as both my physical ancestor and an ancestor of faith who by God's grace helped shape my father's faith and through him, mine as well. Moreover, because every ancestor represents the Creator God to the next generations, I can honor my grandfather as an ancestor of faith regardless of whether he was a believer.

A NEW TESTAMENT VISION OF HONORING ELDERS, LIVING AND DECEASED

Our understanding of the NT vision of honoring our elders is significantly informed by Confucian filial piety, comparable in many ways but also divergent in other ways. Both would ground the honoring of elders in the honoring of one's parents. Proper honoring of parents comes first because only then are other elders in the family, in one's extended family, and in the fictive families (church and society) properly honored. If elders are to be honored as our fathers and mothers, there must first be a genuine attitude of respect and affection. After that, there must be a sense of gratitude and indebtedness that animates our service and support of our elders. And depending on the family context, whether in one's blood family, in the church or in the society, there must be a consideration of material or financial support.

The honor of elders extends from parents to older family members and then to leaders of the communities and the state, radiating outward from one's blood family to the fictive families of the church and society. Elders should then be honored not only as parents but also as older siblings and as leaders, whether formally or informally, on the basis of mature age. What is more, the honor of elders in the NT is grounded in the glory of God as Creator and first

Father of the family of humanity. Elders then are to be honored as emissaries of God, bearing a reflection of his glory for those who come after them.

The NT does not support the veneration of elders who have died in forms and rituals similar to Confucian filial piety. However, it does support the idea that dead ancestors should be honored as ancestors of faith who are used by God to bring life to us, not only physically but also spiritually, by God's redemptive purposes. In this way, Asian evangelicals may give thanks to God for all ancestors.

I dedicate this essay to my late father, Chang Sang Min (May 12, 1938 – June 13, 2022), who taught me how to trust in God's love. *Abeoji, sarang-haeyo, gamsahaeyo!*

BIBLIOGRAPHY

Ahn, Deok Weon. "Liturgical Encounter: A Comparison among the Celebration of All Saints, Ancestor Worship, and Chudo Yebae." *Theology and Praxis* 37 (2013): 105–29.

Baik, Chung-Hyun. "Some Influences of Confucianism on Korean Christian Family Life: Confucian? Christian? Or Confucian-Christian?" *Theology Today* 76, no. 3 (2019): 242–51.

Chan, Simon. "Toward an Asian Evangelical Ecclesiology." In *Asian Christian Theology: Evangelical Perspectives*, edited by Timoteo D. Gener and Stephen T. Pardue, 139–54. Carlisle: Langham Global Library, 2019.

Chen, Diane G. "Filial Piety and Radical Discipleship in Matthew." In *T&T Clark Handbook of Asian American Biblical Hermeneutics*. Edited by Uriah Y. Kim and Seung Ai Yang, 340–50. London: T&T Clark, 2019.

DeSilva, David A. *Honor, Patronage, Kinship & Purity: Unlocking New Testament Culture.* Downers Grove: InterVarsity Press, 2000.

———. "Ruler Cult." *DNTB* 1026–30.

Deuchler, Martina. *The Confucian Transformation of Korea: A Study of Society and Ideology.* Cambridge: Harvard, 1992.

Duncan, John. "The Korean Adoption of Neo-Confucianism: The Social Context." In *Confucianism and the Family*, edited by W. H. Slote and G. A. DeVos, 75–90. Albany: SUNY, 1998.

Finley, M. I. "The Elderly in Classical Antiquity." *Greece & Rome* 28, no. 2 (1981): 156–71.

Gener, Timoteo D., and Stephen T. Pardue, eds. *Asian Christian Theology: Evangelical Perspectives.* Carlisle: Langham Global Library, 2019.

Keener, Craig S. "Family and Household." *DNTB* 356–57.

————. *The IVP Bible Background Commentary: New Testament.* 2nd ed. Downers Grove: InterVarsity Press, 2014.

Kim, Jaewon. "No Country for Old Koreans: Moon Faces Senior Poverty Crisis." *Nikkei Asia.* 29 January 2019. https://asia.nikkei.com/Spotlight/Asia-Insight/ No-country-for-old-Koreans-Moon-faces-senior-poverty-crisis.

Kim, Myung-Hyuk. "Historical Analysis of Ancestor Worship in the Korean Church." In *Christian Alternatives to Ancestor Practices*, edited by Bong Rin Ro, 165–68. Seoul: Asia Theological Association, 1985.

Kim, Paul Mantae. "The Ancestral Rite in Korea: Its Significance and Contextualization from an Evangelical Perspective." *International Journal of Frontier Missiology* 32, no. 3 (2015): 117–27.

Knapp, Keith N. "Reverent Caring: The Parent-son Relationship in Early Medieval Tales of Filial Offspring." In *Filial Piety in Chinese Thought and History*, edited by Alan K. L. Chen and Sor-hoon Tan, 44–70. London: RoutledgeCurzon, 2004.

Lee, Jung Young, ed. *Ancestor Worship and Christianity in Korea.* Studies in Asian Thought and Religion 8. Lampeter: Edwin Mellen, 1988.

Lee, Sungmu. "The Eucharist and the Confucian *Chesa* (Ancestor Rite)." *Worship* 82, no. 4 (2008): 323–38.

Lim, Kar Yong. "The New Testament and the Sociocultural and Religious Realities of the Asian Contexts." In *An Asian Introduction to the New Testament*, edited by J. Thomaskutty, 5–27. Minneapolis: Fortress, 2022.

Lincoln, Andrew T. *Ephesians.* WBC 42. Dallas: Word, 1990.

Ma, Wonsuk. "Three Types of Ancestor Veneration in Asia: An Anthropological Analysis." *JAM* 4, vol. 2 (2002): 201–15.

MacMullen, Ramsay. "Christian Ancestor Worship in Rome." *JBL* 129, no. 3 (2010): 597–613.

————. "The End of Ancestor Worship: Affect and Class." *Historia: Zeitschrift für Alte Geschichte* 63, no. 4 (2014): 487–513.

Nylan, Michael, ed. *The Analects: The Simon Leys Translation, Interpretations.* New York: W. W. Norton & Company, 2014.

Oh, Jung Sun. "A Hermeneutics of Korean Theology of Filial Piety: A Global Theology." *AsJT* 24, no. 2 (2010): 325–46.

Park, Hae Jung. "All Saints Worship: Possible or not in a Korean Protestant Context?" *Theology and Praxis* 45 (2015): 47–74.

Peñamora, Aldrin M., and Bernard K. Wong, eds. *Asian Christian Ethics: Evangelical Perspectives.* Carlisle: Langham Global Library, 2022.

Qin, Daniel. "Confucian Filial Piety and the Fifth Commandment: A Fulfillment Approach." *Asian Journal of Pentecostal Studies* 16, no. 1 (2013): 139–64.

Rainey, Lee Dian. *Confucius and Confucianism: The Essentials*. Chichester: Wiley-Blackwell, 2010.

Ro, Bong Rin, ed. *Christian Alternatives to Ancestor Practices*. Seoul: Asia Theological Association, 1985.

Rosemont Jr., Henry, and Roger T. Ames. *The Chinese Classic of Family Reverence: A Philosophical Translation of the* Xiaojing. Honolulu: University of Hawaii Press, 2009.

Seong, ShinHyung. "Honor Your Father and Your Mother." In *Asian Christian Ethics: Evangelical Perspectives*, edited by Aldrin M. Peñamora and Bernard K. Wong, 61–79. Carlisle: Langham Global Library, 2022.

Son, Bong Ho. "Socio-Philosophical Background for Change of Attitude toward Ancestor Worship." In *Christian Alternatives to Ancestor Practices*, edited by Bong Rin Ro, 235–46. Seoul: Asia Theological Association, 1985.

———. "Ancestor Worship: From the Perspective of Modernization." In *Ancestor Worship and Christianity in Korea*, edited by J. Y. Lee, 61–71. Studies in Asian Thought and Religion 8. Lampeter: Edwin Mellen, 1988.

Thiselton, Anthony C. *The First Epistle to the Corinthians*. NIGTC. Grand Rapids: Eerdmans, 2000.

Tu, Wei-Ming. "Probing the 'Three Bonds" and 'Five Relationships' in Confucian Humanism." In *Confucianism and the Family*, edited by W. H. Slote and G. A. DeVos, 121–36. Albany: SUNY, 1998.

Winter, Bruce W. *Seek the Welfare of the City: Christians as Benefactors and Citizens*. Grand Rapids: Eerdmans, 1994.

Yeo, Khiok-Khng. "The Rhetorical Hermeneutic of 1 Corinthians 8 and Chinese Ancestor Worship." *BibInt* 2, no. 3 (1994): 294–311.

Yoshihara, Hirokatsu. "A Study of 1 Peter 3:18b–20a and 4:6: A Response to the Notion of Christ's Postmortem Evangelism to the Un-evangelized, a View Recently Advocated in Japan, Part 1." *Asian Journal of Pentecostal Studies* 20, no. 2 (2017): 183–97.

———. "A Study of 1 Peter 3:18b–20a and 4:6: A Response to the Notion of Christ's Postmortem Evangelism to the Un-evangelized, a View Recently Advocated in Japan, Part 2." *Asian Journal of Pentecostal Studies* 20, no. 2 (2017): 199–217.

CHAPTER 10

RESPONDING TO PERSECUTION AND MARGINALIZATION OF CHRISTIANS

Chee-Chiew Lee

INTRODUCTION

Christians have been facing opposition, marginalization, and even persecution since the birth of the church. In order for contemporary Asian Christians to respond in accord with the Bible's teaching, it is important that we examine the teachings of the New Testament (NT) in a well-rounded way before we consider how we may respond in our own contexts. Specifically, we will look at what factors led to the persecution of Christians in the NT and how these early Christians responded accordingly.[1] Thereafter, we will do some contemporary reflection by briefly analyzing various contexts in Asia and suggesting how Asian Christians might respond.

It is important that we first define what persecution entails so that we do not exaggerate opposition nor trivialize persecution. "Persecution" in general refers to "unfair or cruel treatment over a long period of time because of race, religion, or political beliefs."[2] In terms of persecution of Christians, this article will adopt Tieszen's definition: "Any unjust action of varying levels of hostility, perpetrated primarily on the basis of religion, and directed at Christians, resulting in varying levels of harm as it is considered from the victim's perspective."[3] Thus, mere rejection of or opposition to the gospel message does not necessarily entail persecution unless it involves physical or verbal violence against the proclaimers.[4]

---

1. For a detailed analysis of the factors of and responses to persecution in the New Testament, see Chee-Chiew Lee, *When Christians Face Persecution: Theological Perspectives from the New Testament* (London: Apollos, 2022), 12–93.
2. *Cambridge Advanced Learner's Dictionary and Thesaurus*, s.v. "Persecution," https://dictionary.cambridge.org/dictionary/english/persecution.
3. Charles L. Tieszen, "Towards Redefining Persecution," *International Journal for Religious Freedom* 1, no. 1 (2008): 76.
4. E.g. in Acts 13:8, Elymas opposed Paul's gospel message but Luke did not depict him inflicting harm on Paul.

FACTORS LEADING TO PERSECUTION
AND MARGINALIZATION

In the four Gospels, Jesus clearly teaches that his disciples will be persecuted because of him (Mark 13:13 // Matt 10:22 // Luke 21:17; John 15:18–21). Based on the descriptions in the NT, Jewish and polytheistic opponents persecute Christians because they perceive Christians to be a threat to: (1) dearly-held traditions (including theological and biblical interpretive traditions); (2) economic losses; and (3) the stability of the society. These sociological factors led to the persecution of Christians during the first century AD. In addition, from the perspective of NT authors, there is a spiritual dimension behind the persecution of Christians – opposition is often associated with the work of the devil (e.g. John 8:33, 44; Acts 13:10; 2 Cor 11:4; 2 Tim 2:25–26), and Revelation 12:9 specifically depicts Satan as the instigator of persecution.

Threat to Dearly-Held Traditions

First-century Greco-Roman cultures, whether Jewish or polytheistic, were steeped in the concept of honor and shame, and people highly valued traditions handed down from past generations. For the post-exilic Jews, obedience to the Mosaic Law was important because they reckoned that their forefathers were exiled due to disobedience (cf. Neh 9:29–35). Covenantal unfaithfulness was the major sin of their ancestors – they had engaged in idolatry by following the nations to worship other gods (2 Kgs 17:7–23; Ezek 20:1–44; Dan 9:1–19). Thus, many post-exilic Jews separated themselves from Gentiles (Ezra 9–10; Neh 8–9).[5] For them, Gentiles can only be included as God's people if they become fully proselytized by worshipping the God of the Jews exclusively, obeying the Mosaic Law (especially male circumcision), and assimilating into the Jewish community.[6] As post-exilic Jews held to monotheism, any divine claims by individuals were regarded as blasphemous (e.g. Luke 5:21; John 10:33).

Therefore, when Christians proclaimed that Jesus was the Son of God and the Messiah, Jews who could not agree with them regarded these claims as blasphemous. Furthermore, Christians also proclaimed that Gentiles could be included as God's people without obeying the Mosaic Law (Acts 15:1, 5),

---

5. The rationale behind this separation likely includes: (1) to avoid defilement as idolatry (cf. Ezek 36:25; 37:23) and the Gentile diet (e.g. Lev 11) were considered unclean; and (2) to avoid being tempted into idolatry like their forefathers (cf. Neh 13:25–27).
6. David C. Sim, "Gentiles, God-Fearers and Proselytes," in *Attitudes to Gentiles in Ancient Judaism and Early Christianity*, eds. David C. Sim and James S. McLaren, LNTS 499 (London: Bloomsbury, 2015), 9–27.

and the apostle Paul advocated for the notion that justification is by believing in Christ and not by obedience to the law (Gal 2:15–3:29; Rom 2:1–5:2). Jews who were zealous for the law perceived these Christian teachings as a threat to their dearly-held traditions. It was not just for tradition's sake, but conceivably their concern that disobedience to the law, as understood in its traditional Jewish interpretation, would incur God's wrath (cf. Neh 13:17–18).

For the polytheists, they believed that their well-being in various aspects of their lives (e.g. family, work, society) were favors bestowed by the gods. They were to reciprocate by honoring and serving the gods through performing rituals. Failure to do so was shameful and amounted to ingratitude. Furthermore, the gods – their benefactors – may then no longer bestow favors to them. Conversely, they believed that disasters (e.g. poor health, poor business, foreign invasion, natural catastrophe) were due to the anger of the gods, and they often attributed this to the negligence of rituals.[7] Several contemporary Asian folk religions also have similar beliefs, whereby offerings are made to the gods or the deceased to appease them, so that they may bless the worshippers and not harm them.[8]

Non-traditional forms of rituals and worship were frowned upon as these were unproven to be acceptable to the gods. In order to avoid disasters, people were to observe the "customs of the ancestors" (*mos maiorum*) strictly and were prohibited from performing new or foreign rituals publicly or privately, unless given official approval.[9] Consequently, polytheists considered Christians' exclusive worship of one God, their refusal to participate in other rituals, and their new rituals as highly dangerous – these not only defied their traditional values of piety and honor to the gods but were considered to incur divine wrath on the entire community.

Furthermore, the Christian theological perspective of other gods as demonic (cf. 1 Cor 10:19–21) is highly offensive to the polytheists. We can

---

7. Harry O. Maier, *New Testament Christianity in the Roman World* (New York: Oxford University Press, 2018), 35. This negligence includes rituals that were incorrectly performed or inappropriate in form.

8. See Stuart H. Blackburn, "Death and Deification: Folk Cults in Hinduism." *History of Religions* 24, no. 3 (1985): 269–71; Ichiro Hori, "Japanese Folk-Beliefs," *American Anthropologist* 61, no. 3 (1959): 418–23; Joseph B. Tamney, "Asian Popular Religions," in *Encyclopedia of Religion and Society*, ed. William H. Swatos, Jr. (Walnut Creek: AltaMira, 1998), 31–32.

9. James R. Harrison, "The Persecution of Christians from Nero to Hadrian," in *Into All the World: Emergent Christianity in Its Jewish and Greco-Roman Context*, ed. Mark Harding and Alanna Nobbs (Grand Rapids: Eerdmans, 2017), 277, 279; Eric M. Orlin, *Temples, Religion, and Politics in the Roman Republic* (Boston: Brill Academic, 2002), 61; Alan Watson, *The State, Law, and Religion: Pagan Rome* (Athens: University of Georgia Press, 1992), 58.

imagine how offended polytheists would be when they heard Christians claiming that the worship of their gods is "detestable idolatry" (1 Pet 4:3 NIV).[10] As some scholars note, even polytheists did not describe religious practices they disapprove of in such a manner.[11]

Threat to Economic Losses

When people adopted the Christian faith in response to evangelistic proclamations, Jewish Christians would leave the Jewish synagogue community (cf. Acts 13:43; 17:4), and Gentile Christians would discontinue their previous polytheistic religious practices (cf. 1 Thess 1:9; 1 Pet 4:3–4). This is unlike most polytheists, who could adopt new gods into their pantheon without renouncing others (some Asian polytheistic religions also have such an expandable pantheon).[12] Having members leaving their religious community is not just a loss of their adherents to this new religion, but a loss of honor of their gods (cf. Acts 19:26–27) and income, as we shall see below. These losses had a direct impact on the livelihood of people and the funding of synagogues, it was not just about personal selfish gains. In present-day Asia, people whose livelihood depends on selling religious products for worship would be in a similar position.

When Paul proclaimed the gospel in synagogues, those who believed and left the synagogue community included not only Jews but also Gentile god-fearers (Acts 17:4, 12). Among them were some prominent Greek women who could have provided benefactions to them as their patrons.[13] For the non-Christian Jews, this would mean loss of funding for the operations of the synagogue. Similarly, in Asia, when more and more people become Christians, other Asian religious places of worship would also suffer loss of income because there would be less people donating to them.

---

10. *Athemitos* "detestable" in 1 Peter 4:13 means "violating canons of decency, wanton, disgusting, unseemly" (*A Greek-English Lexicon of the New Testament and Other Early Christian Literature*, s.v. *athemitos*).

11. Paul J. Achtemeier, *1 Peter*, Hermeneia (Minneapolis: Fortress, 1996), 282; Karen H. Jobes, *1 Peter*, BECNT (Grand Rapids: Baker Academic, 2005), 267.

12. Ralph Anderson, "New Gods," in *The Oxford Handbook of Ancient Greek Religion*, eds. Esther Eidinow and Julia Kindt (New York: Oxford University Press, 2015), 309–23. In some Asian religions, the deceased were frequently deified and added to the pantheon of deities. See Blackburn, "Death and Deification," 258–68; Hori, "Japanese Folk-Beliefs," 417–19.

13. Craig S. Keener, *Acts: An Exegetical Commentary*, 4 vols. (Grand Rapids: Baker Academic, 2012–2015), 2:2095, 3:2542–43; Carolyn Osiek, "*Diakonos* and *Prostatis*: Women's Patronage in Early Christianity," *HTS Teologiese Studies/Theological Studies* 61, nos. 1–2 (2005): 347–70.

For the polytheists, Christian conversion would mean loss of income for those whose livelihood depended on supplying the needs of polytheistic worship, such as craftsmen who made shrines and statues of gods, as well as meat sellers who sold sacrificial meats in the markets.[14] Thus, it is not surprising that Demetris the silversmith of Ephesus and those in his trade strongly opposed Paul (19:24–27).

Threat to Stability of Society

Other than being frequently regarded as subversive in its threat to dearly-held traditions, Christians were also regarded as a threat to the stability of the society, and even seditious for the following reasons. First, conflicts Christians had with other Jews and polytheists often led to social unrest, with opponents bringing charges against Christian missionaries to the authorities (e.g. 16:19–24; 17:5–8; 18:12–16; 19:28–41; see also Suetonius, *Life of Claudius* 25.4).

Second, the proclamation of Jesus as the Messiah (i.e., Christ) carried strong political connotations that could be perceived as seditious, as the Scriptures speak of an ideal king who holds a priestly office and rules over all nations (e.g. Pss 72, 110; cf. Heb 8–9; Rev 17:14), and who will rule eternally after destroying the worldly empire (e.g. Dan 7:13–14; cf. Rev 19:11–21). Although the titles used of Jesus, such as "the Son of God" (e.g. Acts 9:20; Heb 1:3), "the Great High Priest" (e.g. 4:15), "Savior of all people" (e.g. 1 Tim 4:10) were developed from the Jewish Scriptures and traditions, they overlapped with titles that were used of the Roman emperor.[15] Thus, we can understand why the people and officials of Thessalonica were alarmed when the Jews accused Paul and Silas of "defying Caesar's decrees, saying that there is another king, one called Jesus" (Acts 17:7 NIV).[16]

Third, polytheists regarded the refusal of Christians to participate in imperial worship as highly dangerous and seditious. Polytheists showed their loyalty to the Roman emperor and honored him both publicly and privately in a way similar to how they honored their gods.[17] Other than praying and sacrificing to

---

14. E.g. during the early second century, Roman magistrate Pliny the Younger (*Letters* 10.96.10) noted that, because many people in Bithynia-Pontus had become Christians, the sales of sacrificial meats in the market were badly affected.

15. Michael Peppard, *The Son of God in the Roman World: Divine Sonship in Its Social and Political Context* (New York: Oxford University Press, 2011), 31–49; Bruce W. Winter, *Divine Honours for the Caesars: The First Christians' Responses* (Grand Rapids: Eerdmans, 2015), 62–77.

16. Keener, *Acts*, 3:2552–55.

17. Ittai Gradel, *Emperor Worship and Roman Religion* (New York: Clarendon Press, 2002), 13; Gwynaeth McIntyre, *Imperial Cult* (Leiden: Brill, 2019), 65.

their gods for the well-being of the emperor, they also performed these rituals directly to the emperor to honor him for the favors he had bestowed on the people. This is not only because the populace regarded the emperor as a divine being, but also because the emperor would then (like the gods) be obliged to return further favors to them.[18] For the polytheists, failure to participate in imperial worship rituals would not only result in loss of favors, but could be regarded as treason and could invite a bloody Roman military suppression. Thus, local authorities not only promoted imperial worship, but also punished those who refused to practice it (cf. Rev 13:11–17). We will discuss similar situations in contemporary Asia below.

Considering the unrest caused by the opposition of Christians from among the people, the subversive nature of the Christian message in challenging dearly-held traditions, the threat of economic losses for some groups of people due to Christian conversion, as well as the perceived sedition due to the Christian messianic proclamations and non-participation in imperial worship, we can understand why (1) individuals and groups would oppose or even persecute Christians; and (2) the authorities would regard these early Christians as a threat to the stability of the society and thus suppress them. As religion permeated every aspect of first-century life (e.g. privately at home or at work, publicly at trade guilds and municipal gatherings), we can also understand how Christians would be marginalized (e.g. in terms of participation in trade guilds and municipal administration) for fear of incurring the wrath of the gods and the Roman authorities.

RESPONSES TO PERSECUTION AND MARGINALIZATION

The NT reflects diverse ways by which Christians responded to the persecutions they faced. We shall also look at how the NT authors evaluate these various responses and how they encourage their audience to stand firm in their Christian faith. We will also distinguish between the teachings of the NT regarding how Christians *should* respond and how these early Christians *actually* responded when facing persecution.

---

18. Bruce W. Winter, "Divine Imperial Cultic Activities and the Early Church," in Harding, *Into All the World*, 240.

Perseverance

In Acts, Luke portrays the disciples persevering in their faith despite persecution in a way that demonstrates that Jesus is faithful to his promises.[19] First, the disciples understood their suffering for Christ as integral to following Christ (cf. Luke 9:23; Acts 14:22), because Jesus had said that those who would not take up their cross to follow him are not able to be his disciples (Luke 14:27). Jesus had also promised that the Holy Spirit would empower them to be his witnesses and give them wisdom to know what to say before the authorities (Luke 12:11–12; 21:12–15; Acts 1:8). The defense of Peter, Stephen, and Paul before the authorities clearly shows how this promise was fulfilled (4:8–12; 5:29–32; 7:1–53; 23:1–9; 24:10–21; 25:6–7; 26:1–23). In doing so, we may infer that Luke seeks to encourage his audience that they can live in accord with Jesus's teachings when facing persecution, because his promises are true and can be experienced as seen in the lives of the early disciples.

Paul persevered despite persecution, and he also commended the Thessalonians for doing likewise (1 Thess 1:3, 6; 2 Thess 1:4). Like the disciples in Acts, the Thessalonians were joyous despite facing persecution (1 Thess 1:6; cf. Acts 5:41). Paul also reckoned that suffering persecution for Christ is inevitable (1 Thess 3:3–4; Phil 1:29; 2 Tim 3:12) and he was not ashamed of it (Phil 1:20; 2 Tim 1:12). It is noteworthy that, although Paul was not spared from sorrows and fears (2 Cor 6:10; 7:4), he could still be joyous and persevere on because he experienced God's empowerment in his weaknesses (cf. 4:7–10).[20]

For Paul, such suffering is worthwhile for two reasons. First, it serves as evidence of his divinely appointed apostleship (cf. 6:4; 11:23–29) and a mark that he is a true member of God's people (Gal 4:28–31; Phil 1:28).[21] Second, it gives him opportunities to advance the gospel:[22] (1) he could bear witness for Jesus before his persecutors and the prison guards (cf. 1:12–13; 2 Tim 2:9–10); (2) other Christians would be encouraged to do the same when they see his example (Phil 1:14); and (3) sufferings are able to form character and

---

19. See also Scott Cunningham, 'Through Many Tribulations': The Theology of Persecution in Luke-Acts (Sheffield: Sheffield Academic, 1997), 128.

20. Kar Yong Lim, "The Sufferings of Christ Are Abundant in Us" (2 Corinthians 1:5): A Narrative-Dynamics Investigation of Paul's Sufferings in 2 Corinthians, LNTS 399 (London: T&T Clark, 2009), 106.

21. John A. Dunne, Persecution and Participation in Galatians (Tübingen: Mohr Siebeck, 2017), 4–7, 193–95; James A. Kelhoffer, Persecution, Persuasion, and Power: Readiness to Withstand Hardship as a Corroboration of Legitimacy in the New Testament (Tübingen: Mohr Siebeck, 2010), 30–93.

22. See also Lim, Sufferings of Christ, 186–87.

hope (Rom 5:3–4), and no persecution can separate believers from God's love (8:35–39). These reasons became his motivation to persevere.

Jesus taught his disciples to love their enemies and not to repay evil with evil, but instead to pray for them and bless them (Matt 5:43–44; Luke 6:27–28). Paul and Peter continued to teach this in their letters (Rom 12:14–21; 1 Pet 3:8–9), while Luke showed how Stephen demonstrated this teaching with his last breath (Acts 7:60). Although in some cases Paul may have responded to his persecutors in accord with the above teaching by blessing those who cursed him (1 Cor 4:12–13b), he seemed to do the opposite in some other cases (e.g. Acts 13:9–11; 23:3–4; Gal 5:12; Phil 3:2). Scholars have offered various plausible explanations for Paul's strong language (e.g. ancient practice of rhetorical vilification, eccentric personality), and these could constitute one of the possible reasons behind.[23] Yet as I have explained elsewhere, given Paul's hot temper (cf. Acts 15:37–40; Gal 2:11–14), this behavior more likely reflects Paul's life as a typical Christian experience: we know the standards of Scripture, we succeed in some cases, fail in others, but can continue to grow in Christlikeness and improve over time by God's grace.[24]

The recipients of 1 Peter also rejoiced in their suffering for Christ (1 Pet 1:6–9). Peter advocated for holy living against sinful behavior (e.g. 1:14–16; 2:11), quiet submission to those in authority (2:13–3:7), and gentle and respectful defense of one's faith (3:15–16). As Christians were frequently perceived as subversive, this could very likely be a response to such accusations, so that Christians would live such good lives that they were not perceived as a threat to society (cf. 2:12).[25]

I know of a teenage girl who was the first Christian convert in her family. Her father strongly opposed her because he thought that the Chinese should not believe in a "Western" religion. Initially, her father thought that she was rebellious because she would not give up going to church meetings, despite

---

23. Andreas B. du Toit, "Vilification as a Pragmatic Device in Early Christian Epistolography," *Bib* 75, no. 3 (1994): 403–12; John G. Gager with E. Leigh Gibson, "Violent Acts and Violent Language in the Apostle Paul," in *Violence in the New Testament*, ed. Shelly Matthews and E. Leigh Gibson (New York: T&T Clark, 2005), 13–21; Lauri Thurén, *Derhetorizing Paul: A Dynamic Perspective on Pauline Theology and the Law* (Tübingen: Mohr Siebeck, 2000), 66–67.
24. Lee, *When Christians Face Persecution*, 72–73.
25. See also David L. Balch, *Let Wives Be Submissive: The Domestic Code in 1 Peter* (Chico, CA: Scholars Press, 1981), 109; David G. Horrell, "Between Conformity and Resistance: Beyond the Balch-Elliott Debate Towards a Postcolonial Reading of First Peter," in *Reading First Peter with New Eyes: Methodological Reassessments of the Letter of First Peter*, ed. Robert L. Webb and Betsy J. Bauman-Martin, LNTS 364 (London: T&T Clark, 2007), 134–35.

him punishing her repeatedly by beating and scolding her. This teenager would suffer quietly and not retaliate verbally or physically. Other than not compromising her faith, she was obedient to her parents in every other aspect of her daily life. Her life demonstrated the teaching of 1 Peter 4:19 (NIV), "So then, those who suffer according to God's will should commit themselves to their faithful Creator and continue to do good." Eventually, her father relented and even went to church with her.

In Revelation, there are some Christians who persevered in the face of persecution, even to the point of martyrdom (e.g. 2:12; 12:11; 20:4), and Christ commended those among the seven churches who had been faithful (2:2–3, 9, 13, 19; 3:8, 10). Other than Christ's commendation, the conviction that God is righteous and will reward and vindicate faithful believers, as well as punish their oppressors (e.g. 6:9–11; 19:1–21), is a form of motivation and comfort that their suffering will not be in vain. Revelation not only teaches perseverance but also faithful witness for Christ in the face of persecution (e.g. 10:1–11:14; 12:11).[26]

The conviction of eschatological reward and punishment plays a major role in motivating perseverance in the face of persecution. Jesus taught that those who deny him in order to avoid persecution presently, he will deny them at the eschatological judgment; in contrast, those who suffer loss presently for his sake will actually gain life (Matt 16:24–27 // Mark 8:35–38 // Luke 9:24–26). This conviction continues to be seen in the rest of the NT as a motivation and a deterrent (e.g. 2 Tim 2:8–10; Heb 10:26–39; 1 Pet 4:12–16; Rev 14:1–20).

Compromise

Both the pressure of suffering persecution and the temptation to give up one's faith in Christ are very real and can come upon any Christian. The NT authors had not explicitly mentioned cases of people giving up their Christian faith. This may give us a wrong impression that early Christians were mostly faithfully pressing on. However, it is more likely that some Christians were

---

26. For details, see Chee-Chiew Lee, "'Fire from Their Mouths': The Power of Witnessing in the Face of Hostility and Suffering (Rev 11:3–13)," *Central Taiwan Theological Seminary Journal* 4 (2013): 222–27. "Fire from the mouth" symbolizes the proclamation of God's imminent judgment on sinners and the call to repentance. Although Revelation 11:5 uses violent imagery, it does not advocate a violent retaliation to opposition or persecution.

discouraged and tempted to give up, or had even given up, which was why the NT authors had to keep on encouraging their recipients to press on.[27]

Yet, when facing such pressures and temptations, rather than giving up their faith totally, some Christians may instead respond by compromising through cultural assimilation. For both Jewish and Gentile Christians, the social pressure from not participating in traditional religious practices could be very strong. Christians had to face ostracization from family and trade guilds. As we have already seen, this could not only result in being alienated from their original community but could also create economic losses.

Some Corinthian Christians bowed to such social pressure and compromised by participating in polytheistic religious rites, eating food offered to idols, and justifying themselves for doing so. Thus, Paul had to address this issue in 1 Corinthians 8–10. Some Christians in Pergamum and Thyatira had acted similarly in order to avoid persecution, community alienation, and economic losses (Rev 2:14–15, 20; cf. 13:14–16). Both Paul and John taught that such compromise is idolatrous and unfaithful to God, and it would incur God's wrath (1 Cor 10:14–22; Rev 14:9–11). While Acts 15:20 and Revelation advocated a blanket prohibition to eating food offered to idols, Paul taught that the eating of such food without knowing its origin is still acceptable (1 Cor 10:25–33).

Some Christians also faced social pressures to conform to Jewish practices such as circumcision and food laws in order to avoid persecution from the Jews (e.g. Gal 6:12; cf. 4:8–11). Thus, they insisted that Gentile Christians must engage in these Jewish practices, and this is a form of cultural assimilation. For Paul, this goes against the grain of justification by faith and renders Christ's death on the cross ineffective (2:21; 5:2, 4).

In some Asian cultures, families or businesses perform religious rituals regularly, with no segregation between religious and secular lives. Christian converts in such situations often face social pressure as they are often expected to participate in these rituals to show solidarity. The fear of opposition, alienation from their family, and losing their jobs is very real. Christians need both wisdom and courage to know which rituals and practices they can join, and which ones they must resist.

---

27. If there were cases of people who "stopped being Christians" in the early second century (Pliny, *Epistles* 10.96.6), it is not surprising that the second half of the first century was likewise. See also Karen L. King, "Rethinking the Diversity of Ancient Christianity: Responding to Suffering and Persecution," in *Beyond the Gnostic Gospels: Studies Building on the Work of Elaine Pagels*, ed. Eduard Iricinschi et al. (Tübingen: Mohr Siebeck, 2013), 64.

The struggle with fear of persecution is real and can be intense. John and the author of Hebrews were clearly aware of this, and they addressed it in detail.[28] While John clearly teaches that fear of confessing Christ publicly is not the desirable response (e.g. John 9:20–23; 12:42–43), he seemed to withhold his judgment on two Jewish leaders: (1) Joseph of Arimathea, whom John described as a secret disciple (19:38–42); and (2) Nicodemus, whom John did not clearly say whether or not he was a disciple (3:1–9; 7:50–52; 19:39–42). This deliberate ambiguous characterization could be John's way of expressing his understanding of the difficulties involved and allowing some form of accommodation in certain instances. It is also important to note that in Jesus's prayers for his disciples, he prayed for their unity in the face of persecution (17:11–23).

On the one hand, the author of Hebrews clearly taught about who (God, not the persecutors), what (not death or economic losses, but eschatological judgment), and why (eschatological reward and punishment) Christians should fear. On the other hand, he also emphasized that Jesus can empathize with such fear and suffering (Heb 2:17; 4:15; 5:1–9), so that his letter's recipients who felt likewise may be willing to seek help from Christ. Only by relying on Christ can they persevere on in their weakness. He also exhorted his recipients to empathize with and support these suffering Christians (10:24–25; 13:3), so that the community may persevere together.

Adaptation

In response to the perception of outsiders that Christians are subversive, we have seen how 1 Peter adapted certain cultural practices (submission, good works) without compromising the Christian faith. Paul adapted similarly in Romans 13:1–7. As the use of authoritative tradition is a common practice for both Jews and Gentiles, the apostles also adapted this and showed that the Christian faith fulfilled the Jewish Scripture rather than deviating from it (e.g. Acts 15; Rom 4).[29] These are examples of NT Christians adapting cultural practices and norms in a way that is faithful to Christ.

---

28. For details of the following two paragraphs, see Chee-Chiew Lee, "A Theology of Facing Persecution in the Gospel of John," *TynBul* 70, no. 2 (2019): 189–204; "The Rhetoric of Empathy in Hebrews," *NovT* 62, no. 2 (2020): 201–18; "The Use of Scriptures and the Rhetoric of Fear in Hebrews," *BBR* 31, no. 2 (2021): 191–210.
29. Dennis L. Stamps, "The Use of the Old Testament in the New Testament as a Rhetorical Device: A Methodological Proposal," in *Hearing the Old Testament in the New Testament*, ed. S. E. Porter (Grand Rapids: Eerdmans, 2006), 9–37; Christopher D. Stanley, "The Rhetoric

Another instance of adaptation may be seen in Paul's exhortation to pray for the ruling authorities (1 Tim 2:1–4). This practice bears strong resemblance to a contemporaneous Jewish practice in response to the imperial worship rituals. As mentioned earlier, imperial worship was a means by which polytheists honored and expressed their loyalty to their rulers. From the reign of Caesar Augustus (27 BC–AD 14) until the Jewish revolt (AD 66), Jews adapted this ritual practice as follows: (1) they swore their loyalty to the emperor, as well as offered daily sacrifices and prayers to God at the Jerusalem temple for the welfare of the emperor and all peoples;[30] and (2) Jews in the diaspora also offered similar prayers, paid temple taxes to contribute to the sacrifices, and had honorific inscriptions for the emperor in their synagogues.[31] In this way, they showed honor and loyalty to the rulers without compromising their monotheistic faith, and the polytheists in general did not regard the Jews as seditious.[32] Considering this strong resemblance, 1 Timothy 2:1–4 could likely be an adaptation of this Jewish practice as a way to show that Christians were not seditious and did not pose a threat to the society. For suggestions on how Asian Christians can adapt, see "Some Contemporary Reflections" below.

We have seen from the above that Christians in the NT responded to persecution in diverse ways. Some persevered, others compromised or perhaps even gave up their faith in Christ. Even among those who remained faithful to Christ, they may also differ in their responses to the same issue (e.g. public confession or secrecy, food offered to idols). When encouraging their recipients to persevere, NT authors not only continued in Jesus's teachings, they also put forth clearly the motivations that would encourage perseverance and deter unfaithfulness. The NT authors identified with their fellow believers in terms of the reality of fear and suffering, especially the author of Hebrews, who was unique in his emphasis on empathy.

---

of Quotations: An Essay on Method," in *Early Christian Interpretation of the Scriptures of Israel: Investigations and Proposals*, eds. Craig A. Evans and James A. Sanders (Sheffield: Sheffield Academic, 1997), 54–56.

30. Philo, *Embassy* 23 §157; Josephus, *Against Apion* 2.6 §77; *Jewish Antiquities* 17.2.4 §42.

31. Justin K. Hardin, *Galatians and the Imperial Cult: A Critical Analysis of the First-Century Social Context of Paul's Letter* (Tübingen: Mohr Siebeck, 2008), 108–9; Winter, *Divine Honours for the Caesars*, 110–16.

32. Winter, *Divine Honours for the Caesars*, 131. Therefore, as Winter (*Divine Honours for the Caesars*, 117–23) notes, when the Jews ceased such sacrifices at the Jerusalem temple as an act of defiance in AD 66, the Romans saw that clearly as a rebellion and this led to a bloody suppression between AD 66–70.

SOME CONTEMPORARY REFLECTIONS

It is not difficult for us to see the similarities between the NT Christians and contemporary Asian Christians in terms of the factors leading to persecution and their responses to it. Nonetheless, it is also necessary for us to understand that, throughout history, Christians are not the only group of people who face religious persecution.[33] As these factors are frequently common to other religious groups, this will help us appreciate the perspective of opponents and help us formulate our responses thoughtfully, prayerfully, and accordingly.[34]

Dearly-Held Traditional Values

Conflict with dearly held traditional values is the most common factor leading to opposition and sometimes even to persecution. Opponents perceive Christians as subverting their traditional values and seek to fend off this threat. Religious nationalism, fundamentalism, and radicalism represent a spectrum of responses with increasing degree towards the extreme. These movements result in marginalization and even persecution of "others" who differ from their traditions.[35]

Furthermore, the missionary movement from the West to Asia is unfortunately often associated with imperialism, colonization, and certain contemptuous attitudes towards Asians.[36] During the colonial days, Asians who adopted Western practices (e.g. clothing style, language, religion) were reckoned by others to have betrayed their tradition and cultural identity for that of the

---

33. E.g. during the Roman period, worship of the Volsinian goddess Nortia and the Egyptian goddess Isis were rejected, while the latter was outlawed and suppressed. See Eric M. Orlin, *Foreign Cults in Rome: Creating a Roman Empire* (New York: Oxford University Press, 2010), 203–7; Sarolta A. Takács, *Isis and Sarapis in the Roman World*, RGRW 124 (Leiden: Brill, 1995), 56–58. For modern day examples, see Tieszen, "Towards Redefining Persecution," 70–73.

34. For examples of perceptions of Christianity by other Asian religious groups, see Felix Wilfred, ed., *The Oxford Handbook of Christianity in Asia* (New York: Oxford University Press, 2014), 345–455.

35. Sivin Kit, "Inter-Religious Relations," in *Christianity in East and Southeast Asia*, ed. Kenneth R. Ross, Francis D. Alvarez, and Todd M. Johnson (Edinburgh: Edinburgh University Press, 2020), 444; Paul Marshall, "Religious Freedom," in Ross, *Christianity in East and Southeast Asia*, 431; Kar Yong Lim, "A Theology of Suffering and Mission for the Asian Church," in *Asian Christian Theology: Evangelical Perspectives*, ed. Timoteo D. Gener and Stephen T. Pardue (Carlisle: Langham Global Library, 2019), 182.

36. Jude L. Fernando, "The Role of Christianity in Peace and Conflict in Asia," in Wilfred, *The Oxford Handbook of Christianity in Asia*, 284; Lalsangkima Pachuau, "Cultural Identity and Theology in Asia," in Gener and Pardue, *Asian Christian Theology*, 199.

foreign oppressors.[37] This historical baggage continues to be present among some Asians.

An example of such clashes is the veneration of ancestors in East Asian cultures (Chinese, Korean, Japanese). This practice reflects the values of respect, honor, and filial piety, but commonly takes the form of ancestor worship and includes other superstitious beliefs.[38] Thus, faithful Christians who reject participation in this dearly-held traditional form of expression are frequently perceived as unfilial and disrespectful, much like early Christians who rejected participation in imperial worship.[39] Abandonment of traditional religions or social systems (such as the Indian caste system) also provokes similar reactions.[40]

First Peter as a whole and 1 Timothy 4:1–4 prompt us to think about how to adapt cultural norms that address the concerns of those who oppose, but in a way that is faithful to Christ. As Sivin Kit puts it, we have to "re-imagine fresh expressions of faith that are nonetheless still faithful."[41] Pachuau proposes that Christians are "to identify with their cultures and to transform them toward Christlikeness,"[42] while Satyavrata aptly reminds us not to end up with

---

37. See Gandhi's impression of Christianity, he wrote, "Only Christianity was at the time an exception [to religious tolerance]. I developed a sort of dislike for it. And for a reason. In those days Christian missionaries used to stand in a corner near the high school and hold forth, pouring abuse on Hindus and their gods. I could not endure this. I must have stood there to hear them once only, but that was enough to dissuade me from repeating the experiment. About the same time, I heard of a well-known Hindu having been converted to Christianity. It was the talk of the town that, when he was baptized he had to eat beef and drink liquor, that he also had to change his clothes, and that thenceforth he began to go about in European costume including a hat. These things got on my nerves. Surely, thought I, a religion that compelled one to eat beef, drink liquor, and change one's own clothes did not deserve the name. I also heard that the new convert had already begun abusing the religion of his ancestors, their customs and their country. All these things created in me a dislike for Christianity." Mohandas K. Gandhi, *Autobiography: The Story of My Experiments with Truth*, trans. Mahadev H. Desai (New York: Dover, 1983), 29–30.

38. For details, see Nobushige Hozumi, *Ancestor Worship and Japanese Law* (London: Routledge, 2016); Roger L. Janelli and Ton-hŭi Im, *Ancestor Worship and Korean Society* (Stanford: Stanford University Press, 1982); William Lakos, *Chinese Ancestor Worship: A Practice and Ritual Oriented Approach to Understanding Chinese Culture* (Newcastle upon Tyne: Cambridge Scholars, 2010).

39. The Rites Controversy (AD 17th to 18th century) during the Jesuit missions to East Asia is a classic example of such clashes regarding traditional ancestral rites. For an overview, see Claudia von Collani, "The Jesuit Rites Controversy," in *The Oxford Handbook of Jesuits*, ed. Ines G. Županov (New York: Oxford University Press, 2018), 891–917.

40. See also Fernando, "Role of Christianity," 293.

41. Kit, "Inter-Religious Relations," 449.

42. Pachuau, "Cultural Identity and Theology," 218.

pluralism.[43] Bearing these in mind, East Asian Christians may need to think of various alternative expressions of respect and gratefulness to ancestors that can be close to traditional forms but without the worship or superstitious elements in them (such as thanksgiving or memorial services), rather than downright abandoning the tradition.

There are other Asian Christians who have made similar efforts to indigenize their Christian faith.[44] For example, using Matthew 5:17, Paul's approach (Acts 14, 17), and creation theology (Rom 1–2) as biblical bases, Satyavrata cites various Indian Christians who sought to navigate their Christian faith within Indian ancestral traditions using the "fulfillment approach," rather than a downright rejection of traditions.[45] There are more examples from other cultures, but space does not permit us to discuss them here.[46] These are attempts to demonstrate that the gospel is not "Western" but God's plan of salvation for peoples of all cultures.

Another example of such clashes is the offense caused by Christians. For example, Angela Wong notes that some missionaries in the late nineteenth century used "crude depictions of Hindus and Indian culture as idolatrous and demoniac," ultimately provoking "hostile resentment" in their communities.[47] There are similar problems among Asian Christians in other cultures, many of which echo the challenges of some NT Christians. Pachuau aptly reminds us,

> More than ever, we desperately need communication that is fair and just. Modes of communication that deride or dominate others are not acceptable. Unfortunately, the domineering manner by which Christians often "evangelized" in the past were not evangelical by nature. As a result, the word "evangelical" came to assume negative connotations. What is needed, then, is

---

43. Ivan Satyavrata, "Jesus and Other Faiths," in Gener and Pardue, *Asian Christian Theology*, 225–29. "Pluralism" in this case is the view that all kinds of beliefs and practices are equally valid and should be accepted.

44. Julius Bautista, "Christianity in Southeast Asia Colonialism, Nationalism and the Caveats to Conversion," in Wilfred, *Oxford Handbook of Christianity in Asia*, 218; Pachuau, "Cultural Identity and Theology," 201–4; Edmond Tang, "Identity and Marginality: Christianity in East Asia," in Wilfred, 85–86. Tang cited East Asian examples; Bautista Southeast Asian examples; Pachuau cited one Indian and 2 Chinese as examples of different approaches to indigenization.

45. Satyavrata, "Jesus and Other Faiths," 230–32.

46. E.g. Francis K. G. Lim, "Negotiating 'Foreignness', Localizing Faith: Tibetan Catholicism in the Yunnan-Tibet Borderlands" in *Christianity and the State in Asia: Complicity and Conflict*, ed. Julius Bautista and Francis K. G. Lim (London: Routledge, 2009), 79–96.

47. Angela W. C. Wong, "Modernity and Change of Values: Asian Christian Negotiations and Resistance," in Wilfred, *Oxford Handbook of Christianity in Asia*, 211–12.

a gospel-transformed manner of communicating the gospel of transformation.[48]

While it is true that some people may feel offended when the gospel confronts them of their sin and calls them to repentance, we need to distinguish between this and our lack of wisdom and respect in presenting the gospel (cf. 1 Pet 2:17; 3:15).

Stability of the Society

It is understandable that state authorities have the responsibility of maintaining order in society, and as Turner notes, Christian evangelism and conversion "brings with it the possibility of conflict and competition with existing traditions," causing disturbances in society in many instances.[49] Unfortunately, Christians in Asia must reckon with the reality that governing authorities will sometimes perceive them as a threat to social stability and use harsh tactics to restore a perception of order.[50] This is in many ways similar to the situation of New Testament Christians.

Communist regimes frequently perceive Christianity as a threat to the state for a number of reasons, which include: (1) religion (not only Christianity) is incompatible with communist atheistic ideology; (2) the tendency to identify Christians with Western democratic influence and former colonial enemies; (3) influence on society and politics if intellectuals become Christians; and (4) the offensive message of the damnation of non-believers of Christ.[51] These regimes in Asia impose varying degrees of restrictions on Christians and other religious groups.[52] In a noteworthy study, Kim-Kwong Chan lists and evaluates several case studies illustrating how Christian groups in various regions within the same country relate differently to the state with varying outcomes.[53]

---

48. Pachuau, "Cultural Identity and Theology," 218.
49. Bryan S. Turner, "Evangelism, the State, and Subjectivity," in Bautista, *Christianity and the State in Asia*, 18–19.
50. Bhagwan Josh notes one such example: the case of the Gujarat government imposing restrictions on Christian evangelism to curb conversions ("Conversions, Complicity and the State in Post-Independence India," in Bautista, *Christianity and the State in Asia*, 110).
51. Julius Bautista and Francis K. G. Lim, "Introduction," in Bautista, *Christianity and the State in Asia*, 8; Kim-Kwong Chan, "The Christian Community in China: The Leaven Effect," in *Evangelical Christianity and Democracy in Asia*, ed. David H. Lumsdaine (New York: Oxford University Press, 2009), 50; Lim, "A Theology of Suffering and Mission," 183; Marshall, "Religious Freedom," 427; Tang, "Identity and Marginality," 93.
52. For details, see Marshall, "Religious Freedom," 425–29.
53. Chan, "Christian Community in China," 51–78.

In some Asian countries (e.g. Indonesia, Myanmar, India), early Christian conversions usually happened among ethnic minorities who were oppressed or marginalized by the majority population. Some of these groups are also associated with separatist movements and militants.[54] Consequently, Christians in these groups, whether or not they are separatists, became identified with political instability and are also suppressed by the authorities.

Certain core Christian beliefs and values are bound to face opposition and cause a certain level of instability in society. For example, Christians in the region are likely to invite strong reactions by affirming that salvation is available only through Jesus, or that marriage must be a covenant union between a man and a woman. How should Christians manage these oppositions as peace-makers without compromising our beliefs?

In the NT, Romans 13:1–7 and 1 Peter 2:13–17 are examples of attempts to demonstrate through virtuous lives and respect for the authorities that Christians are good citizens and not a threat to the authorities or the stability of the society. On the other hand, Revelation portrays a non-violent resistance to persecution by perseverance and faithful witness.[55] In line with the above biblical principles, the United Nation's Universal Declaration of Human Rights may be an important guideline and protection for both Christians and their opponents.[56] Even if both parties disagree with each other, we need to respectfully allow each party the freedom to hold, express, and practice beliefs different from us or others without using or inciting physical or verbal violence (e.g. hate speech). Nor should people be easily accused of discrimination or intolerance merely because they uphold their beliefs and respectfully seek to explain them with the hope of convincing others. From a Christian eschatological perspective, everyone will be held accountable to God in the final judgment.

With these biblical principles in mind, how then can oppressed Asian Christians relate to state authorities, other traditional majority religious groups, or other rights advocacy groups who oppose them? This is a highly controversial topic that we do not have space here to discuss in detail. It should suffice to say that just as there are diverse responses to persecution in the NT, there are also diverse responses among Asian Christians, even on the same issue or

---

54. Bautista and Lim, "Introduction," 4; Fernando, "Role of Christianity," 287; Turner, "Evangelism, the State, and Subjectivity," 31; David H. Lumsdaine, "Introduction," in Lumsdaine, *Evangelical Christianity and Democracy in Asia*, 14.

55. See also Thomas B. Slater, *Revelation as Civil Disobedience: Witnesses Not Warriors in John's Apocalypse* (Nashville: Abingdon, 2019); Lee, "Fire from Their Mouths," 224–27.

56. Universal Declaration of Human Rights, https://www.un.org/en/about-us/universal-declaration-of-human-rights. See, especially, Articles 16, 18, and 19.

within the same region. This diversity sometimes creates deep rifts among Christians. Jesus's prayer for unity in the Gospel of John and John's ambiguous characterization of Joseph and Nicodemus remind us that we will need to accept such diversity and withhold judgment on others who differ from us. Different regions and cultures in Asia differ in their society's level of tolerance for opposing views and opinions. Thus, Asian Christians in these contexts will need to develop strategies that specifically address their unique circumstances.

ENCOURAGEMENT TO PERSEVERE

We have seen how the NT authors encouraged their recipients who are suffering from persecution by elucidating the eschatological and missional value of such sufferings to motivate them towards persevering in their Christian faith. Not only did these NT authors experience the reality of Jesus's promise of wisdom and providence by the Holy Spirit, their exemplary (though not perfect) lives in accord with Jesus's teachings encouraged others to persevere as well. In many ways, Asian Christians have been emulating the NT authors in these aspects.

It is also important that we also note the author of Hebrews' emphasis on empathy and its effect on both individual and community perseverance. Empathizing with those who suffer persecution – regardless of whether their faith is strong or weak – not only brings comfort to them, but empathy also acts as a catalyst in: (1) encouraging the empathized to be willing to seek help; and (2) inducing the empathizer to help the empathized.[57] If we are critical towards those whom we think are weak, we add to their pain and become a stumbling block to them in getting help.

Even as we empathize with Christians who suffer persecution, perhaps we should also empathize with those who oppose Christians. In cultures that perceive the abandonment of traditions as betrayal, the pain suffered by their community (e.g. non-Christian parents) can also be very intense. Their attempts to pressurize their "deviant" members who have become Christians to conform back to their traditions often stems from what they think is for the good of the deviant. Similarly, state authorities who suppress and "re-educate" their "deviant" Christian citizens often think that they do so for the good of the deviant and for the greater good of society. Empathizing with the opponents does not mean condoning the sometimes extreme, or even inhumane, methods

---

57. Research by modern psychologists have shown that empathy very often precedes altruistic behavior. This was also recognized and practiced by Greco-Roman rhetoricians, including the author of Hebrews. For details, see Lee, "Rhetoric of Empathy," 214–18.

that the opponents employ. Rather, it is to express our understanding of their concerns and for us to address them accordingly. This also does not mean that we deny the existence of malicious persecutors who act out of evil intent.

CONCLUSION

Asian Christians and NT Christians have much in common with regard to the sociological factors leading to persecution, especially in terms of being perceived as a threat to dearly-held traditions and the stability of the society. In this short study, we have seen that, other than the common denominator of faithful perseverance, the NT authors exhibit diverse responses when facing persecution and may differ in their opinions, even with regard to the same issue. This understanding helps us to appreciate the likewise diverse responses to persecution among Christians in our own Asian contexts. While Christians seek to be peace-makers as children of God (cf. Matt 5:9),[58] peace-making has to be in a way that is faithful to Christ and the biblical teachings. The attempt that Paul and 1 Peter took to adapt, rather than accommodate, certain existing traditions to address concerns of their opponents is an important approach for us to consider for our own context. The effort that John and the author of Hebrews took to address the reality of fear and to identify with those who suffer persecution for Christ reminds us that encouraging fellow Christians to persevere takes more than just teaching them what to do and how to respond – empathizing with them is just as important. While we hope that our responses to persecution can have missional effect, address the concerns of our opponents, and promote mutual understanding, it certainly does not imply that we will be able to rid persecution with these efforts. A robust conviction of the eschatological and missional value of suffering persecution for Christ, as well as the experience of the Holy Spirit's wisdom and empowerment, are essential to faithful perseverance for all times (cf. Matt 5:10–12; 10:16–39).

BIBLIOGRAPHY

Achtemeier, Paul J. *1 Peter*. Hermeneia. Minneapolis: Fortress, 1996.

Anderson, Ralph. "New Gods." In *The Oxford Handbook of Ancient Greek Religion*, edited by Esther Eidinow and Julia Kindt, 309–23. New York: Oxford University Press, 2015.

Balch, David L. *Let Wives Be Submissive: The Domestic Code in 1 Peter*. SBLMS 26. Chico: Scholars Press, 1981.

---

58. See also Fernando, "Role of Christianity," 297.

Bautista, Julius. "Christianity in Southeast Asia Colonialism, Nationalism and the Caveats to Conversion." In *The Oxford Handbook of Christianity in Asia*, edited by Felix Wilfred, 215–30. Oxford Handbooks in Religion and Theology. New York: Oxford University Press, 2014.

———, and Francis K. G. Lim. "Introduction." In *Christianity and the State in Asia: Complicity and Conflict*, edited by Julius Bautista and Francis K. G. Lim, 1–17. Routledge Studies in Asian Religion and Philosophy 4. London: Routledge, 2009.

Blackburn, Stuart H. "Death and Deification: Folk Cults in Hinduism." *History of Religions* 24, no. 3 (1985): 255–74.

Chan, Kim-Kwong. "The Christian Community in China: The Leaven Effect." In *Evangelical Christianity and Democracy in Asia*, edited by David H. Lumsdaine, 43–86. Evangelical Christianity and Democracy in the Global South. New York: Oxford University Press, 2009.

Collani, Claudia von. "The Jesuit Rites Controversy." In *The Oxford Handbook of Jesuits*, edited by Ines G. Županov, 891–917. New York: Oxford University Press, 2018.

Cunningham, Scott. *'Through Many Tribulations': The Theology of Persecution in Luke-Acts*. JSNTSup 142. Sheffield: Sheffield Academic, 1997.

Du Toit, Andreas B. "Vilification as a Pragmatic Device in Early Christian Epistolography." *Biblica* 75, no. 3 (1994): 403–12.

Dunne, John A. Persecution and Participation in Galatians. WUNT 2/454. Tübingen: Mohr Siebeck, 2017.

Fernando, Jude L. "The Role of Christianity in Peace and Conflict in Asia." In *The Oxford Handbook of Christianity in Asia*, edited by Felix Wilfred, 283–301. Oxford Handbooks in Religion and Theology. New York: Oxford University Press, 2014.

Gager, John G., and with E. Leigh Gibsom. "Violent Acts and Violent Language in the Apostle Paul." In *Violence in the New Testament*, edited by Shelly Matthews and E. Leigh Gibson, 13–21. New York: T&T Clark, 2005.

Gandhi, Mohandas K. *Autobiography: The Story of My Experiments with Truth*. Translated by Mahadev H. Desai. New York: Dover, 1983.

Gradel, Ittai. *Emperor Worship and Roman Religion*. Oxford Classical Monographs. New York: Clarendon Press, 2002.

Hardin, Justin K. *Galatians and the Imperial Cult: A Critical Analysis of the First-Century Social Context of Paul's Letter*. WUNT 2/237. Tübingen: Mohr Siebeck, 2008.

Hori, Ichiro. "Japanese Folk-Beliefs." *American Anthropologist* 61, no. 3 (1959): 405–24.

Harrison, James R. "The Persecution of Christians from Nero to Hadrian." Pages 266–300 in *Into All the World: Emergent Christianity in Its Jewish and Greco-*

Roman Context. Edited by Mark Harding and Alanna Nobbs. Grand Rapids: Eerdmans, 2017.

Horrell, David G. "Between Conformity and Resistance: Beyond the Balch-Elliott Debate Towards a Postcolonial Reading of First Peter." In *Reading First Peter with New Eyes: Methodological Reassessments of the Letter of First Peter*, edited by Robert L. Webb and Betsy J. Bauman-Martin, 111–43. LNTS 364. London: T&T Clark, 2007.

Hozumi, Nobushige. *Ancestor Worship and Japanese Law.* London: Routledge, 2016.

Janelli, Roger L., and Ton-hūi Im. *Ancestor Worship and Korean Society.* Stanford: Stanford University Press, 1982.

Jobes, Karen H. *1 Peter.* Baker Exegetical Commentary on the New Testament. Grand Rapids: Baker Academic, 2005.

Josh, Bhagwan. "Conversions, Complicity and the State in Post-Independence India." In *Christianity and the State in Asia*, edited by Julius Bautista and Francis K. G. Lim, 97–114. Routledge Studies in Asian Religion and Philosophy 4. London: Routledge, 2009.

Keener, Craig S. *Acts: An Exegetical Commentary.* 4 vols. Grand Rapids: Baker Academic, 2012–2015.

Kelhoffer, James A. *Persecution, Persuasion, and Power: Readiness to Withstand Hardship as a Corroboration of Legitimacy in the New Testament.* WUNT 270. Tübingen: Mohr Siebeck, 2010.

King, Karen L. "Rethinking the Diversity of Ancient Christianity: Responding to Suffering and Persecution." In *Beyond the Gnostic Gospels: Studies Building on the Work of Elaine Pagels*, edited by Eduard Iricinschi, Lance Jenott, Nicola Denzey Lewis, and Philippa Townsend, 60–78. Studien und Texte zu Antike und Christentum 82. Tübingen: Mohr Siebeck, 2013.

Kit, Sivin. "Inter-Religious Relations." In *Christianity in East and Southeast Asia*, edited by Kenneth R. Ross, Francis D. Alvarez, and Todd M. Johnson, 438–62. Edinburgh Companions to Global Christianity. Edinburgh: Edinburgh University Press, 2020.

Lakos, William. *Chinese Ancestor Worship: A Practice and Ritual Oriented Approach to Understanding Chinese Culture.* Newcastle upon Tyne: Cambridge Scholars, 2010.

Lee, Chee-Chiew. "'Fire from Their Mouths': The Power of Witnessing in the Face of Hostility and Suffering (Rev 11:3–13)." *Central Taiwan Theological Seminary Journal* 4 (2013): 204–37.

———. "The Rhetoric of Empathy in Hebrews." *NovT* 62, no. 2 (2020): 201–18.

———. "A Theology of Facing Persecution in the Gospel of John." *TynBul* 70, no. 2 (2019): 189–204.

———"The Use of Scriptures and the Rhetoric of Fear in Hebrews." *BBR* 31, no. 2 (2021): 191–210.

————. *When Christians Face Persecution: Theological Perspectives from the New Testament.* London: Apollos, 2022.

Lim, Francis K. G. "Negotiating 'Foreignness', Localizing Faith: Tibetan Catholicism in the Yunnan-Tibet Borderlands." In *Christianity and the State in Asia*, edited by Julius Bautista and Francis K. G. Lim, 79–96. Routledge Studies in Asian Religion and Philosophy 4. London: Routledge, 2009.

Lim, Kar Yong. *"The Sufferings of Christ Are Abundant in Us" (2 Corinthians 1:5): A Narrative-Dynamics Investigation of Paul's Sufferings in 2 Corinthians.* LNTS 399. London: T&T Clark, 2009.

————. "A Theology of Suffering and Mission for the Asian Church." In *Asian Christian Theology: Evangelical Perspectives*, edited by Timoteo D. Gener and Stephen T. Pardue, 181–98. Carlisle: Langham Global Library, 2019.

Lumsdaine, David H. "Introduction." In *Evangelical Christianity and Democracy in Asia*, edited by David Halloran Lumsdaine, 3–42. Oxford University Press, 2009.

Maier, Harry O. *New Testament Christianity in the Roman World.* Essentials of Biblical Studies. New York: Oxford University Press, 2018.

Marshall, Paul. "Religious Freedom." In *Christianity in East and Southeast Asia*, edited by Kenneth R. Ross, 425–37. Edinburgh: Edinburgh University Press, 2020.

McIntyre, Gwynaeth. *Imperial Cult.* Ancient History. Leiden: Brill, 2019.

Orlin, Eric M. *Foreign Cults in Rome: Creating a Roman Empire.* New York: Oxford University Press, 2010.

————. *Temples, Religion, and Politics in the Roman Republic.* Boston: Brill Academic, 2002.

Osiek, Carolyn. "*Diakonos* and *Prostatis*: Women's Patronage in Early Christianity." *HTS Teologiese Studies/Theological Studies* 61, nos. 1–2 (2005): 347–70.

Pachuau, Lalsangkima. "Cultural Identity and Theology in Asia." In *Asian Christian Theology*, edited by Timoteo D. Gener and Stephen T. Pardue, 199–220. Carlisle: Langham Global Library, 2019.

Peppard, Michael. *The Son of God in the Roman World: Divine Sonship in Its Social and Political Context.* New York: Oxford University Press, 2011.

Satyavrata, Ivan. "Jesus and Other Faiths." In *Asian Christian Theology*, edited by Timoteo D. Gener and Stephen T. Pardue, 221–44. Carlisle: Langham Global Library, 2019.

Sim, David C. "Gentiles, God-Fearers and Proselytes." In *Attitudes to Gentiles in Ancient Judaism and Early Christianity*. Edited by David C. Sim and James S. McLaren, 9–27. LNTS 499. London: Bloomsbury, 2015.

Slater, Thomas B. *Revelation as Civil Disobedience: Witnesses Not Warriors in John's Apocalypse.* Nashville: Abingdon Press, 2019.

Stamps, Dennis L. "The Use of the Old Testament in the New Testament as a Rhetorical Device: A Methodological Proposal." In *Hearing the Old Testament in the New Testament*, edited by S. E. Porter, 9–37. Mcmaster New Testament Studies. Grand Rapids: Eerdmans, 2006.

Stanley, Christopher D. "The Rhetoric of Quotations: An Essay on Method." In *Early Christian Interpretation of the Scriptures of Israel: Investigations and Proposals*, edited by Craig A. Evans and James A. Sanders, 44–58. JSNTSup 148. Sheffield: Sheffield Academic, 1997.

Takács, Sarolta A. *Isis and Sarapis in the Roman World*. RGRW 124. Leiden: Brill, 1995.

Tamney, Joseph B. "Asian Popular Religions." In *Encyclopedia of Religion and Society*, edited by William H. Swatos, Jr, 31–32. Walnut Creek: AltaMira, 1998.

Tang, Edmond. "Identity and Marginality: Christianity in East Asia." In *The Oxford Handbook of Christianity in Asia*, edited by Felix Wilfred, 80–98. Oxford Handbooks in Religion and Theology. New York: Oxford University Press, 2014.

Thurén, Lauri. *Derhetorizing Paul: A Dynamic Perspective on Pauline Theology and the Law*. WUNT 124. Tübingen: Mohr Siebeck, 2000.

Tieszen, Charles L. "Towards Redefining Persecution." *International Journal for Religious Freedom* 1, no. 1 (2008): 67–80.

Turner, Bryan S. "Evangelism, the State, and Subjectivity." In *Christianity and the State in Asia*, edited by Julius Bautista and Francis K. G. Lim, 18–35. Routledge Studies in Asian Religion and Philosophy 4. London: Routledge, 2009.

Watson, Alan. *The State, Law, and Religion: Pagan Rome*. Athens: University of Georgia Press, 1992.

Wilfred, Felix, ed. *The Oxford Handbook of Christianity in Asia*. New York: Oxford University Press, 2014.

Winter, Bruce W. *Divine Honours for the Caesars: The First Christians' Responses*. Grand Rapids: Eerdmans, 2015.

———. "Divine Imperial Cultic Activities and the Early Church." In *Into all the world: Emergent Christianity in its Jewish and Greco-Roman Context*, edited by Mark Harding and Alanna Nobbs, 237–65. Grand Rapids: Eerdmans, 2017.

Wong, Angela W. C. "Modernity and Change of Values: Asian Christian Negotiations and Resistance." In *The Oxford Handbook of Christianity in Asia*, edited by Felix Wilfred, 200–13. Oxford Handbooks in Religion and Theology. New York: Oxford University Press, 2014.

CHAPTER 11

POWERS AND PRINCIPALITIES

The Spirit World in the New Testament and Asian Contexts

Samson L. Uytanlet

INTRODUCTION

A Personal Encounter

Some twenty years ago, a church member and coworker, Christine (not her real name), called me about 9 p.m. because her niece and her two friends had an unusual experience while playing a game they called "spirit of the glass," a game similar to Ouija Board wherein participants attempt to communicate with spirits. When I got to their house, another pastor was already talking and praying with one of the girls and Christine's niece. Jenny (not her real name), the other friend was standing outside the house, so I talked with her. Initially, it was hard to tell whether Jenny was just playing mind games when she said she was seeing behind me some beautiful creatures who were inviting her to go with them to their place. I told her not to agree, and asked her to pray with me. She closed her eyes and asked God to set her free. As soon as she opened her eyes, she started trembling and said that the beautiful creatures she saw earlier transformed and became scary looking, and they were angry and threatening to harm her. We prayed again, until they disappeared from her sight. After several hours, the three girls finally calmed down. Christine's niece stayed and the other two girls went to their homes. We were not able to follow up with the girls because the parents of these girls refused to let us talk with them again.

While incidents like this do not happen often, it was not an isolated event. Those who hear this story may have different explanations about what happened to the three girls, but for them to have experienced it after dabbling with the otherworldly and having three girls experiencing something unusual at the same time can hardly be coincidental. There must be a way to make sense of incidents like this.

Our worldview inevitably affects our perception and level of acceptance about the spirits and activities. Hence, it is important to look at what authoritative sources say about this matter. In this chapter we will consider information we can learn from the various disciplines such as history, anthropology, sociology, and psychology in our study; but the primary approach will be exegetical, literary, and theological study of exorcism based on the NT texts. We will first look at the ancient Jewish beliefs about the spirits and how they inform our understanding of the NT teachings on exorcism. Finally, we will look at how the NT teachings about the spirit world are relevant to our time particularly in the Asian setting.

VARIOUS VIEWS

In the last three decades, there has been a surge of interest on the subject of exorcism among Roman Catholics in the United States.[1] This renewed interest can be seen not only among religious practitioners but also among academics. Some publications in the last thirty years also demonstrate the curiosity of European scholars on the subject of healing and exorcism.[2]

Demonic possessions and exorcisms are explained from various perspectives. First, some are simply skeptical. In the eighteenth century, empiricists like David Hume discount the possibility of miracles because they are contrary to the laws of nature.[3] Skepticism toward miracles are also evident among NT scholars like David F. Strauss. In response to Friedrich Schleiermacher's defense

---

1. Mike Mariani, "Why are Exorcisms on the Rise?," *Atlantic* 62 (2018): 68. In 1999, the Vatican produced the *De exorcismis supplicationibus quibusdam* (Some Prayers for Exorcisms), the revised edition of the document *De exorcizandis obsessis a daemonio* (The Exorcism of the Demon Possessed) in the *Rituale Romanum* (*Roman Ritual*, 1614), almost four centuries after the original was written. A few years earlier (1993), Fr. Gabriel Amorth co-founded the International Association of Exorcists to provide resources for Roman Catholic and Orthodox priests and encourage them to be involved in exorcism. This was partly motivated by the fact that prior to that period, there were more ministers from the Protestant traditions, especially from the Pentecostal and Charismatic movements, who were involved in such ministry.
2. Larry P. Hogan, *Healing in the Second Tempel (sic) Period*, NTOA 21 (Göttingen: Vandenhoeck and Ruprecht, 1992); Todd Klutz, *The Exorcism Stories in Luke-Acts: A Sociostylistic Reading* (New York: Cambridge University Press, 2004); Mikael Tellbe and Tommy Wasserman, *Healing and Exorcism in the Second Temple Judaism and Early Christianity* (Tübingen: Mohr Siebeck, 2019).
3. Craig S. Keener notes that the situation today is different from that of Hume in that many modern reports about the miraculous similar to those from the Gospels are now accessible to present day Gospel scholars (*Miracles: The Credibility of the New Testament Accounts*, 2 vols. [Grand Rapids: Baker Academic, 2011], 1:1). For a more recent evaluation of David Hume's

of the miraculous, Strauss claims, "it is still too indefinite to bring miraculous healings, like those of the possessed, the blind, and those with dropsy, in any way closer to conceivability."[4] After almost three centuries, his ideas have continued to influence on many NT scholars.

Second, the phenomenon of exorcism is also explained from an anthropological perspective. Myrtle S. Langley neither affirms nor denies the existential reality of demons, but proposes that marginality and liminality are the common denominators of those who have experienced some kind of demonic possession and deliverance. In some societies like the Malaysian fishing village of Tawang, direct confrontation is discouraged, so blame is shifted to someone from the spirit world. While one party is in a trance, repressed anger can be released in a socially acceptable way and admission of guilt can be done without losing face. Langley concludes that "a society in transition and a people on its margins were ready to be possessed."[5]

Third, psychotherapy also provides a different explanation for this phenomenon. Demon possession is typically linked with Dissociative Identity Disorder (DID). There are similar symptoms between psychiatric disorders and what is believed to be demonic possession, thus, some have opted to explain incidents of possession as a psychiatric disorder rather than a spiritual phenomenon.[6] In one study, 80 percent of those who had experienced demonic possession had also experienced sexual abuse in the past.[7] Generally speaking, the practice of psychotherapy and spiritual intervention have been separated from each other; however, some call for cooperation between the two fields.[8]

Fourth, in NT studies, assumptions about the NT texts yield various results. Some believe that the accounts of exorcism are historical facts and that

---

philosophical argument against the supernatural, see Olufunso Olubanjo-Olufowobi, "An Assessment of David Hume's Impossibility of Miracle," *Ilorin Journal of Religious Studies* 9, no. 1 (2019): 71–86.

4. David F. Strauss, *The Christ of Faith and the Jesus of History*, trans. Leander E. Keck (Philadelphia: Fortress Press, 1977), 89.

5. Myrtle S. Langley, "Spirit-Possession, Exorcism and Social Context: An Anthropological Perspective with Theological Implications," *Churchman* 94, no. 3 (1980): 228, 242.

6. There are psychiatrists who admit that there are instances that are best explained as a spiritual phenomenon. M. Scott Peck testifies about two incidents during his psychiatric practice that convinced him that not everything can be explained in psychiatric terms (*Glimpses of the Devil: A Psychiatrist's Personal Accounts of Possession, Exorcism, and Redemption* [New York: Free Press, 2005]).

7. Mariani, "Exorcisms on the Rise," 67.

8. Dennis L. Bull, Joan W. Ellason, and Colin A. Ross, "Exorcism Revisited: Positive Outcomes with Dissociative Identity Disorder," *Journal of Psychology and Theology* 26, no. 2 (1998): 195.

demons do exist. Some NT interpreters see references to demons as a literary device to speak about humans or societal structures that embody evil; they are coded language that refer to some Roman rulers who embody evil,[9] rather than an acknowledgment of their existence. The purpose of these accounts of exorcism is to elicit faith, rather than narrate historical accounts.

WHERE CAN WE GO FROM HERE?

There is much to learn from science and other disciplines when we discuss the topic of exorcism. We can observe, however, that one's theological assumptions inevitably affect how we understand this phenomenon. The belief in demonic activities did not begin in the NT. Thus, before we look into the NT teachings about the spirits and their activities in the physical world, we will briefly look at how these beliefs were expressed both in the OT and the pseudepigraphic writings prior to the NT, and how the NT presented and explained these activities.

ANCIENT JEWISH BELIEFS

Some modern beliefs about the supernatural and its manifestation in the physical world may be influenced by what we see in the movies, as Dale E. Custodio warns.[10] Hollywood is not the only source of cinematic stereotypes of demonic manifestation, we see hopping ghosts from Hong Kong movies in the 1980s, or more recently, the Zombies in Korean cinema that may or may not accurately reflect traditional beliefs of one particular group of people. Various cultures experience and describe evil differently. This explains the variety of myths and folklore in different regions of the world, such as the werewolves of the Europeans, or the *tikbalang* and *kapre* in the Philippines. The creation of myths is a way for people to explain the unusual experiences they had, and although it is possible that these experiences can be misinterpreted, dismissing all of them is not the best way to go in our attempt toward understanding. Eyewitness testimonies remain to be invaluable resources for understanding these activities.

Aside from eyewitnesses, written sources must also be considered, particularly the NT where we can read accounts of exorcisms. Exorcism presumes

---

9. Norman A. Beck, *Anti-Roman Cryptograms in the New Testament: Symbolic Messages of Hope and Liberation*, Westminster College Library of Biblical Symbolism 1 (New York: Peter Lang, 1997), 5–6.

10. Dale G. Custodio, "*The Exorcist*: A Hollywood Perspective," in *Principalities and Powers: Reflections in the Asian Context* (Mandaluyong: OMF Literature 2007), 174–75.

demonic activity, and demonic activity presumes a demonic actor. There is no known ancient Jewish writing that attempts to prove the existence of demons, nor is there one that attempts to disprove it. The simplest explanation for this is that ancient writers assume they do, and that even their readers do not question this assumption.

Aside from the NT, other sources of information include the OT, the Second Temple writings, and the Dead Sea Scrolls. They provide the literary resources that reflect the beliefs of ancient Jews about the spirit world and otherworldly beings, both clean/good and unclean/evil, and their activities. Even in rabbinic writings, the belief in evil spirits can be inferred from some of their traditional teachings. For instance, a person who puts out a lamp on a Sabbath out of fear of bad spirits is not considered liable for breaking the Sabbath (Mishnah, Shabbat 2:5). The wide range of available materials from this era show that even within Judaism, the beliefs about the spirit beings are variegated and reflect different traditions. Nonetheless, these various traditions still share a lot in common.[11]

Old Testament

The OT does not contain many accounts of exorcism compared to the NT. One of earliest records of demonic possession is the story of Saul. After the Spirit of the Lord left him to rest on David, an evil spirit (Heb. *ruakh ra'ah*) came upon Saul, as if replacing the Spirit of the Lord, to terrify (Heb. *va'at*) Saul (1 Sam 16:14–16, 23; 18:10; 19:10). The evil Spirit is said to be "from the LORD," which accentuates God's rule even over the evil spirits. It seems that although both good and evil spirits eventually fulfill the Lord's plans, the primary difference is that the good ones consistently do God's commands (for example, Michael was ready to fulfill God's plan for humans [Dan 10:10–14]), and the evil ones do not (for example, Satan was ready to test God and instigate disaster for humans [Job 1–2]).

Saul's servants suggest that they look for someone skilled in playing the lyre to calm Saul down whenever he is tormented by the evil spirit.[12] This sug-

---

11. This is the point wherein Jewish and Christian traditions diverge from their Greco-Roman counterparts. Although other ancient religions express belief in demons, the *daimon* in ancient Greco-Roman writings do not always refer to evil spirits. The term *daimonaō* may mean to be possessed either by an evil god or by a benevolent spirit (Henry George Liddell, et al., *A Greek-English Lexicon*, 9th ed. [Oxford: Clarendon, 1996], s.v. *daimonaō*).

12. In Pseudo-Philo's rewriting of the story, David reminded the spirit that Tartarus is its residence, and "as a stranger on earth and an unwelcome guest to its 'host,' it can rightly be sent back to this place of residence if it does not behave itself" (H. M. Jackson, "Echoes and

gestion may be an indicator that this had been the practice by earlier exorcists. Saul's attitude toward spiritism had been inconsistent also. On the one hand, he expelled the mediums and necromancers out of the land in the early part of his reign (1 Sam 28:3, 9). This is in compliance with Yahweh's commands regarding consulting spiritists (Lev 19:31; 20:6, 27; Deut 18:11). On the other hand, in an attempt to seek counsel from his long-time adviser Samuel after his death, Saul sought the help of the witch of Endor (1 Sam 28:7). This one mistake, unfortunately, is one of the two things that defined his legacy according to the Chronicler: his unfaithfulness to God and his consultation with a medium (1 Chr 10:13).

Two other passages are more conjectural. Solomon, the son of David, is said to be knowledgeable with botanical life (1 Kgs 4:33). Later, Josephus interpreted Solomon's knowledge of plants and nature as part of his skill in expelling demons. Josephus also mentions the magic ring Solomon used in exorcism (*Jewish War* 8.2.5 §§44–47).[13] Another passage is Zechariah 5 which some interpret to be an account of exorcism based on its similarity with some Ugaritic and Mesopotamian incantation texts.[14]

Second Temple Apocalyptic Writings

The belief in wandering spirits, or sometimes known as the "good brothers" (好兄弟, *hǎo xiōngdì*), is the basis for celebrating the Hungry Ghost Festival among some Chinese people scattered throughout Asia. This festival is celebrated on the fifteenth day of the seventh month of the lunar calendar; food is offered to these wandering spirits so that these "good brothers" would resist doing evil and avoid harming those who are alive. The belief in wandering spirits is not exclusively Chinese; some ancient Jews also believed in them. They were said to have taught the Gentiles evil ways (Testament of Napthali 3:5), but are constantly tormented because they scorned the law, have no chance to repent, can only watch the obedient being rewarded and other angels guard the habitation of others, waiting for their future torment while seeing others being tormented, and are consumed with shame before God (4 Ezra 7:81–87).

Demons in the Pseudo-Philonic *Liber Antiquatitum Biblicarum*," *JSJ* 27, no. 1 [1996]: 8).

13. Solomon is also adjured in some later incantation materials (Larry Perkins, "Greater than Solomon [Matt 12:42]," *TJ* 19, no. 2 [1998]: 208–9, 212–13). See also Dennis C. Duling, "Solomon, Exorcism, and the Son of David," *HTR* 68, no. 3 (1975): 235–52.

14. Lena-Sofia Tiemeyer, "Dumping your Toxic Waste Abroad: Exorcism and Healing in Zechariah's Vision Report and Beyond," in *Healing and Exorcism in Second Temple Judaism and Early Christianity* (Tübingen: Mohr Siebeck, 2019), 11–31.

The Jewish apocalyptic tradition is more elaborate in its discussion about spirits. It provides us with a long list of names of angels, the various hierarchies, their activities, and their designated locations (1 Enoch 69:2–3). It also provides us with stories about the origin of demons. According to one Enochic tradition, the fall of these angels results from them leaving the places designated for them to interfere with the affairs of humans; the evil spirits roaming on earth are spirits of the Watchers (15:1–12; esp. v. 9). The fallen angels were also responsible for teaching humans various forms of evil (8:3–4; 64:1–2; 65:6–12). Demons exercise their power over humans, but certain individuals were also given authority over demons, like Phanuel, who exorcized demons to keep them from accusing humans before God (40:7, 9).[15]

Second Temple Writings that Rewrote Old Testament Stories

The story of creation in the Book of Jubilees contains a passing comment about the angel Gabriel's revelation about the various roles of the ministering spirits assigned to the various elements and seasons (Jubilees 2:1–2). The book also traces the origin of demons back to the Watchers who were uprooted from their dominion after taking human wives (5:1–2, 6); as a result, they became the demons misleading Noah's descendants on earth (7:27; 10:2). Like Satan in the canonical Book of Job, Mastema the chief of the spirits negotiated with God to exercise authority over Noah's descendants (Jubilees 10:7–11). God permitted him, but also instructed the demons to teach Noah healing methods, so they taught him to use herbs to heal, a knowledge Noah passed on to Shem (10:10–14).

In another work, Satan is the enemy who wanted to destroy the saints at Sinai (Lives of the Prophets 2:15). He is also called Beliar to whom king Nebuchadnezzar belonged (4:6), who slaughtered the people (4:20), hindered Nathan from confronting David (17:2).

In Pseudo-Philo's rewriting of David's story, the writer briefly recounts how David used a song to cast out demons. In that song, he recounts how demons were created on the second day of creation "from a resounding echo in the chaos." David identifies one of his offspring will rule over the demons. Every time David sang, the evil spirit spared Saul (Pseudo Philo, *Liber antiquitatum biblicarum* 60:1–3). A longer story of demonic activity and exorcism is found in Tobit. The demon Asmodeus fell in love with a human, Raguel's daughter

---

15. Other related work shows satanic control over a person can continue even after a person's death. Only prayers of their living relatives can free them from this (Questions of Ezra 14–18).

Sarah; so, Asmodeus killed the seven men to whom she was betrothed (Tobit 3:8; 6:14). God sent Raphael who disguised himself as a relative of Tobit (3:17), and taught him how to exorcize demons by burning the heart and liver of a fish (6:7; 8:2). The angel also taught him how to heal the eye problem of his father Tobias by making an ointment using fish gall (Tobit 6:8).

Collection of Writings from the Second Temple Period Called "Testaments"

Like the canonical Book of Job, the Testament of Job presents Satan as the one who has access to God that he can enter into a negotiation about the fate of some people (Testament of Job 6:1–8:1; Job 1–2). Unlike the canonical Job, Satan comes as a master of disguises that he can appear as a beggar (Testament of Job 6:4), as the king of Persia (Testament of Job 17:1), or as a bread seller (21:1–23:11). Evil spirits (called "the spirits of Beliar") also have power to cause humans to sin (Testament of Dan 1:6–8; Testament of Asher 1:8).

The most comprehensive discussion about demons is the Testament of Solomon, that introduces the demons by name, their power, and their dwelling places. It also contains dialogues between Solomon and the evil spirits who reveal the methods that can be used to suppress their activities, and the punishments sentenced to them by Solomon. A story that is, perhaps, the most useful for our purposes in this essay is about an old man who complained to Solomon about his disrespectful son. The father wanted the son to be put to death. When Solomon asked the complainant to reconsider his request, Ornias the demon was in the background laughing and revealed to Solomon that the son would die in three days. When Solomon asked how the demon knew, Ornias explained how they could fly up to heaven close enough to God's throne to overhear what God's plans are (Testament of Solomon 20:6–21).

Earlier studies of the Testament of Solomon suggest that it was written by a Jewish author and edited by a Christian; but more recent scholarship is more open to the idea that the work was produced by a Greek speaking Christian.[16] In several instances, the author clearly acknowledges that together with the angelic beings and Solomon, Jesus (who was called "Emmanoel" in this work) can defeat the demonic spirits (6:8; 11:6; 12:3; 15:10–11; 17:4; 22:20).

---

16. Dennis D. Duling, "Testament of Solomon," in *Old Testament Pseudepigrapha*, 1:943.

Dead Sea Scrolls

Filipino faith healers do not follow a handbook guide to determine whether a person is demon possessed or not; but there are some traditional methods for testing which include measuring fingers, placing of matchsticks in between toes, placing coins on eggs, looking at candles through a glass of water, and use of *tawas*, among others.[17] The Dead Sea Scrolls include documents that provide us insights on how exorcism was practiced by some ancient Jews.

The Damascus Document recounts how the Guardian Angels of Heaven were ensnared by their willful heart and disobeyed God's commandments (Damascus Document 2:17–18). The belief that the world is under evil influence is also seen in this document. Belial (the name commonly used to refer to Satan) set three traps for the dwellers of the land: fornication, wealth, defilement of the Temple (Damascus Document 1:12–17). He also raised up Jannes and Jambres (5:18–19), his spirit led people to apostasy (12:2). Another document, the Rule of the Community, emphasizes his control over the wicked (Rule of the Community 1:23–24; 2:19), because the righteous have no place for Belial in their heart (10:21).

Three sets of fragments provide a glimpse into the Qumran community's belief about exorcism. First, the Songs of the Sage for Protection Against Evil Spirits contain two sets of fragments, each one a song of incantation to protect the faithful from evil spirits. The first fragment begins with an acknowledgment of God's power followed by the claim of the instructor:

> And I, the Instructor, proclaim His glorious splendor so as to frighten and te[rrify] all the spirits of the destroying angels, spirits of bastards, demons, Lilith, howlers, and [desert dwellers . . .] and those which fall upon men without warning to lead astray from a spirit of understanding and to make their heart and their [. . .] desolate during the present dominion of wickedness. (Frag. 1, 4–7)

The "lyre of salvation" is used as part of the incantation. A smaller fragment contains the same key words found in the first, "the second [so]ng so as to

---

17. Violeta Villaroman-Bautista, "Possession: Where Psychology, Culture, and Theology Interface," in *Principalities and Powers: Reflections in the Asian Context* (Mandaluyong: OMF Literature, 2007), 48. Eggs and animal bile are used by necromancers who are also consulted by those who believed that it is the spirit of a dead relative that is communicating with the living by causing them sickness or discomfort (Mona P. Bias, "Consulting the Medium of Endor: Parallels and Analogies," in *Principalities and Powers*, 112–15).

frighten those who terrify" (Frag. 8, 4). Second, another document discovered from Cave 4, known as "An Exorcism," identifies male and female Wasting-demon, Fever-demon, Chills-demon, and Chest Pain-demon (i, 3–4). The role of the midwife in the process may reflect a belief in demonic activities during childbirth. Third, the Song to Disperse Demons, also called "A Psalm of Solomon," calls the Lord to smite the demons in his fierce wrath and send them into the great abyss, the lowest Hades (iii, 1–12).

In summary, although there may be various beliefs in ancient Jewish traditions about the origin of evil spirits, with some tracing it back to the story of creation while others to the story of the Watchers, the common element they share is the belief that these beings were the angels who rebelled against God. Their leader may be identified by different names like Satan, Mastema, Belial, or Semyaz, but he and his followers all share the same characteristics, namely, their rebellion against God and hostility against humans which is evidenced in the sins they cause humans to commit, various types of sicknesses they cause humans to suffer, and the accusations against humans they bring before God. The earth was created for humans, but the fallen angels have infiltrated the physical world and by causing humans to rebel against God, these angels laid claim over the realm that is to be ruled by God through humans. There is no standard method for the expulsion of demons: some use incantations/prayers, talisman, or other rituals. In some cases, the name of God is invoked during exorcisms.

DEMONIC ACTIVITIES IN THE NEW TESTAMENT

The research of Violeta V. Bautista on the *sinapian* (demon possessed) yields a *pattern of beliefs* among Filipino Evangelicals concerning the cause of demonic activities on a person (which includes sin, occult activities, psychological/emotional weaknesses and problems) and their manifestations (which includes cognitive disturbance, physical illnesses or unusual strength, changes in behavior and appearance, among others). As a psychotherapist, she observes that many of such manifestations can be linked to psychiatric problems, such as those who hear voices others cannot hear; thus, one cannot immediately conclude that a person is *sinapian* just by looking at these outward manifestations.[18]

---

18. Violeta V. Bautista, "View of *Sapi* by Evangelical Churchworkers: Some Implications for Psychopathology and Counseling," in *Understanding Behavior Bridging Cultures: Readings on an Emerging Global Psychology*, eds. Allan B. I. Bernardo, Natividad A. Dayan, and Allen A. Tan (Malate: DLSU Press, 1998), 184.

Nonetheless, she admits that there are cases when the manifestations are not classifiable under known psychiatric disorders; thus, the possibility of real possession cannot be dismissed. We will now turn to the NT for information.

In the NT, the Evil One is known as Satan, the devil, Beelzebul, and Belial/Beliar (2 Cor 6:15). The first two names are the more commonly used. Although the NT points to human desires as the cause of sins (Matt 15:18–19; Jas 1:14–15), the devil's direct involvement is clear in some instances of temptation, for example, of Jesus (Matt 4:1–11; Mark 1:12–13; Luke 4:1–13), of Judas (Luke 22:3; John 5:29; 13:2, 27), of Ananias (Acts 5:3), of unbelievers (Eph 2:2), and of new converts (1 Tim 3:6).

The NT describes demonic activities in terms of warfare (Eph 6:10–20). Satan schemes (4:27; 2 Cor 2:11; 1 Tim 5:15); thus, believers are to resist him (Jas 4:7) and ask for God's protection (John 17:15). Satan also devours (1 Pet 5:8), comes with disguises (2 Cor 11:14), and hinders God's work (1 Thess 2:18). When Paul talks about his "thorn in the flesh," he specifies that this was a "messenger of Satan" (2 Cor 12:7), perhaps a person who is instrumental in hampering God's work. Satan also takes part in the discipline of wayward believers (1 Cor 5:5; 1 Tim 1:20); and his judgment is sure (Rom 16:20; Heb 2:14).

Stories of Exorcisms

The practice of exorcism is not exclusively Christian. Stories of ritual dancing among the traditional Tanzanian in Segeju, forced vomiting among the Navajos, burning of charms and paper "money" among the Chinese, or chanting of Qur'anic passages among Somalian Muslims are believed to be ways for expelling demons. The Balahi Hindus engage in debates with the demons, Filipino psychic enter trances, and Shamans negotiate with demons to drive them out.[19] Even in Scripture, there are some non-Christian exorcists like the seven sons of Sceva (Acts 19:13–14).

Aside from several passing statements about Jesus casting out demons (Matt 4:24; 8:16; Mark 1:32–34, 39; 16:9; Luke 8:2) and his commands to his disciples to do the same (Matt 10:8; cf. Luke 10:17), the Gospels and Acts recount several stories of exorcisms.

---

19. Keener, *Miracles*, 2:810–11. See "Appendix A: Demons and Exorcism in Antiquity" (769–87) and "Appendix B: Spirit Possession and Exorcism in Societies Today" (788–856) for more examples from the ancient and modern eras.

In some cases, evidences of possession are comparable to symptoms of mental disorder as in the case of the man who lived in a cemetery. He cut himself with stones as if suicidal (Mark 5:5), is uninhibited (Luke 8:27) and fierce (Matt 8:28). No wonder demonic possession can easily be confused with mental illness. His unusual physical strength (Mark 5:3–4; Luke 8:29) and his ability to immediately recognize Jesus's supernatural authority, however, cannot be explained as a psychiatric problem. His return to sanity after Jesus's confrontation with Legion suggests that one of the effects of possession was mental disorder (8:35). However, the confrontation between Jesus and Legion shows that his mental illness was the symptom and demon possession was the problem.

All three Synoptic accounts point to the Gerasene cemetery as the dwelling place of the demon possessed. Tombs do not always connote eeriness. Burial sites can be a "reunion" place for dead family members (e.g. Abraham's family [Gen 23:19; 25:10; 49:31]), a "home" for the departed (e.g. Joseph's request [50:24–25; Josh 24:32]), or a holy site (e.g. tomb of the prophet from Bethel [2 Kgs 23:17]). At times, when two people groups fight for territories, ancestral gravesites legitimize land claims.[20] In the case of Nehemiah, for instance, while he was in Susa and was planning to return to his native land, he sought Artaxerxes's permission to return to Jerusalem, "the place of [his] fathers' graves" (Neh 2:3). In the Gospel accounts, the cemetery is the place of conflict between Jesus and the evil army as the demonic forces have unrightfully claimed this "land of the dead" for themselves.[21]

Aside from the geographical location these evil forces claimed for themselves, they also claimed the physical body and mental faculty of the possessed man. Demonic possession is, in a way, a form of territorial control of the demons over a person's mind and body; and exorcism is the way for God to reclaim the space that is rightfully his.[22] Demonic control over the body manifests in physical illness such as blindness, muteness, and seizures; and in contrast, God's rule over the person includes the restoration of one's health. No wonder healing and exorcism were essential components of Jesus's message of the kingdom of God (Matt 4:23; 9:35; Luke 9:2, 11; 10:9).

---

20. Francesca Stavrakopoulou, *Land of Our Fathers: The Role of Ancestral Veneration in Biblical Land Claims*, Library of Old Testament Studies 473 (London: T&T Clark, 2010), 3.
21. Like the lecherous spirit of a giant man who died in a massacre (Testament of Solomon 17:1–5), the Legion found home among the dead.
22. Patrick Schreiner, *The Body of Jesus: A Spatial Analysis of the Kingdom in Matthew*, LNTS 555 (London: T&T Clark, 2016), 62.

There are accounts of healing in the Gospels that may make one suspect that the sickness might have been related to demonic possession. For instance, when Jesus healed Peter's mother-in-law of her fever, he "rebuked the fever" (4:39); four verses earlier, Jesus did the same thing to the demon (4:35).[23] One may infer that the fever could be related to demonic possession. However, there are instances when the Gospels relate stories of healing without any hint that the disease is related to demonic possession, like the paralytic (Matt 9:1–8), the blind beggar Bartimaeus (Mark 10:46–51), Jairus's daughter, and the bleeding woman (Luke 8:40–56). This suggests that the early witnesses to Jesus's healings and exorcisms could tell the difference between illnesses that result from demonic possession and those that were not. They were also clear about one thing – exorcism is a work of God (11:20).

Occultism: Revelation Received, Repressed, and Rejected

The use of tarot cards and palm reading are popular in many cultures. Among many Chinese, the drawing of lots/sticks (抽籤, *chōuqiān*) is one way to tell a person's future. The OT clearly prohibits involvement in any form of occult practices such as sorcery (Exod 22:18; Deut 18:10), fortune-telling (Lev 19:26; Deut 18:14), and necromancy (Lev 19:31; 20:6, 27; Deut 18:11). This raises the question why the magi were given such an important role in the story of Jesus's birth (Matt 2:1–12).[24] Not only were they implicitly absolved from their occultic practices, they were also a few of the privileged ones who received the revelation from God about the birth of the Messiah; and of all the possible or available methods, they received the revelation by watching stars. No wonder some translations (like ESV, NRSV) prefer translating the Greek word *magoi* (that is, magicians or sorcerers) as "wise men." The image of the magi has been unnecessarily sanitized, and as a result the message of hope for occult practitioners that the magi's story brings is also wiped clean.

Micah's prophecy about the birth of the Messiah comes with an indictment against the Jewish religious leaders. The Messiah's birth (Mic 5:2–3; cf. Matt 2:2, 5–6) would be preceded by God's denouncement of Israel's prophets;

---

23. The word "rebuke" (Greek, *epitimaō*) is equivalent to the Aramaic *ga'ar*, which is often used in the context of putting evil spirits under subjection (Steve Walton, "Why Silence? Reflections on Paul and Jesus Silencing Demonised People in Luke-Acts," in *Healing and Exorcism in Second Temple Judaism and Early Christianity* [Tübingen: Mohr Siebeck, 2019], 104).

24. For a more detailed discussion on this, see Samson L. Uytanlet, *Matthew: A Pastoral and Contextual Commentary*, Asia Bible Commentary Series (Carlisle: Langham Global Library, 2017), 25–29.

they would see no vision and receive no revelation, resulting in their shame (Mic 3:6–7). God's revelation was given to the sorcerers, not to the religious leaders (Matt 2:1–4). Moreover, the prophecy about the Messiah's birth comes with a series of promises to the remnants, one of which is the end of sorcery and fortune-telling (Mic 5:12). The magi found Jesus by following the star, but went home by another way (Matt 2:12), no longer depending on celestial bodies for guidance. God used the occultic practice of the magi to reveal to them about the Messiah, but he did not stop there. They sought Jesus as occult practitioners, they left him as worshippers of the Messiah. This is part of the hope that the gospel brings even for those who delve into occultism.

Although the magi had been involved in practices that opened a doorway for evil spirits to take control of them, there is no hint in Matthew that they had been possessed. To put it another way, despite their involvement in the occult, God clearly intervened and revealed his plan to them. Not all occult practitioners received revelation from God. There are more recent accounts of people getting revelation about the future from other sources.[25] In Scripture, the story of the slave girl possessed by the python spirit (from the Greek, *pneuma puthōn*, translated "spirit of divination" [ESV]) is no different (Acts 16:16–24). She was also a recipient of a revelation, but not from God. This story shows the direct connection between fortune-telling and demonic activity, and the demons in this account provide accurate information and predictions. This recalls the story about the conversation between Solomon and Ornias about how demons know the future (Testament of Solomon 20:6–21). The story is clearly an attempt to explain how demons could know the future.

In an earlier account in the Gospels, an encounter between Jesus and an unclean spirit occurred in a synagogue in Capernaum (Luke 4:31–37; cf. Mark 1:21–28). There is no indication that Jesus initiated the exorcism by approaching the one possessed or that someone from the congregation informed Jesus about it, which suggests that the demon-possessed man had been sitting quietly among the worshippers without anyone even noticing his condition. It was only when Jesus started teaching that the demon called Jesus the "Holy One of God," so he rebuked the demon to silence him.

Similarly, the so-called "python demon" was also silenced after it identified Paul and Silas as the "servants of the Most High God" (Acts 16:17). In Philippi,

---

25. Bautista shares the story of Hezda, who claimed to have been receiving "impressions" about future events from unknown sources ("Possession: Where Psychology, Culture, and Theology Interface," 42).

the "most high god" could easily be understood as a reference to Zeus. Through exorcism, the voice of the demon was repressed. The expulsion of the python spirit did not only liberate the girl from the clutches of unclean spirits, but it also dissociated Paul and Silas from the Greek local deity preventing unnecessary confusions.[26] More importantly, Paul's method of exorcism made it clear that it is only by the name of Jesus that the demons can be expelled (16:18).

Exorcising by the name of Jesus is not a magical ritual as seen in the story of the sons of Sceva. These seven exorcists tried to imitate Paul's method, only to end up embarrassing themselves (19:13–16). One positive result from this incident was the conversion of many Ephesians, including those who had been practicing magic (19:17–19). There were many who practiced magic who brought their books on magic to be burned. There might still be those who did not do so. Luke mentions that the books cost fifty thousand pieces of silver (19:19). If we assume that a piece of silver is equivalent to a day's wage, fifty thousand pieces of silver would be equivalent to a person's wages for more than one hundred thirty-six years of non-stop work. The cost of the books shows the extent of the people's involvement in occultism. This might also explain why there were numerous cases of demonic possession in the city. No wonder that in Paul's Letter to the Ephesians, he closed the letter by discussing about spiritual battle (Eph 6:10–20).

Jesus and Beelzebul

There are two truths that sound contradictory, but nonetheless, clear from the NT: (1) God is "Lord of heaven and earth" (Matt 11:25; Luke 10:21; Acts 17:24), and (2) Satan is the god of this world (2 Cor 4:4; 1 John 5:19). That makes the earth/world (the space occupied by humans) the battleground of God and Satan. Some ancient works explain this conflict in terms of a battle between two spiritual forces: between the Truth, the Beloved and Bride on one side versus the Corrupter/Deceiver/Error on the other (Ode of Solomon 38), or between the Holy Spirit versus the Evil One (14:5, 8; 16:5). In other works, the battles that happen in the spiritual realm are said to be evident in the material, such as the conflict between the communities that isolated themselves in Qumran and the "world" that they left. This is the battle between the sons of light *who dwell within* the kingdom of Belial and the armies of Kittim *which is part of* the kingdom of Belial (Damascus Document 14:9;

---

26. Walton, "Why Silence," 107.

15:3; 18:1). Evil may prevail in the interim, but condemnation awaits Belial and his followers (Wars Scroll 13:1–4).

The idea of this epic battle between the kingdom of God and the kingdom of Satan is also alluded to in the exorcism of the blind/mute man (Matt 12:22–32; Mark 3:22–30; Luke 11:14–26). The material world is their implicit battleground, which includes human bodies as in cases of demonic possession.[27] Through Jesus's exorcism, God reclaimed control over this bodily territory. In Luke's account, the battle did not end in the expulsion of the demons as it looks for seven other spirits for reinforcement (Luke 11:24–26). On the part of the one set free, to avoid recurrence, it requires living "within the reality of God's reign, continuing to hear God's word and persisting in guarding it."[28] Jesus's revelation about the expelled demon calling reinforcements shows the persistence of the Evil One to take what is not rightfully his.

The Pharisees accused Jesus of connivance with Beelzebul, the prince of demons to overcome other demons (Matt 9:34; 12:24, 27; Mark 3:22; Luke 11:15, 18–19; cf. Matt 10:25). Jesus shows the fallacy of their reason because an internal conflict within the kingdom of Beelzebul will only cause its downfall (cf. Isa 19:2).[29] Beelzebul is known as the ruler of demons who also rules the world by raising tyrant rulers, and consequently ruling the world and destroying humanity (see Testament of Solomon 3:6). Thus, Jesus dissociated himself from the prince of demons making it clear that he does not represent the ruler of the world (cf. John 12:31; 14:30; 16:11), but is the "Lord of heaven and earth."

The difference between the extent of God's kingdom and that of the Evil One shows that we are not looking at two equally powerful deities fighting for supremacy. Instead, we have one true King whose kingdom is partially usurped by one who desired to assume God's rule and led the rebellious faction against God. He did so by trying to take some of God's territories and by causing humans to also rebel against their Creator.

---

27. Schreiner correctly points out that demonic possession is a means of "territorial control," and by exorcizing Jesus regains power over a place (*The Body of Jesus*, 62).

28. John T. Carroll, *Luke*, NTL (Louisville: WJKP, 2012), 256.

29. Jesus's response shows that the Pharisees were not merely implying that he was performing a theatric with fellow members of Beelzebul's army in order to deceive those who watch him cast out demons.

Satan in Revelation

The Book of Revelation points to two interrelated spheres where the god of this world asserts control, namely, religion and politics. First, there were demonic influences even within the religious sphere. John warns the Christians of Smyrna of the persecution initiated by the Jews who belong to the "synagogue of Satan" (Rev 2:9–10; cf. 3:9). Likewise, he encourages those in Thyatira to keep themselves away from "Satan's so-called deep secrets" taught by Jezebel because some have already fallen to her trap (2:20–25). He points to Pergamum as the city where Satan's throne is located (2:13).

Second, like earlier apocalyptic writings, the so-called "unholy trinity" in Revelation – the dragon, the beast from the earth, and the beast from the sea – shows the devil's attempt to control human affairs through the state. Satan's demise is expressed in terms of the heavenly battle between the archangel Michael and the dragon. The victory that Michael won in the spiritual realm, Jesus won in the physical realm through his death on the cross so that the devil can no longer continuously accuse humans before God (12:7–11; cf. Col 1:20). The aftermath of Satan's defeat was not his surrender, but his continuous deception of humans by empowering two beasts to continue his purposes. These apocalyptic images may refer to political figures who, albeit unknowingly, fulfill the purposes of the devil. The use of coded language to refer to political or religious leaders who personify evil does not require us to look at Satan or the devil as a mere personification of evil. Instead, we can consider them him as a real being who can be actively involved in human affairs.

THEOLOGICAL REFLECTIONS

The NT teachings about spiritual reality and demonic activities have a lot in common with those from the OT, the Second Temple writings, and the Dead Sea Scrolls. There are, of course, areas of differences as well. I will conclude this chapter by reflecting theologically on the NT teachings about this spiritual reality, drawing insights from them in relation to some Asian beliefs about the spirit world.

First, the NT writers wrote with the assumption that spirit beings exist and that their actions affect the lives of humans. The NT does not provide a comprehensive list of the angelic hierarchy, their designated places in the heavenlies, or their activities similar to those from works like 3 Enoch and the Testament of Adam. Even the Book of Revelation, which uses images common among apocalyptic writings, does not delve into this area. This suggests that angelology and demonology are not the primary concern of the NT. The NT, however, points to how angels fulfill the purposes of God and how unclean spirits obstruct and oppose the work of God. The fact that stories of good and evil angels found their way into ancient Jewish folklores does not automatically mean that their reality is suspect. Folklores are human attempts to make sense of their experiences. *Their explanations may not always be accurate, but the reality that they have experienced is something that cannot be discarded.* This should lead us to seriously consider why different regions have their own local folklores that involve otherworldly beings that harm humans. In the Philippines, for instance, there is the *kapre*, the *aswang*, the *mananaggal*, and the *tiyanak*. Not all experiences with the otherworldly elements can be relegated to the realm of the imagination.

Second, the witnesses of the stories in the Gospels clearly distinguished between diseases that are caused by demonic possession and those that are not. There are mental or physical symptoms of demon possession that are similar to other mental or physical illnesses, but the NT does not blame everything on the devil. In some cultures, evil spirits are convenient scapegoats for societal maladies. Discernment is necessary, therefore, in distinguishing real and imagined cases of demon possessions.

Third, occult practitioners can be found in all Asian countries. The *arbolario* (herbalist) is popular in both rural and some urban areas in the Philippines. The *mangkukulam* (witches) may be despised, but some people may seriously look for one to pronounce curses against an enemy. Consulting a *manghuhula* (fortune-teller) is so common that they can be found even outside the Church of the Black Nazarene in Quiapo, Manila. Although the Scripture clearly condemns all forms of occultic practice as it opens a gateway for demonic influence, the story of the magi in Matthew 2 gives hope for those who are involved in any form of occultic practices.

Fourth, the conflict between God and Satan is described using military imagery that involves, not only the invisible/spiritual realm, but also the physical world as their battleground. God, by virtue of being the Creator, is the real "Lord of heaven and earth." Satan is known as the "god of this world," not because he is a legitimate ruler, but because he is the usurper. The message about God's kingdom must, therefore, be continuously proclaimed. In a few instances, proclamation may be accompanied by supernatural feats; but in most cases, as one study of the South Indian Pentecostal Movement shows, missionary success is not attributable to miracles but through the bold proclamation of the gospel by believers in their families, neighborhood, and workplaces.[30]

Finally, like the OT and other non-canonical writings, the NT presents Satan and his angels as actively interfering in human affairs, whether by tempting them to sin, or sometimes causing them harm. Their work is not always obvious, like the demon possessed man in the synagogue in Capernaum. No one even noticed his condition until Jesus came to teach (Luke 4:31–37). This calls for vigilance on the part of the believers to pray for protection, not only for themselves, but for those in authority (1 Tim 2:1–2). Unlike the stories from the non-canonical writings, exorcisms in the NT are not performed by following certain rituals or reciting certain prayers. Exorcisms are performed by the power of God in the name of Jesus.

BIBLIOGRAPHY

Bautista, Violeta V. "View of *Sapi* by Evangelical Churchworkers: Some Implications for Psychopathology and Counseling." Pages 175–84 in *Understanding Behavior Bridging Cultures: Readings on an Emerging Global Psychology*. Edited by Allan B. I. Bernardo, Natividad A. Dayan, and Allen A. Tan. Malate: DLSU Press, 1998.

———. "Possession: Where Psychology, Culture, and Theology Interface." In *Principalities and Powers: Reflections in the Asian Context*, 41–65. Mandaluyong: OMF Literature, 2007.

Beck, Norman A. *Anti-Roman Cryptograms in the New Testament: Symbolic Messages of Hope and Liberation.* Westminster College Library of Biblical Symbolism 1. New York: Peter Lang, 1997.

Bergunder, Michael. "Miracle Healing and Exorcism: The South Indian Pentecostal Movement in the Context of Popular Hinduism." *International Review of Mission* 90, nos. 356–57 (2001): 103–12.

Bias, Mona P. "Consulting the Medium of Endor: Parallels and Analogies." In *Principalities and Powers: Reflections in the Asian Context*, 100–18. Mandaluyong: OMF Literature, 2007.

Bull, Dennis L., Joan W. Ellason, and Colin A. Ross. "Exorcism Revisited: Positive Outcomes with Dissociative Identity Disorder." *Journal of Psychology and Theology* 26, no. 2 (1998): 188–96.

Carroll, John T. *Luke.* NTL. Louisville: WJKP, 2012.

---

30. Michael Bergunder, "Miracle Healing and Exorcism: The South Indian Pentecostal Movement in the Context of Popular Hinduism," *International Review of Mission* 90, nos. 356–57 (2001): 111.

Charlesworth, James H. *The Old Testament Pseudepigrapha*. 2 vols. New York: Doubleday, 1983–1985.

Custodio, Dale G. "*The Exorcist*: A Hollywood Perspective." In *Principalities and Powers: Reflections in the Asian Context*, 163–75. Mandaluyong: OMF Literature, 2007.

Duling, Dennis C. "Solomon, Exorcism, and the Son of David." *Harvard Theological Review* 68, no. 3 (1975): 235–52.

————. "Testament of Solomon: A New Translation and Introduction." In *The Old Testament Pseudepigrapha*, edited by James H. Charlesworth, 1:935–87. 2 vols. New York: Doubleday, 1983–1985.

Harrington, D. J. "Pseudo-Philo: A New Translation and Introduction." In *The Old Testament Pseudepigrapha*, edited by James H. Charlesworth, 2:297–377. 2 vols. New York: Doubleday, 1983–1985.

Hogan, Larry P. *Healing in the Second Temple Period*. NTOA 21. Göttingen: Vandenhoeck and Ruprecht, 1992.

Jackson, H. M. "Echoes and Demons in the Pseudo-Philonic *Liber Antiquatitum Biblicarum*." *Journal for the Study of Judaism in the Persian, Hellenistic, and Roman Period* 27, no. 1 (1996): 1–20.

Josephus. *The Works of Josephus: Complete and Unabridged. New Updated Version*. Translated by William Whiston. Peabody: Hendrickson, 1987.

Keener, Craig S. *Miracles: The Credibility of the New Testament Accounts*. 2 vols. Grand Rapids: Baker Academic, 2011.

Klutz, Todd. *The Exorcism Stories in Luke-Acts: A Sociostylistic Reading*. SNTSMS 129. New York: Cambridge University Press, 2004.

Langley, Myrtle S. "Spirit-Possession, Exorcism and Social Context: An Anthropological Perspective with Theological Implications." *Churchman* 94, no. 3 (1980): 226–45.

Liddell, Henry George, Robert Scott, and Henry Stuart Jones. *A Greek-English Lexicon*. 9th ed. Oxford: Clarendon, 1996.

Mariani, Mike. "Why are Exorcisms on the Rise?" *Atlantic* 62 (2018): 62–71.

Olubanjo-Olufowobi, Olufunso. "An Assessment of David Hume's Impossibility of Miracle." *Ilorin Journal of Religious Studies* 9, no. 1 (2019): 71–86.

Peck, M. Scott. *Glimpses of the Devil: A Psychiatrist's Personal Accounts of Possession, Exorcism, and Redemption*. New York: Free Press, 2005.

Perkins, Larry. "Greater than Solomon (Matt 12:42)." *Trinity Journal* 19, no. 2 (1998): 207–17.

Schreiner, Patrick. *The Body of Jesus: A Spatial Analysis of the Kingdom in Matthew*. LNTS 555. London: T&T Clark, 2016.

Stavrakopoulou, Francesca. *Land of Our Fathers: The Role of Ancestral Veneration in Biblical Land Claims.* Library of Old Testament Studies 473. London: T&T Clark, 2010.

Strauss, David F. *The Christ of Faith and the Jesus of History.* Translated by Leander E. Keck. Philadelphia: Fortress Press, 1977.

Tellbe, Mikael, and Tommy Wasserman. *Healing and Exorcism in the Second Temple Judaism and Early Christianity.* WUNT 2/511. Tübingen: Mohr Siebeck, 2019.

Tiemeyer, Lena-Sofia. "Dumping your Toxic Waste Abroad: Exorcism and Healing in Zechariah's Vision Report and Beyond." In *Healing and Exorcism in Second Temple Judaism and Early Christianity*, edited by Mikael Tellbe and Tommy Wasserman, 11–31. WUNT 2/511. Tübingen: Mohr Siebeck, 2019.

Uytanlet, Samson L. *Matthew: A Pastoral and Contextual Commentary.* Asia Bible Commentary Series. Carlisle: Langham Global Library, 2017.

Walton, Steve. "Why Silence? Reflections on Paul and Jesus Silencing Demonised People in Luke-Acts." In *Healing and Exorcism in Second Temple Judaism and Early Christianity*, edited by Mikael Tellbe and Tommy Wasserman, 91–112. WUNT 2/511. Tübingen: Mohr Siebeck, 2019.

CHAPTER 12

POWER AND LEADERSHIP

Structures of the World and Jesus's Expectations of Servanthood for Asian Leaders

Alroy Mascrenghe

I was once asked to give an impromptu speech on power and politics. When I reached the stage I sat on a large sofa in the middle of the stage, and said: "This is politics. Large seat, small man – this is politics. Whenever a man has been given a seat bigger than him, he creates politics. The first thing he does is to eliminate anyone who is a threat to him. That is the beginning of all power politics." I was explaining the sad truth that all power politics is created by insecure people.

Unfortunately, this reality is pervasive in the contemporary Asian church, where we hear stories of abuse of power and authority quite frequently. More often than not, those who abuse power and authority also abuse women or money. Thus, lack of integrity in one area is also reflected in other areas. Writing about the church in India, Vishal Mangalwadi laments, "Shamefully, we must confess that very often the institutional church has been the cause or means of perpetuating injustice and poverty."[1] He further adds:

> Christian officers in the government of India and in the secular world are often respected for their integrity and ethical standards, but the same cannot be said about some of the leadership of churches and Christian institutions. And even church leaders who have the personal integrity do not always seem to have the power to judge the sin within the church.[2]

This essay is an effort towards identifying these blind spots of the church and proposing an alternate way.

---

1. Vishal Mangalwadi, *Truth and Social Reform* (London: Hodder & Stoughton, 1989), 112.
2. Mangalwadi, 92.

In this chapter, after a brief discussion about power in general, we will survey the power structures and struggles in the NT from selected passages and try to identify the root causes of the power struggles. In the final section of this essay, we propose a model of leadership for the modern Asian church that is rooted in the Bible's ethical vision.

WHAT IS POWER?

Max Weber famously defined power as "the probability that *one* actor within a social relationship will be in a position to carry out his own will despite resistance, regardless of the basis on which this probability rests."[3] However, the modern definitions of power are more neutral. Power is often understood as something that helps to "achieve the intended results,"[4] and it can be used for either good or bad.[5] The need for power arises because of the inequalities in society, where there are leaders and followers, the strong and the weak.

The power and authority of the church come from Christ himself, who shared with it the power and authority given to him by God the Father (Matt 10:1; 28:18; Phil 2:9–11). Donald Guthrie, looking at the church as Christ's body and Christ as its head, comments: "No authority structure is possible without the supreme authority being vested in Christ himself. Moreover, even here the authority must be understood as organic and not organizational . . . Any officials who are mentioned must be regarded as exercising their various functions under the direction of the head."[6] Thus, the power that is given to the church (leaders) is from Christ himself. However, knowing how power can corrupt people, he warned his disciples not to "lord it over" them (Matt 20:25–28), and his disciples gave the same warning to their successors, the NT church leaders (1 Pet 5:3).

This is also why the NT places a strong emphasis on the character of the church leader (1 Tim 3:1–13; Tit 1:6–9). Not only should the church demand its leaders to be holy, but it must also filter out those who are ineligible to be leaders.

---

3. Max Weber, *Max Weber: The Theory of Social and Economic Organization*, trans. A. M. Henderson and Talcott Parsons (Mansfield Centre: Martino Publishing, 2012), 157.
4. Gilbert W. Fairholm, *Organizational Power Politics: Tactics in Organizational Leadership*, 2nd ed. (Santa Barbara: Praeger/ABC-CLIO, 2009), xiii.
5. Fairholm, xiv.
6. Donald Guthrie, *New Testament Theology* (Leicester, England; Downers Grove: InterVarsity Press, 1981), 760.

POWER STRUGGLES IN THE MINISTRY OF JESUS

The Gospels portray the power struggles between Jesus and the Jewish leaders page after page. In the following section, we will look at some of those episodes – between Jesus and John the Baptist and Jesus and the Pharisees. Interestingly, these stories illustrate strikingly different reactions to Jesus's authoritative power.

Jesus and John

While there were frequent power struggles between Jesus and the Jewish leaders, it is remarkable that there were no power struggles between John the Baptist and Jesus reported in the Gospels. This is even more striking given that from a human perspective, there were good reasons for John to have clashed with Jesus. Jesus, who was younger than John and had come to ministry after him, was becoming more popular than him. The Jews tried to create division between Jesus and John, reporting, for example, that "all are going to him" (John 3:26 ESV), implying that Jesus was becoming more popular than John.

An OT parallel to this would be the conflict between David and Saul. When the crowds praised David, crediting him for killing tens of thousands (1 Sam 18:7), Saul became jealous of David and started his pursuit of David. Yet in John's case, he never turned against Jesus. He understood his God-given role and place in life. "No one can receive anything except what has been given from heaven" (John 3:27 NRSV), John declared. John also confessed Jesus to be the "one more powerful than I" (Mark 1:7 NIV). As noted above, one of the fundamental reasons for all power struggles is insecurity. Leaders often do not realize their calling and the God-given purpose of their lives; instead, they try to live someone else's life. John is a striking example of fighting that instinct.

Jesus and the Pharisees

In a stunning contrast to John the Baptist, the Pharisees engaged in constant power struggles with Jesus. The sect of the Pharisees was one of the most powerful groups mentioned in the NT. The "central characteristic of the Pharisees" was their focus on "biblical law and its interpretation."[7] The Pharisees were the leaders of the masses and were the most influential Jewish group according to Josephus (*Jewish Antiquities* 13.10.6 §298; *Jewish War* 2.8.14 §162).

---

7. Hillel Newman, *Proximity to Power and Jewish Sectarian Groups of the Ancient Period*, ed. Ruth Ludlam, Brill Reference Library of Judaism 25 (Leiden: Brill, 2006), 54.

They had control over the synagogues[8] and they exercised some control over the Sanhedrin, the Jewish ruling council (John 11:47; Acts 5:34) and they even had some influence over Roman rulers (Matt 27:62; cf. Mark 12:13). In addition, they were well-connected with the high priests.[9]

The Pharisees were well-informed. For example, they had messengers who informed them of Jesus's activities. In one instance, Jesus departed from Judea because he knew that the Pharisees had been informed that he was making more disciples than John (John 4:1–2). Whereas John the Baptist publicly confessed that Jesus was the long-expected Messiah, the Pharisees would not tolerate any identification of Jesus as the Messiah. As soon as the people started to doubt whether Jesus was indeed the long-awaited Messiah, they tried to get him arrested (7:25–32). One likely reason for the Jewish leaders to kill him by crucifixion was because that would be a definitive way to challenge his "messianic claims." No messiah would ever die hanging on a tree.[10]

While there could have been professional reasons for Pharisees to seek to kill Jesus, there is no denying that they also had personal motives. At the trial of Jesus before the Sanhedrin, the Jewish leaders accused him of blasphemy, a religious crime, alleging that he claimed to be the son of God (Luke 22:66–71). But before Pilate, they accused him of treason, a political crime, that Jesus was "misleading our nation and forbidding us to give tribute to Caesar, and saying that he himself is Christ, a king" (23:2 ESV). Pilate soon realized that it was because of jealousy that they had delivered Jesus to him (John 15:10). The Pharisees and their sect created trouble even for the NT church long after the death of Jesus (cf. Acts 15:5).

Another possible reason for the clash between the Pharisees and Jesus was that the Pharisees saw an "otherness" in Jesus. He was different from them. He ate with the wrong people, he healed people, he healed them on the wrong day, and he did not follow the same code as the Pharisees. While the Pharisees had power over others, they could not control Jesus. His actions, directly and indirectly, challenged their power base.

When the Jewish leaders questioned the origin of Jesus's authority (soon after he had "cleansed" the temple), he in turn asked them about John's baptism. By asking this, Jesus was not trying to avoid the question or "box them

---

8. Synagogue played a significant role not only in the religious life of the Jewish community but also their social life. Pharisees exercised control over the society by controlling membership to the synagogues (John 12:42).

9. Newman, *Proximity to Power and Jewish Sectarian Groups of the Ancient Period*, 69.

10. Martin Hengel, *The Cross of the Son of God* (London: SCM Press, 1986), 231.

into a corner,"[11] but was answering their question.[12] It was when John baptized Jesus that the Holy Spirit descended on him, and God said, "This is my Son, the Beloved, with whom I am well pleased" (Matt 3:13–17 ESV). It was during Jesus's baptism that John got to know who Jesus really was (John 1:29–34). So, if they accepted John's baptism as coming from God, then they must also accept Jesus's authority as coming from God. This sense of mandate and calling was one of the things that distinguished Jesus's ministry from that of the Pharisees (John 3:17; 6:38; 20:21). Jesus saw his ministry as a calling from God.

According to the Gospel of John, it was the resurrection of Lazarus that eventually led to Jesus's crucifixion. Immediately after this incident, the chief priests and the Pharisees gathered the ruling council (11:47). Their main concern was losing the crowd, "If we let him go on like this, *everyone* will believe in him" (11:48 ESV, emphasis mine). Gospel writers, as well as the Pharisees, saw the Jesus movement and the Pharisaic movement as mutually exclusive. The crowds left the Pharisees and joined Jesus mainly because of his unique teaching and miracles (12:11). The Pharisees were worried that Jesus was establishing an alternative authority with which they struggled to compete.

Jesus also associated with the kind of people whom the Pharisees considered morally and ritually unclean, rather like the untouchables in India. The Pharisees avoided the "tax collectors and sinners," but Jesus welcomed them and often had meals with them. As Scot McKnight aptly says, "Tables can create societies; they can also divide societies."[13] Pharisees used the table as a tool to maintain social stratification,[14] but Jesus used it as a tool to reach out to the marginalized classes.[15] The Pharisees used the dinner table to establish their power base. Part of the self-identity of the Pharisees was formed by the meal table. They would not eat with sinners, not only because sinners were ritually unclean, but also because it would give a wrong message to others about who they, as Pharisees, were. Ironically, part of Jesus's identity was also formed by the table. When questioned why he ate and drank with sinners, he

---

11. John T. Carroll, *Luke: A Commentary*, NTL (Louisville: WJKP, 2012), 391.

12. Joel B. Green, *The Gospel of Luke*, NICNT (Grand Rapids: Eerdmans, 1997), 725–26.

13. Scot McKnight, *The Jesus Creed: Loving God, Loving Others* (Brewster: Paraclete Press, 2014), 36.

14. Green, *The Gospel of Luke*, 571.

15. This issue took a completely different form in the early church when Peter refused to eat with the gentile sinners, because of their "impurity." The use of the word sinners in both places is striking, James D. G. Dunn, *The Theology of Paul the Apostle* (Grand Rapids: Eerdmans, 2008), 192. Again, in the Corinthian church, the Corinthians used the table to maintain social stratification. Something for which they paid heavily with their lives (1 Corinthians 11).

related that to his mandate: "I *have . . . come* to call . . . the sinners" (Luke 5:32 ESV, emphasis mine). So, when Jesus ate with sinners at the same table, he was fulfilling his mission to call sinners. Jesus and the Pharisees both used the dinner table to display their identity. Jesus ate and identified with the sinners claiming that he was sent by God to do exactly that, whereas the Pharisees refrained from eating with sinners to maintain their status quo.

POWER STRUGGLES IN THE NEW TESTAMENT CHURCH

In this section, we will look at two accounts of power struggles in the NT and discuss their relevance to the modern church in Asia.

The Paul-Peter Conflict

Many issues began to arise in the NT church when non-Jewish people started to become members of an "exclusively Jewish community." The much-discussed conflict between Paul and the Judaizers and the ensuing confrontation with Peter was a result of this "Jewish-Gentile mix" (Acts 15 and Gal 2).[16] To summarize the issue: Judaizers from Jerusalem came to Antioch and taught that the Gentile believers must be circumcised in order to be considered full members of the Christian community and to have fellowship with the Jewish Christians. As a result, a conflict arose between Paul and Peter which led to the first church council in Jerusalem that addressed this issue.

We can draw several important lessons from this story. First, Paul was a junior leader who stood up to the most senior leaders in the church. He identifies Peter, John, and James as the "pillars" of the church (2:9). But he still went on to confront them. In most Asian cultures, it is unacceptable for junior leaders to confront senior leaders. For example, in India, the Guru-shishya relationship has impacted the wider society.[17] Some Asian leaders make decisions without consulting others and have little accountability. When it comes to matters of ethics, seniority must not be a shield against confrontation and accountability.

We can see the echo of Paul's words (2:11–14) in Peter's speech (Acts 15:7–11). Peter eventually saw Paul's point of view and spoke boldly in front of the whole assembly. This would not have happened if Paul had not confronted Peter. Senior leaders must be willing to learn from younger leaders.

---

16. Donald Guthrie, *New Testament Theology* (Downers Grove: InterVarsity Press, 1981), 734.
17. Paul R. Brass, "Leadership Power and Honor in a Corrupt System," in *Power and Influence in India: Bosses, Lords and Captains*, ed. Pamela Price and Arild Engelsen Ruud (New Delhi: Routledge India, 2012), 170.

Second, though Dunn claims that Peter is a bridge maker between two schools of thought,[18] Peter could be seen as a people pleaser. Peter refused to eat with the Gentiles only after the group from Jerusalem had come. If the events described in Galatians 2 happened after the events described in Acts 10 (I believe they did), then Peter was given the sanction by God himself not only to preach the gospel to the Gentiles but also to eat with them. However, because the Judaizers were more powerful, Peter possibly took their side and was not willing to be seen eating with the Gentiles. I think Peter's mistake is much more serious than that of the Judaizers. Whereas the Judaizers believed that they still needed to keep the law, Peter knew the truth and was willing to compromise it because he did not want to offend others. He was willing to compromise on something which had been directly revealed to him by God.

We sometimes find people like this in Christian circles whose primary goal is to indiscriminately please those in positions of power. When you put them in committees they will say "yes sir, yes sir" to any decision taken by the committee. What makes their mistakes more disgraceful is that they know the truth, but they are silent because they want to keep their jobs and secure their power.

Third, the NT church held a meeting to solve this issue. Sometimes, people who want to avoid conflicts at any cost do not confront the real issues. The church must come forward to discuss and resolve its issues even if it involves painful confrontations.

Fourth, people from both sides participated in the debate. Sometimes debates are held, and decisions are made without the concerned parties. One classic example is from the Synod of Dort which was gathered to discuss the Arminian "controversy." Simon Episcopus, the leader of the Arminian side, asked to critique Calvinism first and was compelled to leave the Synod when the assembly refused him the right to do so. Hence, the synod proceeded without the Arminian representation and condemned them as heretics![19]

Finally, in his speech to the Jerusalem Council, James quotes from the OT. In making theological and administrative decisions we must go back to the Bible for answers. Basing our views and decisions on the Bible will help us to be impartial to particular parties. And when we go to the Bible, we must

---

18. James Douglas Grant Dunn, *Unity and Diversity in the New Testament: An Inquiry into the Character of Earliest Christianity*, 3rd ed. (London: SCM Press, 2006), 430.
19. Scott Thomas, *The Articles of the Synod of Dort* (Philadelphia: Presbyterian Board of Publication, 1856), 28.

be willing to submit to its authority rather than bend it according to our pre-conceptions or personal interests. As we can see, the Jerusalem Council sets a precedent for the modern church to follow in solving problems. The church in Asia will benefit immensely if it follows these guidelines.

The Paul-Barnabas Conflict

Sometime after the Jerusalem Council, we read of another conflict (Acts 15:36–41). This time it was not about a theological issue but was about a person, John Mark. Mark had failed Barnabas and Paul on an earlier mission trip. Based on this experience, Paul refused to take him on another mission journey, but Barnabas, characteristically, was willing to give him a second chance.

Two things must have made this disagreement more personal and awkward. Firstly, Mark happened to be the cousin of Barnabas (Col 4:10). Secondly, when the disciples were afraid to take Paul into their fellowship, it was Barnabas who took him to the apostles and welcomed him to their fellowship (Acts 9:26–27). Barnabas acts in accord with his character – as his name conveys it – son of encouragement. He was people-oriented and gave others a second chance. Paul, on the other hand, was task-oriented. Unable to solve the issue amicably, they went on their own ways. Sometimes we must let people go their own ways. This is better than letting the power struggles evolve into something that will eventually destroy the whole ministry. Paul and Barnabas seem to have become friends again (1 Cor 9:6; Col 4:10).

This pattern is evident in some Asian settings. For example, political leaders throw mud at each other, and hit each other with their shoes in the parliament (quite so literally in some Asian countries!); and the next day we see them become friends again and form an alliance. Unfortunately, some Asian Christian leaders are slow to reconcile and remain at loggerheads with each other almost for a lifetime.

LEADERSHIP IN THE NT CHURCH

Analyzing the NT church leadership, Robert Johnston divides NT leaders into three categories:[20] the "Charismatic" leaders are those who "received a direct divine call." The best examples for this category are the twelve apostles who were chosen by Christ himself. The "Familial" leaders are the "blood relatives" of Jesus. James and Jude, the brothers of Jesus were both leaders in

---

20. Robert M. Johnston, "Leadership in the Early Church During Its First Hundred Years." *Journal of the Adventist Theological Society* 17, no. 1 (2006): 2.

the church, and when Peter fled the persecution in Jerusalem, James took over the leadership in the Jerusalem church. Notice the "I" in Acts 15:19, "*I* have reached a decision" (NRSV, emphasis mine) which probably means that James chaired the Jerusalem Council. The third category is the "Appointive" leaders who were "elected" by the church. The deacons appointed by the church in Acts 6 are good examples of appointed leaders. In the section below we will see examples of each of these categories.

The Twelve Apostles

NT writers use the term "Twelve" to single out the twelve apostles chosen by Jesus (Acts 6:2). The "Twelve" enjoyed special rights in the NT church. In 1 Corinthians 15:5, Paul picks out Cephas and the Twelve. During the inception of the church, they played an important leadership role – they preached the gospel and helped to form the church (Acts 2:42–43). They were also witnesses to the most important event in their lifetime (and in the history of the world) – the resurrection of Jesus (4:33).[21]

One of the important things the twelve apostles did to help the church grow was to appoint successors. The early church fathers saw themselves as successors to the apostles and saw the importance of the resurrection of Jesus Christ, which was witnessed by the apostles:

> The apostles have preached the Gospel to us from the Lord Jesus Christ; Jesus Christ [has done so] from God. Christ therefore was sent forth by God and the apostles by Christ. Both these appointments, then, were made in an orderly way, according to the will of God. Having therefore received their orders, and being fully assured by the resurrection of our Lord Jesus Christ, and established in the word of God, with full assurance of the Holy Ghost, they went forth proclaiming that the kingdom of God was at hand. (1 Clement 42:1–3)[22]

---

21. This was considered a core characteristic of an apostle, so much so that when there was a need to select a new apostle, this was made a criterion (Acts 1:22). Peter also sees the hand of God in making them as witnesses to Jesus's resurrection (Ajith Fernando, *Acts*, NIVAC [Grand Rapids: Zondervan, 1998], 76). Paul would also assert his authority as an apostle because he has seen the resurrected Christ (1 Cor 9:1). For a discussion of apostolic authority especially Paul's authority as an apostle see John Howard Schütz, *Paul and the Anatomy of Apostolic Authority*, NTL (Cambridge: WJKP, 1975).
22. Clement of Rome, "The First Epistle of Clement to the Corinthians," in *The Apostolic Fathers with Justin Martyr and Irenaeus*, The Ante-Nicene Fathers 1, ed. Alexander Roberts, James Donaldson, and A. Cleveland Coxe (Buffalo: Christian Literature Company, 1885), 16.

This is one of the greatest lessons Asian Church leaders need to learn from the apostles. Instead of looking at the junior leaders as a threat, the church must develop them as successors. The only way for current leaders to move forward in their careers is to help build others who can replace them in their current roles.

The Seven "Deacons"

Deacons, as they came to be called later, were people who were given administrative tasks other than preaching and teaching. Acts 6 records the first conflict in the church between two cultures and serves as a model to solve power struggles in the modern-day church. The Hellenistic Jews complained against the Hebraic Jews because their widows were neglected. The church got together and appointed seven men to deal with this issue. This is the first recorded account of the "division of labor" in the church – while the apostles were tasked with prayer and teaching, the "Seven" were to take care of the food distribution. We must also remember that the men were chosen based on criteria – they must be "men of good repute, full of the Spirit and of wisdom." As I mentioned earlier, the modern-day church must use the criteria given in the NT to select its leaders. It must also be noted that they chose leaders from the neglected/minority community.[23] We can apply this to the church in Asia. When trying to solve the problems of neglected communities (like the scheduled caste communities in India), the church must involve representatives from that community in decision-making.

Elders

There were elders (*presbuteros*) in the early NT church; some were appointed by Paul and Barnabas (Acts 14:23), others emerged in the Jerusalem church itself (15:4, 6, 22–23; 16:4; 21:18). Paul not only appointed elders in the churches he founded, but also instructed Titus to do the same (Tit 1:5). The elders are not simply the old people in the church, but those who held a "recognized position," which is why Paul instructed Timothy to use a predefined criteria to choose them (1 Tim 3:1–7; 5:22–25; Tit 1:5–9).[24] It is noteworthy that while the reference in Acts (14:23) is to appoint elders in every church, Paul instructed Titus to appoint elders in every town. Though this may point

---

23. Darrell L. Bock, *Acts*, BECNT, EPub ed. (Grand Rapids: Baker Academic, 2007), 341.
24. Matthew D. McDill, "The Authority of Church Elders in the New Testament" (PhD diss., Southeastern Baptist Theological Seminary, 2009), 178.

in that direction, we cannot be certain whether the role of the elder evolved from looking after a single church to looking after multiple churches in a city during the period of the apostles.

The elders are frequently mentioned alongside the apostles in Acts. Since the role of the twelve apostles was unique and was not meant to continue, the NT church created other structures. It is noteworthy that these appointed elders were present in the Jerusalem Council and other meetings along with the apostles. While James replaced Peter, the elders replaced the apostles. This is confirmed by Ignatius (discussed below) who instructs the Magnesians to set "presbyters in the place of the assembly of the apostles" (Ignatius, *to the Magnesians* 6:1).

Bishops

The NT refers to bishops (*episkopos*) in Acts 20:28; Philippians 1:1; 1 Timothy 3:1–2; and Titus 1:7. However, whether they are the same as elders or whether they are a group of their own is debated. It was during the later periods that they became bishops of a certain region overseeing many churches. The role of this office seems to have evolved.

Clement of Rome, an early church father, claims that apostles appointed the bishops themselves (1 Clement 44:1). By the time of Ignatius of Antioch (early second century AD), the terms bishops, elders and deacons were well defined and differentiated; a single bishop was named as the head of the church of an area:[25]

> Since therefore I have, in the persons before mentioned, beheld the whole multitude of you in faith and love, I exhort you to study to do all things with a divine harmony, while your bishop presides in the place of God, and your presbyters in the place of the assembly of the apostles, along with your deacons, who are most dear to me, and are entrusted with the ministry of Jesus Christ, who was with the Father before the beginning of time, and in the end was revealed (Ignatius, *to the Magnesians* 6:1–2)

So, there was one bishop supported by many elders and deacons – we find this structure in the churches in Asia Minor.[26] Ignatius also makes the bishop

---

25. G. W. Bromiley, "Bishop, Anglican View," *ISBE*, 1:518.
26. William R. Schoedel, "Ignatius, Epistles of," *ABD* 3:386.

the sole authority for the activities of the church. Without the permission of the bishop, a person cannot even partake in the Eucharist:[27]

> See that ye all follow the bishop, even as Jesus Christ does the Father, and the presbytery as ye would the apostles; and reverence the deacons, as being the institution of God. Let no man do anything connected with the Church without the bishop. Let that be deemed a proper Eucharist, which is [administered] either by the bishop, or by one to whom he has entrusted it . . . It is not lawful without the bishop either to baptize or to celebrate a love-feast. (Ignatius, *to the Smyrnaens* 8:1–2)

Though we see this structure in Ignatius, it was during the later centuries that this developed into a universal structure accepted by all the churches.[28]

In the above section, we saw how the twelve apostles played an important role in the NT church. As part of their "succession planning," they created leadership roles such as elders and bishops, that could outlast them. In the next section, we will propose a model of leadership that is based on the Bible.

BIBLICAL MODEL OF LEADERSHIP

There are different styles of leadership practiced within and outside the church: transformational, transactional, servant, autocratic, democratic, laissez-faire, bureaucratic, charismatic, pacesetting, ethical, affiliative, and coaching. There is a flood of literature on these leadership styles and my intention here is not to add more to it. In the section below I take aspects from the Bible and relate them to these standard styles where relevant.

Leadership Redefined

That there were power struggles among the apostles is very clear from the dubious requests they make of Jesus: they asked Jesus who would be the greatest in the kingdom (Matt 18:1) and they wanted to be granted the right to sit at the right hand of Jesus (20:20–28; Mark 10:35–40), a position of power. This latter request springs from Jesus's promise to give them "seats of authority."[29] No doubt they were upset when Jesus told them that he must die on the cross

---

27. William R. Schoedel, *Ignatius of Antioch: A Commentary on the Letters of Ignatius of Antioch*, ed. Helmut Koester, Hermeneia (Philadelphia: Fortress Press, 1985), 244.

28. Schoedel, "Ignatius, Epistles of," 386.

29. Samson L. Uytanlet and Kiem-Kiok Kwa, *Matthew: A Pastoral and Contextual Commentary* (Carlisle: Langham Global Library, 2017), 208.

as the Messiah – as it upset all their dreams of sitting next to him in his kingdom. In his reply to them in Matthew 20:22–28, Jesus essentially redefined glory and leadership. The first thing he mentions is about his death – the cup and the baptism are metaphors for the suffering and death that he was about to go through (20:28).[30] The path to glory is filled with suffering and leads to death (John 13:31–32).[31] It is through suffering and the cross that Jesus attained glory. It will be the same for his disciples.

Jesus also redefines greatness. The one who must be the leader must be the servant of others (Matt 20:26). Greatness lies not in "lording" over others but in serving them. Jesus cites himself as the supreme example, who came to serve and give his life for many (20:28).[32] When Jesus tells them to be servants, he is not talking about being a servant to all. He is talking about being servants to one another, the fellow apostles. This must have been quite challenging for them given that there was competition among them for positions of power.[33] Servant leaders serve their peers and subordinates to break the spirit of competition.

Humility Defined

While Jesus's foot-washing incident is given enough prominence in Christian literature, the background to the incident is often neglected when discussing leadership principles. It was when Jesus *knew* that he had been given everything by the Father that he chose to wash the feet of his disciples (John 13:3–5). When he realized that his eternal father had given him everything, he chose to wash his disciple's feet. This is completely different from how Nebuchadnezzar reacted when he realized that he had acquired his vast kingdom (Dan 4:28–30): "Is not this great Babylon, which *I have built by my mighty power* as a royal residence and for the glory of my majesty" (4:30 ESV, emphasis mine). Jesus perceived glory as being given by God, whereas Nebuchadnezzar perceived glory as something achieved by human power.

Leaders must imitate Jesus who is the perfect example of a servant leader. The education, experience, and skills of the leader must help him to be humble

---

30. Robert H. Stein, *Mark*, BECNT, EPub ed. (Grand Rapids: Baker Academic, 2008), 485.
31. Uytanlet and Kwa, *Matthew*, 208.
32. Jesus has been often cited as the role model for servant leadership even in secular literature. Corné J. Bekker, "A Modest History of the Concept of Service as Leadership in Four Religious Traditions," in *Servant Leadership: Developments in Theory and Research*, ed. Dirk van Dierendonck and Kathleen Patterson (New York: Palgrave Macmillan, 2010), 64.
33. David W. Bennett, *Metaphors of Ministry: Biblical Images for Leaders and Followers* (Eugene: Wipf & Stock, 2004), 28.

and serve others. Humility is probably the single most important characteristic of leadership. If leaders look at themselves as servants and not as privileged leaders, then the church would certainly be hugely different today!

Strength Redefined

While Jesus emphasized and exemplified servant leadership, he still was a strong leader. People often confuse servant leadership with being a doormat and letting others have their way in everything. S. M. Moon has documented this mindset among Korean church leaders who perceived biblical leadership as weak.[34]

If we apply the well-known way of classifying people as submissive, assertive, and aggressive, Jesus certainly does not appear as a submissive person. Most of his actions are assertive and some are even on the border of being aggressive. Chasing the money changers from the temple would most certainly not count as an example of submissiveness. It was during the final trial and crucifixion that we see him as a "sheep that before its shearers is silent" (Isa 53:7; cf. Acts 8:32 ESV). But even then, when one of the officers of the chief priests struck him, he did not remain silent but challenged him, "If what I said is wrong, bear witness about the wrong; but if what I said is right, why do you strike me?" (John 18:23 ESV). Jesus even challenged the Roman governor Pilate, "You would have no power over me unless it had been given you from above; therefore, the one who handed me over to you is guilty of a greater sin" (19:11 ESV). As C. S. Lewis said, Jesus is "not a tame lion." We need leaders who are humble yet are not afraid to use power and authority for the betterment of the church. As someone said, Christianity must be hard like the nail that pierces the board and be as soft as the board that is pierced – both at the same time!

Leading with Mixed Motives

Leadership often gives us opportunities to make a decision first and then look for reasons. Leaders often work with mixed motives or even wrap their bad intentions with seemingly good actions. That is why the New Testament warns in several places about motives (1 Cor 4:5; Jas 4:3). The story of Samson has a lot to say about intentions. Samson stands as a unique judge in the Book of Judges. All the other judges fought for their people, to deliver them from the

---

34. S. M. Moon, "A Study of Servant Leadership in Korea" (Masters Thesis, Fuller Theological Seminary, 1999).

oppressors. But Samson fought only for himself. All his battles had personal vendetta as their motive: he killed the Palestinians because they had killed his wife, and finally, when he killed three thousand people at the temple of Dagon, it was to revenge his eyes. Today some Christian leaders are like Samson in that they avoid solving problems until they are personally hurt. For example, some pastors will avoid confronting a person who is causing great damage to the community life of the church until the day that person steps on the toes of the pastor. Church leaders must be aware of this Samson mentality and must lay aside personal feelings when making leadership decisions.

Teamwork Redefined

Both Jesus and NT leaders like Paul trained others to take up the baton. They depended on others to get the job done.[35] As Boyer remarks, "leadership development successfully transpires through the prayerful selection, constant association, and comprehensive teaching toward developing leaders."[36] Elements of transformational leadership can be seen in Jesus – he transformed several uneducated people into those who would turn the world upside down. He used transactional methods – he promised rewards for obedience and punishment for disobedience. His leadership also had elements of participative leadership, which avoids the extremes of autocratic and *laissez-faire* leadership. *Laissez-faire* leadership style is where the team members make their own decisions and, the autocratic leadership style is where the leaders make all the decisions. By training the disciples and sending them on a mission on their own, Jesus is making a balance between these two extremes. Jesus tells them what to do, yet at the same time, he gives them the freedom to make their own decisions on the mission trip.

There was no "one-man show" in the NT church or with Jesus. Very sadly, this is not the reality in many Asian churches. Many leaders try to do everything themselves and do not invest in second-level leaders. Some of them get carried away with day-to-day work, so the long-term need to create leaders gets neglected. Some others intentionally avoid creating leaders because they think the younger leaders will become a threat to them. Moses was a wonderful

---

35. Two classic books on the subject are A. B. Bruce, *Training of the Twelve: How Jesus Christ Found and Taught the 12 Apostles* (Edmonton: Adansonia Press, 2018); Robert E. Coleman, *Master Plan of Discipleship* (New Jersey: Fleming H. Revell, 2020).
36. Stuart W. Boyer, *Biblical Leadership Development: Principles for Developing Organizational Leaders at Every Level*, Christian Faith Perspectives in Leadership and Business (Cham: Springer Intl; Imprint: Palgrave Macmillan, 2019), 148.

leader who developed a second-level leader – Joshua. So, when Moses died Joshua led the Israelites into the promised land. However, when Joshua died, there was no one to lead them as he had not developed a successor.

The creation of deacons in the NT church shows that different roles can be delegated to different people. As ministries grow it will be a best practice to have different people play different roles. For example, during the initial stages of the ministry, there may not be enough funds to recruit a person to handle finances, but as the church grows it may be wise to have a separate person handle finances.

Working with a team invariably involves trust. G. G. Brenkert shares three aspects/views of trust: attitudinal, predictability, and voluntarist.[37] In the attitudinal view, trust is seen as the mutual belief that neither party will take advantage of the other's weaknesses. According to the predictable view, trust is the degree to which one's behavior meets the accepted usual behavior. According to the voluntarist view, trust is to deliberately put yourself in a vulnerable situation knowing that nothing bad will happen as a result.[38]

If we apply these to Jesus, he trusted his disciples but never allowed them to take advantage of him. He also never allowed anyone to keep him from doing the will of God or fulfill the purpose for which he was sent to earth. His disciples often let him down – they were not with him during the darkest hours of his life, and one of his closest associates betrayed him to his enemies. But Jesus still trusted these people to build God's kingdom on earth.

Spirit-Led Leadership

The Spirit has been the focus of the church in the last couple of centuries. The focus is on signs and wonders rather than teaching. However, as A. W. Tozer once said, the question should not be whether we have the Holy Spirit, but whether the Holy Spirit has control over us. One of the functions of the Holy Spirit is to judge the world (John 16:8). As Vishal Mangalwadi comments:

> it takes enormous power and discernment to judge the powers and principalities which are committed to corruption and cruelty. But that is what Peter, empowered by the Holy Spirit, was doing

---

37. G. G. Brenkert, "Trust, Morality and International Business," *Business Ethics Quarterly* 8, no. 2 (1998): 295.
38. Brenkert, "Trust," 295.

in his sermon on the day of Pentecost. He charged his audience
with the sin of cruel murder. (Acts 2:23)[39]

Peter shows us that being empowered by the Holy Spirit should lead us to
confront sin and injustice more boldly.

There is one point that is less emphasized in the deacon selection story.
The apostles wanted to devote themselves "to prayer and to serving the word"
(6:4 NRSV). Prayer and preaching are combined here, a rare combination
in today's world that should be encouraged in Christian leaders. Prayerful
preaching will not only help the congregation, but it will also help the preacher
to be led by the spirit.

Leadership without Compromises

Today, church leaders make more compromises than political leaders. The
church compromises with sin. In the prophetic words of Vishal Mangalwadi,
"this loss of perspective . . . which preaches salvation without proclaiming
repentance and justice, reduces the church to a rudderless boat floating at
the mercy of social currents some of which are ghastly in their cruelty and
injustice."[40] As he rightly points out, "when we cease to be the voice of justice
we also become ineffective as channels of salvation."[41] The church should not
think that "speaking the truth in love" is synonymous with lying. As Vishal
Mangalwadi says, "they consider compromise to be wisdom."[42] Christian leaders need to have high standards of moral behavior, not only for their safety
but also to earn the respect of their followers.

Evangelism and Social Work

While the ecumenical churches focus more on social work, the evangelical
churches focus on evangelism. What we need is the right balance between
the two. Some churches in Asia seem to favor social work because it is easy to
raise funds for that cause. A hungry body gets more dollars than an unsaved
soul! If the church is involved in social work, we must make sure that it does
not do it at the cost of spiritual work – which is the church's primary calling.

---

39. Mangalwadi, *Truth and Social Reform*, 90.
40. Mangalwadi, *Truth and Social Reform*, 93.
41. Mangalwadi, *Truth and Social Reform*, 94.
42. Mangalwadi, *Truth and Social Reform*, 93.

God-Fearing Leadership

Wayne Oates demonstrates that the pastor has "symbolic power." The pastor or the leader represents God, reminds people of Jesus Christ, and is led by the Holy Spirit.[43] As such, they should live worthy of the triune God. When the NT church wanted to appoint people for leadership, they looked for people with certain characteristics. This is what Philip Huan calls, "Guarding the 'Gate' of Leadership."[44] He warns, "Guard the 'gate of leadership' responsibly."[45]

It has been observed that leaders in India use fear to attain leadership positions. When followers fear their leaders, they will not oppose them.[46] However, Paul threatens the Corinthian church by invoking the fear of the divine (1 Cor 10:8–10, 22–23; 11:31; 16:22). He even asks "Shall we provoke the Lord to jealousy? Are we stronger than he?" Since the leaders represent God to people, they must use fear of God as a tool to bring about obedience to him. In this respect Paul uses transactional leadership with the Corinthians, trying to "correct them by penalty."[47]

CONCLUSION

Power and authority are God-given tools to achieve the vision he has given us. The goal is the expansion of God's kingdom through mission work and exemplary living. Any activity that hampers that purpose must be avoided. The church must use power for his glory and the expansion of his kingdom. Power must not be (mis)used to cover up the mistakes of the leaders. We must also not take the position where we stop using all power and authority. We, as his disciples must be willing to use power and authority for the greater good of the kingdom and others.

Perhaps the story of Daniel Wilson gives us an example of the proper use of power based on the New Testament principles. Wilson was the bishop of Calcutta from 1832 to 1858, and during his time dealt strongly with the

---

43. Wayne E. Oates, *The Christian Pastor*, 3rd ed., rev. (Philadelphia: Westminster Press, 1982), 65–95.

44. Philip Huan, *Enduring Church Growth: Issues on Discipleship, Leadership, and Followership* (Singapore: Genesis, 2011), 65–73.

45. Huan, *Enduring Church Growth*, 73.

46. Bjorn Alm, "Creating Followers, Gaining Patrons: Leadership Strategies in a Tamil Nadu Village," in *Power and Influence in India: Bosses, Lords and Captains*, ed. Pamela Price and Arild Engelsen Ruud (Routledge India, 2012), 1–19.

47. Bikrant Kesari and Bhupendra Kumar Verma, "Does the Leadership Style Impacts on Employee Outcomes? A Study of Indian Steel Industry," *Global Business Review* 19, no. 6 (2018): 1605.

caste issues within the Anglican church in South India. He believed that caste was not only a "scandal to religion" but was also a "bridge" by which people often returned to their previous religions. In his famous letter, Bishop Wilson asserts that:

> caste must be abandoned decidedly, immediately, finally; and those who profess to belong to Christ must give this proof of their having put off . . . the old . . . and having really put on the new man in Jesus Christ. The gospel recognizes no distinctions such as those of caste imposed by heathen usage . . . condemning those in the lower ranks to perpetual abasement, placing an immovable barrier against all general advance and improvement in society, cutting asunder the bonds of human fellowship on the one hand and preventing those of Christian love on the other.[48]

He would also urge the churches to make everyone sit together and to come to the "Lord's table without any distinction." In some districts, Wilson took the lower caste people by their hands and made them sit next to the higher caste people. This started a "storm of protest" and caused many higher caste people to leave the church in large numbers in the 1840s and 1850s. However, Wilson stood his ground, and eventually, the church started to grow in the 1860s and 1870s as mass conversions started to happen from the lower castes. Wilson used power and his position to eradicate a social evil that was prevalent in his church. In a way consistent with what we see in the New Testament, Wilson set an example of using power for the betterment of the church.

BIBLIOGRAPHY

Alm, Bjorn. "Creating Followers, Gaining Patrons: Leadership Strategies in a Tamil Nadu Village." In *Power and Influence in India: Bosses, Lords and Captains*, edited by Pamela Price and Arild Engelsen Ruud, 1–19. Routledge India, 2012.

Bekker, Corné J. "A Modest History of the Concept of Service as Leadership in Four Religious Traditions." In *Servant Leadership: Developments in Theory and Research*. Edited by Dirk van Dierendonck and Kathleen Patterson, 55–66. New York: Palgrave Macmillan, 2010.

Bennett, David W. *Metaphors of Ministry: Biblical Images for Leaders and Followers*. Eugene: Wipf & Stock Publishers, 2004.

---

48. Cited in Charles Hoole, "Bishop Wilson and the Origins of Dalit Liberation," *Transformation* 21 (2004): 43.

Bock, Darrell L. *Acts*. BECNT, EPub ed. Grand Rapids: Baker Academic, 2007.

Boyer, Stuart W. *Biblical Leadership Development: Principles for Developing Organizational Leaders at Every Level*. Christian Faith Perspectives in Leadership and Business. Cham: Springer Intl; Imprint: Palgrave Macmillan, 2019.

Brass, Paul R. "Leadership Power and Honor in a Corrupt System." In *Power and Influence in India: Bosses, Lords and Captains*, edited by Pamela Price and Arild Engelsen Ruud, 169–92. New Delhi: Routledge India, 2012.

Brenkert, G. G. "Trust, Morality and International Business." *Business Ethics Quarterly* 8, no. 2 (1998): 293–317.

Bromiley, G. W. "Bishop, Anglican View." *ISBE* 1:516–18.

Bruce, A. B. *Training of the Twelve: How Jesus Christ Found and Taught the 12 Apostles*. Edmonton: Adansonia Press, 2018.

Carroll, John T. *Luke: A Commentary*. NTL. Louisville: WJKP, 2012.

Clement of Rome. "The First Epistle of Clement to the Corinthians." In *The Apostolic Fathers with Justin Martyr and Irenaeus*. The Ante-Nicene Fathers 1, edited by Alexander Roberts, James Donaldson, and A. Cleveland Coxe, 5–21. Buffalo: Christian Literature Company, 1885.

Coleman, Robert E. *Master Plan of Discipleship*. New Jersey: Fleming H. Revell, 2020.

Daniel, Monodeep. "Models of Leadership in the Indian Church: An Evaluation" 13, no. 1 (2007): 67–90.

Dunn, James D. G. *The Theology of Paul the Apostle*. Grand Rapids: Eerdmans, 2008.

———. *Unity and Diversity in the New Testament: An Inquiry into the Character of Earliest Christianity*. 3rd ed. London: SCM Press, 2006.

Fairholm, Gilbert W. *Organizational Power Politics: Tactics in Organizational Leadership*. 2nd ed. Santa Barbara: Praeger/ABC-CLIO, 2009.

Fernando, Ajith. *Acts*. NIVAC. Grand Rapids: Zondervan, 1998.

Green, Joel B. *The Gospel of Luke*. NICNT. Grand Rapids: Eerdmans, 1997.

———. *The Gospel of Luke*. NICNT, Epub ed. Grand Rapids: Eerdmans, 1997.

Guthrie, Donald. *New Testament Theology*. Leicester, England; Downers Grove: InterVarsity Press, 1981.

Hengel, Martin. *The Cross of the Son of God*. London: SCM Press, 1986.

Hoole, Charles. "Bishop Wilson and the Origins of Dalit Liberation." *Transformation* 21, no. 1 (2004): 41–45.

Huan, Philip. *Enduring Church Growth: Issues on Discipleship, Leadership, and Followership*. Singapore: Genesis, 2011.

Ignatius of Antioch. "The Epistle of Ignatius to the Magnesians." In *The Apostolic Fathers with Justin Martyr and Irenaeus*. The Ante-Nicene Fathers 1, edited by

Alexander Roberts, James Donaldson, and A. Cleveland Coxe, 59–65. Buffalo: Christian Literature Company, 1885.

———. "The Epistle of Ignatius to the Smyrnæans." In *The Apostolic Fathers with Justin Martyr and Irenaeus*, The Ante-Nicene Fathers 1, edited by Alexander Roberts, James Donaldson, and A. Cleveland Coxe, 89–92. Buffalo: Christian Literature Company, 1885.

Johnston, Robert M. "Leadership in the Early Church During Its First Hundred Years." *Journal of the Adventist Theological Society* 17, no. 1 (2006): 2–17.

Josephus. *The Works of Josephus: Complete and Unabridged*. Translated by William Whiston. Peabody: Hendrickson, 1987.

Kesari, Bikrant, and Bhupendra Kumar Verma. "Does the Leadership Style Impacts on Employee Outcomes? A Study of Indian Steel Industry." *Global Business Review* 19, no. 6 (2018): 1602–21.

MacDonald, Gordon. *Ordering Your Private World*. Expanded ed. Nashville: Oliver-Nelson, 1985.

Mangalwadi, Vishal. *Truth and Social Reform*. London: Hodder & Stoughton, 1989.

McDill, Matthew D. "The Authority of Church Elders in the New Testament." Southeastern Baptist Theological Seminary, 2009.

McKnight, Scot. *The Jesus Creed: Loving God, Loving Others*. Brewster, Massachusetts: Paraclete Press, 2014.

Moon, S. M. "A Study of Servant Leadership in Korea." Masters Thesis. Fuller Theological Seminary, 1999.

Newman, Hillel. *Proximity to Power and Jewish Sectarian Groups of the Ancient Period*. Edited by Ruth Ludlam. Brill Reference Library of Judaism 25. Leiden: Brill, 2006.

Oates, Wayne E. *The Christian Pastor*. 3rd ed. Philadelphia: Westminster Press, 1982.

Schoedel, William R. "Ignatius, Epistles of." *ABD* 3:384–87.

———. *Ignatius of Antioch: A Commentary on the Letters of Ignatius of Antioch*. Edited by Helmut Koester. Hermeneia. Philadelphia: Fortress Press, 1985.

Schütz, John Howard. *Paul and the Anatomy of Apostolic Authority*. NTL. Cambridge: WJKP, 1975.

Stein, Robert H. *Mark*. BECNT, EPub ed. Grand Rapids: Baker Academic, 2008.

Thomas, Scott. *The Articles of the Synod of Dort*. Philadelphia: Presbyterian Board of Publication, 1856.

Uytanlet, Samson L., and Kiem-Kiok Kwa. *Matthew: A Pastoral and Contextual Commentary*. Carlisle: Langham Global Library, 2017.

Weber, Max. *Max Weber: The Theory of Social and Economic Organization*. Translated by A. M. Henderson and Talcott Parsons. Mansfield Centre, CT: Martino Publishing, 2012.

CHAPTER 13

PRACTICING HOSPITALITY

Ancient Cultural Values and the Contemporary Asian Christians

Andrew B. Spurgeon

Every society values hospitality, but each society expresses it differently.[1] This essay explains the multifaceted expressions of hospitality in the New Testament.

Andrei Rublev, a fifteenth-century Russian, painted *The Trinity*.[2] It is a depiction of Abraham and Sarah welcoming three angels under an oak tree in Mamre (Gen 18:1–8). Rublev equates those angels with the Father, Son, and the Holy Spirit. They are sitting at a table with equal space in between them and with similarly colored outfits. On the table is a cup of wine. Behind them is the oak tree. The Father is on the left, the Son is in the middle, and the Holy Spirit is on the right. The Son tilts his head towards the Father, and the Holy Spirit tilts his head towards the Son, implying from whom they proceed. And their gestures

---

1. For hospitality among Tuareg people, Semites, Mediterranean people, Greek, and Romans, see Luis Carlos Marrero Chasbar, "God Crosses Borders, Too: A Sociotheological Perspective on Migration," *Journal of Latin American Theology* 14, no. 1 (2019): 57–70.
2. *The Image* painting by Andrei Rublev, Public Domain, https://commons.wikimedia.org/w/index.php?curid=54421.

communicate intricate details of early Christian theology and the doctrine of hospitality.[3]

Abraham and Sarah's hospitality is the standard for Judeo-Christian hospitality. Cohen calls their hospitality "as a hallmark value of Jewish tradition, as well as . . . [their] love and concern for human beings."[4] Byanungu calls Abraham the "Father of hospitality."[5] The writer of Hebrews refers to this scene and requests that his audience practice hospitality whereby which they could entertain angels (Heb 13:1–2).

Foundational to the Judeo-Christian faith is the conviction that whoever extends hospitality to strangers is offering it to God. The Lord Jesus explains this in a parable.

> Once there lived a king in a middle eastern country. On the day of his coronation, he sat on his throne addressing the people of diverse nations before him. He divided them into those who sided with him and those who opposed him, just as a shepherd separates the sheep from the goats. To those who sided with him, he said, "Come into the kingdom I am preparing for you. While I was hungry, you fed me. While I was thirsty, you gave me a drink. And, while I was a stranger, you took me into your home. You clothed me, healed my wounds, and visited me in my imprisonment." They wondered how and when they fed and clothed the king. He answered, "Truly, I say to you, whatever good you did for one of these little ones, you did that for me." (Matt 25:31–40, paraphrased)[6]

Thus, hospitality is offering a safe space for the needy (including a stranger, homeless, and refugees), accepting them for who they are, and extending God's provisions and protections to them. The Greek word for hospitality, *xenodecheō*, is a combination of the noun "stranger" (*xenos*) and the verb "welcoming"

---

3. For a detailed explanation, see Beringia M. Zen, "Shame to Hospitality: A Post-Holocaust Biblical Hermeneutics" (PhD diss., Graduate Theological Union, Berkeley, 2015), 216–24; Amos Yong, *Renewing Christian Theology: Systematics for a Global Christianity* (Waco: Baylor University Press, 2014), 13–14.

4. Jeffrey M. Cohen, "Abraham's Hospitality," *JBQ* 34, no. 3 (2006): 168.

5. Gosbert Byanungu, "Retrieving Abraham's Human Experience of *El-'Eljon*: Interfaith Implications of Faith in the God of Creation," *ABQ* 26, no. 3 (2007): 281.

6. All translations are mine. For this parable referring to hospitality, see Waldemar Janzen, "Biblical Theology of Hospitality," *Vision* (Winnipeg, Man.) 3, no. 1 (2002): 12.

(*decheō*) – "welcoming a stranger" (1 Tim 5:10).[7] Based on this, Barton defines hospitality as "a social process by means of which the status of someone who is an outsider is changed from *stranger* to *guest* (italics mine)."[8] Nouwen expands: "The paradox of hospitality is that it wants to create emptiness, not a fearful emptiness, but a friendly emptiness where strangers can enter and discover themselves as created free; free to sing their own songs, speak their own languages, and dance their own dances; free also to leave and follow their own vocations. Hospitality is not a subtle invitation to adopt the lifestyle of the host, but the gift of a chance for the guest to find his own."[9] In this, biblical hospitality differs from the contemporary practice of entertaining relatives and friends alone; it extends welcome to perfect strangers.[10] The men on the Emmaus road exemplified biblical hospitality when they invited the unknown traveler saying, "Stay with us since it is the evening" (Luke 24:29). Likewise, Lydia was hospitable when she invited itinerant preachers, whom she never knew, saying, "Come into my house and stay" (Acts 16:15).

HOSPITALITY IN THE OLD TESTAMENT

Hospitality is more than inviting someone into one's house. It is acceptance of others with the intent of blessing them. Such gracious hospitality fills the Old Testament. When the Creator God created a perfect world, visited his image-bearers in the coolness of the evening, and walked with them, it was his hospitality (Gen 3:8). He accepted them for who they were, a creation, regardless of their frailty. By his hospitality, he took Enoch, a human, to his eternal home (5:24). The Lord God called Abram from Ur and promised to prosper him with land and immeasurable descendants because of his hospitality (12:1–4). His hospitality led him to make covenants and bless Isaac, Jacob, and their children. God's hospitality extended even to non-covenantal people like Hagar (16:7–14), Tamar (38), Ruth, Naaman (2 Kgs 5), and the Ninevites (Jonah). On every page in the Old Testament, we see God extending his hospitality to everyone, without prejudice or partiality. Even the law demanded that his people offer gracious hospitality because of his nature:

---

7. Similarly, *philoxenia* and *philoxenos* refer to showing love, *philo*, to strangers, *xenos* (Rom 12:13; 1 Tim 3:2; Tit 1:8; Heb 13:2; 1 Pet 4:9).
8. Stephen C. Barton, "Hospitality," in *DLNT*, 501.
9. Henri J. M. Nouwen, *Reaching Out: The Three Movements of the Spiritual Life* (New York: Image Books, 1986), 68–69.
10. Andrew E. Arterbury, "Breaking the Betrothal Bonds: Hospitality in John 4," *CBQ* 72, no. 1 (2010), 66, and William R. O' Neill, "'No Longer Strangers' (Ephesians 2:19): The Ethics of Migration," *WW* 29, no. 3 (2009): 229.

"YHWH God defends the orphans and widows; *he loves those strangers/refugees who are staying in your midst.* So, you give them food and clothing" (Deut 10:18). The Lord God welcomed all people into an everlasting relationship with him and extended his hospitality to those deserving and undeserving, wicked and good, and poor and rich. God's hospitality has no limit so that a prophet can promise that God will deliver the people from their oppression and feed them food and wine (Amos 9:13–15). God's hospitable heart is the basis for Christian hospitality. As Amos Yong writes, "Christian hospitality is grounded in the hospitable God who through the Incarnation has received creation to himself and through Pentecost has given himself to creation."[11]

HOSPITALITY IN THE NEW TESTAMENT

The New Testament mirrors such open-handed hospitality of God. It begins with Jesus's parents and continues through his childhood and early ministry. Immediately after an assuring dream, the righteous Joseph welcomed his unmarried but pregnant wife, Mary (Matt 1:18–25).[12] Egypt offered refuge and protected the baby Jesus while a ruling king in Judea threatened to kill him (2:13–15). Soon after forty days of starvation and temptation, God sent his angels to serve and feed Jesus, extending his hospitality (4:11). When Antipas beheaded John, Galilee Zebulun and Naphtali sheltered Jesus as expressions of their hospitality (4:12–14).

John the Baptizer exemplified God's hospitality by offering salvation to anyone who was willing to confess their sins and return to God (3:4–5). Similarly, the Lord Jesus extended his hospitality by welcoming Simon and Andrew (4:18–20), James and John (4:21–22), and Matthew (9:9) to be his disciples and friends. He welcomed people who would not be in the inner circle of a rabbi like lepers (8:1–4; 11:5), centurions (8:5–13), demoniacs (8:28–34; 9:32–33; 12:22; 17:14–20), paralytics (9:1–8; 11:4), the unclean (9:20–22), the blind (9:27–31; 20:29–34), the sick and afflicted (8:16–17; 9:35; 12:15; 14:14, 34–36; 21:14), sinners and tax collectors (11:19), and people with disabilities (12:9–14).

---

11. Amos Yong, "The Spirit of Hospitality: Pentecostal Perspectives toward a Performative Theology of Interreligious Encounter," *Missiology* 35, no. 1 (2007): 62.

12. I have drawn principles from the Gospel of Matthew, although these principles apply to the other Gospels. For hospitality in Mark, see Peter Spitaler, "Biblical Concern for the Marginalized: Mark's Stories about Welcoming the Little Ones (Mark 9:33–11:11)," *Ephemerides Theologicae Lovanienses* 87, no. 1 (2011): 89–126.

Jesus's hospitality extended to people from Syria, Galilee, Decapolis, and across the Jordan along with those in Jerusalem and Judea (4:23–25). He always felt a "deep moving compassion" (*splanchnizomai*) for those who were hurting (9:36; 14:14; 15:32; 18:27; 20:34).

Jesus lived a life of welcoming strangers, aliens, refugees, the sick, afflicted, and socially oppressed as his family, such that others called him names: a glutton, drunkard, and friend of tax collectors and sinners (11:19). Nothing more acutely illustrated Jesus's hospitality than the words: "Come to me, every one of you who is striving and burdened, and I will give you rest . . . I am gentle and humble, and your souls will find rest in me" (11:28–30).

When people were hungry, Jesus fed them (14:15–21; 15:29–39). He satisfied Peter's longing to walk on water (14:28–33). All these by his hospitality. When a Canaanite, an age-old enemy, was persistent in receiving healing for her daughter, the Lord offered her healing as a sign of acceptance (15:21–28). He shared intimate times with his disciples, such as inviting them to see his transfiguration (17:1–8). Children received blessings as a sign of his hospitality (19:13–15). As would a good Jew, he celebrated the festivals of the Unleavened Bread and Passover with his family of disciples (26:17–31).

Even as Jesus faced death, he extended hospitality. At Gethsemane, he invited his disciples to stay up and pray with him; he offered them a place to share in his sorrow (26:36–46). Even when Judas came to betray him, he offered forgiveness and called him a "friend" (26:50). When Peter cut the ear of a servant of the high priest, Jesus restored it, showing his gracious acceptance of even that slave (26:51–54). To the enemies who came to arrest him, he offered peace and surrendered himself (26:55). Even his death visualized his hospitality: "Jesus' arms stretched on the beam – extended to release our sin, to receive all in love, to invite us to new life – are the very image of God's unaccountably gracious hospitality to us."[13]

The Lord Jesus's teachings, too, reflected God's hospitality. His kingdom belonged to the poor and persecuted (5:3, 10). The meek inherited the earth, unlike the world's "cut-throat" philosophy of self-advancement (5:5).

Jesus's disciples were to extend his hospitality. They were taught to overcome anger against siblings and settle differences without seeking retribution (5:21–22, 25–26). They were to offer hospitality by loving their enemies and praying for those who persecuted them (5:43–48). They provided for the

---

13. Marjorie J. Thompson, *Soul Feast: An Invitation to the Christian Spiritual Life* (Louisville: WJKP, 1995), 124.

needs of the poor (6:2–4). They sought God's hospitality in providing them their daily bread, canceling their spiritual debts, and protecting them from the evil one (6:11–13; 6:25–34; 7:7–11). True hospitality was forgiving others as God forgave them (6:14–15). While traveling, the disciples were not to be fickle-minded and change residences; instead, they should find a noble person and stay with that host until they complete their tasks (10:11). When entering a host's home, they should greet them and offer them peace (10:12–13). If the people would not provide hospitality, they were to go to another place (10:23; 11:21–24).

All who welcomed the disciples not only welcomed the Lord Jesus who sent them but also the Father who sent Jesus. They will receive a just reward for their hospitality (10:40–42). The once-raised wall of separation between the Jews and Gentiles over the Sabbath and kosher food existed no longer: saving lives was more important than the Sabbath, and what came from a person's mouth mattered more than what went in (12:11–12; 15:10–11, 17–20). Disciples were to honor and accept the local and international governments by paying taxes (17:24–27; 22:15–21). When someone sinned, they were to confront that person privately – giving that person a place to save face (18:15–16). Forgiveness was to be unconditional and generous as they are extensions of God's hospitality (18:21–22). Whereas the world rejected eunuchs, the disciples were to welcome them because some have made themselves eunuchs for the kingdom of God (19:11–12). Those who showed hospitality to the poor by giving away their wealth and uplifted the poor entered the kingdom (19:16–24). God accepted the wealthy even when others did not (19:25–26). Greatness in God's rule began with serving others, the essence of hospitality (20:25–28). The Father's house was a house of prayer for all nations (21:12–13). Sinners, prostitutes, and tax-collectors would be accepted in God's family before the self-righteous (21:31–32). The kingdom belonged to anyone willing to accept the invitation and enter it, without any biases (22:1–14). The greatest command of loving God included loving and accepting one's neighbor as they loved and accepted themselves (22:34–40). True worshippers served others (23:1–12). Hospitality was proselytizing and helping the disciples grow in their love of God (23:15). Vigilant disciples entered as faithful bridesmaids into the banquet of the groom (25:1–13). Hospitality was an expression of one's love for God (25:31–46). Their great commission was to reach all nations and disciple them (28:16–20).

Seeing Jesus's hospitality, others showed hospitality. Peter's mother-in-law waited on Jesus (8:14–15). Matthew welcomed other tax-collectors and sinners into his home, just as the Lord welcomed him into his life and ministry (9:9–13). A synagogue leader welcomed Jesus into his home to heal his dying daughter (9:18–31). The disciples extended God's hospitality by healing people with diseases and sickness and freed them from the oppression of demons (10:1, 8). They generously admitted people in God's kingdom (16:19; 18:18). When the Lord needed a donkey to ride, an unknown family offered their donkey (21:1–3). The people laid their garments on the donkey for him to ride on (21:6–7). At Bethany, Simon the leper welcomed him to his home (26:6–13). A lady expressed hospitality by pouring an alabaster jar of expensive perfume on the Lord's head (26:7). Simon the Cyrene offered hospitality by carrying the cross of Jesus (27:32–33). And, Joseph of Arimathea gave his freshly hewn grave to bury Jesus (27:57–61).

The above examples are just the tip of the iceberg of the biblical depiction of hospitality. Other examples of hospitality include the shepherd's commitment to retrieve the lost sheep (Luke 15:4–7), the father's reception of the prodigal son and his brother (15:11–32), Martha's hospitality of feeding Jesus and his disciples (10:38–41), Jesus's acceptance of the prisoner on the cross into his paradise (23:43), the bride and groom's invitation of Jesus to their wedding (John 2:1–11), Jesus's reception of Nicodemus (3:1–15), the woman's acceptance of Jesus at the well (4:7–30),[14] the reception of Jesus by the Samaritans (4:39–42), John's acceptance to care for Jesus's mother (19:26–27), and Jesus preparing food for the disciples (21:12).

Biblical hospitality is welcoming someone completely foreign to us: a stranger from out of town, a non-resident of our city, state, or country, and someone who has no home or is expelled from their home because of political unrest and turmoil. It is also extending the same hospitality to those familiar to us, our family and friends. God's hospitality forms the basis for our hospitality: "Both testaments . . . present the God-human relationship metaphorically as a host-guest relationship and call on human beings to extend God's hosting role toward other human beings."[15] Hospitality is receiving others and giving them a safe space for them to be who they are. It is welcoming someone "unknown and vulnerable into our life-world, to create space for something foreign, to offer room, to accommodate, care for, and protect" them.[16]

---

14. Arterbury sees Jesus's discussion with the woman at the well as an "ancient custom of hospitality" ("Breaking the Betrothal Bonds," 65).
15. Janzen, "Biblical Theology of Hospitality," 4.
16. Tobias Brandner, "Hosts and Guests: Hospitality as an Emerging Paradigm in Mission," *International Review of Mission* 102, no. 1 (2013): 96.

HOSPITALITY IN THE NEW TESTAMENT CHURCHES

The NT churches understood the importance of hospitality and continued to offer it.[17] When the disciples gathered after the Lord's resurrection, they included the Lord's mother and his brothers – those who missed their son and brother (Acts 1:14). On the day of Pentecost, the Spirit of God came on Jews and God-fearing people alike, expressing God's hospitality (2:1–12). Those who accepted the gospel opened their homes for preaching, fellowship, communion, and prayer (2:42, 46–47; 5:42). They shared everything in common so that none had any needs (2:44; 4:32). They even sold their properties and possessions to help those in need expressing their hospitality (2:44–45; 4:34–36).

Their zeal for hospitality tore down racial tensions. When the Hellenistic widows were overlooked in the distribution of food, the apostles appointed deacons to serve them (6:1–6). Philip went to the Samaritans and offered healing and deliverance from demon oppressions (8:4–8). Peter, John, and Philip extended God's gift of the Holy Spirit to the Samaritans as an expression of hospitality (8:14–17). Philip went south and welcomed an Ethiopian eunuch, a social outcast, into God's covenant (8:26–40). Ananias hosted Saul who once persecuted the church (9:10–19). Christians in Damascus showed hospitality to Saul despite his past and protected him by helping him escape a threat to his life (9:19; 9:23–25). In Jerusalem, Barnabas welcomed Saul even when others were afraid of him (9:27). Peter broke the Jew-Gentile chasm by visiting Cornelius's family and staying with them and eating their non-kosher food (10:1–48). When he returned to the Jews and they questioned him about eating food with the Gentiles, he shared how God had extended his grace and hospitality even to the Gentiles (11:1–18). Upon the prophet Agabus's prophecy that a severe famine was coming in the Roman world, the disciples gathered funds to help the poor Christians in Judea, a sign of their generous hospitality (11:27–30). At the Jerusalem Council, the apostles welcomed the Gentiles into their fellowship without demanding that they undergo circumcision and keep the Jewish laws (15:1–35). A frightened but saved jailor opened his home for the apostles (16:33–34). Aquila and Priscilla extended their hospitality to Paul and Apollos (18:1–3, 26). They even sent Apollos to Achaia with the instruction to the churches there to welcome him (18:27).

---

17. This section deals with materials in the Book of Acts. Luke's respect for Theophilus to give a faithful account to him is also an expression of hospitality.

Following the Lord's example of welcoming the sick, healing them, and restoring them to their family and community, the early Christians did the same. They healed the lame (3:1–10; 14:8–9), the sick (5:15), those with impure spirits (5:16; 19:12), the paralyzed (9:32–35), and raised the dead (9:36–42; 20:7–12). Yong sees these acts of healing as expressions of God's hospitality and writes, "The charismatic gifts of healing and miraculous powers manifest in the early church remain significant for Christian mission since it is through such encounters with God that people are often initially moved to repentance and experience conversion."[18]

Following the examples of the apostles, others showed hospitality. These include Simon in Joppa (9:43), Jason in Thessalonica (17:7), Aquilla and Priscilla in Corinth (18:1–3), Titus Justus in Corinth (16:7), Lydia in Philippi (16:13–15),[19] Philip in Caesarea (21:8), Mnason in Jerusalem (21:16), people of Malta (28:1–2), Publius the chief official of Malta (28:7),[20] Philemon (Phlm 22), and Gaius of Corinth (Rom 16:23). In addition, several wealthy Christians opened their homes for congregations to meet: Mary (Acts 12:12), Aquila and Priscilla (Rom 16:5), Aristobulus (16:10), Narcissus (16:11), Hermas (16:14), Olympas (16:15), Archippus (Phlm 2), "an elect lady" (2 John), and Gaius (3 John).

Their hospitality extended in more ways than offering food, health, or hosting someone. Stephen offered forgiveness to those who stoned him as a sign of his hospitality (Acts 7:59–60). Macedonia welcomed Paul; as a result, people like Lydia, the jailor in Philippi, Philippians, Thessalonians, and the Corinthians heard the gospel (16:6–10). Leaders from Ephesus gathered around Paul, wept, prayed, embraced, and sent him off to minister in other places, another expression of hospitality (20:36–37). The women and children of Tyre accompanied him in such an expression of hospitality (21:3–5). A commander chose to protect the life of Paul by his hospitality (23:12–35). The centurion Julius allowed Paul to visit his friends in Sidon to receive provisions because of his hospitable heart (27:3). Soldiers, who had once planned to kill the prisoners, spared their lives because the centurion wanted to spare Paul's life (27:42–44). With so much expression of hospitality in the early church, the Book of Acts aptly ends saying, "Paul stayed two whole years in his rented

---

18. Yong, "The Spirit of Hospitality," 63.
19. For Lydia's hospitality, see Jody B. Fleming, "Spiritual Generosity: Biblical Hospitality in the Story of Lydia (Acts 16:14–16, 40)," *Missiology* 47, no. 1 (2019): 51–63.
20. For a detailed study, see Joshua W. Jipp, "Hospitable Barbarians: Luke's Ethnic Reasoning in Acts 28:1–10," *JTS* 68, no. 1 (2017): 23–45.

quarters and *welcomed* everyone who came to him, preaching God's kingdom and teaching about the Lord Jesus Christ, with boldness and no restriction" (28:30–31).

HOSPITALITY INSTRUCTED

The apostles were committed to hospitality. Paul, the author of Hebrews, Peter, and John instructed their congregations to practice hospitality since it reflected God's nature and offered a safe space to newcomers to the Christian faith and outsiders.

Paul said to the Romans, "Love that is sincere . . . *practices hospitality*" (Rom 12:9, 13).[21] In the previous verses, he explained how genuine love expressed itself in many ways. One of them is hospitality. Soon after instructing them, Paul asked them to welcome Phoebe, someone unknown to them, and offer her hospitality (16:1–2).

To Timothy, Paul instructed that Christians must commit to caring for the widows in the congregation (1 Tim 5:3–16). As the congregation chose to support a widow, she must have met a few criteria such as, being at least sixty years old, shown marital faithfulness, and done good works including raising children, showing *hospitality*, serving God's people, helping those in trouble, and devoting herself to the ministry of doing good deeds (5:9–10). The principle here is "reciprocity: the widow is to receive hospitality from the church household because, as a former householder, she has been hospitable herself."[22]

The writer of Hebrews instructed his Jewish audience, "Do not *neglect* hospitality since through it some have entertained angels *unknowingly*" (Heb 13:2).[23] The writer made a play on words with two related words: neglect (*epi-lanthaono-mai*) and unknowingly (*lanthano*). If they neglected hospitality, they would miss opportunities to entertain strangers who might have been angels from God. He was alluding to Abraham and Sarah welcoming the three angelic theophanies (Gen 18:1–8). He wanted the readers to imitate the example of their fore-parents.[24]

---

21. For the structure of this passage, see Andrew B. Spurgeon, *Romans: A Pastoral and Contextual Commentary* (Carlisle: Langham Global Library, 2020), 209; Douglas J. Moo, *Romans* (Grand Rapids: Zondervan, 2000), 409.

22. Barton, "Hospitality," 504.

23. The writer also uses the word for "stranger" (*xenia*) twice for emphasis: do not neglect hospitality (*filo-xenia*) because by hospitality (*xenizō*; lit. "hospitality-zing") some have entertained angels.

24. Abdul Rashied Omar, a Muslim, explains that the exhortation in Hebrews 13:2 to show hospitality to strangers resonates with Islamic teaching and it could be a pathway to open

Peter instructed his audience: "The completion of all things is near. Therefore, be alert and vigilant towards prayer, having constant love for one another . . . and *be hospitable to one another* without murmuring" (1 Pet 4:7–9). Without a doubt, his failure to stay alert and vigilant on the night of betrayal and his denial of the Lord Jesus formed the background of Peter's instructions (Matt 26:36–46, 69–75). He did not want his audience to be like his former self. Instead, he wanted them to love one another and show hospitality without murmuring.

Finally, the apostle John exhorted the elder Gaius who was hospitable to him, saying, "Let us be obligated to *welcome* one another so that we may become coworkers in the truth" (3 John 8). True reception of a person is the essence of hospitality.

PRACTICAL IMPLEMENTATION OF HOSPITALITY

Hospitality is ingrained in the hearts of Asians. We welcome people into our homes and offer them what we have. When someone asks for help, we go the extra mile. In Vietnamese culture, "One must do everything for one's friend. It is never a burden but rather an honor and a privilege to be asked by a friend [to do something] . . . A 'no' is indeed unthinkable!"[25]

Yet, we can do more. I have selected a few practical implications of hospitality beyond what we often consider. The list is by no means complete.

Walking with someone

In many cultures, walking with someone to a destination shows hospitality.[26] When John's disciples inquired of the Lord where he stayed, he asked them to follow him, walk with him, and see where he stayed (John 1:37–39). He instructed his disciples, "Whenever someone insists that you walk with him/her for a mile, you walk two" (Matt 5:41). On the road to Emmaus, the resurrected Lord walked with two guests until they reached their destination (Luke 24:13–32). Similarly, we can accompany people on their physical, emotional, and spiritual journeys.

---

communication between Christians, Hebrews, and Muslims. Abdul Rashied Omar, "Embracing the 'other' as an Extension of the Self: Muslim Reflections on the Epistle to the Hebrews 13:2," *AThR* 91, no. 3 (2009): 440–41.

25. Van Thanh Nguyen, "'An Asian View of Biblical Hospitality' (Luke 11:5–8)," *BR* 53 (2008): 25.

26. For Africans practicing this, see Carolyn Butler, "Hospitality and Spiritual Direction," *The Way* 52, no. 3 (2013): 67.

Visiting Prisoners

In the Lord's parable, the king says, "You clothed me, healed my wound, and *visited me in my imprisonment*" (Matt 25:36). Visiting prisoners and showing hospitality are truly services done to the almighty king. Brandner, ministering in prisons in Hong Kong, writes, "Here, my own feeling of being a stranger, including my occasional feeling of homesickness . . . resonates with the alienation of inmates and their longing for home and safety."[27] One way to show them hospitality is to visit them and make them part of the family.

Eating with People

The Lord Jesus enjoyed eating with the people, even sinful ones (11:19). In his culture, eating was more than sustaining one's body; it was a social association. To eat with someone was to associate, agree, and appreciate that person. Green writes:

> To share a meal with others involved including them as extended family. . . . People did not want to involve themselves at a table that would undermine their own status in the wider community. . . . For many Jews, including Pharisees, the table was the focus of issues of clean and contaminated, acceptable and unacceptable.[28]

This was why the religious leaders hated that Jesus ate with sinners and tax collectors; he was agreeing with their lifestyles. In reality, he was reforming them, as seen in the lives of Zacchaeus and Matthew. With his presence at their table, they became Abraham's children. Brandner writes, "When host and guest meet, it is foremost by *joint celebration and joint meals*, an aspect that traditional Chinese hospitality reflects particularly strongly."[29]

When people refused to eat with one another, it showed prejudice, as in the case of Cephas in Antioch. He ate with the Gentiles until his own people came. Then he withdrew (Gal 2:11–12). Paul considered it a hypocritical act and opposed Cephas openly (2:13–14). In contrast, when they showed hospitality regardless of whether they were Hellenistic or Hebraic widows, it exemplified God's nature of hospitality (Acts 6:1–4). May we hasten to eat with strangers and social outcasts to bring them to God's kingdom.

---

27. Brandner, "Hosts and Guests," 98.
28. Joel B. Green, "Embodying the Gospel: Two Exemplary Practices," *Journal of Spiritual Formation & Soul Care* 7, no. 1 (2014): 18.
29. Brander, "Hosts and Guests," 100.

Caring for the Overseas/Migrant Workers

In many Asian cultures, one member of the family goes off to another country to work and provide for the needs of the family. We call them overseas foreign or migrant workers. The families of these workers go through extensive trauma. Rodríguez writes:

> Human displacement . . . has deep repercussions in people's lives. It affects those who stay in the home country and those who immigrate. . . . Some will be beneficial, such as the well-being that a good job might provide. Others might be negative, such as emotional pain or a drop in one's self-esteem.[30]

Most overseas/migrant workers are lonely on holidays and festive days. In addition, they "lack native roots in terms of customary arrangements, social constructions and political organization."[31] Christians and churches should extend hospitality to the overseas/migrant workers and their families. In turn, we will reap blessings: "The migrant workers and refugees living among us will also *enrich our churches*, not simply by adding to the numbers on our membership lists, but *by causing us to grow in wholeness*" (italics added).[32] Sihombing compares them with Onesimus and exhorts the churches to receive them as "more than a slave," that is, "beloved brother and sister in the flesh and the Lord" (Phlm 16).[33]

Hospitality and the Emotionally Needy

Hospitality is being there for someone hurting emotionally. The Lord Jesus asked the disciples three times to stay awake with him and pray while he begged the Father to remove his cup (Matt 26:36–46). The disciples failed to show hospitality. Paul, in a similar situation, pleaded with Timothy to hurry to his aid because everyone had deserted him except for Luke (2 Tim 4:9–13). When people are lonely and dejected, we can extend hospitality, which "are often aimed at alleviating suffering, bringing comfort, or simply providing a friendly presence to a stranger or someone in need. This has been a long-standing duty for the people of God."[34]

---

30. Augusto Rodríguez, "God's Protection of Immigrants: A Personal Reflection from a Hispanic Pastoral Perspective," *Journal of Latin American Theology* 3, no. 2 (2008): 80.
31. Batara Sihombing, "Hospitality and Indonesian Migrant Workers," *Mission Studies* 30, no. 2 (2013): 167.
32. Brandner, "Hosts and Guests," 100.
33. Sihombing, "Hospitality and Indonesian Migrant Workers," 178.
34. Fleming, "Spiritual Generosity," 52.

In Theological Education

Theological education is a great place to show hospitality. The disciples of the Lord received their training in daily living – eating, healing, protecting the innocent, and showing justice. They learned their theology of hospitality by accepting others and offering them a safe space in God's kingdom. Christian educators should redesign classrooms into a safe space, a hospitable place. Shaw writes, "Developing hospitable space in the classroom is . . . in itself an essential theological act. When we welcome students as guests, this very act of hospitality communicates dramatically the divine reconciling work that is at the heart of our educational mandate."[35] Teachers who imitate Jesus's teaching principle not only leave long-lasting impressions on their students but also destroy the power gap that exists between teachers and students in Asia.

Interreligious Dialogues

Christianity, with its message of exclusive faith, is often seen as a religion of hate. But, the New Testament shows that in claiming exclusivity, the speakers always offer hospitality. Jesus told the woman at the well, "You worship whom you do not comprehend; we worship whom we know. Salvation is from the Jews" (John 4:22) – a message of exclusivity. Immediately he said, "But a time is coming and has come when the true worshippers will worship the Father in Spirit and truth" (4:23). That was hospitality: extending worship to anyone who followed the Father's guidance in worship. Paul imitated Jesus's pattern of speaking the truth while extending hospitality. He said to the Athenians, "You worship an unknown God" (Acts 17:23), but he immediately explained to them the greatness of the Creator God who could not stay in any temples built by humans, which included the temple in Jerusalem (17:24–25). Instead, the Creator God lived in the whole earth, his creation, and was available to the Athenians, which was a form of hospitality. In interreligious dialogues, we must offer a safe place for people of other faiths to express their views. Only then can both parties have deep discussions.[36] Such hospitality will open common grounds for meaningful conversions to occur and could even lead

---

35. Perry W. H. Shaw, "A Welcome Guest: Ministerial Training as an Act of Hospitality," *Christian Education Journal* 8, no. 1 (2011): 9. For how libraries can show hospitality, see Carisse Mickey Berryhill, "The Guest Brings the Blessing: Hospitality in Theological Librarianship," *ATLA Summary of Proceedings* 67 (2013): 84–89.
36. For further discussions, see Mary C. Boys and Scott C. Alexander, "Christian Hospitality and Pastoral Practices from a Roman Catholic Perspective," *Theological Education* 47, no. 1 (2012): 47–73.

to evangelism.[37] Smith writes, "Hospitality . . . empowers the church of Jesus Christ to reach to those outside the Body of Christ who sense no immediate need to enter the environment where Christians worship and fellowship (cf. Rom 12:13)."[38] Our hospitality opens ways for interfaith dialogues, evangelism, and missions.

Hospitality to People with Disabilities

The actress Dale Evans Rogers and her husband Roy eagerly anticipated the birth of their daughter, Robin. She was born with Down's Syndrome. Some advised them to "put her away" in a foster home. Instead, they lovingly raised her.[39] In Asia, persons with disabilities often face shame from others. They ask parents what wrong they did for their child to be born with disabilities (cf. John 9:2). Even in churches, persons with disabilities are treated as "guests" rather than fellow worshippers. Agustina Christiani says, "For people with disabilities, inclusion means that they are part of the church, and they can fully participate in every aspect of church life. They are the church, not just guests."[40] Hospitality is offering a safe space for everyone, which includes not drawing special attention to one's disability and seeing that person as God's creation, a person of equal value.[41] Jesus modeled this when he offered healing and miracles without demeaning the recipients. Hospitality breaks down the "us" versus "them" attitude.[42]

Hospitality and Undocumented People

Undocumented people are those who reside in a country without legal immigration status. They may have outstayed their legal visas, smuggled into the country illegally by a loving parent or a ruthless exploiter, or voluntarily entered a country to escape atrocities in their home countries. Regardless, they have no legal status in the country, and often they stay in the shadows and

---

37. Martin William Mittelstadt, "Eat, Drink, and Be Merry: A Theology of Hospitality in Luke-Acts," *WW* 34, no. 2 (2014): 139.
38. Robert Smith, "Paul's Quest for a Holy Church: Romans 14:1–15:13," *Wesleyan Theological Journal* 42, no. 1 (2007): 103.
39. Dale Evans Rogers, *Angel Unaware: A Touching Story of Love and Loss* (Grand Rapids: Fleming H. Revell, 1953). The title is borrowed from Hebrews 13:2.
40. An oral presentation from the ATA Consultation, "Ethics with a Human Face," presented on 16 September 2021.
41. But the churches must be conscious to make provisions for the physically challenged such as providing ramps, elevators, braille signage, sign language speakers, etc.
42. Gerald McKenny, "Disability and the Christian Ethics of Solidarity," *Fu Jen International Religious Studies* 6, no. 1 (2012): 9.

fear what might happen to them if they are caught. David was in a similar situation when Saul plotted to kill him. He fled to Gath and pretended to be a madman just to escape his death (1 Sam 21:10–15). The Philippians thought Paul was an undocumented migrant, beat him, and imprisoned him, only to be confronted by his true identity (Acts 16:16–40). Regardless of our political views, we should care for the undocumented while they are "strangers" in our land. Senapatiratne and Aadland compare the undocumented people's situation to that of those who fled to the sanctuary cities in the Old Testament for protection under covenant and say, "All humans [including the undocumented residents] are on one side of the covenant, and God – as the second party of the covenant – is on the other side."[43] Kim and Ahn explain that we live in a "supranational" world without boundaries. In such a world:

> Rather than criminalizing undocumented migrants, we must develop a culture of inclusion and hospitality with a new sense of responsibility in today's post-national context. The concept of "post-national" refers to a global phenomenon in which the traditional "nation states" are gradually transformed into "supra-national" entities.[44]

Kivisto and Mahn concur and exhort churches to extend hospitality to the undocumented and immigrants.[45] Extending hospitality without violating the country's laws is always a fine balancing act.

Hospitality in Church Gathering

Some visitors find entering a church threatening: new faces, practices, songs, sermons, and even clothing. Hospitality is seeking such new visitors and making them feel comfortable in a new atmosphere. Vogels writes:

> In Tahiti, every person received a flower before entering the church on Sundays, so one obviously felt very welcome. Hospitality may also include saying goodbye to people when they leave the church,

---

43. Timothy Senapatiratne and Brien Aadland, "A Contemporary Theology of Sanctuary as It Relates to Undocumented and Displaced People," *WW* 39, no. 2 (2019): 142.

44. Uriah Y. Kim and Ilsup Ahn, "The Post-National Responsibility toward Undocumented Immigrants: The Practice of Hesed and a New Ethics of Friendship," *The Covenant Quarterly* 71, nos. 3–4 (2013): 3.

45. Peter Kivisto and Jason A. Mahn, "Radical Hospitality: Sociotheological Reflections on Postville, Iowa," *WW* 29, no. 3 (2009): 252–61. Miguel H. Diaz, too, interprets "strangers" in Leviticus 19:9 as migrating people("On Loving Strangers: Encountering the Mystery of God in the Face of Migrants," *WW* 29, no. 3 [2009]: 234–42).

or even perhaps offering coffee after the celebration in the parish hall.[46]

Inviting the visitors to the fellowship meal and eating with them would certainly make them feel comfortable and accepted. It may even open a way for
them to continue to come and become members of the local congregation.

The Lord's Supper as Hospitality

When the Corinthians desecrated the Lord's Supper with divisions and glut-
tony, Paul wished that they did not celebrate the Lord's Supper at all (1 Cor
11:18–34). Just as the Corinthians divided over leaders saying, "I am of Paul,"
"I am of Apollos," or "I am of Cephas" (1:12), they segregated at the Lord's
meal. Similarly, even now, the Lord's Supper (or holy communion) must be a
place where people of all races, colors, and nationalities unite based on their
faith. "The communion table remains the central and constant symbol of this
hospitality."[47] So, we must participate in the Lord's Supper with reverence and
make it a safe space, a place to "welcome or receive one another" (11:33). In
a world divided by ethnic and caste conflicts, the Lord's table could become
a symbol of unity among Christians and a witness to the world that God's
people crossover borders and boundaries at the table to be united.

Hospitality and Caring for the Poor

The Lord Jesus, the apostles, and early Christians were committed to helping
the poor.[48] Early churches shared everything in common, even sold their properties so that they could care for the poor (Acts 2:44–45; 4:34–36). As soon
as Agabus prophesied that a severe famine would take over the entire Roman
world, the disciples in Antioch gathered funds to help the Christians in Judea
who were poor (11:28–30). The apostles imposed no restrictions on those
who ministered among the Gentiles except to care for the poor (Gal 2:10).
Hospitality "expresses itself in generosity to one another and the creation of
a community in which there is communal care and the sharing of resources
for the benefit of the poor."[49] If we are committed to hospitality, then we are
also committed to providing for the needs of the poor.

---

46. Walter Vogels, "Hospitality in Biblical Perspective," *Liturgical Ministry* 11 (2002): 161.
47. Janzen, "Biblical Theology of Hospitality," 13.
48. For a detailed study, see Andrew B. Spurgeon, "Paul: Passionate to Help the Poor," *JAM* 13, no. 2 (2012): 15–23.
49. I. Howard Marshall, "Holiness in the Book of Acts," in *Holiness and Ecclesiology in the New Testament*, ed. Kent E. Brower and Andy Johnson (Grand Rapids: Eerdmans, 2007), 125.

Hospitality and Impurity

In India, caste distinction persists. People belong to high and low castes, and some do not even have a caste (the untouchables or Dalits). The high caste people consider the low caste people as unclean and would not eat with them. Peter was like them. He did not want to eat non-kosher food or enter the house of the Gentile Cornelius and eat with him, but God forced him to do the same (Acts 10:1–48).[50] The new covenant canceled any caste or class distinction and opened the way for Jews and Gentiles, free and slave, male and female, and Brahmins and Dalits to eat and fellowship together. This includes people marrying without any reference to one's caste and celebrating birthdays, weddings, and other celebrations by inviting people who were shunned by others because of their caste or color. For Christians, no one is *untouchable*, low-caste, or impure.

Hospitality to Missionaries

Jesus, Philip, Paul, Peter, Apollos were itinerant preachers and missionaries. Many Christians showed hospitality to them, including Susanna and Joanna (Luke 8:3), Aquila and Priscilla (Acts 18:1–3), Lydia (16:13–15), Philip (21:8), Mnason (21:16), Phoebe (Rom 16:2), Gaius (16:23), and Philemon (Phlm 22). Arterbury writes, "In expressions of early Christian hospitality, an association develops between the custom of hospitality and traveling missionaries."[51] By inviting itinerant preachers and missionaries into our homes and churches, offering them fellowship, food, and missionary support, we excel in hospitality.

Conclusion

Hospitality is risky. While it offers a safe space to those we invite to share in our lives, it also makes us vulnerable. In Victor Hugo's novel, *Les Misérables*, a priest offers room and board to a jail-breaker, Jean Valjean, only to find his household silver stolen. "To offer hospitality to the stranger is to welcome something unknown and vulnerable into our life-world, to create space for something foreign, to offer room, to accommodate, care for, and protect the alien."[52] And yet, that's the call for all Christians: "Do not *neglect* hospitality since through it some have entertained angels *unknowingly*" (Heb 13:1–2).

---

50. In Antioch, he had difficulty eating with Gentiles until Paul rebuked him (Gal 2:11–16).
51. Arterbury, "Breaking the Betrothal Bonds," 68.
52. Brandner, "Hosts and Guests," 96.

Hospitality, in all its manifestations, offers a profound message of reconciliation. In Paul's words, "*Welcome* one another as *Christ welcomed you* for the glory of God" (Rom 15:7). Those of us who have been unconditionally reconciled to God by the offerings of the Lord Jesus Christ, in turn, offer ourselves unconditionally to others (Matt 18:21–35). That is hospitality!

BIBLIOGRAPHY

Arterbury, Andrew E. "Breaking the Betrothal Bonds: Hospitality in John 4." *CBQ* 72, no. 1 (2010): 63–83.

Barton, S. C. "Hospitality." *DLNT* 501–7.

Boys, Mary C., and Scott C Alexander, "Christian Hospitality and Pastoral Practices from a Roman Catholic Perspective." *Theological Education* 47, no. 1 (2012): 47–73.

Brandner, Tobias. "Hosts and Guests: Hospitality as an Emerging Paradigm in Mission." *International Review of Mission* 102, no. 1 (2013): 94–102.

Butler, Carolyn. "Hospitality and Spiritual Direction." *The Way* 52, no. 3 (2013): 65–75.

Byanungu, Gosbert. "Retrieving Abraham's Human Experience of *El-'Eljon*: Interfaith Implications of Faith in the God of Creation." *ABQ* 26 no. 3 (2007): 261–83.

Chasbar, Luis Carlos Marrero. "God Crosses Borders, Too: A Sociotheological Perspective on Migration." *Journal of Latin American Theology* 14, no. 1 (2019): 57–70.

Cohen, Jeffrey M. "Abraham's Hospitality." *JBQ* 34, no. 3 (2006): 168–73.

Díaz, Miguel H. "On Loving Strangers: Encountering the Mystery of God in the Face of Migrants." *WW* 29, no. 3 (2009): 234–42.

Fleming, Jody B. "Spiritual Generosity: Biblical Hospitality in the Story of Lydia (Acts 16:14–16, 40)." *Missiology* 47, no. 1 (2019): 51–63.

Green, Joel B. "Embodying the Gospel: Two Exemplary Practices." *Journal of Spiritual Formation & Soul Care* 7, no. 1 (2014): 11–21.

Janzen, Waldemar. "Biblical Theology of Hospitality." *Vision: A Journal for Church and Theology* 6 no. 1 (2005): 4–15.

Jipp, Joshua W. "Hospitable Barbarians: Luke's Ethnic Reasoning in Acts 28:1–10." *The Journal of Theological Studies* 68, no. 1 (2017): 23–45.

Kim, Uriah Y., and Ilsup Ahn, "The Post-National Responsibility toward Undocumented Immigrants: The Practice of Hesed and a New Ethics of Friendship." *The Covenant Quarterly* 71, no. 3–4 (2013): 3–19.

Kivisto, Peter, and Jason A. Mahn, "Radical Hospitality: Sociotheological Reflections on Postville, Iowa." *WW* 29, no. 3 (2009): 252–61.

Marshall, I. Howard. "Holiness in the Book of Acts." Pages 114–28 in *Holiness and Ecclesiology in the New Testament*. Edited by Kent E. Brower and Andy Johnson. Eerdmans, 2007.

McKenny, Gerald. "Disability and the Christian Ethics of Solidarity." *Fu Jen International Religious Studies* 6, no. 1 (2012): 9–23.

Mittelstadt, Martin William. "Eat, Drink, and Be Merry: A Theology of Hospitality in Luke-Acts." *WW* 34, no. 2 (2014): 131–39.

Nouwen, Henri J. M. *Reaching Out: The Three Movements of the Spiritual Life*. New York: Image Books, 1986.

Omar, Abdul Rashied. "Embracing the 'other' as an Extension of the Self: Muslim Reflections on the Epistle to the Hebrews 13:2." *AThR* 91, no. 3 (2009): 433–41.

O'Neill, William R. "'No Longer Strangers' (Ephesians 2:19): The Ethics of Migration." *WW* 29, no. 3 (2009): 229–34.

Rodríguez, Augusto. "God's Protection of Immigrants: A Personal Reflection from a Hispanic Pastoral Perspective," *Journal of Latin American Theology* 3, no. 2 (2008): 80–92.

Rogers, Dale Evans. *Angel Unaware: A Touching Story of Love and Loss*. Grand Rapids: Fleming H. Revell, 1953.

Senapatiratne, Timothy, and Brien Aadland, "A Contemporary Theology of Sanctuary as It Relates to Undocumented and Displaced People." *WW* 39, no. 2 (2019): 138–47.

Shaw, Perry W. H. "A Welcome Guest: Ministerial Training as an Act of Hospitality." *Christian Education Journal* 8, no. 1 (2011): 8–26.

Sihombing, Batara. "Hospitality and Indonesian Migrant Workers." *Mission Studies* 30, no. 2 (2013): 162–80.

Smith, Robert. "Paul's Quest for a Holy Church: Romans 14:1–15:13." *Wesleyan Theological Journal* 42, no. 1 (2007): 103–19.

Spitaler, Peter. "Biblical Concern for the Marginalized: Mark's Stories about Welcoming the Little Ones (Mk 9,33–11,11)." *Ephemerides Theologicae Lovanienses* 87, no. 1 (2011): 89–126.

Spurgeon, Andrew B. "Paul: Passionate to Help the Poor." *JAM* 13, no. 2 (2012): 15–23.

Thompson, Marjorie J. *Soul Feast: An Invitation to the Christian Spiritual Life*. Louisville: WJKP, 1995.

Van Thanh, Nguyen. "'An Asian View of Biblical Hospitality' (Luke 11:5–8)." *BR* 53 (2008): 25–39.

Vogels, Walter. "Hospitality in Biblical Perspective." *Liturgical Ministry* 11 (2002): 161–73.

Yong, Amos. "The Spirit of Hospitality: Pentecostal Perspectives toward a Performative Theology of Interreligious Encounter." *Missiology* 35, no. 1 (2007): 55–73.

———. *Renewing Christian Theology: Systematics for a Global Christianity*. Waco: Baylor University Press, 2014.

Zen, Beringia M. "Shame to Hospitality: A Post-Holocaust Biblical Hermeneutics." PhD diss., Graduate Theological Union, Berkeley, California, 2015.

CONTRIBUTORS

Steven S. H. Chang received his PhD from the University of Aberdeen and is currently professor of New Testament and director of the PhD program at Torch Trinity Graduate University in Seoul, Korea, where he has been a member of faculty since 2001. He is contributor to *A Hybrid World: Diaspora, Hybridity, and Missio Dei* (William Carey, 2020) and *Scattered and Gathered: A Global Compendium of Diaspora Missiology* (Langham Global Library, 2020). He and his wife, Lisa, pastor the English congregation at Hallelujah Church in Seongnam, Korea, and they have two grown children.

Bennet Lawrence received his PhD from Asia Graduate School of Theology and is currently the regional secretary of Asia Theology Association India. He is the author of *Legalistic Nomism: A Socio-Rhetorical Reading of Paul's Letter to the Galatians* (ISPCK, 2015), *Comparative Characterization in the Sermon on the Mount: Characterization of the Ideal Disciple* (Wipf & Stock, 2017), and *Approaches to the New Testament* (SAIACS Press, 2018). He is married to Joyce, and their daughter's name is Netanya.

Chee-Chiew Lee is professor of New Testament at Singapore Bible College. Her publications include *When Christians Face Persecution* (IVP, 2022), *Interpreting New Testament Epistles* (in Chinese), and *The Blessing of Abraham, the Spirit, and Justification in Galatians* (Wipf & Stock, 2013). She also serves on the editorial board for Langham Chinese Bible Commentary and on the advisory board of Evangelical Quarterly. She enjoys sightseeing.

Siang-Nuan Leong is a senior lecturer at the School of Theology, TCA College. Her PhD research at the University of Edinburgh was on the book of Revelation. Two essays were published based on her dissertation: "The Teaching Point of Revelation Clothed in Beasts and Harlots" in *Honouring the Past, Looking to the Future: Essays from the 2014 International Congress of Ethnic Chinese Biblical Scholars* (Chinese University of Hong Kong Press, 2014) and "Death of a Queen or Goddess? Overtones to Jezebel's Vilification at her Death Scene in the Hebrew Bible" in *Voices: Postgraduate Perspectives on Inter-disciplinarity* (Cambridge Scholars Publishing, 2011). She enjoys teaching biblical interpretation, as well as bridging faith and culture.

Alroy Mascrenghe writes commentaries to the books of the Bible in the Tamil language. He is the author of *Samson as God's Adulterous Wife* (Peter Lang, 2019). He is an honorary research associate at the University of Cape Town.

Narry F. Santos is associate professor of Christian ministry and intercultural leadership at Tyndale University in Toronto, vice president of the Evangelical Missiological Society Canada, and part-time senior pastor of Greenhills Christian Fellowship (GCF) Peel and GCF York in Canada. He has a PhD in New Testament (Dallas Theological Seminary, 1994) and another in Philippine Studies (University of the Philippines, 2006). He wrote several books, including *Family Relations in the Gospel of Mark* (Peter Lang, 2021) and *Slave of All* (Bloomsbury, 2003), edited mission compendiums and contributed chapters in diaspora books and biblical articles in academic journals. He has been married for thirty-five years, has two grown daughters and two grandchildren.

Andrew B. Spurgeon is a professor of New Testament Studies at Singapore Bible College. He is the publications Secretary for the Asia Theological Association, an accrediting agency, and the general editor of the Asia Bible Commentary Series. He is the author of *Twin Cultures Separated by Centuries: An Indian Reading of 1 Corinthians* (Langham, 2016), *James* (co-authored; ATA/Langham, 2018), and *Romans* (ATA/Langham, 2020). He and his wife live in Singapore.

Joyce Wai-Lan Sun is an associate professor of China Graduate School of Theology in Hong Kong. She is the author of *This Is True Grace: The Shaping of Social Behavioural Instructions by Theology in 1 Peter* (Langham Academic, 2016) and a contributor to *Best Practice Guidelines for Theological Libraries Serving Doctoral Programs* (Langham Global Library, 2021). Her book *1 Timothy: How to Behave in the Household of God* (in Chinese) was awarded the 2023 Outstanding Theological Academic Research Work by Rev. Dr. Lienhwa Chow Memorial Foundation.

Thawng Ceu Hnin is the academic dean and a professor of New Testament at Hindustan Bible Institute and College, India. He contributed essays including "Discourse Analysis" and "Performance Criticism" in *Approaches to the New Testament: A Handbook for Students and Pastors* (SAIACS Press, 2021), and "The Letter to Philemon" in *An Asian Introduction to the New Testament* (Fortress Press, 2021).

Johnson Thomaskutty is professor of New Testament in the department of biblical studies at The United Theological College, Bengaluru, India. He is the author of *Dialogue in the Book of Signs: A Polyvalent Analysis of John 1:19–12:50* (Brill, 2015), *Saint Thomas the Apostle: New Testament, Apocrypha, and Historical Traditions* (T&T Clark, 2018), and editor of *An Asian Introduction to the New Testament* (Fortress, 2022). His upcoming works include a commentary on John in the Asia Bible Commentary Series (Langham Global Library) and *Asian Biblical Hermeneutics* (Fortress Press).

Samson L. Uytanlet is associate professor of New Testament at the Asian Theological Seminary, Philippines. His works include *Luke-Acts and Jewish Historiography* (Mohr-Siebeck, 2014), *Manual for Sojourners* (Wipf & Stock, 2023), and two volumes for the Asia Bible Commentary Series, *Matthew* (Langham Global Library, 2017) and *2 Peter & Jude* (Langham Global Library, 2023). He is married to Juliet and they have one son.

Xiaxia E. Xue is an associate professor of New Testament at China Graduate School of Theology (CGST), Hong Kong. She has written *Paul's Viewpoint on God, Israel, and the Gentiles in Romans 9–11* (Langham Academic, 2015), which has been translated into Chinese (Tien Dao Publishing House, HK, 2018). She chose the area of New Testament studies, because she has been deeply touched by the life stories of many biblical figures and wanted to reflect on their struggles, confusions, and sufferings in their own historical context.

Kazuhiko Yamazaki-Ransom serves as the academic dean of Covenant Seminary in Tokyo and as the associate pastor of Tsurumi Covenant Church in Yokohama. He is the author of *The Roman Empire in Luke's Narrative* (T&T Clark, 2010) and a contributor to *Dictionary of Jesus and the Gospels*, 2nd ed. (IVP, 2013). He currently lives in Yokohama with his family.

AUTHOR INDEX

SUBJECT INDEX

SCRIPTURE INDEX

OLD TESTAMENT

NEW TESTAMENT

Asia Theological Association

54 Scout Madriñan St. Quezon City 1103, Philippines
Email: ataasia@gmail.com Telefax: (632) 410 0312

OUR MISSION

The Asia Theological Association (ATA) is a body of theological institutions, committed to evangelical faith and scholarship, networking together to serve the Church in equipping the people of God for the mission of the Lord Jesus Christ.

OUR COMMITMENT

The ATA is committed to serving its members in the development of evangelical, biblical theology by strengthening interaction, enhancing scholarship, promoting academic excellence, fostering spiritual and ministerial formation and mobilizing resources to fulfill God's global mission within diverse Asian cultures.

OUR TASK

Affirming our mission and commitment, ATA seeks to:

- **Strengthen** interaction through inter-institutional fellowship and programs, regional and continental activities, faculty and student exchange programs.
- **Enhance** scholarship through consultations, workshops, seminars, publications, and research fellowships.
- **Promote** academic excellence through accreditation standards, faculty and curriculum development.
- **Foster** spiritual and ministerial formation by providing mentor models, encouraging the development of ministerial skills and a Christian ethos.
- **Mobilize** resources through library development, information technology and infra-structural development.

To learn more about ATA, visit www.ataasia.com or facebook.com/AsiaTheologicalAssociation

Langham Literature, along with its publishing work, is a ministry of Langham Partnership.

Langham Partnership is a global fellowship working in pursuit of the vision God entrusted to its founder John Stott –

> *to facilitate the growth of the church in maturity and Christ-likeness through raising the standards of biblical preaching and teaching.*

Our vision is to see churches in the Majority World equipped for mission and growing to maturity in Christ through the ministry of pastors and leaders who believe, teach and live by the word of God.

Our mission is to strengthen the ministry of the word of God through:

- nurturing national movements for biblical preaching
- fostering the creation and distribution of evangelical literature
- enhancing evangelical theological education

especially in countries where churches are under-resourced.

Our ministry

Langham Preaching partners with national leaders to nurture indigenous biblical preaching movements for pastors and lay preachers all around the world. With the support of a team of trainers from many countries, a multi-level programme of seminars provides practical training, and is followed by a programme for training local facilitators. Local preachers' groups and national and regional networks ensure continuity and ongoing development, seeking to build vigorous movements committed to Bible exposition.

Langham Literature provides Majority World preachers, scholars and seminary libraries with evangelical books and electronic resources through publishing and distribution, grants and discounts. The programme also fosters the creation of indigenous evangelical books in many languages, through writer's grants, strengthening local evangelical publishing houses, and investment in major regional literature projects, such as one volume Bible commentaries like the *Africa Bible Commentary* and the *South Asia Bible Commentary*.

Langham Scholars provides financial support for evangelical doctoral students from the Majority World so that, when they return home, they may train pastors and other Christian leaders with sound, biblical and theological teaching. This programme equips those who equip others. Langham Scholars also works in partnership with Majority World seminaries in strengthening evangelical theological education. A growing number of Langham Scholars study in high quality doctoral programmes in the Majority World itself. As well as teaching the next generation of pastors, graduated Langham Scholars exercise significant influence through their writing and leadership.

To learn more about Langham Partnership and the work we do visit **langham.org**

9 781839 737114